D1500477

The Architecture of Ireland
from the earliest times to 1880

For Frank Hoelbeck
with much love and great expectations!
Muriel.

The Architecture of Ireland from the earliest times to 1880

Maurice Craig

B. T. BATSFORD LTD. LONDON
EASON & SON LTD. DUBLIN

For
Catherine and Fergus
and especially
for
Michael

Frontispiece Dublin: the Custom House from the South-East, taken in
about 1950 when that part of the river over which it presides was still alive
with shipping, in this case two vessels belonging to Messrs Arthur
Guinness, Son and Co.

© Maurice Craig 1982
First published 1982
First paperback edition 1989

All rights reserved. No part of this publication
may be reproduced, in any form
or by any means,
without permission from the Publisher

ISBN 0 7134 2587 3

Typeset and printed in Great Britain by
Butler & Tanner Ltd, Frome and London
for the publishers
B. T. Batsford Ltd,
4 Fitzhardinge Street
London W1H 0AH
and
Eason & Son Ltd,
65 Middle Abbey Street
Dublin 1

The author and the publishers wish to
acknowledge the generous help of the following,
who have made this publication possible:
The Alfred Beit Foundation
Allied Irish Banks
The American Irish Foundation
The Arts Council of Northern Ireland
The Bank of Ireland
The Heritage Trust
The Irish Architectural Archive
Sean Mulcahy
Consuelo and Brian O'Connor
Nicholas Robinson
The Trinity College Dublin Trust

Contents

Preface

There are many interesting buildings, and perhaps even some important ones, which may not be found in the following pages. Though Ireland is a small country, her history is long, and certain types of building have been at certain times reasonably abundant. Since my intention has been to study problems rather than periods, a particular building has sometimes been taken as a representative of a whole class. It would not be seemly that out of so small a country should come an unreasonably large book.

The scale of treatment may seem to some readers anomalous in places: some topics are treated at perhaps unexpected length and others rather briefly dismissed. In part this is the result of what I may call temporal perspective: things remote in time become foreshortened and take up less space, while nearer things bulk larger. As a general rule (subject to many exceptions) older buildings are rarer and those more recent are more plentiful.

But more significant than this is the inequality of treatment by my predecessors. The early Christian and mediaeval periods, for example, have been so well dealt with by Leask and his predecessors and even by later scholars that, except in the field of castles, he may be taken as having said, usually, the last word. The eighteenth century has also had plenty of exposure, though some false folk-beliefs remain resistant, and some dark places are still in need of light.

By contrast, the transition from mediaeval to modern, hitherto largely neglected, has here been given some attempt at what seems to be its due. With the honourable exceptions of Waterman and Jope, and very recently of Dr Loeber, nobody has given it much attention. Even more marked has been the total neglect of Catholic church-building between 1760 and 1840, and for this injustice I have tried to compensate. In an ideal world, the writer of such a general work as this would be able to rely on specialist forerunners who had worked up each period or problem to a roughly similar level. As things are, he is reduced to doing some of the work himself.

Decoration, as distinct from architecture, has been virtually omitted as a matter of policy. Those interested can follow it in the pages of Curran, whose book, however, is in need of amplification. A more serious omission, perhaps, is that of vernacular architecture in most of the senses of that word. It proved, in the event, impossible to accommodate some aspects of the vernacular in the book's scheme of composition.

Not all, however. It has been said by one authority that all we mean by calling a building 'vernacular' is that we do not know the name of its designer. On another showing, any building is 'vernacular' if it was not so much 'designed' as assembled on site by a master-builder or at least someone other than a drawing-board 'architect'. The narrowest definition I know is that which requires a 'vernacular' building to have been erected by someone other than a professional builder: by, for example, the united efforts of the able-bodied of a small community over a period of days. The definition which I personally favour is one which returns to the linguistic root of the expression, and calls any building vernacular when it is more or less anonymous and in the stylistic idiom of its time and place and built of local materials. By at least two of these definitions the houses in Merrion Square are 'vernacular': they are all much the same and they are all slightly different and most of them are not by people we should today call 'architects'.

The same, even more evidently, goes for the great mass of Catholic and other non-conformist churches of the early nineteenth century. They are unmistakably in the idiom of their time, and the fruit of communal effort. The pity is that they are so little regarded and in such great danger.

Consideration of the whole body of Irish building from the seventeenth century to the nineteenth disposes of the notion, still not quite dead, that there was some kind of alien style which was temporarily imposed on the country. There is no escaping the fact that the rich build more grandly than the poor. But between Castletown Co Kildare (fig. 136) and Ballynahinch Co Clare (fig. 153) there is no essential difference except that one is very much larger and built of richer materials than the other. Ballyboughlin (fig. 155) is perhaps about half-way between them. In stylistic terms there is complete continuity.

A word about place names and other proper names in or from the Irish language. It has proved impossible to achieve any approach to consistency in this thorny matter. For many centuries Irish names, whether of places or of families, have been trans-literated into English, and in many cases these anglicised forms, e.g. Tipperary, Galway, O'Brien, Costello, are the most familiar even to most Irish people, let alone to outsiders. But it is now over 50 years since Macalister ridiculed the barbarous orthography of 'Errigal Keerogue', and even the less sensitive of us now write 'Connacht'. One of the principal purposes for which Macalister advocated such reform, the steering of strangers away from excusable mispronunciations, seems nearly as remote of attainment as ever, though the newsreaders have in the past ten years had some much-needed practice.

So I have resorted to compromise. When the site or monument seems nowadays more familiar in its purer Irish form, I write, for example, Sceilg Mhichíl, and I drop the final e from Clonmacnois because I like it better without. But East of the Shannon I almost invariably use anglicised forms, and for such places as Philipstown and Maryborough I use the names most appropriate for the context in which the buildings occur.

I am grateful to An Taisce the National Trust for Ireland, to An Foras Forbartha the National Institute for Physical Planning and Research, and to the Representative Body of the Church of Ireland, in whose service I had opportunities to visit and inspect buildings which might not otherwise have come my way.

Much of Chapters 3 to 11 formed the substance of the Rhind Lectures for the year 1980, delivered in Edinburgh University under the auspices of the Society of Anti-quaries of Scotland, an opportunity for which I am also grateful.

List of Illustrations

Page

Page

Acknowledgments

I wish to thank the following for help given in various ways: C. E. B. Brett, Tony Byrne, Hugh Charlton, Cork City Planning Office, Richard Dann, Liam de Paor, Edward Diestelkamp, Hugh Dixon, Pierre du Prey, the late N. W. English, William Garner, the Knight of Glin, David Griffin, Peter Harbison, Roger Hill, C. P. Hyland, D. Newman Johnson, Paul Kerrigan, Dr Elisabeth Kieven, Percy Le Clerc, John Lenahan, Rolf Loeber, Edward McParland, F. X. Martin O. S. A., Kenneth Milne, G. F. Mitchell, Niall Montgomery, Brian O'Carroll, Frederick O'Dwyer, Liam Raftis, Sean Rothery, Alistair Rowan, Nicholas Sheaff, Jeanne Sheehy, Roger Stalley, Barrie Trinder, Diarmuid and Elizabeth Twohig, Michael Walsh-Kemyss, the late Dudley Waterman and Jeremy Williams.

In addition to the printed books cited elsewhere, I have made extensive use of three unpublished theses, placed at my disposal by their authors:

'Gothic Revival Architecture in Ireland' Ph.D. Yale 1970 by Douglas Scott Richardson.

'The Public Work of Architects in Ireland during the neoclassical period' Ph.D. Cambridge 1975 by Edward McParland.

'The Irish Palladians' Harvard (not submitted) by Desmond Fitz-Gerald, Knight of Glin.

I have also been allowed to consult the very voluminous materials collected for *The Buildings of Ireland* under the direction of Professor Alistair Rowan.

Great as my indebtedness is to these, they cannot be held responsible for any errors into which I may have fallen.

The author and publishers are grateful to the following for permission to reproduce the following illustrations:

Bord Failte: 44, 49, 52, 168; Cambridge University Collection (copyright reserved): 3, 4, 5, 265; College Studios: 127, 130; Commissioners of Public Works in Ireland: 11, 12, 26, 28, 33, 37, 38, 40, 41, 45, 50, 55, 62, 63, 64, 65, 80, 90; Michael Craig: 53, 144, 196, 200; David H. Davison: 24; David H. Davison (Pieterse-Davison International Ltd), 42, 126, (Trinity College Library) 124; George Eogan: 2; William Garner: 72, 74, 142; William Garner (Irish Architectural Archive, National Heritage Inventory Collection): 1, 61, 68, 69, 72, 73, 76, 79, 83, 93, 101, 103, 105, 113, 133, 135, 153, 154, 156, 171, 172, 175, 176, 177, 178, 179, 180, 181, 182, 183, 188, 189, 190, 191, 192, 202, 204, 210, 211, 212, 216, 217, 224, 226, 240, 244, 251, 257, 260, 261, 268, 272, 273, 277; Dr Joachim Gerstenberg: frontispiece; Desmond Fitz-Gerald, Knight of Glin: 115; David Griffin: 140; Irish Architectural Archive (David Davison photo): 116, 136; Irish Architectural Archive (Patrick Rossmore photo): 194, 213, 255, 266; P. Kerrigan and R. Stapleton: 242; Mrs A. K. Leask: 19, 59; Dr W. A. McCutcheon, Ulster Museum: 276; T. H. Mason & Sons: 132; Mrs Renate Moores and R. A. Stalley: 27, 32, 36, 43; Dr D. Pochin Mould: 58, 122, 243; National Gallery of Ireland:

230; National Library of Ireland: 219, 259, 271; Northern Ireland Archaeological Survey: 31, 57, 167, 185, 186, 256; John O'Connell: 99, 110; Sean Rothery: 274; Royal Archaeological Institute: 199; Royal Irish Academy: 25, 214; R. A. Stalley, 25: Leo Swan: 78, 258; The Board of Trinity College Dublin: 124 and 252; Ulster Museum: 160; Jeremy Williams: 109.

Illustrations not credited are by the author.

Readers familiar with Ireland will notice that several of the best known and finest buildings are illustrated inadequately or in some cases not at all. Many of these have been repeatedly depicted elsewhere, though not always in publications widely available outside Ireland.

The reason for this is that the disposable space was given by preference to buildings and types of building hitherto under-represented but necessary to the argument of the book.

Among those not illustrated at all are the buildings on Sceilg Mhicíl, the oratory of Gallerus, any Round Towers (except for the sectional drawing on p. 33), Bunratty and Blarney Castles, Queen's College Cork, and, among country houses, Woodlands Co Dublin, Powerscourt Co Wicklow, Castle Coole Co Fermanagh and Dromore Castle Co Limerick.

Of buildings in Dublin, Dr Steevens' Hospital and the Broadstone Station would have been included if space had permitted, and the old Parliament House and the Four Courts would have been represented by more than their plans alone. The same is true of Trim Castle, Beaulieu and Mount Ievers (pp. 66, 144 and 179), and I would have liked to show Castletown Cox more fully than by the single detail on p. 197. Finally, I should like to have included an exterior of the Trinity College Museum building, the interior of which is shown on p. 295.

Over almost the whole field of history—especially modern
history—the increase in knowledge has brought a decrease
of certainty: too many perspectives and too few principles.

    C. V. Wedgwood, *Truth and Opinion*, 1960

The Stubbornness of our language has sometimes forced
me to deviate from the *conditional* into the *indicative* mood.

    Gibbon, *Decline and Fall of the Roman Empire*,
    Chapter XXI note *s*

We talk too much. We should talk less and draw more.

    Goethe, *Conversations with J. D. Falk*, 1809

Cows are very fond of being photographed, and, unlike
architecture, don't move.

    Oscar Wilde, letter of 21 April 1900

Serious historians fear nothing more than seeing their
labours counted amongst the arts.

    J. H. Huizinga, *Dutch Civilisation* (The Aesthetic
    Element in Historical Thought), English edition 1968

CHAPTER ONE

Prehistoric

Those who arrive in Ireland, whether by choice of ticket or accident of birth, come to realise that they are in a Western European country. To be sure, it is not quite like other Western European countries: the ingredients may be much the same, but the proportions are different. Surprising as it may seem to find an almost total lack of mediaeval churches, it is perhaps equally striking to be faced with a profusion of very complete, though ruined, later mediaeval friaries; and, still more striking, to see them in empty countryside instead of in urban situations where, by the standards of other countries, we should expect to find them. There are, it is true, a few categories of building which are peculiar to Ireland: such are, for example, Round Towers, spirit-groceries and ball-alleys.

The Round Towers are known to have been common, and nearly a hundred of them remain in recognisable form: a little over 30 of them substantially complete. Spirit-groceries are less immediately recognisable: they are not so much a building-type as a way of using internal space. They are, grievously, on the wane. Ball-alleys are, as often as not, adaptations of existing buildings: whenever a high blank wall is to be found it is likely that someone has added or adapted two cheek-walls to make a ball-alley. They, too, are on the decline, but are still to be seen; especially near the barracks of the Garda Síochána.

The old adage, that to live in England you need to be deaf, whereas in Ireland the advantage is to the blind, has much truth in it. The casual visitor is sometimes oppressed by the thought that everything within sight is made of cement, self-coloured. Nothing of any antiquity in Ireland is made of anything but stone, and nearly all the stone is grey. The somewhat melancholy but undeniably appealing beauty of large tracts of the West, is matched only by the ingenuity of garage-proprietors and hoteliers in enlivening the foreground with irrelevant banalities. Yet in time the eye can train itself to disregard what is actually to be seen, and to dwell only on what is worth seeing. That is the intention of this book.

How did it all begin? With the megalithic monuments of course: how else? But here we are immediately in a difficulty. Many if not all of the most spectacular megalithic monuments were not intended to be seen: certainly not in the form in which they now appear. Many of them were originally covered with mounds of earth or cairns of stones, and whatever they once looked like, it bore little resemblance to what they look like now. But the present appearance of, for example, Durham Cathedral, does not represent the intentions of any of the generations who helped to build it. It must at one time have been as little to our taste as would have been the Parthenon, boldly painted in primary colours, as we are assured it was.

So, if megaliths are to be considered at all, in this context, we must judge them by what they mean to us, and not at all in the light of their original form or even purpose. Whereas the stone circles of the bronze age, being ritual sites, were presumably experienced as architecture by those who erected them, the megalithic tombs of

1

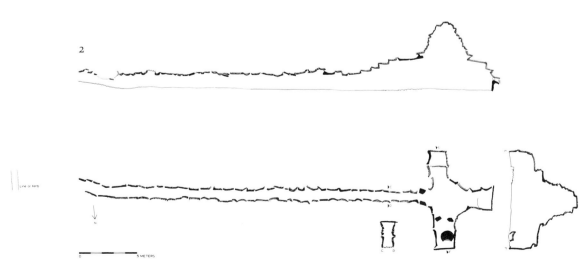

2

the neolithic phase can only be taken as we find them: sometimes accidentally impressive, sometimes not.

Though there are stone circles in Ireland they do not bear comparison with the major examples in other countries, and few of them rank among our most impressive megalithic monuments. With them, as with some other classes of field-monument, the pleasure of seeking and finding them, and the satisfaction to be had in reaching them, is apt to exceed the amount of strictly aesthetic enjoyment which they afford. The typical 'recumbent circle' of Drumbeg Co Cork, for example, is not hard to find, and is very instructive especially in association with the neighbouring monuments. But the fact that few of its stones are higher than a bar-counter, and most of them about the height of a bar-stool, is an obstacle to its being called architecture. At the opposite corner of the country Ballynoe circle in Co Down is 108 feet in diameter, has an outer and an inner circle and contains over 50 large stones, and is somewhat more impressive, though by no means typical.

The passage-graves of the Boyne culture, on the other hand, whatever their original external appearance may have been, offer, internally, a spatial experience rich in drama. At the end of a long, low, narrow passage, the cruciform tomb-chamber at Newgrange, 20 feet high and over 15 feet across, is roofed on the corbel principle, that is to say with large stone over large stone gradually oversailing and approaching each other until a single stone is enough to bridge the gap. This method of construction depends for its stability on the presence of a great deal of superincumbent tailweight. We shall see that in very much later applications of the corbel principle this consideration was not always kept in view.

The accepted date for these monuments is now about 2500 BC, that is to say within a very few centuries of the Pyramids, which, in a remote and crude way, they somewhat resemble. The family is spread right across Ireland, from the three great tumuli of Dowth, Knowth and Newgrange, to the series which occupy the three-mile long ridge of Slieve-na-Calliagh in Meath, and the Western groups at Carrowkeel near Boyle and Carrowmore near Sligo, with outliers in North Co Dublin and in the hills South of the capital. A mere handful are found further South, in Limerick, Tipperary and Kilkenny. As with other monuments the world over (for example Byzantine churches) it would seem that the biggest and best examples are the earliest: the later members of the series are impoverished and degenerate. Two examples, Fourknocks Co Dublin and Knockmany Co Tyrone, have been roofed with modern domes in such a way that daylight illuminates the carvings which, at Fourknocks, include a very funny face.[1] Knowth is still under excavation by Professor Eogan, and has yielded up two opposed passages and chambers (fig. 2).

The type of structure called by prehistorians a dolmen or, more recently, a portal-dolmen, is at once almost the simplest possible type of structure and among the most arresting, especially in certain contexts. Archaeologists have so far been unable either to date them with any precision, or to say for certain whether all of them, or if only some of them how many, were originally covered with mounds of earth or cairns of stone. These two uncertainties are of course interdependent: it is because the mound or cairn, if any, has been removed, that no contents remain by which the monument can be dated.

Neither problem is any concern of ours. We may find it hard to believe that a structure so expressive should have been immediately covered up, until we remember that where religion and magic are concerned, no amount of trouble may be spared on work destined never to be seen again. We may reflect also that, for all we know to the contrary, there may have been a period during which the dolmen was visible

1 Dunboyne, Co Meath: a traditional spirit grocery of a type now increasingly hard to find, though formerly ubiquitous

2 Knowth, Co Meath: plan and section of the passage and chamber in the great neolithic cairn first opened in recent years. The drawing by Professor George Eogan. The familiar plan and section of the neighbouring Newgrange has been frequently published: that of Knowth is less familiar, therefore given here

to the public at large before being covered up, like a Mormon temple today. We may speculate on whether it would have been cheaper to give a box-like outline to a large stone, using primitive tools, or to go looking for one which naturally possessed the desired arrisses (sharp edges). Legananny dolmen looks very much as though the stones have been tooled.

The one thing of which we may be certain is that to primitive man, no more than to ourselves, one stone was much like another stone. They had to make do, to a much greater extent than we must, with what lay to hand, but like all artists before and since, they sought to elicit what was most expressive in the material they used.

The expression can be startlingly diverse, considering how simple is the formula. A capstone supported by three or more uprights: that is all. But at Kilclooney it looks like some kind of a flying-machine, at Proleek like a juggling-act, at Poulnabrone like a house of cards, and at Legananny like a coffin shouldered by a bearing-party. Elsewhere, and especially in the case of the so-called 'earth-fast' dolmens, the suggestion is of a half-formed creature struggling to free itself from the matrix of earth. But if these images are in our minds that does not mean that they have ever been in anybody else's. Later in these pages, when the builders may be presumed to have been people rather more like ourselves, some conjectures will be offered as to what may have been in their minds: but not yet.

For those who are not prehistorians, the appeal of these monuments must often lie in the conjunction of the monument and its setting, whether at Duntryleague where the passage-grave on the North-West spur of the Galtees looks over the rich Limerick plain, or at the court-cairn called Ossian's Grave which commands a view down Glenaan over Cushendall to the North Channel, or where the 'Graves of the Leinstermen' on the Arra Mountains face across the broad Shannon to the wild hills of Clare.

But lest anyone be tempted to follow in the footsteps of George Moore to what he called 'the loveliest prospect that ever greeted mortal eyes', namely the view from Mount Venus over the city and bay of Dublin towards the hill of Howth, let him be warned in Moore's own words: 'Mount Venus has passed away, never to be revived again.'[2] The dolmen is still there, in the beech-dell past the ilexes as Moore described it, and also past a deal of barbed-wire and miscellaneous rubbish. But the house, which Moore dreamed of restoring and living in, is now unrecognizably ruined, and the whole neighbourhood polluted by the encroachment of the Dublin suburbs. Some of the other dolmens in the Dublin region are better worth the visiting today: Brenanstown (Glendruid) for example, described by Dr Harbison as 'looking like a bird about to take off',[3] or Kiltiernan, which in the eyes of an earlier writer 'has the appearance of a sphinx-like monster, advancing out of the rocky hill on some half-dozen short and rickety legs.'[4]★

Other countries can show bigger, and perhaps better, dolmens than those of Ireland; but in the matter of the dry-stone forts it is admitted that, in North-Western Europe at least, Ireland stands alone. The great fort of 'Dun Aenghus' on Inis Mór, on the edge of its cliff, with the Atlantic boiling and snarling 300 feet below, as though seeking to devour what remains of the fort, is a scene of Miltonic grandeur, deservedly famous. The pastoral setting of Staigue Fort in Kerry (fig. 3), regular, round and bland, nestling in a gently sloping valley opening to the South, could hardly be in

---

★ The English travel writer Diana Petry holds the record for dolmen-similes: 'a flying saucer landed in the bog', 'a fungus sprouting up from the earth', 'a huge coffin carried by three pall-bearers', 'a gigantic spider advancing on one', 'like some trapped monster' (all from *Wonders of Ireland* 1969).

3 Staigue Fort, Co Kerry: the very regular system of staircases on the inner face of the wall is under suspicion of having been tidied up during the nineteenth century (as at other sites, especially the Grianán in Co Donegal) but appears much as at present in Wilkinson's book of 1845

4 The Doon Fort, Naran, Co Donegal: a dry-stone fort similar to the Grianán of Aileach or to Staigue, of uncertain date but akin to the early Christian enclosures

5 Dun Conor, Inishmaan, Aran islands, Co Galway: a massive dry-stone fort of uncertain date, containing the remains of subsidiary structures. Note the internal terracing

3

4

5

greater contrast, and is perhaps equally familiar even to those who have never visited either. Much less familiar than these, and in fact hardly ever mentioned or illustrated, is the mysterious and remote structure, variously called The Bawan, The Doon Fort (fig. 4) and O'Boyle's Fort, which occupies the whole of a rocky island in the black water of Doon Lough near Naran in Co Donegal. In superficial contrast to all these is the essentially similar Grianán of Aileach which stands on top of a large domed hill at the neck of the Inishowen peninsula a few miles from Derry.

These are round or approximately round, except of course for Dun Aengus which, like Cahercommaun in Co Clare, is in principle a semicircle, or rather a series of concentric semicircles. Others are more or less oval such as Dun Conor (fig. 5) on Inish Maan which is nearly twice as long as it is wide, or Dun Oghil on Inis Mór which is much less oval, as well as being smaller, measuring 91 feet by 75.

The distribution of these buildings is overwhelmingly Western. In round figures, 20 or 25 major examples are known, and all of these are in the counties of the Western seaboard except for a few in Co Down and one which is in Co Wicklow. This one, Rathgaill near Tullow, is among the very largest, the outermost of its four rings enclosing 18 acres. It is also one of the least impressive, since the innermost ring, though 18 feet thick at the base, is much collapsed, and compared with it the outer rings are meagre and stringy. But most of the better-known Western forts were drastically 'tidied-up' in the nineteenth century—how drastically may be gauged from the fact that the Grianán which now has four V-shaped stone stairways, had originally only two. Fortunately the third Earl of Dunraven had a steam-yacht, an enormous brass-and-mahogany camera, an inexhaustible interest in Irish antiquities, and friends such as George Petrie and Margaret Stokes. Let an extract from a letter from Petrie to Dunraven speak for itself. The year is 1857:

> The weather was glorious, and we scarcely left a church, or grave, or cloghan, a Saint, or a Dun of a Firbolg, in the three islands unvisited or unexamined. Alas that from the want of a protecting hand, these singularly interesting remains should be doomed to utter ruin! The Duns or Cahers particularly, are now only vestiges of the monuments which astonished me by their barbaric grandeur on my visit to these islands in 1822, and it made me melancholy to see the devastations which unthinking man, and not the elements, had made in a few years.[5]

In a few more years, the activities of the Board of Works, all thinking men, had brought order out of chaos: but at a price. Happily, however, the fruit of the collaboration of Dunraven and Margaret Stokes, those two massive volumes so modestly entitled *Notes on Irish Architecture*, have preserved for us the appearance of many of the forts as they were before the hand of the restorer was laid upon them.

Margaret Stokes was a careful observer, and noted, for example, that at Dun Conor the inner wall was built in three concentric rings, the inner one seven feet thick, the middle one five feet six inches (with two smooth faces) and the outer one also five feet six inches, making a total thickness of 18 feet.[6] Some of the forts, notably Dun Beg and the Grianán, have wall-passages, and often they have guard-chambers commanding the entrance, though in some, such as Knockdrum Co Cork, the guard must have had to crouch there in great discomfort. At the promontory fort of Dun Beg on the Dingle peninsula these works at the entrance are of unusual complexity.[7]

In common with many of the earthen forts, the dry-stone forts commonly have one or more souterrains in them: underground structures whose purpose is still uncertain, but was probably connected with storage and perhaps temporary concealment. In some of the forts can be traced the foundations of small buildings:

sometimes round and sometimes rectangular. Among the most striking features found in some forts and pre-eminently in Staigue and its fairly near neighbour Cahergall is the regular network of branching stairways lining the interior: so regular as to invite the suspicion that their primary purpose is decorative. It is not surprising that the older antiquaries hazarded the opinion that Staigue and its relatives may have been amphitheatres intended for some spectacle. It would certainly be possible so to use them to this very day.

Being of dry stone construction, which naturally varies in quality but is seen at its best perhaps in Cahergall, the walls are built with a slight inward slope or 'batter' which was to be one of the most persistent characteristics of Irish building for many centuries to come.

There are to be found structures intermediate between the earth fort and the stone fort, such, for example, as the gigantic enclosure at Mooghaun in Co Clare, where the earthen banks are revetted in stone. A stone fort on an island, such as the Bawan, is not such a very different proposition from an artificial island or crannóg, especially when, as at Fair Head in Co Antrim, the crannóg has an oval dry-stone revetment all round it.

It is understandable that archaeologists should be cautious about both the typology and the dating of these buildings, and their presumed purpose. Dr Raftery has emphasised[8] that in stony terrain they are the analogue of the earthen forts (*rath* or *lis*) so exceedingly common over the country as a whole (a good recent estimate is 30,000–40,000). But by virtue of their materials they have features—lintelled door-ways with upper relieving-lintels for example—which cannot exist in an earthen structure. Their distribution presents even more acute problems. Part of the explan-ation for their existence may well be that which accounts for the network of dry-stone field-walls in so many areas: that there is nowhere else to put the stones, and no field until the stones have been somehow disposed of. Yet even if there was more soil-cover in ancient times than there is today, it is difficult to see an adequate economic basis for structures so demonstrative as these.

The fact that the limestone of Co Clare and the Aran islands has cleavage planes which help it to split into usefully-shaped stones, would have been an encouragement to good workmanship. But little is known about the level of technology obtaining when the forts were built, since the rocky substratum generally precludes excavation. As for their actual age, Professor Evans thinks[9] that there is 'a strong probability' that the *site* (note the caution) of Staigue, like that of the Grianán, belongs to the pagan iron age (i.e. before AD 400), while recent excavation has shown that the central ring of Rathgaill, though of the expected thickness, dates 'to the mediaeval period or later'.[10]

The suggestion has recently been made[11] that these forts are almost entirely symbols of wealth and status, and hardly intended for serious defence. This is an attractive idea, not least because it places these ancient and mysterious structures in the same box as the comical castellated houses of the early nineteenth century. The wealth of the iron age, and of many succeeding centuries, was measured in cattle, and one of the principal functions of the Irish rath must have been for the folding in of beasts. Any magnate who had gathered his kinsfolk and his cattle behind the triple ramparts of Dun Aengus for a last stand, would have his back to the wall in an exact sense of that phrase.

Three of the forts: Dun Aengus and Dubh Cathair (both on Inismór) and Ballykinvarga (on the Clare mainland near Kilfenora) have an additional feature not yet mentioned: the famous *chevaux de frise*. This consists of the largest possible number of spike-shaped stones which can be stuck into crannies in the bare rock, from which they protrude at a variety of angles: more adapted, one would suppose, to the discouragement of an armoured division or a float-down of paratroops than of the warriors who people the plays of Mr Yeats. The thought occurs again that it was because the spike-shaped stones and the cracks in the rocks were there, that someone had the idea of disposing them in such a decorative way.

Dunraven and Stokes were not the only observers to bracket the stone forts with the earliest surviving Christian churches. Whatever their relationship in time, they are obviously related in feeling and in technique, and insofar as the early Christian churches are, or were, surrounded by cashels, the categories overlap. The brochs of Scotland may be thought of as intermediate in type between an Irish stone fort and a Christian Round Tower, and it is perhaps significant that their distribution seems sometimes to defy the criteria of common sense:

> Here [on Rousay] within a distance of no more than 500 yards one is astounded to find the remains of three brochs, and, in view of the labour involved in the building of even one, this concentration is, indeed, a quite extraordinary, and as yet inexplicable, phenomenon.[12]

CHAPTER TWO

Early Christian

There are, scattered more or less all over Ireland, though like most other buildings a little more thickly in the Midlands than in the extreme North or South, several hundred small churches, mostly in a state of advanced ruin, which are described as 'Early Christian'. Their touchingly primitive character is beyond dispute. Their actual age is another matter entirely: still very uncertain, and likely to remain so.

What is certain is that an important phase of architecture, lasting for at least 300 years from, say, 450 to 750 or later, has disappeared completely and can be known only by inference.[1] The fact that the first Irish churches were of timber is attested both by the literary evidence and by the clearly imitative character of some details in the stone churches which survive. Thus, though there is doubtless good reason to associate certain important sites with early missionary saints such as Enda of Aran, Ciaran of Clonmacnois, Laisren of Devenish, Finian of Clonard, Colmcille of Derry and the rest, most, if not all of whom, were historical figures of the fifth to sixth centuries, there are no good grounds for supposing that any of the surviving buildings on even the most favoured of these sites go back to the original foundation.

There is no certainty about the age of the buildings: the most that can be said is that there is rough general agreement about the primitive character of some of them and the more developed character of others. There are some favoured sites which have been sealed, so to speak; if not quite so effectively as Pompeii or Herculaneum, nevertheless sealed. They have been favoured not from their point of view, but from ours. Thus Inismurray in Co Sligo (fig. 6) disappears from the annalistic record in 802 and does not surface again until 1612. Nendrum in Co Down (fig. 8) similarly vanishes in 974 and is rediscovered only in 1844. Seven to nine hundred years of oblivion, even if initiated by a lethal spoliation, is a kind of blessing. The most spectacular of all Irish Early Christian sites, Sceilg Mhicíl on the jagged Great Skellig island eight miles out in the Atlantic off the Kerry coast, has virtually no known history. It belongs, of course, to that group of high places dedicated to the Archangel of which the most splendid adorns the estuary of the Sélune on the border between Normandy and Brittany. But it is hardly so typical as Inismurray or Nendrum.[2]

The cashel which surrounds the monastic precinct at Inismurray[3] off the North-Western coast is barely distinguishable from those we have already seen in the preceding chapter. Within it are grouped a number of dry-stone beehive huts on the corbelled principle, and three rectangular buildings of which the largest and the smallest were certainly churches; the smaller of these has a stone roof, also corbelled. At Nendrum[4] which like Inismurray is on an island, though in a very much more sheltered situation being in a large landlocked tidal inlet and not in the open Atlantic, there is a triple cashel, a number of beehive huts mostly between the middle and inner walls, a church and one other rectangular building, and a Round Tower.

The early monks favoured island sites, as conducive to austerity and to peace. Though vulnerable to Viking raids, such situations have tended to preserve them since, and many of the most characteristic and attractive sites are on islands. But there

26

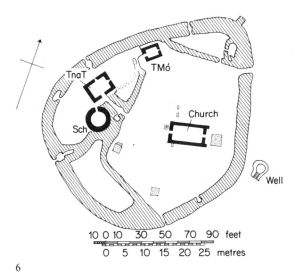

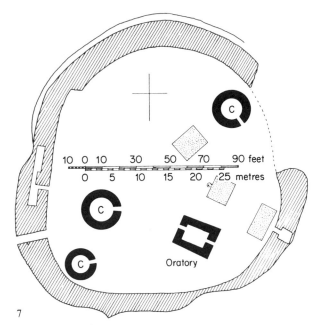

6

7

6 Inismurray, Co Sligo: plan of the monastic enclosure, after Wakeman. Teach na Teine (the fire-house) and Teampall Molaise (Molaise's (Laisren's) House) are near the North-West wall, close to the circular schoolhouse

7 Illauntannig (Oiléan tSeanaigh), Co Kerry: another monastic enclosure, also on an Atlantic island, with an oratory, three clocháns 'C' and other, less decipherable remains. Plan after Dunraven

8 Nendrum, Co Down: plan of the two inner rings of the monastic enclosure, on an island in Strangford Lough, after Lawlor. The finds from the site (excavated in 1922-4) are in the Ulster Museum, Belfast, and give a very vivid idea of the life of a tenth-century Irish monastery

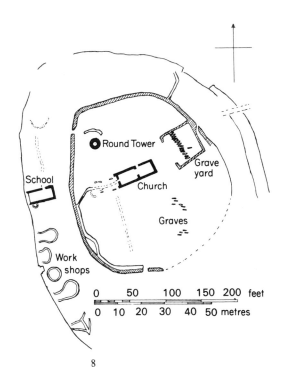

8

is a great variety of situation: Peakaun is up on a slope of the great Glen of Aherlow, Liathmore in the middle of a large bog, Monahincha on a little tump which was once an island but can now be reached dry-shod, Clonamery and St Mullins close to the rivers Nore and Barrow, Aghowle some distance up the foothills of the Wicklow massif, Bovevagh, Dungiven and Banagher a similar distance up the foothills of the Sperrins, St John's Point on a low spit running out into the Irish Sea. Some other ancient sites, of similar origins to these, are now in towns of some consequence such as Kilkenny, Roscrea or Clones. What survives in these places may be a primitive church, or one in the developed Romanesque in fragmentary form, or a house-shaped tomb, or a Round Tower, or some combination of these. It is a matter of accident, for in their origins all these places must have been something like Inismurray or Nendrum.

But perhaps the island sites come most prominently to mind. All down the Western seaboard there is hardly an island without its ancient church: Tory, Inishglora, Duvillaun, Inishkea, Ardilaun, Saint MacDara's Island, Scattery, Illauntannig in the Maharees, Clear Island the most Southerly of all. Even on the Eastern coast, Dalkey island, on the doorstep of the capital, has an ancient church, and so had Ireland's Eye. Quite different in atmosphere are those on islands in inland lakes, Devenish, White Island and Inishmacsaint in Lower Lough Erne, Aghalurcher, Galloon, Trinity Island and others on Upper Lough Erne and Lough Oughter, where it is hard to say whether the land is interrupted by water or the water interrupted by land. There are others on the greater lakes of the West, such as Inchagoill on Lough Corrib, and two famous sites on those widenings of the great river Shannon which are called Lough Ree and Lough Derg: Inishcleraun and Inishcaltra respectively. The most famous site of all, Clonmacnois, is also on the Shannon, not strictly on an island but probably almost completely surrounded by water in the winters of a thousand years ago, and still approached by a causeway.

The earliest surviving Irish churches clearly derive from two traditions: the corbelled tradition of the Clochán or bee-hive 'hut', and a tradition imitating construction in timber. As Mlle Henry has pointed out, the 'huts' are a good deal bigger than most people realise: some of those at Sceilg Mhicíl are 30 feet in diameter and 18 feet high.

One line of development which derives entirely from the corbelling tradition and owes nothing to timber is represented by the two small Sceilg Mhicíl oratories and by several on the mainland, of which much the best known and best-preserved is that of Gallarus in the Dingle peninsula. Many of the bee-hive cells are round both inside and out, and resemble, not so much the *trulli* of the Alberobello region in Apulia with which they are sometimes compared, as those further to the South East beyond Lecce, which have a round domical outline rather than a conical one.[5] Those on Sceilg Mhicíl are externally domical but their plan is rectangular inside, and beside them stand the two oratories which are essentially oblong.

At Gallarus, and others less well preserved such as Kilmalkedar, this principle has been carried a stage further, so that there is a linear roof-ridge on the axis of the plan.★ The gables slope inwards, and indeed curve also, as do the 'walls', so that the roof begins in effect at ground-level. But as Leask has observed[6] the longer sides are inherently unstable and tend to sag inwards at the middle. For this reason all except Gallarus have collapsed. Others, such as Kilmalkedar and Temple Cashel, survive in an instructive state of partial ruin.

The West door of Gallarus has a flat stone lintel, not nearly so deep as in some

★ Compare the *bories* of Vaucluse.

more developed buildings, and its tiny East window has an arch formed of two stones externally and three on the inside, laid more or less radially. The builders appear to have known the principle of the arch, even if they did not place a great deal of faith in it. Elsewhere, and when convenient, arched window-heads were cut out of a single stone: examples are too numerous to specify.

Gallarus and its fellows are built with considerable skill of relatively small stones. In what appears to be the next generation the most striking features are the smallness of the churches and the great size of the stones used in their construction. Teampull Benen, for example, on Inismór Island, has in its South wall one large square stone which contributes one-third of the whole visible surface, and three other stones of phenomenal size in the same wall. But the whole church is less than 15 feet long overall. St MacDara's (fig. 11) has an almost equally small number of similarly large stones, and is only 21 feet long. But while at Teampull Benen the stones are squared, at St MacDara's they are like carefully fitted crazy paving. This, in a sense, is just what they are, for in both buildings the large visible stones are laid on edge, and the middle of the rather thick walls filled up with unbonded stones.

The lintel-stones of the West doorways, by contrast, are very massive indeed and are generally through stones, as are many of the jamb-stones. The coigns also, while not differentiated from the rest of the walling, are large and well squared. The jambs of the doorways, and, to a lesser extent generally, the angles of the buildings themselves, have the batter inherited from the dry-stone forts. As to the amount or nature of the mortar used in these early churches, this is not easy to determine, what with leaching out and repointing in later times. Sea-shells, sand, clay and mud are reported by the observers of a century ago. All or any of these would act as mortar of a kind.[7]

Striking as the minute size of many of these churches is, it is worth remembering that some few churches of similar character were in fact quite large: notably the 'Cathedral' at Glendalough which, though much altered is essentially of early date, and is 48 feet long by 30 feet wide.[8] The literary evidence suggests also the existence of large churches of timber; but since they no longer exist they have no place in this narrative.

For many years the principal interest of Irish pre-twelfth-century architecture was thought to be that it represented an independent primitive effort unaffected by the influence of Rome. But already by the seventh century Irish civilisation had been deeply influenced by Rome, through the Christian church, and this is almost certainly earlier than any surviving Irish Christian building. In the words of Leask, 'a theory deriving the inclined jambs from Classic source is not untenable';[9] and when a doorway with inclined jambs has also an architrave round it, it presents a very Mediterranean appearance. It must be admitted that otherwise, apart from their simplicity and directness, early Irish buildings are not very classical. They have, of course, neither aisles nor arcades.

The elements deriving from wooden construction are very obvious and telling. Paradoxically, it is not easy to deal with them in isolation from the elements deriving from the corbelling tradition: the attempt must nevertheless be made.

The antae with which many early churches are provided are essentially prolongations of the side-walls beyond the plane of the front and often also the back (i.e. East and West). They are usually, though not always, of the same width as the thickness of the walls. At Glendalough Cathedral they are a little less. The most probable explanation for their presence is that they represent the corner-posts of timber buildings. Occasionally, as at St Laisren's, Devenish, Temple-na-Hoe at

9 Agha, Co Carlow: the South-East corner of the early church, the masonry of rounded field-stones fitted to carefully chosen spawls. The other (West) end of the church is later, in masonry of a different, but almost equally striking character

10 Devenish Island, Co Fermanagh: gable-stone from St Laisren's oratory, after MacKenna and Leask. On the left the stone is seen as in position on the right-hand slope of the gable, with the simulated overlapping slate-slopes shown dotted. A is the continuous slope of the barge-course at the gable-verge. B is the intermittent slope of the individual courses of the solid stone roof. After MacKenna and Leask

11 St MacDara's Island, Co Galway: the church after its recent restoration by the Office of Public Works. The original stones, found in situ, were used for the reinstatement of the top and central slopes of the roof. The finials are modern, on the model of the damaged West finial found in situ. The new West finial has been carved with the saint's figure and accompanying ornament in the spirit of the original. It is here in shadow

9

10

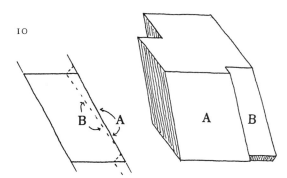

11

Ardfert, and the East end of Tuamgraney and Monahincha, their place is taken by engaged three-quarter columns with capitals.

At St MacDara's Island, at Kilmalkedar, and apparently also at St Laisren's, Devenish,[10] the antae or columns continue up the sides of the gable as an oversailing barge-course to meet at the top. At Kilmalkedar especially it is clear that this is a reminiscence of an 'elbow-cruck' timber structure, even though there are quasi-capitals at eaves-level. When they meet at the top, they sometimes cross in the form of the so-called 'winged-finial', which is known in North Germany, Scandinavia and Iceland, and of which some examples in stone still survive in Ireland (fig. 11).

It is fortunate that there are contemporary 'models' of early Irish churches still in existence: on three scales of reduction. The stone tombs at Banagher, Bovevagh, Clones and elsewhere are essentially models of churches: that at Clones even has the winged finial worked in the solid. Somewhat smaller, and also made of stone, are the miniature churches which stand on top of some of the ninth-century High Crosses of Monasterboice and Durrow. Finally, and on an even smaller scale, there are the portable reliquaries in similar form, such as the Lough Erne shrine, the Lemanaghan shrine and the Breac Mogue.[11] At Muiredach's Cross, Monasterboice, the wooden shingles of the roof-covering are even carved in miniature.

The appearance of overlapping shingles or slabs is, or rather was, imitated in a full-size church which may serve as an introduction to the whole category of stone-roofed churches. The consideration of this category will, in due course, carry us forward right through the middle ages to the seventeenth century. St Laisren's oratory at Devenish (fig. 10), already mentioned, had a corbelled stone roof of which the outer stones were extremely artfully cut to simulate overlapping shingles or slabs. Under this, and continuous with it, was a corbelled vault of pointed form. The roof-pitch was steep, as that of such a roof must be: in this case just over 60 degrees. It is now thought to be twelfth century.

The slope of the stone roof at St MacDara's Island is somewhat greater: about 63 degrees. From both gable-ends and at the eaves, substantial parts of the stone roof have survived *in situ* down to our own time, but the unsoundness of the construction, which at Gallerus had produced a sag, has here led to collapse. However, as these words are being written, the Board of Works is reconstructing the roof of this tiny church. Leask thought that both during construction and during the early life of the building, the two slopes were held apart by timber beams, and that when these decayed the roof fell in.

In his familiar diagram of the evolution of the Irish stone roof, Leask has made clear how, early on, the place of these timber props was taken by a 'strainer-arch' half-way up the roof-slope, and how this developed into the mature double roof with a more or less habitable overcroft as at Killaloe or Cormac's Chapel. He had the great advantage of dismantling St Molua's on Friar's Island in the Shannon when, like the temples at Philae, it was faced with hydro-electric inundation, and of putting it together again on dry land. Its little stone-roofed chancel had a small void in the apex, which would not otherwise have come to light, and, lower down, notches for the propping-beams.

There is one small, early, church which has a unique feature seeming to derive from timber construction. Though much ruined and reconstructed, Labba Molaga near Mitchelstown, Co Cork, has a West doorway made of three stones: two jambs and a carefully fitted lintel: the only such doorway with vertical monolithic jambs. If, as Raftery suggests, the earth-forts are the equivalents in timbered country of the stone forts of the West, then one would expect them to have had post-and-lintel doorways of timber;[12] and this Labba Molaga doorway looks like a translation into stone of such an entrance. The jambs are inclined inwards as they are in the more usual kind of doorway.[13]

No doubt it is true to say, as Conant does, that 'the old Irish churches are widowed now without their furnishings'.[14] What is exposed is, in Seán O'Faolain's phrase, the stillness of the classic bone; as much may be said of the brothel at Ephesus. The soft furnishings have gone, and so has all the turmoil of the flesh.

The atmosphere of these early Christian sites is not easy to convey to those who have not seen them. Photographs can give some idea, especially of those on island sites. But no photograph can convey the remote and plaintive beauty of Monahincha or of St Peakaun's, like the music of an archaic flute.

Nothing has so far been said about decoration. The first form in which it appears can hardly be called decoration: a raised architrave round the openings of windows and especially of doors. In a few cases—Fore, Clonamery, Antrim Round Tower, Inishmurray, Gallen—there is a cross, always very beautifully executed, and all different. At St Mary's, Glendalough, the cross is on the underside of the lintel.

Since the Round Towers are always associated with early churches they must be introduced at some point, and it seems appropriate to do so here. Confusion no longer rages over their origin and meaning, though there is still some disagreement about their date. I may as well say straight away that in my opinion they were built over a period extending from the tenth century to beyond the end of the twelfth.[15] Their doorways and windows are precisely similar to those of the churches, and range, as do those of the churches, from the simplest lintelled types to round-headed examples and through to the fully developed Romanesque with receding orders and 'tangential' gable-pediments. A few are physically connected with churches and actually form part of them, and to deny these the title of Round Towers seems to me contrary to common sense. It has recently been suggested that they are not quite so distinctively Irish as they are generally held to be. This view, also, seems to me to be a little perverse. The pair of towers in the early ninth-century St Gallen plan are symmetrically disposed as part of an architectural ensemble utterly unlike anything in Ireland. While the idea of a tall tapering minaret-like tower from which to look out and ring a hand-bell is unlikely to have originated in Ireland, the Irish annalistic name for them means 'bell-house' and that, among other things, is what they were.[16]

The cylindrical campanili of Ravenna are not really very like the Irish towers, and the East Anglian examples are of twelfth century and later date and seem to be an independent development resulting from having to build in flint.

For long regarded, and employed, as a symbol of Irish nationhood, and by the irreverent as a symbol of another kind altogether, the Round Towers have struck the imagination of visitor after visitor. Many travellers are unprepared for the fact that Ireland is a very flat country: neither the topographical engravers of the past nor the tourist promoters of the present are at pains to emphasise this. The extreme verticality of the towers is thus all the more salient. From one notable visitor they provoked a most curious reaction. Robert Byron printed a picture of one of them as an example of what he called 'Mobile Composition achieved by an economy of vertical lines', and went on to say: 'Its lack of inspiration suits a country where all human effort seems slightly out of place.'[17] No doubt his short visit to Ireland coincided with a period of low barometric pressure. We all know the feeling.

The Round Towers are a remarkably homogeneous group, and variations are few. The distribution of existing and known examples is the expected one for Christian monuments of their date. It is worthwhile to point out that within modern times examples still stood in the cities of Dublin and Derry (doubtless in Cork as well), and that there are, even now, three within eight miles of Dublin and three within 14 miles of Belfast. But most are of course in the Midlands.

Their most common diameter is about 17 to 18 feet at the base. They all taper, and sometimes they have entasis as well, giving them a subtle silhouette like that of a Greek column.★ Lack of inspiration forsooth. All the complete examples (which include some modern restorations) have a conical stone roof on the corbel principle, in at least one case of herringbone masonry. The towers are commonly built on very shallow foundations, with the result that some—not many—lean a little. At least one has a skeleton lying, half inside and half outside, under the four-foot wall.

The door is, with only two known exceptions, well above ground level, usually eight or nine feet up. The doors of those at Castledermot and Scattery Island are at ground level. Internally there are or were four or five timber floors carried on offsets, and lit by small windows. At the top there are usually four windows: occasionally six as at Kilkenny. There were never any stairs; ladders served instead.

Two of the very finest of the towers, those at Devenish and at Ardmore, display as much contrast as the series can show. Devenish is shorter than most complete examples, being only just over five diameters high (81 feet) and has very slight negative entasis (a slightly hollow outline). It also has a carved band of Romanesque ornament sometimes called a cornice but in fact a frieze, just below the cap, interrupted by four finely carved heads. Ardmore, on the other hand, is not only one of the tallest of the towers (about 95 feet), but tapers more than any other tower, and has three external string-courses at which, additionally to the taper, the diameter diminishes slightly. Dysert O'Dea may have been similar.

The tower at Kinneigh, Co Cork, stands on a six-sided base some 18 to 20 feet high: Clondalkin and Rattoo also have slightly unusual bases. Dromiskin is exceptionally short (49 feet) yet complete with cap. But the typical tower is one such as Cashel or Killala, in both of which the masonry is particularly good: the former in Margaret Stokes's 'second' style, the latter in her 'third'. It is by no means proven that her four styles are necessarily sequent: much depends on the stone available in each locality. The character of the openings is a better guide to date. The towers of Timahoe Co Leix (fig. 12) and Kildare have Hiberno-Romanesque doorways of several orders with, at Kildare, a tangent gablet, comparable to the church doorways of the mature phase of that style.

In at least one of the towers, Monasterboice,[18] a doorway with a comparatively elaborate architrave, which I take to be midway between the simply lintelled and the Romanesque, has a round head formed not with arch-stones, but cut out of the horizontal coursing of the tower as a whole. This would be very anomalous in the door of a church; so it seems that the builders knew that a true arch formed on a curve of tight radius is inherently unstable. The door at Scattery, which is believed to be among the earliest, is similarly constructed.

A small number of churches have, or are known to have had, a Round Tower forming part of the church. The best known of these is perhaps 'St Kevin's Kitchen' at Glendalough, a double-stone-roofed church which has, tangentially over its West gable, a belfry of Round Tower form. Leask dated the church to the ninth century and regarded the belfry as an addition, though of course an early addition. Trinity Church, also at Glendalough, is a later nave-and-chancel church with a small square

---

★ The surviving tower at Devenish seems to have a small amount of *negative* entasis, i.e. to be slightly concave in outline. But all such effects, when very small, may have been overridden by a plaster finish.

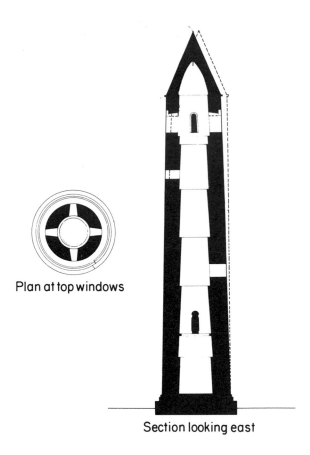

Plan at top windows

Section looking east

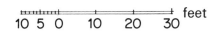

10 5 0   10   20   30   feet

12

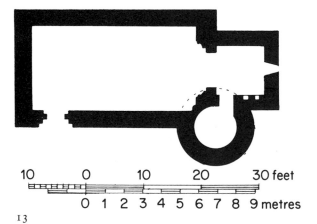

10   0   10   20   30 feet

0 1 2 3 4 5 6 7 8 9 metres

13

12 Timahoe, Co Leix: plan and section of the Round Tower (Office of Public Works). This tower, like that of Kildare, has an elaborate Romanesque door in several orders, but is otherwise entirely typical

13 Clonmacnois, Co Offaly: Teampull Finghín with MacCarthy's Tower attached to the South of the chancel. Plan after Brash. The capstones of the tower are laid herringbone-wise

Western compartment on which there stood until 1818, supported by a vault, a Round Tower said to have been 60 feet high. St Nessan's Church on Ireland's Eye, of very similar form to Trinity, had, by contrast, a Round Tower supported by the vault of its chancel.★

St Finghín's at Clonmacnois (fig. 13) is also a nave-and-chancel church of the mid-to-late twelfth century. On the South side, at the junction of nave and chancel, and opening off the chancel though partly corbelled-out over the nave, is a particularly well built Round Tower some 56 feet high, that is to say about two-thirds the usual scale. The quasi-transeptal position of the tower strongly recalls Cormac's Chapel: in fact the actual North tower of Cormac's Chapel, with its pyramidal stone roof, is nothing but a square version of the Round Tower design, and doubtless the South tower was originally like that also. (The position of the South-West porch recalls Cormac's Chapel also, most forcibly).

Among the spurious or unproven examples of Round Towers attached to churches are Tamlaght Finlagan Co Derry, Trummery Co Antrim, St Michael-le-Pole's, Dublin, and Killashee Co Kildare. The last of these still exists and is indeed round but is not a capitalised Round Tower, being of mediaeval date. At Lusk, Kilmallock and Dysert O'Dea, true Round Towers were incorporated by the mediaeval builders into constructions of their own.†

A handful of Round Towers overseas can be confidently regarded as outliers of the Irish group. The nearest is in the bailey of Peel Castle in Man, where there is also a church of early Irish type. The towers at Brechin and Abernethy, both in the neighbourhood of Dundee, have also been classified as Irish in their affinities. At Deerness in Orkney, and St Magnus, in Egilshay, there are or were churches with Round Towers which, as illustrated by Dunraven, look temptingly Irish.[19] The pair at Deerness flanked what appears to be the West end of a simple church in a manner perhaps too symmetrical to be convincingly Irish: more like Gernrode or St Pantaleon, Cologne: but in such a situation we know not what cross-currents of influence may have intermingled. St Magnus, Egilshay, still stands.

Considered as a national architectural type, the Round Towers are not unworthy of the role in which they have been cast. Professor Conant calls them 'the most poetic of the Celtic architectural creations.'[20] What they lack in complexity of plan they amply atone for in subtlety of profile, and are none the poorer for having emerged from the fog of mystery in which they were shrouded for so long.

★ Trinity Church and Reefert Church both have stone barge-brackets to receive the ends of timber barge-boards. These uncommon features are found also at Teampull Chronain Co Clare (near Carran) and, more surprisingly and hitherto unnoticed, on the ruined South transept of Clonfert Cathedral, perhaps reused.

† At Ferns Co Wexford the Augustinian monastery has a curious belfry, square below but rising into something very like an Irish Round Tower, illustrated in *78th Report of Commissioners of Public Works in Ireland*, 1909-10, p 17 (measured drawings).

CHAPTER THREE

Romanesque

The Irish trabeate (square-headed) West door is capable of considerable variety. At Killeavy Co Armagh, and Tuamgraney Co Clare, the enormous size of the stones, and above all of the lintels, is most expressive. At Tuamgraney a plain broad architrave is worked on these huge stones: similarly at Fore, with the addition of a broad band above the architrave, interrupted by a slightly canted cross in a circle. At Clonamery (fig. 14) a maltese cross, likewise in low relief, stands on a short shaft which itself stands on the architrave. At Aghowle Co Wicklow (fig. 15) there is a plain frame of three receding planes, the outermost of which is a little proud of the wall-face, and the innermost of which is twice as broad as the others, giving a massively monumental effect. At Temple Martin, four miles East of Dingle, the architrave is slightly sunk and bordered by a delicate moulding which makes it look very classical.[1] At Ratass the lintel is gigantic, the architrave broad and bold, and the surrounding ashlar of an impressive scale. At St Mary's, Glendalough, the inclination of the jambs is more marked than usual, and the architrave relatively narrow.

The doorway at Banagher Co Derry, also has its jambs very much inclined, but resembles Aghowle both in its external architrave and in having a semicircular rere-arch. Structurally similar to both of these, the doorway at Maghera, Co Derry, is unique in having a great crucifixion scene in relief on the inner of the planes of the surround. Unfortunately it is now so placed, inside a later tower, that it is almost impossible to see or to photograph. Leask put it just before AD 1100, but Stalley suggests a date about 50 years later because the jambs have Irish Urnes-style decoration.

A limited number of early lintelled doorways have relieving-arches over them, formed flush with the rest of the masonry. Both St Kevin's and the cathedral at Glendalough are so constructed: the former unusually narrow and the latter unusually wide. At Britway Co Cork, the architrave is carried up round the relieving-arch which is formed of five rather regular stones, while the lintel has something of the look of an afterthought.

These primitive doorways are perhaps the most distinctive and the most perennially satisfying features to be found in the whole course of Irish architecture. In their own terms they are the last word and cannot possibly be improved upon.

They were not, of course, the last word. The next step was to make the doorways round-headed, a step which took place in perhaps the year 1000 or so, and which led by imperceptible gradations to the full development of Irish Romanesque.

Throughout this period plan-forms remained extremely primitive. The earliest churches were simple rectangles: as Leask has noted they begin with a proportion of less than 1.5:1, and get longer as they get later. The only development is to add a chancel narrower and shorter than the nave: examples of this plan which are integral (as opposed to additions) and which appear to be early[2] are Trinity, Reefert and St Kieran's, all at Glendalough, and all pre-Romanesque in style, in the sense that they have plain lintelled, semicircular or triangular-headed openings and virtually no decoration. Monahincha Co Tipperary, which is later and has a Romanesque West door and chancel-arch, has the same plan as Trinity and Reefert and very similar dimensions: it is less than 50 feet long overall.[3] In fact, right to the end of the Romanesque period no further elaboration of plan was developed, except for the tower at St Finghín's already mentioned, the quasi-transeptal towers at Cormac's Chapel, and the *porticus* to North and South of the chancel at Rahan: two small chambers corresponding to the *prothesis* and *diaconicon* of the Eastern church, and found also in a few French and English churches of the seventh century. There were no aisles, no arcades, no apses, no underground *confessios*, nothing to compare with, for example, Brixworth or Reculver, Repton or Wing.

Trinity Glendalough, Reefert, St Flannan's and Monahincha have no windows in their North walls. This characteristic was to reappear in the seventeenth century, and very markedly in the early nineteenth. So few mediaeval parish churches survive that generalisation is hazardous: but, among smaller aisleless examples, Drumacoo has an almost windowless North wall; not that the windows in the South or any other walls of the early churches would admit much light: we must think of the interiors as having been very dark, and a North window would have been of little use.

Since churches with residential West ends are a feature of the mediaeval period, it is worth glancing at the possibility that some of the small early stone churches were lived in. The evidence is almost entirely linguistic and very flimsy: the name of Gallarus, St Molaise's 'house' (Devenish), 'Teach' Molaise (Inismurray), St Mochta's (Louth), St Declan's (Ardmore), St Columb's 'House' (Kells), the Priest's 'House' (Glendalough), Labba Molaga which means the *bed* of the saint and where there is a kind of table-tomb on which, or in which, he may have rested during life, like John Donne. Such austerities were part of the order of the day, and beside the hardness of the 'bed' the absence of a hearth seems to be quite in key. 'Molaise (i.e. Laisren) loved to live in a house of hard stone' we read.[4] It seems to me impossible to separate the general drift of this evidence from Bede's suggestion that in the eighth century Irish monks learned to build in stone 'juxta morem Romanorum . . . de lapide'[5]. that is to say, with mortar, and that anchorites very possibly lived in what we now call 'churches' or 'oratories'. This is very far from saying that any of the surviving buildings are as old as that. As we have already seen, mortar is a not very sharply definable substance, and a whole family of wooden structures have vanished without trace.

It is time to turn again to a subject which is closely related to plan-form and to use: namely the story of the stone roof. The desire to vault is perennially recurrent in Western architecture. To cover a building, and especially a church, with a roof of some monumental and incombustible material has been, one suspects, at times as much an aesthetic aspiration as a practical necessity. There are numerous records of the burning of monastic complexes, but so far as I know none of the stone-roofed churches shows any sign of having been burnt. There are 900 entries in the annals recording the burning or plundering of churches between AD 615 and AD 1546, and some of these entries cover a large number of such acts.[6]

Vaulting, however, is usually an end in itself. In the Byzantine and Gothic traditions it becomes a matter of vaults helping to support each other over complex and interdependent spaces. In Ireland, as we have already seen, plans were both simple and small. The first step taken to counter the inward-sagging tendency of the corbelled roof was the insertion of a 'propping-arch', leaving a triangular space above it, for example at St Columb's, Kells (Meath) and, with modifications, St Kevin's, Glendalough. The width spanned in both these examples is less than 15 feet.

The total number of surviving stone roofs of the special Irish type is very small: about nine or ten. Nor is there much evidence that they were ever much more numerous. But the spread of their distribution is impressively wide. St Laisren's in Fermanagh may be slightly anomalous and something of an outlier, but from Louth to Kells (Meath) to Glendalough to Cashel in Tipperary to Killaloe in Clare to Kilmalkedar in Kerry, not counting mediaeval examples not strictly comparable, is a wide sweep and enough to establish the type as national rather than local.

By the time the span is 17 feet or more, the corbel principle has effectively been abandoned. Instead there is a half-round barrel-vault, with a sharply pointed vault sitting on top of it, so steep as to exert very little thrust, and by its weight serving to stabilise the walls beneath. All that is left of the corbel principle is the outer covering of horizontally bedded stones shaped to look like slates or slabs.

If Leask's reconstruction of St Laisren's at Devenish (fig. 10) be correct,[7] that building could represent a transition from the St MacDara's Island type to the later type: that is to say like the top half of Cormac's Chapel standing on the ground, arched within and in a sense corbelled externally.

St Flannan's, Killaloe and Cormac's Chapel (fig. 18) are the two widest spans among the Irish roofs, being 17 feet 6 inches and 17 feet 8 inches respectively. Both were so well designed and so well carried out that neither has needed serious attention. Both are of the twelfth century, and so is Kilmalkedar—the church, not the small oratory—of which the span is or was 17 feet 3 inches. Only the first four or five courses of the lower vault remain *in situ*, and these appear to be horizontally bedded. Perhaps this is why it fell down. As Leask remarks,[8] the introduction of mortar would increase the frictional coefficient and help corbelled structures to stay up for a little longer. But in the long run there was no future for the Irish stone roof.

Not that it disappeared completely. Stone-roofed churches crop up at wide intervals right through the Middle Ages, and by that I do not mean churches with vaults protected by timber-framed roofs such as are found in England or France, but roofs made of stone and nothing else: at St Doulough's Co Dublin, in the thirteenth century, at Ardrass, Co Kildare, and Taghmon Co Westmeath, in the fifteenth, at Hollywood Co Wicklow, late in the seventeenth, and in the curious constructions of John Semple[9] in the nineteenth. If it be objected that these are too far apart in time to constitute a tradition, let it be remembered that Leask accepts[10] the date of 814 for St Columb's Kells, which is a full 300 years before the known date of Cormac's Chapel, which is no doubt the point of highest achievement.

Most of the development of Irish Romanesque is concentrated on West fronts, and particularly doorways, and on chancel-arches. But the related subject of windows, which has so far been merely glanced at, should first be disposed of.

Windows are always small: very small indeed, even in relation to the size of the churches. In this respect, as in others, there is continuity right through from the Early Christian to the end of the Romanesque. The West window of Cormac's Chapel is quite exceptional with an external width of three feet. As already mentioned, windows often have round heads cut out of a single stone: both those without ornament and those which, as at Iniscealtra and Devenish, are framed by a moulding.

Triangular heads are also very common. In a few cases the head is cut out of a single stone: for example in the top storey of Cashel Round Tower, but most commonly two stones meet with a vertical joint. This type is very common indeed. At Roscrea Round Tower it is backed by a semicircular rere-arch (all these very small windows have of course very wide internal splays), and in Monasterboice

14

15

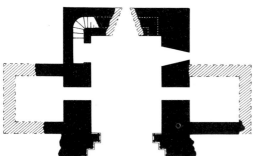

MODERN
ROOF-SLOPE

5   0   5   10   15   20   25

feet

WIDTH OF ORIGINAL NAVE UNKNOWN

16

17

Round Tower there is a window with a triangular head made of two stones meeting thus:

George Wilkinson developed an ingenious theory that by making openings of two stones propping each other up, and then advancing by scooping out the intrados of each stone in a curve, the Irish builders had already invented the pointed arch for themselves.[11] (So did the Egyptians, at the pyramids of Mycerinus and Khephren.) He gives several interesting examples in support of this, without, however, making his case, as it seems to me. On the contrary, he goes on to illustrate very tellingly how the mediaeval Irish builders used the pointed arch without fully understanding its structural principles. This is fully in accord with what we know of Irish gothic: namely, that the Irish builders did not show any interest in exploiting the structural possibilities of the style. Since gothic is primarily a constructional method, it follows, as we shall see later, that gothic is in Ireland an affair of pointed openings, some decoration, and of very little else.

To return to our windows. It is obvious that almost any very small-scale stone structure will stand up: so there is not much point in pursuing further the structural nature of these openings. In decorative terms, when they are surrounded by a moulding, this commonly goes right round the window including the bottom where the sill might otherwise be: there are good examples at Iniscealtra, Devenish, Rath Co Clare, and Ratass Co Kerry, and internally at Temple Melaghlin Clonmacnois, where it goes round a pair of windows. There is sometimes a horizontal moulding at impost-level, flanking the window but not used as an impost: this occurs externally at Temple Melaghlin and also at Devenish. At Trinity, Glendalough, there is a curious kind of drip-moulding worked in the solid above the round head of the window, rather like that on the lintel of St Kevin's Church, and at Temple na Skellig, both at Glendalough.

As Leask has noted, citing Ballintober, Killaloe, Knockmoy and others, the habit of running the architrave or moulded frame right round the bottom of the window carried over into the period of transitional gothic. He regards this as deriving perhaps from the windows at Killeshin and Kilpeakaun, which are worth closer attention for another reason altogether.[12]

In these, very small, windows, the arch-head is semicircular and formed with a single stone. But the windows are framed externally by a band with a triangular head, which at Kilpeakaun is enriched with delicate carving. These frames are in effect miniature versions of the pediment-gables which as we shall presently see, are characteristic of the developed Romanesque. There are two small circular windows: one, now re-set in the East gable of the larger church at Rahan, and another so much restored that it is difficult to believe in more than one or two of its stones as original, in the West gable of Freshford.

There are something under 20 Romanesque and pre-Romanesque chancel-arches surviving: mostly of very moderate span—between five and nine feet is very usual— and mostly very similar in character to the doorways. Some are very plain, and these

14 Clonamery, Co Kilkenny: the West door of the ?eleventh-century church. Note the plain 'architrave' worked on the jamb-stones and lintel, and the maltese cross. The Round Tower at Antrim has a doorway with a cross in a similar position

15 Aghowle, Co Wicklow: the West door of the church, lintelled on the outside but with a semi-circular rear-arch

16 Rahan, Co Offaly: plan and section (after Leask) of the larger church. Presumed original structures now disappeared are diagonally hatched. The compartments to North and South of the chancel are equated with the prothesis and diakonikon of the Eastern churches. The stairs seems to have passed above the head of the East window and traces of its emergence into the upper chamber seem still to be seen. The exterior of the East window is nineteenth-century restoration-work, and above it an ancient wheel-window has been re-set, but the inner mouldings of the lower window may be in part original

17 Clonmacnois, Co Offaly: late twelfth-century windows in the East wall of Teampull Rí or Melaghlin

include some early examples such as Trinity and Reefert at Glendalough, St Flannan's Killaloe, and Inchagoill. But simplicity does not always mean an early date, and there are plenty of simple chancel-arches which appear to be seventeenth century.

Among the decorated examples, Rahan Co Offaly has curious bulbous bases, and capitals in the form of human heads with curly moustaches and beards such as we shall meet again elsewhere. This arch used to be assigned to a very early date, but the date of about 1100 given to it by Leask or even a date 50 years later may now be accepted. The actual arch is quite plain, and so is that at Iniscealtra except for being in three simple orders. The Iniscealtra capitals have a strong flavour of the globe-artichoke about them, and the bases too are vegetable in character.

A unique chancel-arch, reconstructed in this century up to impost-level, is that at Kilteel Co Kildare. The four capitals are particularly fine male heads with interlaced hair and beards, like those at Killeshin, carved in what appears to be a fine-grained granite, but the jambs are adorned with small-scale figure-carvings of scriptural subjects, a little like the figure-panel in the Freshford doorway but more animated, and with some resemblance to the sculptures on the High Crosses.

But without doubt the most splendid of all Irish chancel-arches is that of Tuam Cathedral. It has a very curious history. The visitor now sees it acting as portal to a small nearly square chancel with three narrow East windows with wide splays, through which a retro-choir of some size can be seen. Small as the chancel is, the arch, with a span of nearly 16 feet, is the widest in Ireland, and correspondingly rich. Behind and above the spectator is the cathedral of 1861, by Sir Thomas Deane, which covers the site of the Romanesque cathedral to which the chancel originally belonged. At some time in the Middle Ages, perhaps in the mid-fifteenth century, the original cathedral nave fell into disrepair. It may have been finally destroyed by a fire in 1787. At all events, the Romanesque chancel was made to serve as the West doorway of the building to the East (described above as a retro-choir), a door being punched through the central East window for the purpose. A print of 1862[13] shows it in this state, with a tower of friary type over the junction between twelfth and fifteenth century. The retro-choir now serves as the chapter-house and contains a splendid set of seventeenth-century Italian marquetry stalls. So there is more than one reason for going to Tuam.

The capitals of the chancel-arch, which has five orders, are carved in very low relief, and bear strangely oriental faces of which that on the South side in particular is one of the most unforgettable sights in the whole of Irish architecture.

The date of the Tuam arch is probably late in the third quarter of the twelfth century. By this time the third and final phase of the Irish Romanesque had been going for 40 years, and was already nearing its end. It has recently been persuasively argued by Mr Liam de Paor[14] that the most elaborate single building of the style, Cormac's Chapel (fig. 18), is in fact among the very earliest. It is, as has long been known, securely dated to the years 1127-1134.

All other Irish Romanesque buildings are to some extent fragmentary. Only Cormac's Chapel is complete and, except for a little judicious restoration, intact. Yet its non-Irish characteristics are among the most obvious things about it.

To begin with, it has no batter. Insofar as its walls diminish they do so by reduction at offsets, like buildings in other countries. It has not, and never had, anything much in the way of a West front. This may have been owing to the topography of the site: not of course the present topography which has made the Chapel into, as it were, one of those opening off the South transept of the mediaeval cathedral, but whatever layout (which will have included the Round Tower) may have been there before

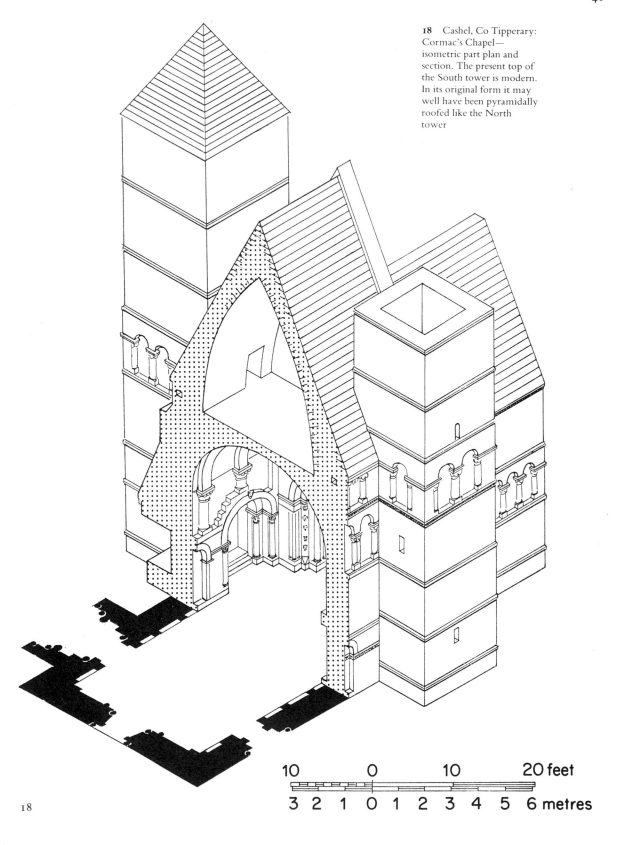

18 Cashel, Co Tipperary: Cormac's Chapel— isometric part plan and section. The present top of the South tower is modern. In its original form it may well have been pyramidally roofed like the North tower

10   0   10   20 feet

3 2 1 0 1 2 3 4 5 6 metres

Cormac's Chapel was built. Its principal entrance was to the North, near the West end of the nave, and opposite is a less important entrance in the same position as that of Temple Finghín at Clonmacnois.

The arches of these two doorways have tympana, which are an un-Irish feature except insofar as they appear in one or two buildings obviously derivative from Cashel, such as Kilmalkedar. The use of blind arcading both inside and outside is likewise without Irish precedent, though it started a fashion. It is true that two of the Glendalough doorways are solid with masonry between lintel and relieving-arch, but this is not at all the same thing as a recessed tympanum with carving in relief: a strange beast over the South doorway, and over the North another strange beast, possibly a lion, treading down two other beasts while himself being shot at by a centaur wearing a Norman-type helmet with a long straight nose-piece: a bizarre scene.

This North portal, which is flanked to the East by a deep recess which looks like an external tomb-recess and may indeed be one (though the North side of the church is a curious place for it to be) has also, in its high gable-pediment, the most unequivocal translation of timber-forms into stone to be seen in any Irish building. The vertical, sloping and horizontal bands of stone, enriched with the zig-zag chevron ornament, are the clearest possible representations of timber beams. The rosettes, too, as Leask remarks, have an air of being made of plaster though they are of course of stone.[15] The North porch is brimful of puzzles: why to the North? what does the sculpture mean? why so strong a suggestion of timber here and not elsewhere in the church?

For a building of its date, Cormac's Chapel is unusually coherent. As de Paor says, 'it is an entity ... a piece of *architecture* as hardly any other Irish Romanesque church is'.[16] Nevertheless both Leask and de Paor have detected signs of a change of plan, such as almost any building will reveal if looked at hard enough. Most obviously, the axis of the nave is somewhat North of the chancel-axis, which suggests to Leask that after the building of the chancel and the South wall of the nave, it was decided to widen the latter. Both towers have doorways opening Eastwards and therefore outwards. Though both have been tampered with they appear to be original, and as anomalous as the towers themselves. The function of the high-pitched stone roof is, among other things, to stabilise the massive barrel-vault underneath it. This applies less to the chancel, both because it is smaller all round and because it is roofed with a ribbed groin-vault which appears to be the earliest such vault in Ireland.

As de Paor rightly remarks, too much has been made of the Rhenish affinities of Cormac's Chapel and there are as good or better grounds for predicating English influence. King Cormac MacCarthy who built it was already under the influence of English ecclesiastical reformers, and the eclectic character of the design and detail draws on England, Germany and France. Small as it is, Cormac's Chapel is of unusual power in its own right, and when to this is added its marvellous situation on St Patrick's Rock, the result is unforgettable.[17]

It was immediately and widely influential: no doubt in the usual double sense of emulation by building-owners and migration of craftsmen. Some of the post-Cormac buildings are remote and rustic: for example Kilmalkedar, where there is a blank tympanum over the West door and where the wall-arcading of Cashel has been transformed into a colonnade of dumpy engaged columns high up on the inner faces of the walls.

The pediment-gable, seen at the North porch at Cashel, became one of the most noted marks of the Irish Romanesque, used, except for Cashel itself and the Round

20

19 Killeshin, Co Leix: the
West door, drawn by H. G.
Leask. The absence of
inward inclination of the
jambs is, he suggested, due
to its having been rebuilt.
The inscription was
laboriously defaced by a
religious zealot in the early
nineteenth century. Eight
of the voussoirs—randomly
disposed, one in the inner
order, three in the
intermediate and four in
the outer—are of dark
brown sandstone, leading
one to conjecture that the
whole was originally
painted. The shallow
carving is of very great
subtlety to which neither
drawings nor photographs
can do full justice

20 Killeshin: the
doorway, detail

Tower at Kildare, always in West fronts. An exception is the very simple, almost schematic, example at Ballyhay Co Cork. For the finer points of sequence and influence the reader must go to specialised studies: here, let us look at them in a convenient order. Not far from Cashel to the North-East are the doorways of Freshford and Killeshin (fig. 19): not far apart in date but contrasted in several ways. Killeshin, a ruin on a green hillside just West of Carlow, has a splendid set of capital-heads, a great wealth of low-relief carving of the utmost subtlety and delicacy, a keystone-head slightly off-centre, and a gable tangent to the outermost ring of the arch (fig. 20). The now defaced inscription is credited to Dermot MacMurrough who died in 1171. The jambs have no inclination, but this may just possibly be the result of a rebuilding.

At Freshford the doorway is more of a porch, projecting a considerable distance from the West gable of the church in the village street. The steep gable is carried on a figured but much weathered frieze. The decoration of the soffit includes the head of a beast devouring with evident relish two human heads, one in each corner of his mouth. Here, also, there is an inscription, commemorating the artificer and the patron, neither otherwise known. The doorway is the tallest of the series, and the jambs are slightly inclined.

Far to the West of Cashel, at Ardfert in Co Kerry, the ruined mediaeval cathedral incorporates what must be the lower part of the West front of its predecessor, the incomplete remains of an arcade of five bays, of which the central bay, higher and wider than the others, is the doorway, while the rest are blank. In itself it is not very inspiring, but it is a close relative of the West front of St Cronan's, Roscrea (figs 21 and 22), which is yet the greatest possible contrast to it in every other way. Where Ardfert is fragmentary, Roscrea is complete, where one is low and dumpy the other is slender and elegant, and, alas, in contrast to the seclusion of Ardfert, St Cronan's is so placed that every articulated truck from Dublin to Limerick thunders and belches within feet of it.

This West front is a most assured and accomplished piece of design. The arcade is held within a pair of bold antae which have roll-moulded corners. The central arch, that of the door, is twice the width of the others, and hence twice the height also. There is a continuous impost broken in and out across all the arches and the recesses, and the plinth is likewise broken out to form pedestals for all the piers. A tangential gable over the doorway rises from the same level as the minor gables over the minor arches. In the main gable the rosettes of Cormac's Chapel reappear, but in place of the central vertical member is a statue of the saint. A string-course with pellet-ornament touches the tops of the little gables but is interrupted by the main one. In its way it is as classical as the façade of St Gilles-du-Gard, though the layout of the elevation is perhaps closer to St Pierre d'Aulnay in Saintonge or to Angoulême Cathedral.[18] Only the West gable survives: the rest of the church was destroyed as recently as 1812. It does not appear to have been otherwise remarkable.★

There is no batter or inwards inclination of the jambs at Roscrea, except slightly in the inner orders of the central opening. A moment's reflection will show that such a classically ordered elevation could not have accommodated the usual such effects.

At Clonfert Cathedral, on the other hand, where the West front is likewise contained by a pair of antae, the inclination of the jambs is the most extreme in any Irish church, made all the more conspicuous by the numerous orders of the doorway and by the insertion in the fifteenth century of an inner order in blue limestone with

★ The extreme state of decay and present deterioration of St Cronan's must be noted, with regret. It seems to be largely inevitable, because of the use of sandstone.

21

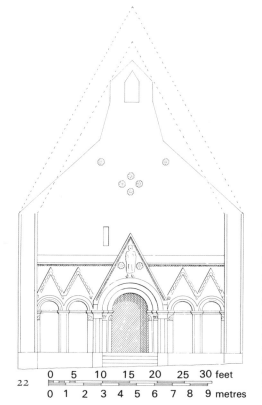

22

0 5 10 15 20 25 30 feet

0 1 2 3 4 5 6 7 8 9 metres

21 Roscrea, Co
Tipperary: St Cronan's
church, the West gable

22 Roscrea: West
elevation of St Cronan's,
after a nineteenth-century
survey by the Office of
Public Works. The exact
number and position of the
rosettes is uncertain, as they
are/were in very low relief
and time has dealt hardly
with the sandstone

its jambs standing primly upright. This great doorway (figs 23 and 24) by far the finest in Ireland, is freely placed in the centre of the façade, and not tied to the antae in any way. It is the tallest such feature in Ireland, reaching over 30 feet from the ground. The innermost but one order of the arch is made of dogs' heads biting the torus moulding. The gable is tangent, with an angle of about 67 degrees, and contains, immediately above the main arch, a miniature arcade of five narrow arches, with human heads peering out from under each arch. Above this is a diaper pattern of triangles, every other triangle containing a head. In the spandrels over the haunches of the main arch three more human heads are disposed on each side, with that kind of *horror vacui* which, centuries later, sometimes governed the placing of binder's tools on a book-cover.

The superlatives which have been lavished on this marvellous doorway seem to me entirely deserved. Though the rest of the little cathedral has been rebuilt, most of the rebuilding is either thirteenth or fifteenth century. Over the West front there now stands a typical tower of fifteenth-century friary type. It reminds us, by its slight batter, that the future of this feature was henceforth to lie in the profile of church-tower, castle or dwelling-house, and no longer, save very rarely as at Jerpoint, in the inclination of the jambs of doors or windows.

Clonfert dates from after 1167, the Tuam chancel arch from a decade or more later.[19] Other buildings of the last phase of the Romanesque were being carried out at much the same time: St Saviour's Priory at Glendalough and the Nuns' Church at Clonmacnois. Both are nave-and-chancel churches of similar proportions and about the same size, the former about 65 feet overall, the latter just under 60. Both were extensively reconstructed about a century ago. Neither seems ever to have had inclined jambs to door, arch or window.

The Nuns' Church is itself a mid-to-late twelfth-century restoration of an earlier building: a fact which accounts for the discontinuities and discrepancies of scale between the jambs and the arch-rings of its chancel-arch. The West doorway is entirely of the later period, and has on its second order a series of animal masks such as we have already seen at Clonfert, holding a roll in their mouths. The West door and chancel-arch form a memorable sequence.

The decoration at St Saviour's is at least equally varied, but there is no West doorway. The chancel was vaulted in stone and may have had an Irish double vault. But the principal interest of this church is that to the North of the nave, with which it shares a wall, is a building evidently of domestic character, perhaps the only surviving immediately pre-Cistercian monastic structure other than a church or Round Tower. Apart from the fact that it had a staircase at its East end, not much more can be said about it. It may originally have been a quasi-transept adjoining the Eastern half only of the nave (a little like Monaincha) but this is uncertain: if it was, it was later extended to match the nave in length. It already represents a kind of half-way house between the Celtic type of clachan-like monastery and the rectilinear continental model.[20]

To match the use of animal-heads at Clonfert and Clonmacnois, there is a similar display of human heads at a small number of other late Romanesque churches, deriving perhaps from the Cashel chancel-arch. It is tempting to see in this the survival of the pagan 'head-cult': after all, it is recorded that as late as 1457, 300 years after the date of these churches, one of the Maguires adorned the posts of his garden with 16 heads of his enemies, the O'Rourkes. On the other hand, 'the heads of kings and heroes were also preserved and honoured.'[21] Either way, the parade of heads ranged ear-to-ear as we see them at Inchagoill, Ballysodare and, above all, at Dysert

23

24

23 Clonfert Cathedral: the West doorway, detail of the North jamb

24 Clonfert, Co Galway: the West doorway of the Cathedral, third quarter of the twelfth century. The innermost order, in limestone, with its vertical jambs and standing saints, is 300 years later

O'Dea is much removed in spirit from the very classical placing of a single head as a keystone, such as Killeshin or Clonkeen. The fact that the Dysert O'Dea doorway is a late and imperfect reconstruction has not robbed it of its barbaric splendour. Three or four animal heads have strayed in among the human ones.

Another church which is also a reconstruction stands apart from the rest. The West gable—one cannot call it a West *front* because it has no door—of the cathedral of Ardmore Co Waterford, is a near neighbour to the elegant and unique Round Tower. The cathedral is unique but in no wise elegant. Two very large semicircular wall arcades themselves contain three and five much smaller arches respectively, and sitting straight on the tops of the two large arches is an arcade of 12 little arches which, like those below, are filled with miscellaneous and much-weathered figure sculpture. Ardmore is a beautiful place and its tower one of the finest, but the cathedral is little more than a curiosity.

There are many more Romanesque churches and fragments of churches than can be mentioned here. Most of them conform in one way or another to the types already mentioned. Some distance to the East of the church still in use at Rahan there is another, smaller, ruined church. The West door of this small church is itself small and has the usual late Romanesque combination of boldly modelled chevrons with delicate surface-decoration on the intervening spaces. But there is one important difference between this and other such doorways: it is carved, not in the usual sandstone, but in the hard blue limestone of the district. Limestone was about to come into its own. Just over the horizon were the Anglo-Normans. Not only did they have sharper chisels than the native Irish: they had sharper swords as well.

CHAPTER FOUR

Cistercian Gothic

The Anglo-Norman penetration of Ireland had an ecclesiastical and a military wing. More accurately perhaps, the ecclesiastical penetration of 1140 onwards can be seen as the shock-wave which, travelling ahead of the primary convulsion, gives warning of its approach. The Irish church prepared itself in stages for assimilation into the European system. The Synod of Rathbreasail in 1110 divided Ireland into 24 dioceses, a number increased at the Synod of Kells, 42 years later, to 36, which are, with few exceptions, those still existing.[1] At the same time (1152) four of the sees, Armagh, Cashel, Dublin and Tuam were elevated into archbishoprics, which correspond roughly to the four provinces of Ulster, Munster, Leinster and Connacht.

By this time Malachy O Morgair, the Archbishop of Armagh, had invited the Augustinians to Bangor (1140) and the Cistercians to Mellifont (1142). St Mary's Abbey, Dublin (originally Savignac) dates from 1139. At all these places large regular churches of complex plan, totally unlike anything hitherto seen in Ireland, had been put in hand. Malachy's own experiences illustrate the sequence of events in a peculiarly vivid way. In about 1120 he took charge of the abbey at Bangor which had been destroyed by pirates, and in a few days built an 'oratory, himself handling the axe among the workmen'. It was, of course, of timber. Twenty years later 'it seemed good to Malachy that a stone oratory should be erected at Bangor like those which he had seen constructed in other regions. And when he began to lay the foundations, the natives wondered, because in that land no such buildings were to be found'.[2] One is irresistibly reminded of Peter the Great, whose log cabin, built with his own hands on the banks of the Neva, is still piously preserved, surrounded by the noble and enduring city which he did not live to see. Peter's ideas, gleaned, like those of Malachy, from foreign travel, cannot have seemed more alien to his fellow-Russians than did those of Malachy to his fellow-Irishmen.

On 6 May, 1169, Robert FitzStephen and Maurice Prendergast, with less than 400 men, landed at Baginbun on the Wexford coast. They were soon followed by Maurice FitzGerald and Raymond leGros, and within little more than a year came Richard de Clare, Earl of Pembroke and Strigul, better known as Strongbow, with a further thousand followers.

The political background to the Anglo-Norman invasion does not concern us, but its political effects do, because they are reflected in the architecture. Non-Irish readers may need to be reminded that it was not a conquest like that of 1066 in the neighbouring island. A century after the landing they had mastered most of Leinster and Munster, but the interpenetration of social institutions had already begun: the 'demoralisation' of the Anglo-Normans (looked at one way round) or the 'Gaelic recovery' (looked at from the other side).

But the one incontrovertible fact is a startling and irreversible change of scale. In the years when the Ile de France was being covered with its 'white robe of churches', much of Ireland was being enlaced with a network of great abbeys and strong castles.

The castles were at first of timber, perched on their motes★ (and account, incidentally, for the ubiquity of placenames such as Brittas (breteche) or Pallas (palisade) or those incorporating the word mote, including of course Moate itself). But within 20 or 30 years stone donjons of a very massive and permanent kind replaced them.

Dublin fell to the invaders in 1170. But even here the ecclesiastics had anticipated the secular arm, for Laurence O Toole the Archbishop had brought Augustinian Canons regular into Christ Church Cathedral seven years before. John de Courcy set out from Dublin and took Downpatrick in 1176. He married the daughter of the king of Man and kept princely state himself, founding Inch Abbey and (through his wife) Grey Abbey, and beginning the castles of Carrickfergus and Dundrum. The great castle of Trim, apparently begun by Hugh de Lacy in 1172 or so, was burnt in the following year, and must therefore have been of timber. There is much confusion about the genesis of its successor, the present castle, but no doubt about its size. It probably took about 30 years to build. In the meantime de Lacy had got into trouble with the king of England for marrying the daughter of Rory O Conor, King of Connacht.[3] Far to the South-West Adare castle had been begun by the end of the century, and not far away from it the abbey of Monasternenagh, a daughter of Mellifont. In the North-West Boyle Abbey was another daughter-house of Mellifont, and though it is a very long way from Burgundy to Boyle, the building there was among the most up-to-date of the Irish Cistercian houses.[4]

The general pattern was the parallel appearance of the great castle with its feudal and manorial system, and the great abbey with an administrative structure of similarly Roman inspiration. The Gaelic kings, however, did not take to castle-building in stone as quickly as the invader barons. Though Dermot MacMurrough of Leinster is said to have had a palace of stone at Ferns, nothing is known about it. In the early thirteenth century Cathal Crovderg O Conor, king of Connacht, founded Abbey Knockmoy for the Cistercians and Ballintubber for the Augustinians, and is thought to have retired to Knockmoy before his death in 1224.[5] If so, he would have been following the example of his elder brother, the last High King, who died in the Abbey of Cong in 1198. Founding abbeys was one thing, but building castles was another.

As Dr Stalley remarks, when the Irish went out on grabbing expeditions they grabbed cattle, whereas the Normans grabbed land and took steps to hold on to it by building a castle.[6] It was to be some time before the Gaels were to learn to grab the actual castles, and to hold on to them.

Many years ago, Professor R. A. S. Macalister, in a moment of perhaps understandable impatience, remarked that the motto of post-Norman Ireland was 'Ah sure 'twill do, 'tis only temporary.' He had in mind the fall in the standards of craftsmanship in the mediaeval period, and the disorderly nature of much Irish gothic when measured by the standards of the Continent or even of England. A much more recent writer, himself also an archaeologist, has observed that in present-day Ireland 'virtually nothing is made or done that is not in some way slipshod.'[7] If both these

---

★ The word 'mote' with a long o is one of those words which, like 'ditch' and 'dike' has ambivalent connotations of convexity and concavity. I deplore the recent tendency to substitute the abrupt, ugly and alien usage 'motte' (which in Hiberno-English has a homonym of startlingly different meaning). 'Mote' is an old-established and respectable usage which should be good enough for us. The concave meaning can be adequately conveyed by the spelling 'moat'.

statements were true, the rest of this book would be anticlimax and would be worth writing only out of a sense of duty. Fortunately things are not so simple.

It is true that the impact of such a formidable social and political system shook the Gaelic world-view very profoundly indeed. Irish Gothic is often anomalous and almost always incomplete. It is also true that in our own time, under the impact of post-industrial technology, the Irish building craftsman seems to have died the death with remarkable rapidity. How rapidly may be gauged from the fact that I myself watched the high-quality ashlar and decorative carving of the Munster and Leinster Bank in Dame Street being carried out *in situ* only a quarter of a century ago. The place to look for Irish craftsmanship today is elsewhere, in precision industries where it matters that things should be done right.

Practically nothing built in mediaeval Ireland is fit to be put up against the corresponding buildings in other countries. Even Dr Stalley, who knows much more about Irish gothic than Macalister ever did, has to admit that 'Irish Gothic of the later Middle Ages is unpredictable and full of anachronisms. It defies the normal categories of style, producing unusual combinations, which are often refreshingly original.'[8] They will, of course, refresh only those who already know what to expect.

There is no need to make excuses for Clonfert Cathedral or for the Four Courts: both are the equal of anything comparable to be seen anywhere. But it is not so easy to explain why anyone who has not yet experienced Pontigny, Fontenay, Durham, Vézelay or Chartres should be lured away to look at Athassel or Kilkenny or even the Rock of Cashel, unless of course they are already at Shannon Airport with a few days to spare. As illustrations of Irish mediaeval history Irish gothic buildings are of course very instructive; but the history is as complicated and inconclusive as the buildings themselves, and the buildings do not elucidate it: they match it.

'To the last', wrote Macalister, 'the native architects could never master the principles of gothic.'[9] Leask, who devoted much of his life to the study of Irish mediaeval building, never answers this reproach directly, but contents himself, in his great book on the churches, with the description of what was done, leaving aside altogether the question of what was *not* done. Champneys, writing in 1910, 18 years before Macalister, entitles his tenth chapter 'Pure Gothic Architecture Established in Ireland', and, being an Englishman, and a very fair-minded one, can find nothing worse to say of Boyle and Knockmoy than that 'they are very Irish in the dislike of their builders to be fettered by rules and precedents and symmetry.'[10] Of the fifteenth-century builders (to anticipate) he says 'they solved architectural problems in their own way' and of the buildings: 'any complete church or monastery of the period, most of its parts and much of its ornament could not possibly, as they stand, occur elsewhere than in Ireland ... the buildings are unmistakably Irish'.[11]

It is evident that we must take a look at the various criteria which have been put forward as defining gothic, from Viollet-le-Duc to Sir John Summerson and Dr John Harvey, and make up our own minds whether, by any of them, Irish mediaeval architecture should qualify.

Insofar as the use of the pointed arch means gothic, all these buildings are of course gothic, but that does not take us very far. Even the castles, right down to and including the latest of the tower-houses, use the pointed arch, but have no other attributes peculiar to gothic. It has been said, I do not remember by whom, that gothic is an architecture of small stones whereas classic is an architecture of large ones. This is certainly true in Ireland. The eye is not drawn to look at the actual texture of the wall in most Irish mediaeval buildings. The features of cut stone—windows, arches, doorways—simply occur in this medium as and when they are called for. This can be said irrespective of whether the wall was originally lime-plastered or not, as in very many cases it probably was. It is rare to find any large feature built of ashlar stone: the tower of Rosserk Friary Co Mayo is an example, and so is much of St Nicholas Galway.

Gothic as a way of building grounded in structural functionalism is of very limited occurrence in Ireland, because in the last resort this means vaulting and the preparation for vaulting, and the whittling away of supports to their minimum safe area. The total amount of vaulting in the whole of Irish mediaeval architecture is not great: the two Dublin cathedrals as originally built, the cathedral at Newtown Trim which has virtually disappeared, the presbyteries and sometimes the crossings of a dozen great abbeys or priories, in one case a transept, a few chapter-houses. Very small spaces, such as Cistercian or Cistercian-inspired Eastward chapels, or the interiors of the narrow friary towers of the fifteenth century, or the little thirteenth-century chapel in Ferns castle, have rib-vaults, but these hardly modify the total picture.

Some of the most distinctive features of Irish mediaeval church architecture are virtually incompatible with vaulting: for example the tendency to light a choir by a row of many closely-spaced lancets—as many as nine in each of two buildings at Ardfert, and eight at Sligo—the habit of placing clerestory windows over the piers instead of the usual position over the arches. It has been suggested that this widely diffused habit originated at the now vanished abbey church of Mellifont (fig. 25) (vanished, that is, as regards the nave and its clerestory). If so, it was an early departure from the norm.

When we turn from the 'truthful expression of structure' aspect of gothic to the psychological interpretations of the style, the field is hardly more fertile. What has become of 'the ambition to dissolve architecture from the substantial to the insubstantial'?[12] What has become of that 'aesthetic intention . . . the destruction of mass',[13] or of the 'nervous passion for multiplication',[14] which are characteristic of gothic, the architecture of aedicules? There is more deployment of aedicular themes in Roscrea and Freshford alone than in most Irish buildings from between 1200 and 1500. In small things, such as the Chapter House of St Canice's Kilkenny, or St John's Priory in the same city, or the enigmatic structure, perhaps an Easter Sepulchre, in Holy Cross Abbey, there is a glimpse of that attenuated and disembodied gothic, apparently freed from gravitation, which is so characteristic of other countries, but such glimpses are few and far between.

As for Lethaby's vision of a gothic art inspired by the mystery of the great forests of the North, or John Harvey's upward flame-like leap,[15] there is little enough of either of these in most Irish examples. It will be urged, no doubt, that money is the limiting factor: Ireland, we are told, has always been too poor.

I am not economist enough to understand, still less to explain why, when materials, skill and manpower are present, a community should still be unable to carry out building-work; something to do with 'surplus' and 'capital formation' I dare say. The fact remains that twice during the Middle Ages, during the late twelfth to early thirteenth century, and again in the fifteenth, there was a spectacular increase in building output. But certain things which were done elsewhere were not done here. Perhaps because nobody wanted to do them?

In developed gothic, loads are concentrated on points instead of being evenly distributed along the length of a wall. A high vaulted space is thus ideally flanked by lower aisles to afford, or to conceal, abutment. But, with rare exceptions, the Eastern limbs of Irish churches (which are the parts most likely to be vaulted if there is to be any vaulting at all) are without aisles: for example the cathedrals of Killaloe, Ardfert, Kildare, Leighlin as first built, and Cloyne, not to mention Cashel.

The cathedral of Limerick, one of the very earliest, though much altered over the centuries, shows traces in its nave-aisles of transverse arches which derive directly from Burgundian models, where they are part of a system of North–South barrel-vaults designed to abut the East–West barrel-vault higher up. Clapham thought Limerick Cathedral earlier than any surviving Irish Cistercian church (through which the Burgundian influence will have come).[16] It was built in the last quarter of the twelfth century by King Donal Mór O Brien, who, though he had lost Limerick to the Anglo-Normans in 1175, had got it back and now held it as a liege to Henry II of England.

Insofar as Limerick Cathedral is Romanesque it is imported Romanesque.[*] The same is true, though more importantly, of Christ Church Cathedral, Dublin, the older, by some 50 years, of the two Dublin cathedrals. Christ Church is, in fact, nothing more nor less than a totally English building erected in Ireland. Even the stone was imported, from Dundry and elsewhere, though this, which was and is a common practice since stone is more easily and cheaply transported by water than by land, is of less significance than the English origin of the designers and the craftsmen.[17]

All that now remains of Christ Church are the transepts and the North wall of the nave: the rest is by George Edmund Street. Dublin had been a Viking settlement for 300 years, and the cathedral was indeed a Viking foundation of 1038, but even the unusual crypt is part of the Anglo-Norman work begun soon after their capture of the town a century and a half later. The reason that nothing has been said about Viking architecture in Dublin or in Ireland is that nothing remains of it, unless we are to count the recently excavated post-and-wattle work of which the value, though great, is hardly architectural, or decorative details in Irish work at such places as Kilmore, Killeshin or Rathblamaic.

The transepts of Christ Church are a-bristle with chevrons like contemporary Norman work in England. The arches are round-headed, except that the paired sub-arches within the main triforium arches are slightly pointed, and the vault also is pointed. Something similar is to be seen in the retro-choir of Chichester, of much the same date, or at Winchester. The East end of Christ Church, which survives now only in the crypt and in Street's reconstruction, is very odd: a chevet of indeterminately polygonal form,[†] with three parallel chapels to the East of it, the middle one projecting further East than the others.

Another rather un-Irish round-arched building of note is the celebrated lavabo at Mellifont. It was built when the monks had been established for about 60 years in the Mattock valley, while the abbey church still stood in its original form. It projected into the South side of the cloister garth opposite the refectory. Seven or eight similar buildings once existed in English monasteries. Only four of its eight arches now remain, and its top storey which presumably contained the cistern, appears to have been rebuilt, so that it is difficult to know just what it looked like. Though the arches are round, the mouldings have already a gothic flavour. There is a whiff of the Irish Romanesque in the way the openings have their mouldings carried round the sills. There was a similar structure at Dunbrody.

---

[*] For example, the thick wall-passage at clerestory level, an English characteristic, never found in Cistercian building (Stalley).

[†] It has some resemblance to the Saxon church at Wing, Buckinghamshire.

The main bulk of transitional work in Ireland is to be found in the Cistercian abbeys. Not all of them were daughters of Mellifont. In the North-East, under the lordship of John de Courcy, Inch Abbey and Grey Abbey were colonised from Furness and Holm Cultram respectively. St Mary's, Dublin, was of obscure origin but had apparently become Savignac by 1147, at which date it transferred its allegiance to Cîteaux, while in the South-East Duiske (Graignamanagh) was started by monks from Stanley in Wiltshire under the protection of William the Marshal, whose patronage extended also over Tintern Minor in Wexford, an offshoot of its more famous namesake in Monmouthshire. Dunbrody, also in Co Wexford, was a daughter of St Mary's, Dublin, founded in 1182 but its earliest surviving parts built, as Leask thinks, some 30 years later.[18] Speaking generally, the buildings of this group, where they survive, show their English or Welsh parentage and have little that is recognisably Irish about them, except insofar as they were modified in the fifteenth century when Irish manners were in the ascendant.

It is worth remarking that Duiske shows a strong relationship to Strata Florida in Cardiganshire, a building which appears to have provided the model for the 'perpyn-walls' found in several Irish Cistercian churches (but except for Buildwas, not in England) and also for the North transept door of Kilkenny Cathedral.

The family of Mellifont, by contrast, show in various ways the traces of the native Romanesque. Bective, Baltinglass, Boyle and Monasternenagh were the first generation. From Baltinglass descended Jerpoint, and from Boyle descended Knockmoy, in 1163-5 and 1189 respectively.

It is a paradox that the Cistercian order, which distrusted art as a distraction from devotion, should have promoted so much noble architecture. In practice, it was not so much art as ornament which they distrusted, and even here they fortunately fell short of their own ideals. The Cistercian plan was very influential in Ireland: its transeptal chapels are to be found at Ballintubber and Athassel which were Augustinian, at Cashel Cathedral and, with a peculiarly felicitous modification, at St Canice's Cathedral Kilkenny, also. Whether a central tower is to be called an 'ornament' or part of the architecture is perhaps debatable: the Cistercians legislated against such a feature as early as 1157, yet by the turn of the century the monks of Boyle had planned a crossing tower. The stones of Boyle are *pierres parlantes* indeed, eloquent of many contradictions as will appear.

So much of the abbey church of Mellifont itself has disappeared that the places in which to study detail are Baltinglass and Jerpoint. The alternating square and circular piers of the South arcade at Baltinglass (fig. 26), though with English affinities are decorated with 'much simplified Irish motives' (Leask) and the bases of the transept arches are also Irish in character. The foundation had the protection (for what it was worth) of Dermot MacMurrough. Some 35 miles to the South-West, Jerpoint on the river Nore lay in the kingdom of Ossory ruled in 1180 by the MacGiollaphadraigs (Fitzpatrick) but soon to pass into the power of William the Marshal, the son-in-law of Strongbow. The strongly Irish character of its East end[19] suggests that it was not so much founded as taken over by the Cistercians from Baltinglass.* Its Irish character is continued in the arcade capitals which are like those of Baltinglass only more so, and in the transept-windows which actually have inclined jambs: perhaps the last known appearance of this feature.

When we look at these abbey churches we have to bear in mind that to parse the building structurally is not at all the same thing as to parse it in terms of its functional

---

* Mr Stalley doubts this.

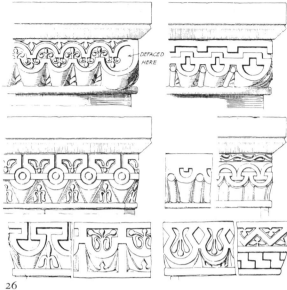

26

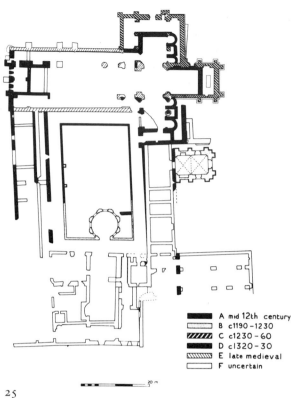

A mid 12th century
B c1190 – 1230
C c1230 – 60
D c1320 – 30
E late medieval
F uncertain

20 m

25

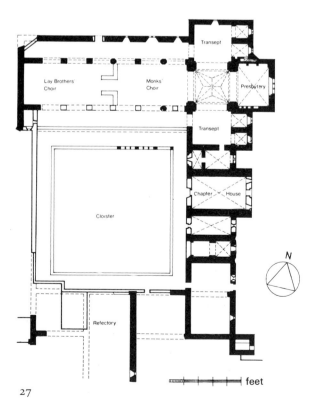

Transept

Lay Brothers' Choir

Monks' Choir

Presbytery

Transept

Chapter House

Cloister

Refectory

N

feet

27

25 Mellifont, Co Louth: plan (R. Stalley). The early round-apsed chapels are shown, and the West end standing on a crypt made necessary by a fall in the ground. Only the octagonal lavabo and the chapter-house now stand more than a few feet above the ground

26 Baltinglass, Co Wicklow: capitals in the Cistercian abbey. Here, and at Jerpoint, some flavour of the Irish Romanesque has been carried over into a building of essentially continental type. (OPW)

27 Jerpoint, Co Kilkenny: plan (R. Stalley)

divisions. There was a wall—sometimes quite a solid wall—some distance down the nave from the crossing, and this divided the monks' choir from the choir of the lay brethren. Leask labels the latter 'nave' on his plans, which is apt to lead to confusion. It helps to refer to the East end, beyond the crossing, as the 'presbytery' while remembering that in current Irish usage this means at least two other, quite different, things.

The principal glories of Jerpoint (fig. 27), the splendid central tower and the cloister sculptures, belong to the fifteenth century and will later be considered in the context of the developments of that fertile time. At Boyle, on the other hand, there is nothing later than the thirteenth century. But it took 60 years—from 1161 until after 1220—to build the church alone, and as a result it displays a bewildering diversity of styles exceeding even that of many English cathedrals. The first four bays of the South arcade of the nave have magnificent cylindrical piers, built—most unusually for Ireland—of coursed ashlar, with square bases and octagonal caps, both of which are more restrained, though more architectural, in their decoration than those of Baltinglass or Jerpoint.

It cannot have helped matters forward when the local de Burgo (Norman) and the local O Conor (Irish) joined forces in 1202 and took three days off to amuse themselves by despoiling the abbey.[20] The North arcade of the nave consists of compound piers of roughly octagonal plan, carrying arches which are only just pointed, as against those on the South side which are round. The Western four bays of the nave are carried on square piers with attached triple shafts, typical of Western English architecture and of Christ Church Dublin, but the carving of the capitals here begins to have an Irish flavour. This is even more the case with the corbels inserted elsewhere in the nave at about the same time, which belong to the 'school of the West' whose very distinctive work is to be seen at Cong, Knockmoy, Inishmaine, Ballintubber and elsewhere.

Nevertheless, in all its inconsequentiality, Boyle is of rather consistently English inspiration which, as Mr Stalley observes, is surprising since the abbey was politically well outside the area of Anglo-Norman influence, and its abbot was deeply involved between 1217 and 1228 on the Irish side in the bitter conflict, within the Order, between Irish and English, known to history as the 'conspiracy of Mellifont'. This is an interesting early instance of a persistently recurring feature of art-history in Ireland: the fact that cultural nationalism and its political counterpart are by no means invariably found together, and are, indeed, at certain crucial epochs, to be found on opposite sides from one another. We shall meet this again.

The most remote of the Cistercian houses, psychologically if not in strict geographic distance, is Corcomroe in North Clare, chosen by Yeats as the setting for *The Dreaming of the Bones*: most aptly, for a more desolate bony place it would be hard to find. As befits the situation there is only one Eastward chapel to each transept, though the presbytery is vaulted, and everything is much smaller than usual, as though such a stony ground could put forth only a stunted plant. Within a stone's throw are the three primitive churches of Oughtmama.

Dunbrody Abbey in Co Wexford is very large (by Irish standards) but also rather dull: partly because it was always rather austere, partly because much which is known to have been impressive has now disappeared, but mostly, perhaps, because its massive crossing-tower (which like all except Boyle and Grey is a later insertion) lacks refinement of outline and suffers by comparison with Jerpoint.

The Augustinian order was on the scene as early as the Cistercian, and, as we know, their church-plans sometimes followed the Cistercian model. Athassel Priory,

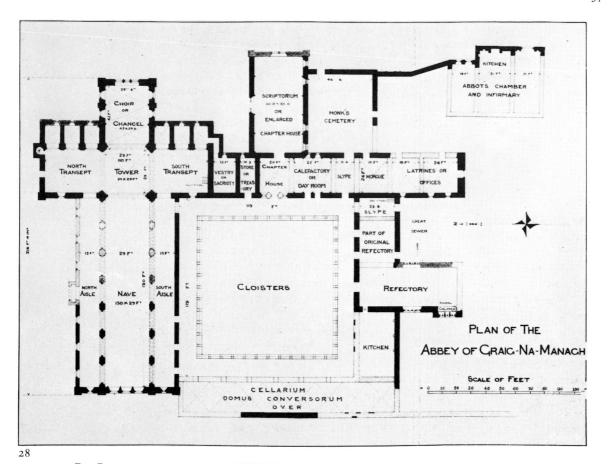

PLAN OF THE
ABBEY OF GRAIG-NA-MANACH

SCALE OF FEET

0 10 20 30 40 50 60 70 80 90 100

Within plan (img_2) labels:

KITCHEN
ABBOTS CHAMBER AND INFIRMARY

CHOIR OR CHANCEL 45×29·6

SCRIPTORIUM 60·0×35·0 OR ENLARGED CHAPTER HOUSE

MONK'S CEMETERY

NORTH TRANSEPT

TOWER 29×29 FT

SOUTH TRANSEPT

VESTRY OR SACRISTY

STORE OR TREASURY

CHAPTER HOUSE

CALEFACTORY OR DAY ROOM

SLYPE

MORGUE

LATRINES OR OFFICES

SLYPE

PART OF ORIGINAL REFECTORY

GREAT SEWER

NORTH AISLE

NAVE 130×29 FT

SOUTH AISLE

CLOISTERS

REFECTORY

KITCHEN

CELLARIUM DOMUS CONVERSORUM OVER

28

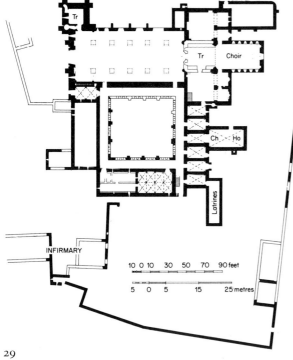

Tr Choir Ch Ho Latrines INFIRMARY

10 0 10 30 50 70 90 feet
5 0 5 15 25 metres

29

28 Graignamanagh, Co Kilkenny: Duiske Abbey (Cistercian)—plan (OPW). Much of the conventual complex survives among the buildings of the town, while the abbey church—the largest in Ireland—has been restored in recent years

29 Athassel, Augustinian Priory: plan. The tower at the crossing is a late insertion, and the thirteenth-century West door appears to have been rebuilt in its present position at the East end of the nave. For some mysterious reason, the plan of Athassel has hitherto usually been given upside-down

to the West of Cashel in Co Tipperary (fig. 29), is one of the largest monastic layouts in the country, and still a very impressive sight. As usual, it is of various dates, with a crossing tower still largely extant and, in the North-West corner of the nave (as at St Patrick's Cathedral, Dublin) a massive belfry of which only a few courses now remain. The outstanding decorative feature of the church is the doorway leading from the nave into the crossing-space: it is very like the West doorway of Grey Abbey in Co Down. Athassel impresses by the amplitude of its layout and by the brooding atmosphere of its setting in low-lying meadows by the river Suir. It is sadly ruined, except for the East end, and even that is not vaulted. But the aisles had rib-vaults.

It is otherwise at Ballintubber Co Mayo (not to be confused with Ballintober Co Roscommon, where there is a fine castle) which is much smaller and has had the good fortune to be one of the few monastic churches in Ireland to be sympathetically and skilfully reinstated for Catholic worship in modern times. It has the usual Eastward chapels opening off the transepts, and a simple aisleless nave, the whole very pure and harmonious in style. The vaulting-ribs spring from wall-shafts which never reach the ground, but taper into points: a feature of the Western style and oddly like the corbelled machicoulis of 300–400 years later. Some of the carved detail rivals that of Tuam in fantasy.

Ballintober exemplifies the tendency in the thirteenth century—whatever about the fifteenth (see page 85)—for establishments to get smaller as they get further West: we have already noted Corcomroe. (To this rule, as to others, Boyle is of course a notable exception.) At Kilmacduagh ('O'Heyne's Monastery') for example, and at Inishmaine, an island in Lough Mask, there are moderate-sized nave-and-chancel churches, the former with remains of monastic buildings, on a scale little greater than St Saviour's at Glendalough. Both these churches have the paired narrow East windows which are so very characteristic of the first quarter of the thirteenth century. We have already seen paired East windows at St Saviour's, both within a single frame.* Here they are individually framed, both inside and out, and the frames go all the way round in the Irish fashion. At Inishmaine the treatment is beautifully simple: at Kilmacduagh two of the roll-mouldings on the internal frames are treated as columns and given little capitals at different heights, which at least makes better sense than the two central capitals in the Killaloe East window which support nothing. Other examples are at Temple Ri, Clonmacnois, where, internally, the whole composition is underlined by a final 'rule' as it were, a sill-like moulding signifying 'finis' to the whole. Externally, the two are linked by a continuous impost moulding.

But by far the finest of these paired East windows is the one at Clonfert cathedral, the greatest imaginable contrast to the intricately textured West portal, yet in its own way no less masterly. Externally the pair are linked by a common sill and a miniature gable with a blank roundel punched in it. Internally their wide splays are panelled with a pair of round-headed panels to each splay, eight in all, and three capitals at impost-level where the outermost roll changes, as at Kilmacduagh, from being a column to being an arch-member. The quality of the design is matched by the workmanship. Evidently nothing but the best would do for Clonfert, and two centuries later this was still true. The triple East window at Tuam is of similar quality.

There is another pair of East windows at Killone, a small nunnery (one of very

---

* Also at Aghowle, Co Wicklow.

few) founded, like Limerick Cathedral, by King Donal Mor O Brien, which are quite different in feeling. They have a pair of boldly-chevron-moulded internal arches supported on three dwarf wall-shafts, and transversely through the wall across both windows goes a trefoil-headed passage, much like those which thread their way through the triforium of large churches. At Drumacoo and at Inchcleraun there are paired East windows;* but by this time frankly and pointedly gothic.

---

* There are similar windows also at Adare Castle, illustrated in Leask, *Irish Castles*, 1941, p. 35 fig. 22.

CHAPTER FIVE

Castles and Churches

Ireland is full of castles, but the greater number of these are comparatively small, and date from the later Middle Ages (i.e. from *c*. 1400 to 1650), during which period they were the usual residence of a landed gentleman, whatever his descent might be. We are now concerned not with these, but with much larger constructions of more military purpose: those built in the thirteenth century by the Anglo-Normans to consolidate their grip on the lands which they had conquered.

Nobody knows which of the surviving stone castles is the oldest in Ireland. Claims of great—indeed pre-Norman—antiquity have been made for Reginald's Tower in Waterford, claims, which rather surprisingly, are not dismissed out of hand by Leask. It is in fact part of the city walls and is very unlikely to be any earlier than other town walls in Ireland which are, generally speaking, of the second half of the thirteenth century. It has a decided batter, which might, just possibly, indicate that it had been built by Irish masons under the orders of the Scandinavians who possessed the city.

As we have seen, there is talk of a stone palace at Ferns before the invasion, and this is included in the list of seven 'castles' which then existed. But various things make it unlikely that they were of stone: notably the rapidity of their construction and their proneness to destruction by fire. There is also the fact that at Henry II's request, a 'wonderful structure of wattle-work'[1] was erected outside the walls of Dublin in 1171, by way of demonstration of the Irish style of secular building. What little we know of the pre-Norman walled cities, notably Dublin itself, is archaeological rather than architectural.

One thing can be said: at least three types of donjon or 'keep' to use the less authentic but more familiar word, were on the scene at a very early age: the nearly square rectangle, represented by Carrickfergus (figs 30 and 31) and Adare; the cylindrical, whether free-standing as at Dundrum (fig. 32) or Inchiquin Co Cork, or engaged in the curtain as at Nenagh; and its variant the polygon, such as Shanid, Dungarvan and Castleknock, both now in fragmentary state, and Athlone, much modified in the Napoleonic period. In addition there was the longish rectangular hall-over-basement type represented by Athenry and Greencastle Co Down, where it is free-standing inside the curtilage, and at Trim (fig. 38) a 20-sided shape arrived at by adding to a normal square design a slender protrusion in the middle of each wall. This was such a bad idea that it was only done twice: here and at Castle Rushen in the Isle of Man. Admittedly, the late-fourteenth century tower at Warkworth in Northumberland has a not dissimilar outline with all the corners chamfered off, but its plan-form is essentially different.

Trim was a bad idea from the military point of view only. In visual terms it is perhaps the most impressive of all Irish castles, and, taking one thing with another—the mass of its donjon, the extent and variety of its walls, the interest of its various gate-buildings, and the fair state of preservation of the whole—it deserves its reputation as the king of the castles.

As early, or nearly as early, as these, is the group which Leask calls the 'towered or

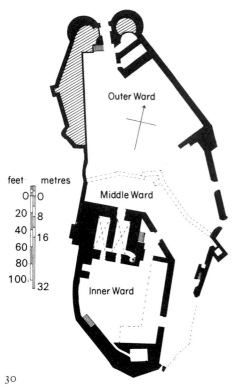

Outer Ward

Middle Ward

Inner Ward

feet metres
0 — 0
20 — 8
40 — 16
60 —
80 —
100 — 32

30

30 Carrickfergus Castle, Co Antrim: plan. The keep is between the middle and inner wards, the harbour is on the West (left) and the waters of Belfast Lough on the South and East, while the double-towered gatehouse faces the land. Like Carlingford, Roche and other thirteenth-century castles, it has a plan-form dictated by the shape of the rock on which it stands

31 Carrickfergus Castle from the North-East. To the left of the donjon can be seen the curtain between the middle and inner wards, and the tower and seaward postern of about 1200, and to the right the twin-towered landward gate

31

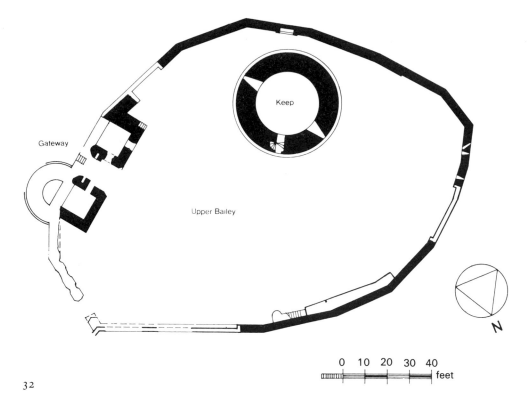

Keep

Gateway

Upper Bailey

N

0 10 20 30 40
feet

32

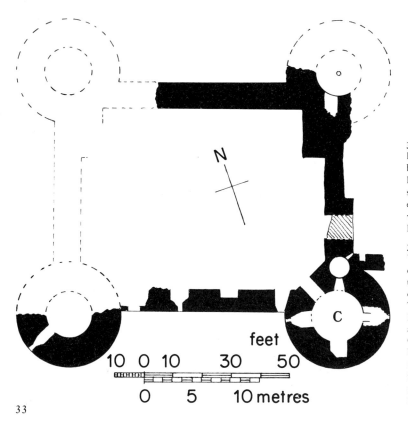

N

C

feet

10 0 10   30   50

0   5   10 metres

33

32 Dundrum Castle, Co Down: the cylindrical keep built probably by Hugh de Lacy *c.* 1205–10, free-standing in its irregular enceinte. The gate-tower was of the familiar double-D type

33 Ferns Castle, Co Wexford: plan. The decorated chapel is in the tower marked C. The castles at Carlow, Terryglass Co Tipperary, Enniscorthy Co Wexford and probably also Dunluce Co Antrim as originally built, are of this form. Quin (see p. 91), though similar, is on a larger scale and was presumably not completely roofed over

turreted keeps'[2] which are rectangles with a cylindrical tower at each corner. They appear to be an Irish invention: that is to say, there are no known earlier English models, and when the form does appear in England, as at Woodford and Nunney, it is a century later. The Irish thirteenth-century examples are all fragmentary: only half of Carlow, and slightly more than half of Ferns, are present. Only one tower of Lea stands to any height, Enniscorthy seems to have been rebuilt in the sixteenth century, and Terryglass stands only a few feet high. Dunluce in its original form seems to have been of this type. But there are enough of them to constitute a family, and a family furthermore of apparently Irish origin. How far (if at all) they can be related to the reappearance of a similar form in the late sixteenth to early seventeenth century, and whether the relationship is, however tenuous, direct, or must be traced via exportation to England and re-importation from thence, is still an open question and one which belongs to a later chapter.[3] For the present we may note that they have a predominantly though not exclusively South-Eastern distribution.

Less than 50 years later comes a group which is obviously related to the royal works in England which culminated in the concentric castles of North Wales, notably Beaumaris and Harlech. The Irish examples, of which Roscommon (fig. 37) is the most conspicuous and Dublin was by far the most important, include a number of royal castles: those just mentioned, as well as Dungarvan and Limerick. Though neither Dublin nor Limerick is quite symmetrical, both were built in towns which already existed, so as to take advantage of rivers, yet their resemblance to the nearly symmetrical castles such as Roscommon is unmistakable. In all of them the most conspicuous feature is the twin-towered gatehouse, double-bowed at the outside and flat on the inside: another such gatehouse of slightly different plan survives in fair preservation at Ballyloughan Co Carlow (fig. 34). These 'keepless' castles, as Leask calls them,[4] seem to belong to the last 20 years of the thirteenth century.[5] None of them now has the outer defences which are so striking at Harlech and Beaumaris, though it is quite likely that an outer palisade of earth and timber may have existed at Roscommon. Not far from Roscommon, Ballintober (Co Roscommon) and Ballymote (Co Sligo) are de Burgo castles of the same type, which before long had fallen to the O Conors. Ballintober has polygonal towers where the others have them semi-cylindrical or D-shaped.

Castles, as everybody knows, were not built primarily for architectural effect, and as everybody also knows, their impact on the modern visitor may owe as much to their natural situation as to art. The Normans' primary interest, as we have seen, was in holding land, and so their major castles were so placed as to dominate the most fertile territories. Should there happen to be a rock commanding a harbour, there they built a castle: such are Carlingford and Carrickfergus, and in both cases the shape of the rock dictated in part the form of the castle. Inland, not far from Carlingford, the de Verdons who had arrived with Prince John in 1185, could not resist the temptation to fortify the rock near Dundalk which to this day is called, simply and in Norman-French, Roche (figs 35 and 36). It has a twin-towered gatehouse very like that of Ballyloughan, and beside it a very considerable hall 58 feet by 30, lit by three great windows safely elevated on top of the cliff.

There were other rock-founded castles, notably Dunamase Co Leix and, a good deal later, Carrigogunnell in Co Limerick, but picturesque as they are, they have been so much knocked about that they can now hardly be considered as architecture. Dunluce Castle, on its sea-girt rock off the Antrim coast, has little about it of the thirteenth century, though it may go back to that time, but a profusion of Jacobean gables instead. It is well-nigh as impractical as Dun Aenghus, and for similar reasons.

34

35

34 Ballyloughan Castle, Co Carlow, from the South. The double-towered gatehouse is thirteenth century, but the building visible in the distance is a seventeenth-century T-plan house, built of stone looted from the castle

35 Roche Castle, Co Louth, from the North-East, showing the double-D gate-tower, the three windows of the hall, and the deep declivity on which the latter stands

It seems to have started life as a four-square enclosure with cylindrical angle-towers, of which two remain in part. At Grannagh or Granny Castle on the Suir above Waterford there are similar remains in a less spectacular setting.

The square keeps were normally divided at basement-level into two long vaulted spaces. At Carrickfergus★ this division is continued in later work higher up, and on the second floor culminates in a great arch spanning the principal hall, inserted at a date so far unknown. The keep of Trim, so anomalous in other respects, conforms to type in being divided into two not quite equal rectangles on its two lower floors. The chapel is in the room over the entrance, which is in one of the square projections, on the East side. These projections add greatly to the striking effect of the tower, but so do the corner turrets which, even now, rise above the general level of the wall-top without the slight set-back which occurs in the main wall some 15 feet below the top. They thus detach themselves very slightly from the main mass, but they stand entirely on the solid: in other words their total thickness, some 11 feet, is no greater than that of the main wall beneath.

The exact date of this remarkable tower remains something of a mystery. The latest and most likely suggestion is that there is no exact date: that it was perhaps begun during the five years 1210-15 when Prince John held it, and completed by the de Lacys afterwards, or begun in the 1190's and finished 30 years later. Neither theory is entirely satisfactory.[6]

The large bailey is surrounded by a curtain-wall built soon after 1220 and incorporating D-plan towers, and, on the South, a fine oval gate-tower with a barbican in the form of a totally enclosed drawbridge, a very up-to-date type of defence.

The town of Trim is, or rather was, surrounded by a wall which encompassed both sides of the Boyne, with the castle at the South-East corner, on the left bank. Little remains of it but one insignificant gate and of course the castle part. Further down the Boyne, at Drogheda, the river bisects another town which, for a time, looked as though it, and not Dublin, might be the capital of the Anglo-Norman colony. To be precise, there were two towns, Drogheda towards Uriel, founded in 1229, and Drogheda towards Meath, founded 20 years later. They were not united until 1412. One gate of the Southern town survived, only to be demolished, most disgracefully, in recent years.

The castle was in the Southern town but nothing remains of it save the mote. But St Laurence's Gate in the Northern town is the finest thing of its kind in the country: not strictly a gate but a forework or barbican. It has a high arch between the two towers, as at Dover Castle and later at other Irish sites, and it has the characteristic Irish stepped battlements, though these may be of later mediaeval date.

The principal towns of the coast and of the Pale were walled: besides those already mentioned (Dublin, Drogheda and Trim), there were Carlingford, Wexford, Waterford, New Ross, Youghal. Inland Kilkenny (fig. 41), Kilmallock and Athenry, and on the Western seaboard Limerick and Galway. There is an impressive run of town-wall at Athenry, but otherwise little to see but the occasional tower or gate of modest size, in many cases late mediaeval or later still: nothing comparable to York or Beverley or a dozen towns in France.

The domestic architecture of the mediaeval towns has vanished, but the street-plan remains, most clearly traceable today in such towns as Kilkenny, Wexford and Ennis. Town churches have been a little more fortunate, and when they are added to the

★ Too late for citation has appeared T. E. McNeill, *Carrickfergus Castle*, Belfast, H.M.S.O., 1981.

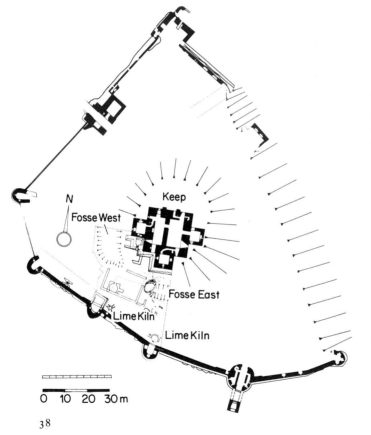

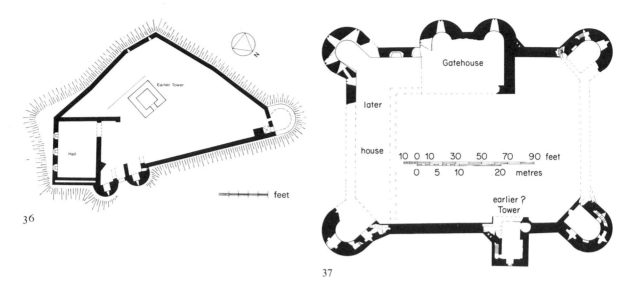

N

Earlier Tower

Hall

feet

36

Gatehouse

later

house

10 0 10   30   50   70   90 feet

0   5   10   20 metres

earlier ?
Tower

37

N

Keep

Fosse West

Fosse East

Lime Kiln

Lime Kiln

0 10 20 30 m

38

39

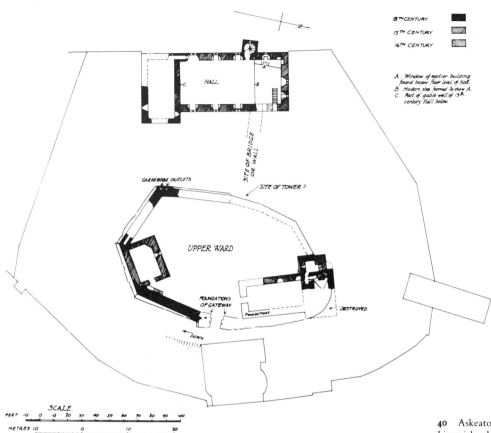

13TH CENTURY
15TH CENTURY
16TH CENTURY

A. Window of earlier building found below floor level of Hall.
B. Modern step formed to show A.
C. Part of gable wall of 13th century Hall below.

HALL

C

SITE OF BRIDGE OR WALL

GARDEROBE OUTLETS

SITE OF TOWER ?

UPPER WARD

FOUNDATIONS OF GATEWAY

FOUNDATIONS

DESTROYED

DOWN

SCALE

FEET 10 0 0 10 20 30 40 50 60 70 80 90 100
METRES 10   0   10   20

40

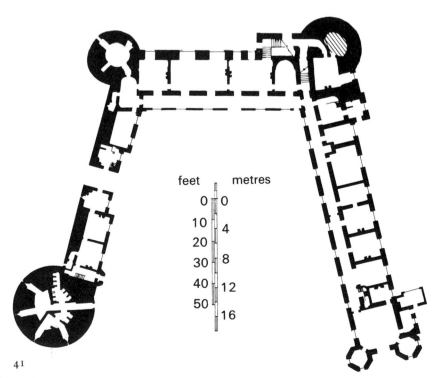

feet   metres

0   0
10   4
20
30   8
40   12
50   16

41

40 Askeaton Castle, Co Limerick: plan at level of upper ward. The castle is most notable for its large fifteenth-century hall rising straight out of the river on its West side (top of the plan). Mediaeval halls are concentrated in Co Limerick: there are two each in the castles of Adare and Newcastle West, and another remarkable specimen, probably thirteenth century, at Tomdeeley. The building shown in outline on the East (bottom) of this plan is a remarkable stone house with classical details in brick, which may be as early as 1700

41 Kilkenny Castle: plan as at present. The North-East, North-West and South-West towers are thirteenth century, and much, no doubt, of the North and West external walls. Otherwise it has been repeatedly remodelled, including the insertion of late-mediaeval wattle-centre vaults in the thirteenth-century towers

cathedrals, not all of which are in towns, they make a modest showing which we must now examine.

A little has already been said about Limerick and Christ Church Dublin. The nave of the latter was begun in about 1213, under the direction of the anonymous artist called 'the Christ Church master', an Englishman from Worcestershire who had already worked at Droitwich and Overbury. He produced a very suave design which links the triforium and clerestory in a single tall storey of the same height as the nave arcade below. This survives in the six bays on the North side. The nave, like the choir, was vaulted, but the vault and the South wall fell down in 1562, more probably as a result of neglect and maltreatment than through faulty design or workmanship, though there was plenty of that in mediaeval Ireland as elsewhere.

Christ Church[7] had a wide influence on subsequent churches in one minor particular: the use of banded shafts. At Christ Church these are of imported Purbeck stone, and being fragile, it was no doubt thought prudent to limit their length for transport by sea, with the result that they are banded at rather frequent intervals. Something similar may be seen at New Ross, Cashel, Graignamanagh, Ardfert Cathedral, Ennis friary and elsewhere. The distribution of buildings in the South-East where Dundry stone from Somerset was used in the thirteenth century, has been studied by Mr Dudley Waterman.[8] It comprises some 38 buildings, mostly churches but including half-a-dozen castles, between Drogheda and Kinsale, coastally, and up the valleys of the Nore, Barrow, Suir and Slaney. And where the English stone went, the English design tended to go too.

Among these churches is St Patrick's Cathedral, Dublin (fig. 42),[9] a building just as English in its genesis as Christ Church: indeed more so. It is true that there existed a church of St Patrick *in insula*, outside the city walls, well before 1170. But it was the death of Archbishop St Laurence O'Toole in 1181, and the appearance of John Comyn in the following year, which brought matters to a head. Comyn was a servant of Henry II, who, on the death of the archbishop, arranged for Comyn to fill his place, and sent him off to Rome where in 1182 the compliant Pope Lucius put him through the grades of priest and bishop in rapid order.

Having no relish for a chapter of Augustinian canons regular and a cathedral and palace within the lay jurisdiction of the city, Comyn resolved on the creation of a collegiate establishment of secular canons, and apparently rebuilt or enlarged St Patrick's for the purpose, in the years following 1191. He himself died in 1212, but his successor Henry de Loundres shared his distrust of the monastic establishment at Christ Church, and in about 1220 raised St Patrick's to the status of a cathedral. Rebuilding began in about 1220 and the church was consecrated in 1254, though the Lady Chapel or retro-choir was not finished until 1270 or so.

St Patrick's is a deeply-loved building, which makes it difficult to write about with the detachment which, no doubt, it deserves. The record shows that it has suffered at least as much as Christ Church, and in some ways more. It is certain that of its many restorations the operations of 1860 onwards had not the benefit of the formidable scholarship with which, at much the same time, Christ Church was being transformed by George Edmund Street. Yet there is a persistent sense that it has survived, that in some special way it is *still there*.

St Patrick's is heavy with history, as few other buildings in Ireland are. It is, among other things, a kind of national pantheon, for all that it is in the possession of a minority faith.

Though it is the largest mediaeval church in Ireland, it is somewhat smaller than Hereford or Southwell, and about the same size as Ripon. But it has a harmony

42 Dublin: St Patrick's Cathedral, the nave, second quarter of the thirteenth century. The simulated vaulting overhead is part of the mid-nineteenth century restoration, but the vault over the choir, seen in the distance beyond the darkness of the crossing, is a true vault, of the late nineteenth century

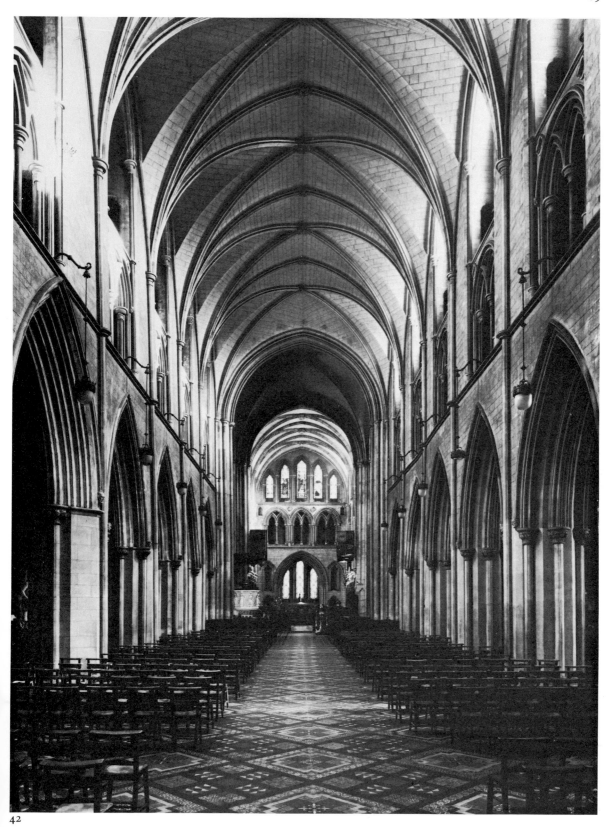

throughout its parts which few English cathedrals, except Salisbury, can match. It is Salisbury of which one is reminded when looking at St Patrick's from the North-East or South-East. Even as shown in Malton's print of 1792 taken from the South-East, it bore a striking resemblance to Salisbury, notably in the way in which the roof of the Lady Chapel is hipped to accommodate the five-light East window of the choir. One surprising difference is that there are more flying buttresses to be seen than at Salisbury, at least round the East end. Like Salisbury, St Patrick's is provided with aisles to East and West of the transepts. The bay design of the nave is the same as that of the choir but a little plainer. The whole church was vaulted,* but most of the nave vault fell in about 1544, no doubt for similar causes to those of the Christ Church catastrophe. The present stone vault over the choir is probably the third, and dates from 1901–04, replacing one of lath-and-plaster which in turn replaced a stone vault of 1681, itself a replacement of the original vault. The present covering over the nave is a simulated vault of lath-and-plaster. It is safe to presume that this fact is unknown to all but a very few of the thousands who frequent the cathedral, and that they are equally oblivious of the fact that the choir has a vault which is not simulated. During the quieter parts of Divine Service, the eye, and the attention, of the critic is apt to be drawn towards the central triforium arch over the altar, provoking speculation once again as to why it was made fractionally narrower than the arches to each side of it, instead of fractionally wider or even the same. The effect, it must be conceded, is not so obtrusive as at the notorious West front of Peterborough; but no less than that, it is a measure of the distance separating the mediaeval mind from our own.

Unlike the designer of Salisbury, the designer of St Patrick's quickened the rhythm of events to take account of the smaller scale of the Lady Chapel, putting in two lancets to each bay instead of one. Though the Lady Chapel was apparently rebuilt from the ground up by Carpenter in the 1840s, it carries much conviction, and the exterior is much as shown in the 1792 print. It is a rare Irish instance of that elongated elegance of the late thirteenth century which is common enough in England.

The great tower at the North-West corner of the nave, Minot's Tower, is so called because it was rebuilt by Archbishop Thomas Minot after the destruction or severe damage of its predecessor by a fire in 1362.† In the early fourteenth century it had had a steeple, but the present stone spire was added, rather surprisingly it may seem, but very successfully, by Dean Corbet, with George Semple as architect, in 1749, four years after the death of Swift.

They say that, here and there, the informed eye, assisted by faith, can find a few palpably mediaeval stones in St Patrick's. This may well be true, and if true, the better. But it is not of the essence. The building has survived in spirit, and that is what matters.

Since the few remaining cathedrals and parish churches of thirteenth-century origin embody in nearly every case features of a later mediaeval date, it will be convenient to take them as they stand, at this stage in the narrative. The great majority of the friaries, on the other hand, and one most important abbey, are primarily fifteenth century in character and will therefore be left over for that chapter.

---

* There is some doubt whether the nave, or indeed the choir, was vaulted in mediaeval times (Stalley).

† Either it took over 30 years to repair or there were two separate catastrophes. Neither is incredible. The Papal Registers are not clear on the point (Stalley).

But first there is one building to be disposed of which does not fit into any series, but by common consent and process of elimination must be of the thirteenth century. This is the church of St Doulough a few miles North of Dublin. It is much easier to describe than it is to diagnose. It is just under 40 feet long with an average width of about 16 feet and entirely built of stone. It divides into three approximately equal parts. The East and West parts have high-pitched stone roofs and over the centre is an approximately square tower, the top chamber of which is inaccessible from the interior, which has two storeys of rude vaulting. There are no large stones to be seen, nor any moulded stones of demonstrably early date. The East and West top vaults are of different heights, the West being higher and continuing through the tower space where it is groined; there is a corresponding change in the upper floor level but this takes place at the West face of the tower whereas the change in the vault is at the East face. There are two staircases, both on the South side.

Traditionally the ground-floor compartment on the West, which is walled off from the rest but with a window in the wall, was a hermit's or anchorite's cell. There are a very great many small windows in very odd places: some of them clearly recent.

It is impossible to say much about St Doulough's except that it is undoubtedly ancient, undoubtedly related to the stone-roofed group of churches, and apparently without surviving parallels. There is some slight evidence for its having had a transeptal limb to the North of the tower, and it may even have been cruciform.[10]

One of the earliest, simplest and most attractive of the Irish cathedrals is that of Killaloe. Killaloe has never been a town of any size, but it is close to the ancient seat of the Dal Cais at Kincora, and was founded by King Donal Mor O Brien in about 1185. Though part of the West half of the nave, and most of the North transept, have been remodelled, it survives as an essentially thirteenth-century structure, cruciform and aisleless. The choir is very regular, with buttresses and lancets and a triple-lancet East window of strangely hybrid character. There are interesting corbel-capitals of the Western school which may possibly indicate an original intention to vault. The crossing-tower was heightened between 1794 and 1803 and left with an unusual and picturesque silhouette, but in about 1890 this was altered and given conventional Irish stepped battlements. Built into the South-West corner of the nave is a notable Hiberno-Romanesque portal, originally a West door but now facing into the church. Externally there is the remains of a pointed arch, which shows up as early as Harris's print of 1739. Leask dates the church to the first quarter of the thirteenth century. It has great charm and atmosphere, and accompanied as it is by two notable stone-roofed predecessors it makes a whole very well worth visiting, situated as it now is in the heart of a centre of aquatic tourism.[11]

The Cathedral at Newtown Trim, of which little now remains, was of similar date and very large, over 230 feet long, as might be expected in such a situation, in the de Lacy lordship. It is known to have had an aisled nave and Eastward chapels.[12]

The large town church of St Mary's, New Ross is of similar date. The roofless chancel is aisleless, but there are long transepts of which the Southern has two Eastward chapels. The three-light East window has banded shafts in the Christ Church manner. The nave has gone but is believed to have had aisles. The scale and grandeur of the church reflects the fact that it was built under the patronage of the elder William the Marshal, to whose wife Isobel it contains a monument which may mark a heart-burial.[13]

Killaloe lay in Irish territory deeply affected by the Anglo-Norman penetration. New Ross was a completely Anglo-Norman bridgehead and trading town. The ancient and sacred acropolis of Cashel (fig. 44), equidistant between them, in

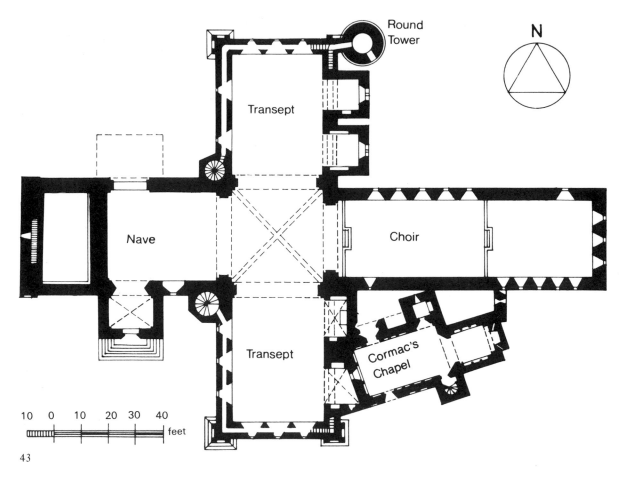

43

43 Cashel, Co Tipperary:
plan of the Cathedral,
Round Tower and
Cormac's Chapel, with the
Archbishop's castle/palace
at the West end of the nave

Tipperary (otherwise Ormond or East Munster) was in Irish, and ecclesiastical, hands, and here, between 1224 and 1289, under three successive archbishops—Marianus O Brien, David MacKelly and David MacCarwill—a cathedral for the archdiocese was built (fig. 43).[14] The site is constricted, and the cathedral touches Cormac's Chapel at two points, and touches also the Round Tower. Its Eastward chapels follow the rather unusual plan of those at Baltinglass, in being separated from each other by narrow and completely useless spaces.* Its choir is laid out on generous lines, though never vaulted nor intended to be. The crossing-space, at 33 feet 6 inches square, is the largest in Ireland, comfortably exceeding St Patrick's Dublin. It is vaulted and surmounted by a massive tower. The nave, by contrast, is very short and stops abruptly, arrested by the solid bulk of the archbishop's castle or palace, built probably in the early fifteenth century by archbishop Richard O'Hedian, which rivals the mass of the crossing-tower.

In the spandrels over the piers between the choir lancets are set strange little windows with colonettes, arched heads and sills in the form of inverted arches. The massive clasping buttresses at the ends of the transepts are relieved by tall niches terminating in gabled heads. The circular windows in the transept-gables have quatrefoil tracery very precisely cut but set askew as though to indicate magnetic variation: another inexplicable quirk of the mediaeval mind.

But after all is said, it is perhaps the incomparable situation of this cathedral and its relation to its companions, as much as its purely architectural qualities, which puts it in a special class.

The cathedral of Ardfert (fig. 45) has already been mentioned because of its fragmentary Hiberno-Romanesque West front. As it stands it is very like a friary church, with a long thin nave-cum-chancel, a south aisle and a long South transept with one Eastward chapel opening off it. Very typical are the nine closely grouped lancets in the South wall of the choir, and the almost over-scale stepped battlements along the wall-tops. There is in fact a Franciscan friary only a few yards away, and it, too, has the nine lancets, aisle and transept. The cathedral has banded shafts, but the friary not, and the friary is slightly the later of the two.

Mediaeval churches roofed and in use, especially continuous use, are so rare in Ireland that they can all be enumerated even in a general account. The oldest is no doubt Tuamgraney church, Co Clare, which has Hiberno-Romanesque features, and though of two periods, is all early and simple. Of the few larger examples that remain, several are in the coastal or near-coastal towns of Co Cork: St Mary's collegiate church, Youghal, St Colman's Cathedral, Cloyne, and St Multose parish church, Kinsale. All three are of thirteenth-century origin, and all have been through diverse vicissitudes. But these churches, which in England would be unremarkable, stand out in an Irish context. (The biggest and best surviving Irish mediaeval parish church, St Nicholas Galway, will be described later because it is substantially an early fourteenth-century building.)

Cloyne was originally somewhat similar to New Ross, except for having had unusually narrow aisles (only six feet in the clear) which were later widened. The East wall of the South transept has a triplet of lancets flanked by two pairs. The North door has the kind of occurrence very typical of mediaeval Irish buildings: the sudden irruption of a primitive mask emerging asymmetrically from the chamfer of the arch, and a sunken quatrefoil doodle on the vertical face of the other half of the arch, while below the stops effloresce upwards in free foliage.[15]

---

* The same feature occurs again at the Franciscan Friary of Adare and at La Trinité at Caen.

44

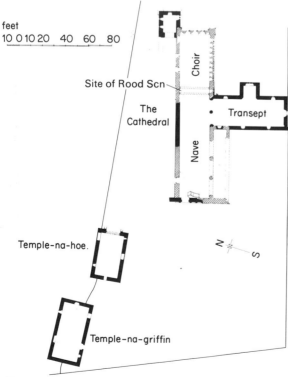

feet
10 0 10 20 40 60 80

Site of Rood Scn

The
Cathedral

Choir

Transept

Nave

N

S

Temple-na-hoe.

Temple-na-griffin

44 Cashel: the Rock, from the North-East. Cormac's Chapel is just visible above the walls of the choir, the Round Tower adjoins the North transept, and the archbishop's castle is on the right at the West end of the nave

45 Ardfert, Co Kerry: the Cathedral, Temple-na-hoe and Temple-na-griffin. The thirteenth-century parts are diagonally hatched: earlier and later parts are in black. Nobody has ever been able to explain why the Romanesque West front of the cathedral and the stretch of early masonry in the middle of the North wall are out of line with one another. The transept is, of course fifteenth-century

45

The large parish churches of Youghal and Kinsale[16] have both been altered and added to (and indeed subtracted from and, in the case of Youghal, devastated and laid roofless in the mid-sixteenth century) so that, though full of interest, neither is now an example of any style or date. At Youghal the tower is, most unusually, free-standing between the North transept and the North nave aisle. At Kinsale it is, also unusually, over the Westernmost bay of the North nave aisle. Neither has a clerestory, and like Cloyne, they have plain, unmoulded, pointed arches supported on square piers. The interest of their tombs and fittings belongs to the guide-book rather than to the architectural history.

Other parish churches still in use are even more fragmentary, such as St Nicholas, Carrickfergus, Holy Trinity, Fethard, St Audoen, Dublin and St Nicholas, Dundalk. The cathedral of Down (Downpatrick) has, in some rarified metaphysical sense, survived, and is extremely attractive for quite different reasons.

Very rarely the plan of a mediaeval building leaps out from the page of a textbook and proclaims itself classical, final and complete and not like other plans. Such, in England, is that of Durham, and such in Ireland is that of St Canice's Cathedral (figs 46 and 47) Kilkenny.[17] In the present building the plan is intact except for one small alteration: the expansion Eastwards and also a little Southwards of the most Southerly of the four chapels which open off the transepts. The Lady Chapel, now used as the chapter house, is less than 50 years later than the rest of the building, and though it was apparently rebuilt in the 1866 restoration it feels perfectly harmonious.

Serenity and harmony prevail throughout this building. It seems a happy accident that when the thirteenth-century crossing-tower fell in 1332 it was rebuilt to a lower outline, only a few feet above the ridges of nave and chancel. Were the cathedral in a low-lying situation like that of Killaloe, this might be a blemish, but situated as it is on an early Christian hilltop site, in close proximity to a Round Tower, it gains by having this very level profile.

As in so many Irish churches, there is no triforium, but this time the clerestory windows, repeating the plan of the piers of the nave arcade, which are elegant quatrefoils, are over the nave arches and not over the piers. The chapels *en échelon* act as aisles to the choir for nearly two-thirds of its length, and at its East end it has nine lancets, three to the East and three each to North and South, all with trefoiled rere-arches and banded shafts in the Christ Church manner. The windows are considerably varied, apparently from the beginning, and include round-headed lancets in the transepts.

The West door is a more elaborate version of the West door of Wells cathedral, reminding us again of the West of England affinities of so much thirteenth-century work in South-Eastern Ireland, and the North transept door is related to a door at Strata Florida.

The nave arcade has quatrefoil piers of modest height supporting pointed arches, above which are the deep splays and sloping sills of the segmental-pointed rere-arches to the external quatrefoils. There is rather more than a hint that the contrasting colours of sandstone and limestone were here exploited to produce a banded effect somewhat like that at Vézelay.

The West window has a most curious feature. Below the raised sill of the central light is a scaled-down model of the West door, but facing into the church where the original faces, of course, outwards. This little aedicule is about one-third the height of its exemplar; and is of course blind, but there is a panel of three quatrefoils externally. It is traversed by a wall-passage as at the East end of Killone.

There are no vaults, nor ever were there, except that over the crossing, a fine

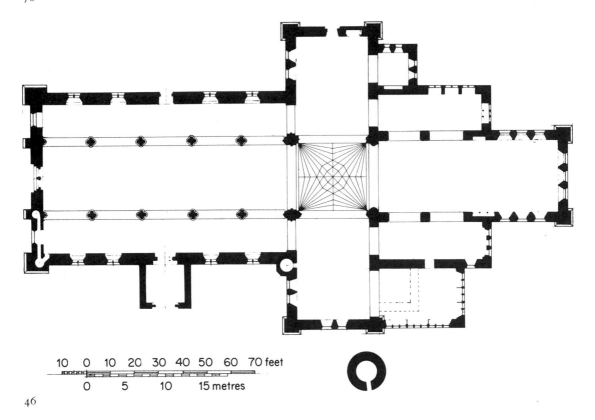

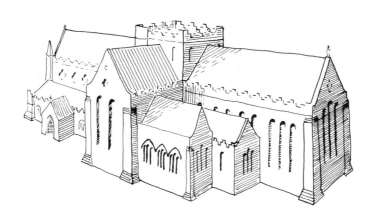

10 0   10 20 30 40 50 60 70 feet

0   5   10   15 metres

46

47

fifteenth-century lierne vault of 30 feet span. The timber hammer-beam roofs are part of the restoration by Sir Thomas Newenham Deane of 1866. (There are no mediaeval roofs left in Ireland except that of Dunsoghly Castle near Dublin.) Among the chief glories of the cathedral is the fine series of tombs which are late mediaeval in style though dating from the sixteenth and seventeenth centuries. Considering the accounts of what happened to it in Cromwellian times, St Canice's has survived remarkably well: better, it may be thought, than any other large Irish cathedral, and even the nineteenth-century restorers have laid a light hand on it. The worst thing that happened to it was the injudicious removal of the plaster from the interior: but when taste and knowledge have recovered, that can easily be set right.

There are two other mediaeval churches in Kilkenny, St Mary's of which in its present form little need be said, and the mid thirteenth-century St John's Priory of which the Lady Chapel, still in use as a parish church, closely resembles that of St Canice's, and is also a nineteenth-century reconstruction, in this case of five three-light windows instead of three.

Kilkenny still has an intensely mediaeval atmosphere: perhaps it is the only town in Ireland which has. Not far away are two other thirteenth-century churches related to St Canice's: Thomastown which is very fragmentary, and Gowran of which a good deal more remains. Both are ruined and have early nineteenth-century Prot-estant churches 'camping-out' in the remains. The master who worked on the West end of St Canice's and has been identified as the 'Gowran master' worked also at Thomastown.[18]

The next-door diocese is Leighlin, where there is a little cathedral of great charm and little coherence of design, which started life as a long chancel with a slightly wider and shorter nave, and now has a roofless North transept, the South one having disappeared, a slender vaulted tower over the West end of the chancel, and a late mediaeval chapel North of the choirs, together with much else of an irregular nature. At Ferns, which diocese adjoins both Ossory (Kilkenny) and Leighlin and is united with them, there is a group of buildings and fragments of which nobody has been able to make any sense. The present anomalously shaped Protestant cathedral is easily related to the original aisled and transepted building of which it represents, however partially and unworthily, the presbytery. But some 70 feet due East of this, on the same axis, is a building with the usual row of closely set lancets, in this case seven in each of the North and South walls. It looks just like an Eastward chapel or retro-choir to the cathedral, except that its floor level is four feet lower. Various explana-tions have been put forward: none of them very satisfactory. It is rather short and wide for a chancel: on the other hand the height of the sills would allow for stalls, perhaps for the Augustinians of Dermot Macmurrough's earlier foundation which stands close by.[19]

One more thirteenth-century cathedral remains to be described: one which was re-constituted and brought back from almost total destruction: the cathedral of Kildare.[20] Built probably between 1229 and 1270, begun by the first Anglo-Norman bishop of the diocese, it was (and again is) a simple cruciform church of moderate size (145 feet overall) without aisles but with a massive central tower. By the beginning of the eighteenth century the chancel, North transept, three-quarters of the tower and much of the West wall had gone, and so had the Eastward chapels if they ever existed. Most surprisingly, in the year following the disestablishment of the Church of Ireland, George Edmund Street was called in to re-edify it. The work was completed in 25 years; and whether because there was less money to spare than at Christ Church, or because the building was a simpler one in the first place, the

46 Kilkenny, St Canice's Cathedral: plan. The original form of the South-Eastern chapel is shown dotted. To the South of the transept the Round Tower was, of course, there first. The four crossing-piers were reconstructed after the fall of the original tower in 1332

47 St Canice's from the South-East

result is a great deal more satisfactory and carries more conviction. Its most striking feature is that at parapet level the intervals between the buttresses are spanned by wide arches a short distance out from the wall–face, constituting a kind of large-scale machicoulis of picturesque effect but undeniably military purpose. It was not long since the abbess of Kildare had, at the instance of king Dermot, been forcibly bedded with a common soldier in order to render her canonically unfit to continue in office,[21] so that he could give the job to one of his female relations. Whether these defences could have prevented such an occurrence or not, they vividly express the military aspect of the ecclesiastical situation in that place and at that time.

CHAPTER SIX

Friaries Etc.

By the close of the thirteenth century things were beginning to go ill for the Anglo-Norman colony. There was a little cloud to be seen on the horizon, no bigger than a man's hand. The justiciar Wogan called a parliament in Dublin in 1297, at which expressions of disquiet were heard. The Gaelic clan system, with its attendant outlook, had begun to infect the colonial families, and there were mutterings of disapprobation about the 'degenerate English' who were showing ominous signs of going native: the kind of thing which 70 years later, in the Statutes of Kilkenny, found expression in colourful and frequently-quoted language. But by then, the cause was irremediably lost. Paradoxically there had been a strong movement in the early 1270s, led by the Archbishop of Cashel, to have the benefit of English law extended to those Irish dwelling in the 'land of peace', meaning the large part of Ireland under Norman control, a benefit for which they were prepared to pay handsomely in cash.[1] It seems that it was the personal decision of Edward I himself to refuse the offer, a refusal which recalls George III's personal refusal to implement understandings in the Union of 1800.

The colony was by now some 130 years in existence. The military momentum had been lost. The grafting of feudal institutions on to the existing social structure had produced an unstable result. Historians, with hindsight, say that by 1300 the tide had turned. Typically in such situations, expenditure on defence mounted, and during the 1270s and 1280s large sums were spent on the castles at Athlone and Rinndown, and on building the new castle at Roscommon:[2] all three, be it noted, close together and forming a foothold in Connacht West of the Shannon, beyond which Richard de Burgo's great lordship stretched to Sligo and the sea. His castle of Ballintober was built in emulation of Roscommon, while of his other great castle 'Northburgh' at Greencastle in Inishowen, little but a fragmentary gate-tower survives.

There is record of work on the castles of Roscrea and Quin in the closing years of the century; but the one exists now in a seventeenth-century remodelling and the other was transmuted into a Franciscan friary in the fifteenth. After the turn of the century there is little record of castle-building.[3] Almost the only example of note is Ballymoon Co Carlow, and this is an unusual building, not very like any other, the nearest (not very close) parallel being at Ballyculhane Co Limerick. Dated 'with reasonable certainty' (Leask) to about 1310, it is a practically square enclosure with walls eight feet thick, with here and there, comparatively slender projections (only one of which is on a corner) containing a lavish provision of garderobes: in plain English, privies. The only thing which is clear about the building is that there must have been a substantial amount of lean-to accommodation up against the outer wall, perhaps for the whole perimeter, as sketched in on Leask's drawing. The details, as one would expect in Co Carlow, are very well wrought and very well preserved. Nobody knows who built it or why, nor indeed whether it was ever finished.[4]

There was rather more ecclesiastical building between 1300 and 1350, though in this field, too, the volume is beginning to tail off by comparison with the spate of activity in the previous century. One of the most attractive fourteenth-century church buildings is the choir of Tuam Cathedral[5] (already mentioned on page 40 as a 'retro-choir') which now does duty as the chapter house. Formerly assigned by Clapham to the late fourteenth century, but subsequently by Leask to about 1310, it has a somewhat fortified aspect, faintly recalling Les Saintes Maries de la Mer in Provence, though less severe. Its buttresses have pretty little niches in them, and the very varied tracery of its windows is among the earliest properly so called,* in Ireland. The Archbishop was English and the tracery is of English character. The present starveling battlements are a poor substitute for what was no doubt there originally. Even as it is, the arches—really too large to be called machicoulis—resting alternately on the buttresses and the intermediate corbels, give bold relief though, unlike those of Kildare Cathedral, they are not actually separated from the wall.

The largest and most intact church which appears to date from the fourteenth century though incorporating much enlargement of the fifteenth and early sixteenth centuries, is the collegiate church of St Nicholas Galway (fig. 48),[6] still in use by the Church of Ireland. Galway, a strictly Anglo-Norman foundation, was very much isolated and left to its own devices in the later Middle Ages to the extent that by 1476 it had gone so far as to adopt the Roman law of the Empire instead of the English common law. Though this isolation had hardly taken effect at the time of the church's foundation, it must have helped to give it the very individual character which it has kept to this day.

As first built in about 1330 it had a choir without aisles, North and South transepts, and an aisled nave of four bays: a plan much like that of Cloyne cathedral, and of much the same size. Over the next two centuries it was altered and added to, like many a similar church in England. The South aisle was widened in 1486 onwards, the crossing-piers strengthened and the tower added at about the same time, the North aisle widened (as to its Eastern half) in 1538, and (as to the rest) in 1583. Much of this work† was done at the expense of the important Galway family of Lynch, who also lengthened the South transept to act as their private chapel and burying-place, in 1561. A North chapel (now roofless) was added at right-angles to the North aisle, probably in the middle of the sixteenth century, and in the second bay of the South aisle there is a porch with a rib-vaulted ceiling which must be after 1510, a very late date for rib-vaulting in Ireland, unless, as Leask suggests, the vaulting is re-used from a porch which gave on to the aisle before it was widened. Its external detail is of the very last phase of gothic.

The widening of the aisles gave the church its three-gabled West façade which is so conspicuous. For the rest, its most salient external features are the 30 splendidly varied gargoyles, some of them double with divergent spouts, which adorn the South parapet, the variety of the window-tracery, and the massing of the central tower. The interior is rich, by Irish standards, in tombs and other fittings.

The widespread destruction and disorganisation which followed on the Bruce invasions of 1315-18, followed, after little more than 30 years, by the arrival in Ireland of the Black Death, made the remainder of the fourteenth century a time of sparse achievement in architecture. But during the first half of it, at least, there was some activity in the building of friaries, and though the first friars arrived well before the middle of the thirteenth century, and though the great bulk of their

---

* i.e. not counting 'switchline' tracery.

† A good deal of it is in ashlar masonry.

surviving buildings date from the fifteenth, the phenomenon as a whole may conveniently be considered here: too late from one point of view, too early from another.

The orders principally concerned are the Franciscans and the Dominicans, both of whom arrived early in the thirteenth century, followed some 40 to 50 years later by the Carmelites and the Augustinians. As in other countries, there were also a few houses of less prominent orders.[7]

The pattern at first was the familiar one of settlement in or near the larger towns. Thus some remains are, naturally, found in such towns as Drogheda, Kilkenny, Kilmallock and Athenry, which last was a walled town of considerable extent.

As in England, the rate of survival of buildings of the mendicant orders in the larger towns is low, though this is much less markedly the case in Ireland where the towns themselves did not expand so much after the Middle Ages, and where the Dissolution took effect both later and less completely. But the really startling contrast is to be seen in the country, and especially in the West, where more than a dozen friaries remain, though roofless, virtually intact: a circumstance not paralleled in any other country, and one which makes Ireland the *locus classicus* for the study of mendicant architecture.

The figures, as given by Gwynn and Hadcock in *Mediaeval Religious Houses*, speak for themselves. During nearly two centuries, they tell us, from 1349 to 1539, not a single new monastery,★ was founded, whereas the same period saw the building of 60 new mendicant houses, plus a further 44 of the third order or 'tertiaries' who lived under a less strict rule. They say furthermore that there are 'remains or ruins of some interest' of 36 Franciscan houses, 29 Dominican, 16 Augustinian, 15 nunneries of various kinds, 13 Carmelite and 21 of the Franciscan Third Order: a grand total of 160, not counting the oddments such as the Trinitarians at Adare or the Fratres Cruciferi at Newtown Trim. These figures, it is true, give a much exaggerated idea of what is actually to be seen. Almost all the Third Order houses are small and insignificant with the exception of Rosserk, and few nunneries can show as much as Killone or Monasternagalliaghduff (otherwise St Catherine de O'Conyl or simply Old Abbey).

But when all deductions have been made, the total is still most impressive. Besides the 12 or more which are virtually complete, another three dozen or so can show substantial remains, while there are six or seven abbeys or priories which by reason of extensive rebuilding or enlargement during the period, fall to be considered within the same general view. This is a much lower figure than the 160 deducible from Gwynn and Hadcock: but obviously the extent of remains required to identify an establishment known from documentary sources is much less than that required to engage the interest of the historian of architecture.

In the larger towns it is common for little more than a friary tower to have survived.† Such is the tower of the Franciscan friary in Kilkenny, one of the very earliest of such towers to be built (about 1347) and most significantly (being in the 'land of peace') without the batter so characteristic of most of them. Here it is accompanied by the splendid seven-light East window of similar date. At Waterford both Franciscan and Dominican towers survive: at Drogheda and Roscrea the

---

★ That is to say a true *monastery* as opposed to friaries which in Ireland are often loosely and confusingly called 'abbeys'.

† A good deal more than the tower survives at Waterford Franciscan Friary, later known as the 'French Church'.

Dominican and Franciscan towers respectively stand widowed. The friary towers, as a class, will be described presently.

Among the very few works assignable to the fourteenth century are friaries at Adare and Athenry. The former, an Augustinian house, was built in about 1320 and re-roofed in the early nineteenth century as the Protestant church, which it still is, with a South aisle widened in the fifteenth century and a tower of that date also, and a miniature cloister three bays in each direction.

At Athenry the fourteenth-century work consisted of an Eastward extension and the addition of an aisle and transept. Friary churches were long and narrow to begin with, but almost without exception an aisle, usually to the South, and a 'preaching transept' was added in the fourteenth and still more the fifteenth centuries, to fit them for their new and more evangelical role.

The long South transept which is such a conspicuous feature of the Dominican Friary ('Black Abbey') in Kilkenny (fig. 49), was erected, in Leask's opinion, some time after 1324. Its fine South window displays very prominently the pointed trefoil which Leask[8] calls 'a sure mark of fourteenth-century work in Ireland': a late thirteenth-century English motif which had crossed the Irish Sea. If Leask's dating is right, this must have been a-building just as the bizarre series of events for which fourteenth-century Kilkenny is renowned were being enacted: the proceedings taken by Bishop Richard de Ledrede against Dame Alice Kyteler and others for sorcery.[9]

The truth is that the colony was suffering in manpower and in morale, not merely through the infection from the Irishry which has already been hinted at, but also through being dragged into the vortex of disturbances on the other side of the Irish Sea: in this case the quarrel between the great houses of Mortimer and Despenser, of which the Kilkenny witch-hunt was but a peripheral eddy. Bishop de Ledrede (who was a Franciscan) was yet not so preoccupied with political problems that he could not, towards the end of his long reign (1316–60), put in hand the repair of the crossing and chancel of St Canice's, damaged by the fall of the tower. (The crossing-vault, however, is of the following century).

The friars, of whatever order, were in origin part of the colony, and only the Franciscans enjoyed, at first, any independence from the English province. By the end of the thirteenth century there were Irish friars, in fair numbers, in the Anglo-Norman houses. In 1291 they came to blows at Cork, and in 1312 the Pope, ready as usual to act (in Bernard Shaw's words) as John Bull's policeman, deprived them of the right to elect their own provincial. There was more trouble of the same kind in 1325. An attempt by the Irish Dominicans to gain independence in 1378 was quashed by a compliant Pope at the request of Richard II. The Augustinians fared a little better, but not much. However, be the de jure position what it might, the mendicant orders had, by the end of the fourteenth century, become thoroughly penetrated by Irish or hibernicised Normans.

It is a rule of all human institutions that they degenerate and become corrupt. Periodically the moulds must be broken and recast: the institutions must be reformed or superseded by others. This happened to conventual life in Ireland in the Middle Ages: twice, in rather rapid succession. The monasteries proper, Cistercians and others, had fallen into predictable ways: too few monks, too many monasteries too close together; as instance Holycross, Kilcooley and Hore in an 18-mile triangle, Duiske and Jerpoint squabbling in their contiguous valleys, only nine miles apart. Such conditions favoured the rise of the friars, who were closer to the people. But the friars themselves, from quite early in the fourteenth century, were taking up another reform, of Italian origin. This was the Observant movement: a very simple

48 Galway: St Nicholas
Church, plan

49 Kilkenny: the 'Black
Abbey' (Dominican friary).
The tower was built by
James Schortall whose
tomb was erected in 1537?
Conspicuous in this picture
is the long preaching-
transept, in this case on the
South side

48

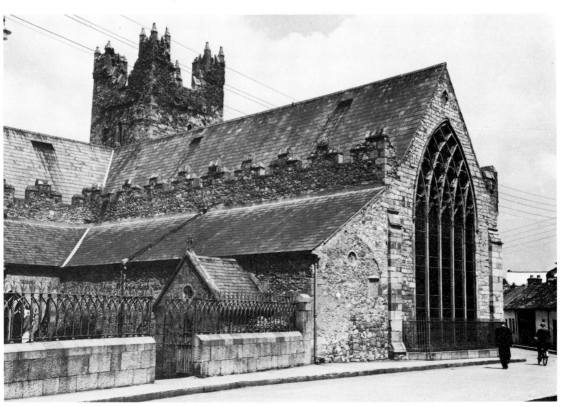

49

affair which consisted of nothing more than the voluntary re-adoption of the order's rule in its pristine purity. But because it was voluntary, some houses became 'Observant' while others remained what was called 'Conventual'.[10]

It would be too crude to say that the fresh foundations were Observant while the existing ones remained Conventual, or to identify the Observant movement exclusively with the Irish membership of the orders, as opposed to the Anglo-Irish. But that is the general tendency, and it goes far to explain the flowering of the friaries in sequestered situations in the following century.

For the rest, we must bear in mind that the devastation of the Bruces' wars did more damage to the Norman than to the Gael, and still more markedly, that insofar as the Black Death affected Ireland it hit the towns (which were Anglo-Norman) much harder than it hit the country (which was predominantly Gaelic). Finally, when the Gaelic resurgence got under way it brought into a position of political and military advantage families who were not town-dwellers by habit.

So, of some 50 representative friaries founded between 1300 and 1508, 29 were founded by Gaelic families and a further half-dozen by hibernicised Normans such as the de Burgos, de Berminghams, Fitzgeralds and Nangles: in round figures altogether some 70 per cent of the total.

In proportion as mendicant friars (and indeed Cistercian monks also) adhere to the primitive strictness of their rule, they do not leave impressive buildings behind them. At least, that is the theoretical position. Neither friars nor Cistercians, for example, were supposed to build towers. Fortunately for us, that is not quite how it worked in practice. The vaulting and tracery of Holycross, the tower and cloisters of Jerpoint, are perhaps the chief glories of fifteenth-century architecture, and both are Cistercian. Towers were added to nine Cistercian abbeys during the fifteenth century, and 19 friary towers, mostly Franciscan, date from the same century: some of them additions, but many coeval with the churches, including several which were Observant.

In fact, the largest and best-preserved of the friaries, Ross or Rosserrilly, some 14 miles North of Galway, was an Observant house, and probably founded as such, though its precise origins are in doubt. It seems to have been founded by a very obscure family called Gannard, probably very late in the fifteenth century. It has a complex plan with an extra courtyard North of the cloister, and the usual graceful slender tower centrally over the church. But, as one would expect from a late foundation, it is relatively plainly finished. Owing to the protection of the Clanrickarde Burkes, it survived in fitful occupation till about the middle of the seventeenth century. This was by no means exceptional.

Generalisations about the friaries are necessarily based on those in the West, where the survival rate was highest, and where in any case most of the fifteenth-century and later foundations were placed. All the pre-fifteenth-century Augustinian foundations were in the South and East, and all those after 1400 in the West.

Whereas in the Cistercian and other monastic houses the claustral buildings had generally been placed to the South of the church (with the single exception of Hore Abbey), the domestic buildings of the friaries lay generally to the North: nobody seems to know why. There are exceptions to this rule also: notably Askeaton where not only is the cloister to the South, but the refectory abuts on to its South side, at right angles: a feature found also at the Cistercian houses of Mellifont and Jerpoint.

The friary cloisters are also markedly smaller than those of the abbeys: a little over 30 feet square is normal. Quin, which is not quite square, is 37 feet in the clear on its longer dimension; but the cloister of Rosserrilly (which is the largest of all the friaries) is one of the smallest at about 25 feet square. (For comparison, the Dunbrody cloister is over 90 feet square).* In part this smallness seems to derive from the relationship between church and cloister. The Western section of a Cistercian church was always about twice the length of the Eastern part, so that the cloister took its scale from the larger unit. The long, narrow friary churches, by contrast, were divided into two equal parts: one with plenty of light for the friars to read their service-books by, the other filled with numinous gloom for the benefit of the unlettered laity. The cloister usually but not always corresponded more or less to the Western section, and its dimensions in the clear were at most one-third of the total length of the church. Friars who went out and about among the people had less need of space within their walls than had the enclosed orders.

Another difference generally to be found between the friary cloisters and those of the abbeys is that the former are integral: that is to say that instead of being single-storey arcades with lean-to roofs, they constitute part of the ground floor of the surrounding buildings, except of course on the side next to the church. Some friaries which have now no trace of a cloister arcade, such as Kilcrea, Sherkin Island, or the little Third Order house at Rosserk, may have, and in some cases certainly had, lean-to cloisters. But the integral type is commoner. Creevelea Co Leitrim, the latest of all, is of the lean-to type.

During the fifteenth century, also, many Cistercian cloisters were rebuilt. The only surviving early cloister, in fact, is the partly reconstructed one at Mellifont, carried on pairs of plain columns. In its typically Irish fifteenth-century form as at Jerpoint, this has been transformed into the arcade carried on 'dumb-bell' piers: piers consisting of two three-quarter columns with a stone web between them. But there is a kind, intermediate in time, though not in type, between these, and represented at Athassel where, according to Leask, it may be as early as the late fourteenth century or as late as 1447-plus. It is hardly to be called an arcade, being rather a wall punched with small openings, their cusped ogee-heads formed each of two stones, but with wide splays to round-headed rere-arches on the inside. Unlike the others, it was designed to be glazed.

Askeaton may be the earliest[11] among the friary cloisters, and is in many ways typical. The cloisters are integral, and consist of slightly pointed arches on dumb-bell piers, in groups of three openings separated by somewhat more substantial piers, and over all a continuous barrel-vault, very small and dark. (The passage is only six feet wide).† Askeaton is unusually regular, having four units of three to each side. Quin also is regular (fig. 55), but not a square, having six double bays in one direction and seven in the other. As well as twos and threes they are found in fives, at Rosserrilly and Moyne, and in one case (at Fore of course) in fours.

The integral cloisters are often buttressed at the thick piers. At Muckross, exceptionally, all the piers are buttressed, which gives a rich effect. At Quin the buttresses are very deep and narrow and die into the wall-face at twice the height of the arcade. The purpose was no doubt in part to relieve the blank expanse of wall below the upper windows, which are high up and surprisingly large. The columns and bases at Quin, as also at Sligo, are varied with twist patterns and the like in the usual mediaeval way.

---

* The cloister of Sligo Dominican friary is somewhat larger at 50 feet by 43 feet 6 inches. Plan in official guide to the monument.

† On the inside of the Askeaton arcade there are very extraordinary cranked shafts leading to simple capitals which, in conjunction with the shafts, look like nothing so much as rainwater-heads and downpipes.

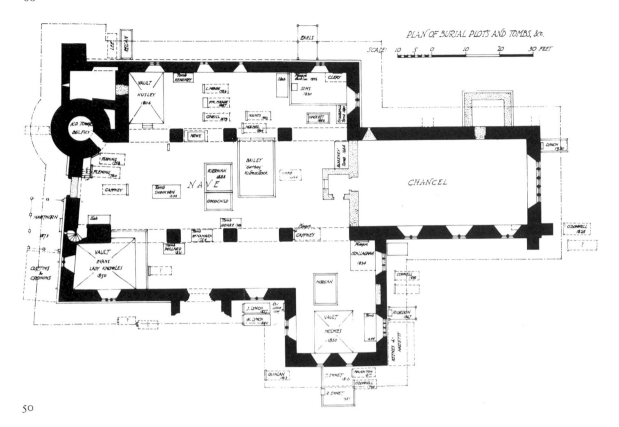

PLAN OF BURIAL PLOTS AND TOMBS, &c.

SCALE: 10 5 0 10 20 30 FEET

50

51

Sometimes the openings are grouped under a massive arch of flattened form and deep projection: in the Augustinian friary at Adare these arches are on the courtyard side, while in the Franciscan friary close by they face towards the ambulatory. So also at Ardfert. There is something rather similar at Bective, where the original Cistercian cloister was replaced by an integral one in the fifteenth century. The Bective cloister is related in its details to those at Fore and at Holy Cross.

At this point it is profitable to lay aside for the moment the distinction between friaries and abbeys (as we have already done by glancing briefly at Athassel and Fore), because the characteristic fifteenth-century Irish detail is common to both. It may be seen, for example, in the recently reconstructed cloister of the Augustinian priory of Clontuskert Co Galway, where little bits of carving suddenly break out from plane surfaces in the typical Irish manner.[12] Of all the fifteenth-century cloisters that of Jerpoint is the most spectacular (it, also, is a twentieth-century re-erection).

The Jerpoint cloister has the webs between the pillars enlivened with high-relief carvings of dragons, apes, members of the Butler family, ladies and ecclesiastics: a spirited assemblage which is related to the local school of tomb-sculpture and in part inspired by the marginal drawings on manuscripts. The arches are semicircular, which should surprise nobody since there was no century during which round arches were not used, and at Muckross (c. 1460) they are found in the cloister side by side with bluntly pointed ones, just as at Jerpoint they have capitals and bases of thirteenth-century style but fifteenth-century date.[13]

At the same time Jerpoint was also beautified by the insertion of its crossing-tower, without doubt the finest in all Ireland, with its slight batter (found also at Dunbrody), still boasting (as Dunbrody does not) its elaborately stepped Irish battlements rising to stepped corner turrets. Jerpoint has little recorded history during the fifteenth century, but it clearly flourished under the protection of the Ormonde Butlers who had bought William the Marshal's great castle of Kilkenny in 1391.

The other Cistercian abbey which lay within the Butler domains and was so transformed at this time that it can virtually be regarded as a fifteenth-century building, is Holy Cross (fig. 52).[14] The Holy Cross cloisters are inferior in interest to those of Jerpoint, and its tower, though comely, rises only a short distance above the ridges. But the elaborately vaulted east end, vaulted throughout except where the night-stair descends into the South transept, is unique in Ireland and of excellent quality. Above the vaults there are living-spaces, which would seem odd in most countries but are paralleled in both ancient and modern Ireland.

The windows of Holy Cross are elaborately varied, cusped and uncusped, geometric and reticulated; the most conspicuous being the great six-light East window which has a companion of similar but more elongated design at the West end of the nave. But the glory of the abbey lies in two internal features of the utmost refinement and delicacy: the sedilia and the enigmatic structure which replaces the solid wall between the two Eastward chapels of the South transept. The former is probably of about 1450–55 but is like English work of the previous century.* The latter is anomalous and has been variously described as a tomb, a 'waking-place' and a place in which to display the relic which gave the abbey its name. The last seems the most probable conjecture. More enjoyable, in some ways, than either of these is the little

50 Kilmallock, Co Limerick: the Collegiate church of Saints Peter and Paul, incorporating the pre-existing Round Tower in the North-West corner of the nave. Mostly thirteenth to fifteenth century

51 Timoleague, Co Cork: the Friary from the South. The slender battered tower is very typical

---

* The royal tomb at Ennis friary resembled the Holy Cross sedilia (Leask, *Churches* III 173 and C. O'Brien in *The Architectural and Topographical Record*, p. 157), and so does the Mac con Mara tomb at nearby Quin (ibid.).

52

52   Holy Cross Abbey, Co
Tipperary: the church from
the East, after its recent
restoration by W. P. Le
Clerc. Though the abbey is
of thirteenth-century
foundation, all the Eastern
parts seen here are of the
later fifteenth century

53   Rosserk, Co Mayo:
detail of the piscina in the
church of the Franciscan
Third Order friary. This
little relief miniature of the
Round Tower at
neighbouring Killala is
exactly one foot high.
Another example of
miniature buildings in relief
may be seen at Northesk
Co Cork. Drawn by
Michael Craig

53

owl on the North-West crossing-pier, in no particular place, just caught by the mason in whose fantasy he settled there: but caught on the wing.[15]

Another fifteenth-century reconstruction at Kilcooly, 15 miles to the East, resulted in an unusual stone screen between the South transept and the sacristy, and two decorated seat-niches in the Western crossing-piers. Here, as at Holy Cross, Butler coats of arms suggest who paid for most of this; but Abbot Philip, who had been to England to collect alms after the abbey had been sacked by roughnecks, is commemorated also. He died in 1463.[16]

A very few of the friaries received stout square towers like those of the Cistercians, but this was exceptional: Burrishoole (Dominican) is an example. The tower of the 'Black Abbey' (also Dominican) in Kilkenny is intermediate in thickness between a Cistercian tower and a typical friary tower: it has a moderate batter, is finished at the top much like Jerpoint, and is very satisfying in design. It is fifteenth-century in style, but in date probably early in the sixteenth (fig. 49).[17]

The typical friary towers, which are with few exceptions either fifteenth-century insertions or integral parts of friaries built then or even later, are tall and slender, appreciably narrower than the church. They stand, generally, on a pair of walls rather close together, running North and South, with a pair of arches, also rather narrow, separating the nave from the choir. In a few cases (Caher (Augustinian), Cashel (Dominican), Muckross (Franciscan) Creevelea (Franciscan)), the tower is oblong and relatively thin from East to West, but the usual thing is for the 'shoulders' to slope inwards (sometimes inside the roof, sometimes outside it) so that the tower itself is square or nearly so. They naturally look taller and slenderer now, emerging from a mass of gabled ruins, than they did when the roofs were intact.

There is no fixed relationship between the tower and the other parts of the plan: even the transept can, on occasion (as at Moyne) extend Eastwards as far as the East wall of the tower, while the relationship between tower and cloister is even more fluid. Thus at Rosserrilly the doorway into the tower lies well to the West of the axis of the cloister, while at Muckross the East cloister-walk is directly prolonged into the passage under the tower. Very nearly the same thing happens at Quin (figs 54 and 55), where the whole plan is closely similar to that at Muckross, and there is little to choose in date between them. Both took about 20 years to build. At Quin, the earlier of the two by perhaps ten years, the plan was ingeniously fitted in to the outer walls of a great quadrangular thirteenth-century de Clare castle, by then in ruins.* The bases of three of its four massive three-quarter round corner towers may still be seen.

In general the friaries, especially those which are most complete, show at their best the massing of many gable-ended forms, with differing ridge-levels, building up to the slender central tower. In detail they abound in small-scale felicities of carving in which sympathy for the hard Irish limestone blends with fantasy and a revival of earlier forms and themes: an abundance of gothic motifs, so to speak, without the gothic motive itself.[18]

This is perhaps most notably evident in the tombs, which almost fall to be considered as pieces of architecture in their own right. At Kilconnell Franciscan friary, for example, a building not otherwise very notable except for its slender tower, there are two sharply contrasted tomb-niches: one, rigidly geometric in its setting-out and bristling with cusps, and the other with *legato* tracery of flamboyant type (fig. 56). Both are works of the utmost virtuosity. The first-mentioned may be

---

* Other friaries – Carrick-on-Suir, Timoleague and perhaps Enniscorthy, apparently succeeded to castles.

54

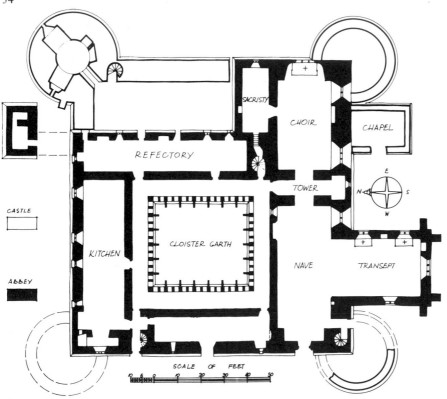

54 Quin Franciscan Friary, Co Clare, from the South-West. The deep recesses in which the choir windows (to the right) are sunk are the result of the thickness of the wall of the castle within which the friary is built. It was effectively founded in 1433. The slender tower is entirely typical of Irish friaries, especially in the West

55 Quin friary: plan. The detached ablutionary block to the North of the refectory and reached by a bridge is worthy of notice (OPW)

that of Malachy O'Kelly who died in 1464: though the cusping would be by then over 150 years out of date in England; Leask thinks it may be later still. The other tomb has a splendid set of figures in its frontal, including a rather large number of French saints, to match the tracery.[19]

At Cahan Abbey in Dungiven, Co Derry, there is a tomb fully equal in quality to these (fig. 57). It is that of Cooey na Gall who died in 1385, though whether the tomb is quite so early as that has been questioned. The tracery is of swirling flamboyance, with small cusps over a nearly semicircular arch below which reposes in effigy the occupant, the panels of the frontal occupied by six of the mercenary soldiers or gallowglasses who gave Cooey his nickname 'Cooey of the Foreigners'. It is a little surprising that a comparatively petty chieftain should have been able to command such work in a rather remote part of the country; but more surprising still if, as has been suggested, his memory still had power to command it some 15 or 20 years after his death. There are other tombs of similar quality at various places including the Dominican Friary at Strade, Co Mayo.

The subject of Irish window tracery is quite unmanageable in a book of this scale. Justice has been done to it, with the necessary illustrations, both by Champneys and by Leask; and to them and to more recent work by Roger Stalley, the reader is referred.[20]

Inevitably the question will be asked: who actually *built* the friaries? The answer must be, as it will be for many buildings in the succeeding centuries, that the masonry was done by masons, the carpentry by carpenters, the heaving and hauling by the unskilled, and that someone representing the client had a general responsibility for the design (in outline at least) and for how the money was spent. The cloisters at Kilconnell, for instance, are rich in variety of masons' marks, while we know that at the Franciscan Friary in Clonmel[21] in 1318 Friar John de Nasse was *magister operum* or master of the works (for what that is worth). The best documented of all is probably the Franciscan house at Adare[22]: the church was built first, then the tower and transept, one walk of the cloister, the East and probably the North ranges, the infirmary, and perhaps last of all the completion of all four sides of the cloister: the whole taking over half a century, with the Earl of Kildare and his wife prominent among the benefactors. Over 200 years earlier the Dominican priory of Athenry[23] had apparently been built rather more rapidly, with Milo de Bermingham building the church, Phelim O'Conor the refectory, Eugene O'Heyne the dormitory, Cornelius O'Kelly the chapter-house, and others the cloister, infirmary, great guesthouse, etc.

At Kells-in-Ossory, Co Kilkenny, there is a complex of which one cannot be certain which century to assign it to, nor indeed whether it should be classified as ecclesiastical or military. This is the Augustinian priory (fig. 58) which, though founded in the twelfth century, appears to be mostly of the fourteenth or fifteenth, and is the largest monastic enclosure in Ireland. In layout it is not unlike Athassel, and like Athassel the church had a North-Western tower, as at St Patrick's Cathedral in Dublin. At both there are two large enclosures, of similar size, in one of which the priory itself is placed. The other, or 'outer bailey', is at Athassel now fragmentary, but at Kells it survives in the form of an irregular tetragon furnished with five great towers and a gatehouse, not counting the various towers belonging to the church itself. No doubt it sheltered the service-settlement of laity attached to the priory.

At least one parish church, that of Clonmines Co Wexford, was conceived and carried out as a fortified building, and indeed looks more like a castle than a church until you get inside it. Nook Co Wexford, is 'semi-fortified'. Another not dissimilar

56

56 Kilconnell, Co
Galway: flamboyant tomb,
probably about 1475

57 Dungiven, Co Derry:
the tomb of Cooey na Gall
in Cahan Abbey. Cooey
died in 1385, though the
tomb looks later. The little
kilted figures in the panels
are his mercenaries from
which he got his nickname.
This tomb is among the
four or five finest in
mediaeval Ireland

57

58

58 Kells-in-Ossory, Co
Kilkenny: the Augustinian
Priory from the air. It is the
most complete monastic
fortification in the country.
The tower visible near the
left (East) corner of the
enclosure is over the
crossing of the priory
church. The lower part of a
North-Western tower (as at
Athassel and St Patrick's,
Dublin) may be seen

building, not very far away, at Aghaviller in South Co Kilkenny, seems to have been fortified at a later date and perhaps to have vacillated between ecclesiastical and secular uses. It was quite common for parish churches to have a residential West end, in the form of a tower-house, sometimes with a residential room overhanging the West end of the church, as at Taghmon Co Westmeath, where the church is barrel-vaulted for the whole of its length, and has a marked base-batter. The tower is here an addition, though an early one. The churches at Fenagh Co Leitrim have residential spaces carried on vaults within the West end. The practice of housing the clergy under the same roof as the church itself did not stop with the end of the Middle Ages: eighteenth- and early nineteenth-century examples are known from a variety of faiths: Catholic (e.g. Tullaherin Co Kilkenny, at Taghmon itself (1844) (fig. 184) and many others), Moravian (Ballinderry Co Antrim) (fig. 186), Methodist (Castlebar Co Mayo) (fig. 188) and probably others. St Mel's Cathedral Longford (fig. 187) is a nineteenth-century example, and so, for that matter, is the West tower of Cashel Cathedral in the fifteenth. But the mediaeval residential West towers are commonest round Dublin and on the edges of the Pale, and their appearance is bound up with the development of the tower-house type, to which we must now turn.

CHAPTER SEVEN

Tower-houses

Castles are, by a comfortable margin, the commonest kind of antiquity in the Irish countryside, if purely earthen structures are excluded. The figures given by Leask[1] add up to about 2,800, which makes them something like one-tenth as common as raths, and much commoner than mediaeval churches, even if churches in very fragmentary state are counted in. Leask's figures are crude, in the sense that they include Norman motes at one end, and seventeenth-century semi-fortified houses at the other, which between them account for perhaps 15 per cent of the total. If these were to be omitted, the startling imbalance revealed by the analysis of the figures would be reinforced rather than mitigated.

How uneven the distribution is may be gauged from the fact that over half the total are to be found in the five counties with the highest scores: Limerick, Cork, Galway, Tipperary and Clare in that order. Even more strikingly, perhaps, the first three counties account for well over one-third of the national total. Admittedly Cork, Galway and Tipperary are unusually large counties, and Clare a little above the average: but Limerick is of average size only. The English Pale, on the most generous computation, can be made to yield up only 200 or so examples: a fact which has some bearing on the problem of the genesis of the Irish tower-house which we must presently consider.

The vast majority of these 'castles' are fortified private residences of the fifteenth, sixteenth and seventeenth centuries, and predominantly of the sixteenth: the homes of minor notabilities, whether Irish or Anglo-Norman (such as we must now begin to call by their historical name of the 'Old English'.)

A closer study of their distribution yields some expected correspondences, and some surprises. For example, rather over half of the castles are either West of the Shannon or in Cork, Limerick and Kerry. If a line is drawn from Dublin to Galway, 70 per cent of the castles will be found to lie South of it. The distribution resembles that of several other classes of building (e.g. monastic foundations, country houses) in that South-central Ulster (Cavan-Fermanagh-Monaghan) is noticeably empty.

If, on the basis of these figures, the densities per county are estimated, Limerick is still away out in front with a density of ·380 towers per square mile followed by Kilkenny with ·245 and Tipperary with ·154. This accords with expectations, for these are rich lands intensively colonised by the Anglo-Normans. Clare scores high with ·148, with Wexford not far behind at ·130. Cork and Galway are equal at ·112: both unusually large counties. Even the Pale recovers somewhat under this treatment, because Dublin, Louth and Kildare are in ninth, tenth and eleventh place respectively, while Meath scrapes in to the top half (at No 16) with a quotient of ·065. (For comparison, the really poor counties have quotients of ·012 and ·013.)

These figures must not, of course, be taken too seriously, since they reflect the position as known in modern times, partly from buildings marked on the six-inch Ordnance Survey maps, and partly from the work of observers in the field. The high score of Limerick no doubt owes something to the intense and prolonged activity of T.J. Westropp:[2] but it is objectively real for all that.

Why should Limerick have one and a half times as many castles as its nearest competitor, and over four times the national average? Were there, formerly, as many or more in some other parts of the country? More to the purpose, perhaps, than either of these questions, how are these late castles related to the baronial castles of the thirteenth century?

All these questions may be re-stated in the form of a single question: if the towers did not begin to be built till about 1430, where did all the people of substance live during the preceding 150 years?

According to Prof. James Lydon 'the only significant development in manorial lay-out in the later Middle Ages was the appearance of the tower house', which he attributes to the progressive breakdown of the feudal system in the 'land of peace'.[3] Before that, it seems that the lesser feudatories occupied moated manors containing buildings of no great substance. Recent aerial research has revealed increasing numbers of these sites, but the buildings have not survived. Nor have the buildings which doubtless formed the living-quarters in the larger raths. When the tower-house did arrive, it was a national version of a widespread building-type, erected indiscriminately by Gael, gaelicised Norman, and Old English.

A very few unfortified dwellings of the earlier Middle Ages do exist, such as the 'Glebe House' at Kilmacduagh and the 'Chancellor's House' and 'St Brendan's House' at Kilmalkedar. These are all two-storey buildings which relied for their safety on being within ecclesiastical enclosures. The central building of Athenry Castle, entered at first-floor level over a vaulted basement, and measuring externally some 54 feet by 35, is rather more like a tower-house.[4] So is Greencastle Co Down. Of similar (thirteenth-century) date is another such 'keep', less well preserved, at Cargin on Lough Corrib, and the enigmatic building at Tomdeeley Co Limerick looks like a thirteenth-century hall on a vaulted basement. Other Co Limerick castles have halls over vaults: Askeaton, Adare and Newcastle West. All these last three were additional to the donjons of their respective castles.

Firm dates are hard to come by. One promising date is 1429, in which year the Dublin Parliament authorised a subsidy of ten pounds to whoever might build, in Dublin, Meath, Kildare or Louth a 'castle or tower' of sufficient strength 20 feet by 16 and 40 feet or more in height, later modified to minimum internal dimensions of 15 feet by 12 in Co Meath, and a limit put on their numbers in 1449.[5] There is a small tower at Donore Co Meath which has been regarded as an example of a 'ten pound' castle: but it is much smaller than the average tower-house.★ It has rounded corners, a feature found widely and sporadically, and a winding staircase in a small cylindrical corner-tower, to which the door is immediately adjacent. In these last two respects it is untypical, but it is typical in having a vault over the first floor.

Still in pursuit of reliable dating, we may look at Kilclief Co Down which is ascribed very colourably to Bishop John Cely who held the see of Down from 1412 to 1441 at which date he was deprived for living in adultery in the castle.[6] This is quite appreciably larger. It has a four-turreted silhouette, but two of these are sitting on top of the corners, while the other two project in one direction, creating a hollow or bay between them, which is spanned at a high level by a great arch. The entrance is sideways into one of the towers, which contains also the stairs. This high external

---

★ It measures only 12 feet 9 inches by 19 feet 9 inches internally.

arch type of defence is found in two or three other Co Down castles (Audley's, Jordan's), and at both front and back of Bunratty Co Clare, at Donamon Co Roscommon, and at what is left of Listowel Co Kerry. They may all have been inspired by the gatehouse at Dover Castle, and there is a rather similar feature at the gatehouse of Ballyadams Co Kildare.

The essence of the tower-houses is their verticality: in them the various organs—entrance-hall, guardroom, bedrooms, kitchen, principal living-room—are disposed on top of one another instead of being laid out side-by-side on the ground as in an English hall-house. In all but the latest tower-houses there is at least one vault: sometimes over the ground floor which, in such cases, we must regard as a basement, sometimes over the first floor, sometimes near the top alone, forming the floor of the principal chamber. It is not uncommon for there to be two vaults: one low down and one high up. There are usually four or five storeys altogether: sometimes as few as three, sometimes as many as six.

In addition to the by now almost ubiquitous Irish batter to the walls, there is usually a talus or base-batter as well: the genial purpose of this feature was to cause missiles dropped from the battlements to bounce outwards and discomfit the attackers. It also looks very nice.

As Leask observes, the similarity in style and detail between the friary towers and the (always much more numerous) house-castles indicates that the same masons were at work on both: he suggests that they worked first for the friars and afterwards for the laity.[7] So far as dating criteria are available, they operate in one direction only: they can hardly ever be used to prove that a building must be early, because the builders were so eclectic that they were quite capable of resurrecting (that is to say copying) a 100 or 200 year-old feature because it took their fancy.

Some things, however, carry a *prima facie* suggestion of early date: such, for example, is the absence of fireplaces. Carrigaphooka Co Cork, for example, has no fireplaces at all. But at Clara Co Kilkenny (fig. 59), the only original fireplace is in the second-floor room, while the top (fourth-floor) room, which was the best-lit and principal living-room, had a central hearth and hence a louvre in the roof: this in the late fifteenth-century.[8] The castle of Burnchurch, not far away and similar in style, has a simple but well-crafted fireplace at second-floor level, but in the top room there is one very like the Clara one, suggesting an evolutionary step forward. But if we look at Carrigaphooka, Clara and Burnchurch in respect of their stairs, the story is different, since Carrigaphooka has long straight mural stairs, Clara has a winding stair in one corner, while Burnchurch reverts again to the straight mural stairs. The castle at the West end of Cashel Cathedral, probably built before 1440, has an enormously long straight mural stair also.

There are some grounds for thinking that a standard form of plan established itself about the middle of the tower-building period. This is the plan in which the entrance is in or near the middle of one of the short sides, with the staircase to one side (usually the left) and a guard-room opposite. The short passage between them always has a murdering-hole in its stone roof. It leads directly into the lowest apartment, the loops of which are for ventilation and some light rather than for defence. To reach the upper floors you must turn back and go up the staircase. In some castles the position of the staircase changes at one of the upper floors, so that an attacker who had managed to get so far might be momentarily disorientated and have to hesitate, or run across a room and thus expose himself. This end of the plan is, even in late towers, vaulted or at least made of stone, even when there are no other vaults. In the very latest towers not only are there no vaults but even the stairs are of timber (e.g.

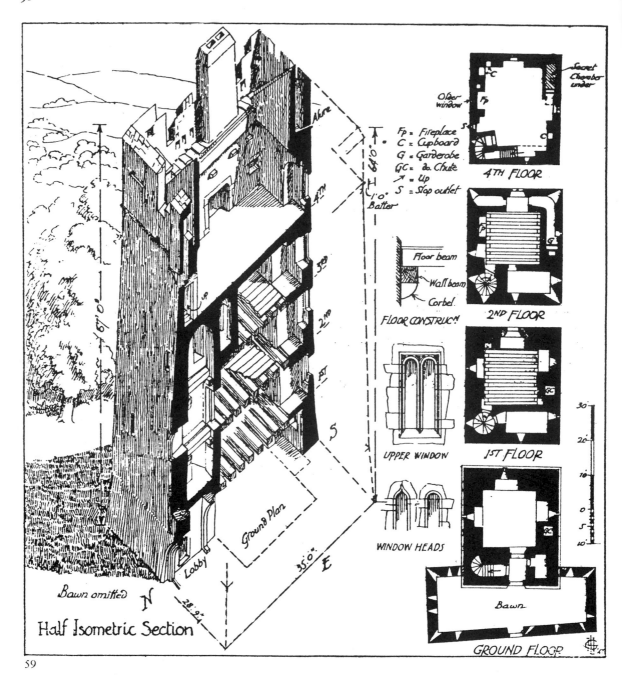

59 Clara Castle, Co Kilkenny: plans and isometric section by H. G. Leask. The unusually small bawn is to be noted

Lismore near Eyrecourt), but when this stage has been reached it is doubtful whether the tower is any longer entitled to be called a 'castle' in any useful sense.

The builders usually formed the haunches of the high vaults as hollows: a convenient place in which to put secret-chambers, etc (as at Clara where a room was reached through an apparent lavatory-seat) as well as to lighten the structure. This can be seen very well at Carrigafoyle Co Kerry where the destruction of an end wall has exposed the section very neatly (fig. 68). The vaults were generally constructed by laying a wickerwork mat over the timber falsework, lathering on plenty of lime-mortar and sticking the voussoirs into this with more mortar on top.[9] A great many Irish mediaeval and post-mediaeval stone vaults are made of stones which are neither themselves wedge-shaped nor truly radially laid. In a sense the result is a kind of concrete in the Roman sense of the term. Termonfeckin Co Louth has a corbelled roof of a very archaic appearance.

The high parapets, stepped in the Irish fashion, often rested on the self-draining wall-walk. As a result the parapets have often fallen off, for the following reason: the wall-walk is made of a succession of long through-stones laid over-and-under like tiles, so that each alternate stone acts as both gutter and spout. Since they are laid at a slight outward slope and the rather thin parapet, sometimes as much as ten feet high, is balanced on top of this, it is apt to slither off and fall to the ground, even though the sloping stones are, in principle, often squared level to receive the bottom course of the parapet.

The only surviving original roof on any Irish castle, that of Dunsoghly Co Dublin, is a 'gambrel' roof, which starts off as a hipped roof but ends up with small gables at each end of the ridge.[10] Many castles have gables inboard of the wall-walk, which means that they sometimes have to be corbelled inwards, as they are at Clara. Sometimes the parapets are carried up at the ends to form elongated turrets with their own high-level wall-walks, and the roof butts against these as though they were gables. Gables flush with the external face of the wall are generally of late date: those at Athenry are of course additions. But even very late structures such as Derryhivenny can have wall-walks outboard of their gables and of course Ightermurragh (see p. 130).

When the gables are flush, defensive cover is provided by corner machicoulis or 'bartizans': Danganbrack Co Clare is a good example. Bartizans protruding from the corners half-way up the wall appear to be a distinctively Irish feature: they are very decorative and can be seen at their best at Clare Island, Fantstown, Aughnanure (fig. 64) or Ballymalis. At Ballynacarriga Co Cork and Fiddaun Co Galway, they are very low down. The angle-loop, which also normally occurs about half-way up the building, is also peculiarly Irish: it is a slit right on the arris of the corner, widening internally into an embrasure, and well adapted for small-arms.★

It has been well observed, in connexion with the tower-houses of Scotland, that 'with the introduction of small-arms the axis of defence changed from the vertical to the horizontal.'[11] Less reliance was placed on shooting or dropping things from the battlements, though to the very end there was a machicoulis over the door. The 'bawn' evidently came to play a larger part in defence.

★ Found, however, in some Scottish castles such as Noltland (W. D. Simpson, *Scottish Castles* 1959 fig. 15). The Desmond Castle, Kinsale (a town house of perhaps the sixteenth century) has large windows on the corners (quite like the 1930s) as part of a completely symmetrical first-floor fenestration. But this is exceptional. See W. Garner, *Kinsale*, Dublin 1980 p. 30.

All of these towers had originally some kind of an enclosure connected with them, ranging from the small fore-court, hardly larger in area than the tower itself, at Clara, to such enormous square enclosures as those of Knockkelly near Fethard or Ballynakill near Roscrea (fig. 103), in which the tower itself stands free. The Irish name for these is *bádhún*, in common anglicised use by 1537 as 'bawn', meaning an enclosure for cattle. There was in the North of England and in Scotland a word 'barmekin' of totally different derivation but roughly similar meaning. This may have assisted the immediate adoption of 'bawn' by the planters of the seventeenth century, and its incorporation into numerous place-names.

In the nature of things, the bawns have been raided as convenient sources of stone much more than the towers themselves. But a good many survive intact, notably the medium-sized ones with angle-towers such as Rathmacknee, Pallas and Derryhiv-enny.[12] Some, such as Clonony Co Offaly, have a decorative gatehouse and enfilade defence by bastions. Others are irregular polygons, and follow natural features. They can be very picturesque, as at Dungory near Kinvara Co Galway (fig. 60).

None of these towers could have sustained an artillery-attack, nor indeed any protracted siege, nor were they expected to. The extreme difficulty and expense of moving heavy ordnance across country restricted its use to major strong-points and goes far to explain the prolonged survival of the tower-house when it had become, strictly speaking, obsolete.

The towers did not always, or even perhaps generally, stand alone. There was often a hall of flimsier construction which was more comfortable if less secure. The creasing of such a building up against one wall of the tower can sometimes be seen, as at Knockkelly and Kilcash. In some later Wexford examples such as Coolhull (fig. 61) and Slade the extensions, though later than the towers, are not much later and not much lower: at Coolhull in fact the finished building is a longish two-storey rectangle. Some oblong hall-castles such as Kindlestown Co Wicklow and Rathum-ney Co Wexford are, rather uncertainly, assigned to the fourteenth or even thirteenth century.

While the windows in the earlier towers are very small, and even in the upper storeys are only one- or two-light ogee-headed openings, in the later towers, prob-ably from about 1550 onwards, square-headed mullion-and-transom windows appear, which are not only fairly generous in size but are also regularly arranged, either vertically over one another as at Knockkelly, or even side by side in two storeys as at Tinnehinch Co Carlow: as regular as a house in Fitzwilliam Square. Here, again, by this time the building should probably be called a 'house' rather than any kind of 'castle'. Needless to say, larger windows were often made in early towers as soon as it was thought safe to do so, and it was not uncommon for a tower to be cut down a storey or two so that, with gables at each end, regular fenestration and perhaps even a new doorway in the middle of one of the long sides, it put on a pretty good imitation of a house. Such, probably, are Ballinahinch Co Limerick (near Kilfinnane) and Garruragh Co Clare (near Tulla).

External decoration is sparing, as might be expected. In the later towers, or those which were remodelled or repaired, the oversailing stepped-battlements are carried on long corbels several courses high in the form of inverted pyramids.* These have some resemblance to the (internal) corbels of the Western school of church-building 300 years earlier. As with all mediaeval military building, it is impossible to determine

---

* Those at Blarney have a subtly concave profile.

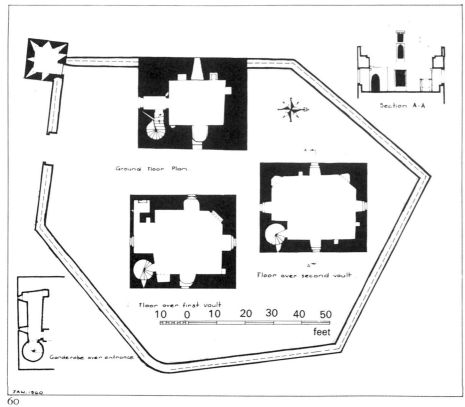

Section A-A

Ground Floor Plan

Floor over second vault

Floor over first vault

10 0 10 20 30 40 50

feet

Garderobe over entrance

JAN. 1960

60

60   Dungory (Dunguaire) Castle, Co Galway: plan (OPW). This castle has been re-roofed in recent years

61   Coolhull Castle, Co Wexford: one of a family of oblong castles in the South-East, which include Slade and Rathumney. Coolhull is of the late sixteenth century

61

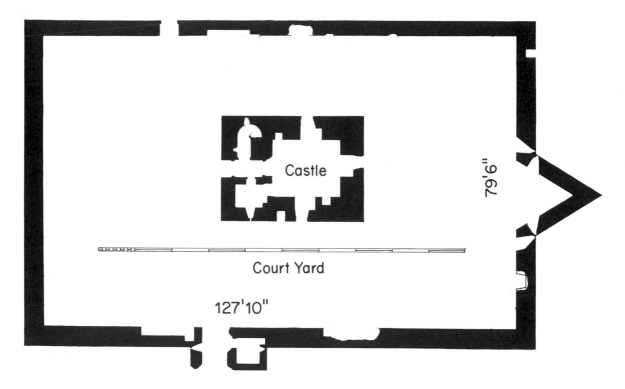

Castle

79'6"

Court Yard

127'10"

Ground Plan

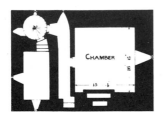

FOURTH FLOOR

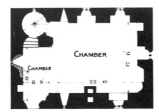

FIFTH FLOOR

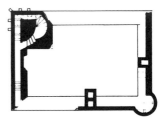

PLAN AT ROOF LEVEL

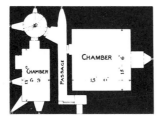

FIRST FLOOR

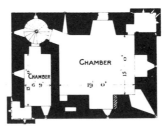

SECOND FLOOR

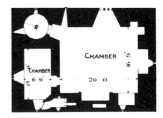

THIRD FLOOR

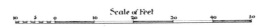

Scale of Feet

OVERLEAF
63 and **64** Aughnanure
Castle, Oughterard, Co
Galway: plans and
elevations (Commissioners
of Public Works). A very
complete and typical
example of a late Western
tower-house with low-
hung bartizans, a circular
dovecote, and, unusually,
an outer and inner bawn

65 Ballynahow Castle,
Co Tipperary: plans,
section and details (OPW).
Above the vaulted
entrance-level, the main
spaces are rectangular with
subsidiary spaces fitted in to
the rest of the circle.
Round castles such as this
are rare

what should be put down to necessity and what to the love of display. At all events these machicoulis cast as fine a shadow as any bold Italian cornice.

There is occasionally a little ornamentation at the ends of label-moulds, though seldom so elaborate as that at Dunnaman Co Limerick. In late examples it is common for the end of the label to be dog-legged through two opposed right-angles at its termination. Sometimes there is a little fanciful revived Romanesque ornament in the spandrels, as at Donore Co Westmeath or elaboration of ventilator-holes as at Coole Co Offaly. There is ornamentation of reveals at Ardamullivane and Aughnan-ure (figs 63 and 64), both in Co Galway, and carvings of religious subjects in the very spacious upper hall of Ballynacarriga Co Cork (near Dunmanway).

It will be remembered that in the supposedly early instance of Donore the corners of the building are rounded: this is found in other towers in Northern Leinster, but also as far afield as Lohort Co Cork.[13] But except for the Louth-Down group, the towers are generally of a simple, rectangular plan. The larger towers such as Dun-soghly, Blarney and Bunratty have projections; but these will be considered later.

There is a small class of cylindrical tower-houses: so small that it is worth attempt-ing to enumerate them all, omitting those which appear to be thirteenth-century (and hence not tower-houses). They are: Cloughoughter, Co Cavan (which is dubiously claimed for the fourteenth century); Carrigabrack, East of Fermoy Co Cork; Knockagh near Templemore Co Tipperary; Ballysheeda near Cappawhite Co Tipperary; Synone, Ballynahow (fig. 65) and Farney, all near Thurles in Co Tipperary; Golden in the same county; Crannagh now attached to an eighteenth-century house near Templetuohy in the same county; Balief Co Kilkenny; Grants-town near Rathdowney Co Leix; Barrow Harbour Co Kerry; Newtown near Gort in Co Galway; Doonagore Co Clare also by the sea; Faunarooska, Burren Co Clare; and Newtown at the North edge of the Burren, also in Co Clare (fig. 67).

The last of these is in some ways the most interesting, being in form a cylinder impaled upon a pyramid. Over the door (which is in the pyramid) there is a notch in the elliptical curve traced by the cylinder, and in this notch is a gunhole covering a wide sector of the sloping wall below. At some other castles, for example Ballyna-mona (fig. 66) on the Awbeg river, there is a feature using the same principle, which is not easy to describe. On each face of the building there is what looks at first sight like the 'ghost' or creasing of a pitched roof, but is in fact a triangular plane, about a foot deep at the top, decreasing to nothing at the base. In the apex there is a gunhole. Aesthetically the effect is very subtle.

In waterside castles the bawn, if it survives, may incorporate a small dock: such is the case at Carrigafoyle and at Galey Co Roscommon, while at two towers on Strangford Lough, both now rather fragmentary, a boat-house was incorporated into the bottom storey.[14]

Though, as we have already seen, a satisfyingly large number of towers may still be found standing in the rich green pastures which they were built to dominate, especially in the counties of Kilkenny, Tipperary, Limerick and Cork, a great many more are so sited as to give the impression of being there to defend what is not worth defending. Perched on rocky outcrops in a barren landscape, reflected in the melan-choly waters of a hundred Western lakes, seeming to grow out of the stone on which they stand, they are at once the delight of the tourist and something of a problem to the historical geographer. Few sites could be more desolate or un-promising, for example, than Newtown, two miles due West of Gort and a similar distance South-West of Coole where Yeats saw the swans.

Yeats was, in fact, among the first to succumb to the modern taste for romantic

62 Fiddaun Castle, Co
Galway: ground plan. The
very complete bawn is of
an unusual shape. (OPW)

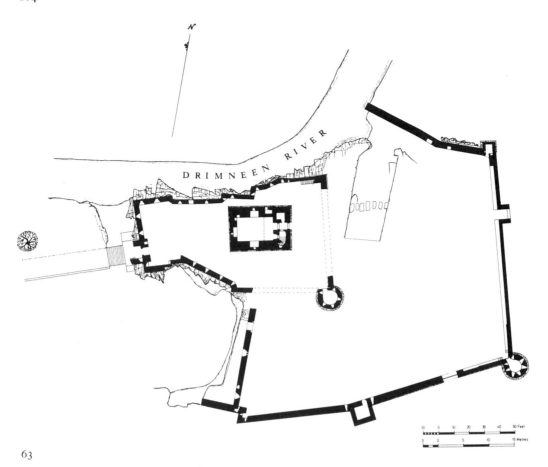

D R I M N E E N   R I V E R

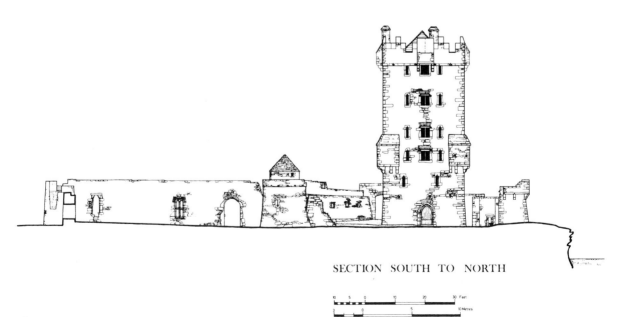

SECTION SOUTH TO NORTH

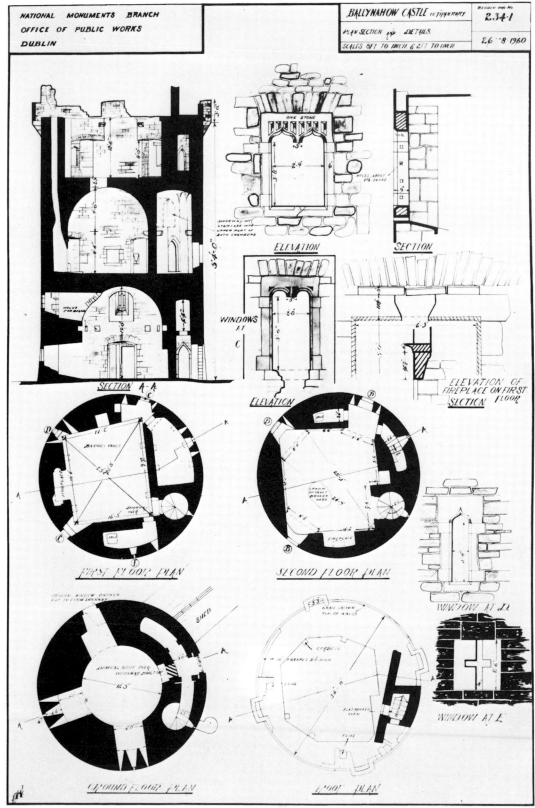

NATIONAL MONUMENTS BRANCH
OFFICE OF PUBLIC WORKS
DUBLIN

BALLYNAHOW CASTLE CO TIPPERARY

2.34.1

PLAN SECTION AND DETAILS

26 – 8 1960

SCALES 8FT TO 1INCH & 2FT TO 1INCH

ELEVATION

SECTION

WINDOWS AT C

ELEVATION

ELEVATION OF FIREPLACE ON FIRST FLOOR

SECTION A-A

SECTION

FIRST FLOOR PLAN

SECOND FLOOR PLAN

WINDOW AT D

GROUND FLOOR PLAN

ROOF PLAN

WINDOW AT E

discomfort in such a tower. In strict truth it was mostly his wife and children who were left in the otherwise not very interesting little tower at Ballylee while he sat in St Stephen's Green or in Oxford, polishing up his verses, or stumped America on a lecture-tour. It seems, however, from an example not very far away that romanticism and the brute realities of the seventeenth century may have overlapped, however briefly. The O'Madden castle at Lismore near Eyrecourt in Co Galway is now a ruin with one side completely missing; but it is clear that it never had any vaults, nor any stone stairs; but it had a wooden stair and still has other late features such as three remarkably regular rows of gothick windows which do not appear to be alterations. Yet it has a working bartizan on one corner, and a batter, and is undoubtedly a real-life tower-house, though with a residential wing which seems little, if at all, later than the tower.

The towers have survived best in those parts of the country where the friaries also have tended to survive, though for slightly different reasons. The towers were and are protected by no such feelings of reverence as have sometimes served to ward off the despoilers of church buildings. On the contrary, the towers were often mistakenly thought of as 'Norman' structures, and as such fair game for patriotic plunderers. The survival of so many in the West is mainly due, we can hardly doubt, to their being situated on land where nobody has since thought it worth while to build a house, and so to use them as convenient stone-quarries.

Some few of these castles are appreciably larger than the general run. One such is Blarney, which for quite other reasons is perhaps more widely known than any other building in Ireland.[15] Supposedly built in 1446 by Cormac MacCarthy 'the Strong', it is, at least in its lower part, exceptionally massive for a building of that date: nearly 40 feet across of which less than 15 are hollow. Higher up the walls get thinner and the rooms get bigger. It was built in two stages: first a comparatively slender tower containing the stairs and some small rooms, and then the massive block just described. The whole is crowned with high stepped battlements borne on long inverted-pyramid corbels, slightly hollowed.

Except for the fact that the earlier tower prolongs one side, Blarney is a simple rectangle.[16] The castle of Dunsoghly Co Dublin, has a more complex outline. At each corner there is a turret, in two different sizes: large at the North-West and South-East, not so large at the North-East and South-West. The two larger turrets contain rooms some eight or nine feet square, while one of the smaller ones contains the staircase. This plan, a rectangle with four 'flankers', is one which had a considerable future before it in the late sixteenth to early seventeenth century. Dunsoghly was built in the fifteenth century by Thomas Plunkett, Chief Justice of the King's Bench, only seven or eight miles from Dublin.

Dunsoghly retains its original roof framing, something which would not be at all remarkable in England but is virtually unique in Ireland. It is a straightforward arch-braced collar roof with short crown-posts carrying a medial purlin and braced downwards to the collar and upwards to the purlin. It has curved windbraces and the ends are treated as a gambrel roof.

Just why so few Irish mediaeval roofs should have survived is not easy to say. Though the vast majority of the towers are now roofless, there is not much evidence that very many of them were burned, and a fair number were still occupied until recently, and indeed the period of occupation of a few at least has in our own time overlapped with the period of re-roofing and reoccupation. But where 'old' roofs have survived they turn out not to be very old nor usually of much quality: non-descript nineteenth-century roofs of softwood. Their main framing must originally

66 Ballynamona Castle, Co Cork. The curious gable-shaped recesses enable shot-holes at their apexes to command the whole of the wall at ground-level. Compare Newtown Co Clare

108

67

68

have been of oak, which was plentiful in Ireland down to the sixteenth century. We might have expected the law of averages to have permitted the survival of more than one complete specimen. But the Irish climate and the Irish temperament between them bear more harshly on things made of wood than on things made of stone: that is to say very harshly indeed.

Beside the castle of Dunsoghly is a small low building ornamented with a panel of the instruments of the Passion, dated 1573 with the initials of Sir John Plunket and his wife Genet Sarsfield: this was the chapel. The bawn contained several other outbuildings and was further strengthened in the seventeenth century with outer defences of an up-to-date kind.

Until recently the latest datable tower-house was thought to be Derryhivenny Co Galway, where the bawn (clearly of the same build as the tower) bears the date 1643. There is, however, a gate tower at Castle Ffrench Co Galway, which bears an inscription saying that 'The tower and this work [i.e. the gatehouse] was built by Iasper French Anno Dom 1683', which indicates that the primary residence, the 'tower', which we know to have been demolished at the construction of the present house in the 1770s, was then less than a century old and is the latest-erected tower-house so far known.

The bawn at Ballygrennan Co Limerick, has a very large tower without corner-turrets and a number of other gabled and tall-chimneyed ruins within the same enclosure, apparently of the sixteenth to seventeenth centuries. In the even more impressive bawn at Ballynakill Co Tipperary, near Roscrea, a tower of moderate size near the centre of the square has been more than doubled in volume by a late-seventeenth century undefendable addition with a blind top storey ornamented with ovals and lozenges in the artisan-mannerist style. The castle at Clonony Co Offaly has a bawn with a picturesque gateway but, more significantly, spear-shaped bastions at the corners.

The largest, and nowadays the best-known, of the tower-houses in the direct mediaeval succession is Bunratty Co Clare, some eight miles West of Limerick on the North bank of the Shannon, in the territory of the Macnamara or MacConmara family by whom it was built in the mid-fifteenth century.[17] It was probably finished in about 1467 and is archaic in having a central-hearth hall, but the upper parts of the corner towers in particular were remodelled by Donchadh O'Brien the 'Great' (fourth) Earl of Thomond who succeeded in 1581. The plaster decoration of hall and chapel and of another room dates from his time and is among the earliest in Ireland, and the brick vaulting which still survives in one top of one of the towers is likewise among the earliest brick in the country.

The most conspicuous external features of Bunratty are the high arches which span the space between the towers both to the North and the South. The South arch is a later modification. The arches recall the similar features at Kilclief, Donamon (Co Roscommon) and Listowel (Co Kerry), but Bunratty is on so large a scale that the room over the North arch (which is deeper than the South arch) is the lord's solar, communicating with the private chapel in the North-East flanker, and furnished with a peep-hole for keeping an eye on what went on in the Great Hall below, as at Hatfield.

The castle has a profusion of small winding staircases, a liberal provision of no less than 14 privies, and even a bathroom of a primitive kind. Though there was a small service kitchen near the hall, the main cookery must have been done in a separate building outside, as so often in mediaeval times. One way and another, there are ample indications that The O'Brien and Earl of Thomond lived in considerable state.

67 Newtown Castle, Burren, Co Clare. Both the pyramidal spurs at the base and the triangular recess between them are to enable shot-holes to command the base of the wall

68 Carrigafoyle Castle, Co Kerry: the damage shows the section of the building very neatly, including the rooms in the haunches of the high vault. The bawn, visible on the left, enclosed a private harbour

The great hall measures 47 feet by 30 feet, and though the plan is primitive in such details as stairs and fireplaces, it already approaches in scale and in general outline the developed rectangle-with-flankers type of semi-fortified house which first appears, near Dublin, in the last quarter of the sixteenth century, exactly at the same time as the Great Earl was carrying out those modifications to Bunratty which, latest among the testimonies of its history, the recent restoration permitted to survive.

Since this was written Dr Kevin Danaher has drawn attention to a roof which may be fifteenth-century, that of the Desmond Hall in the castle of Newcastle West Co Limerick, which has affinities with late seventeenth-century roofs at Honfleur, Normandy. See *The Archaeological Journal*, Vol. 138 for 1981, p. 257.

CHAPTER EIGHT

The End of the Middle Ages

Mediaeval Irish towns were very combustible, and opportunities for burning them were frequently offered and not seldom taken. They also burned by accident: for example the fire of Cork in 1622 which destroyed nearly 1500 houses. Without doubt most of the buildings so burned were of timber construction, and so, at least until the middle of the seventeenth century, were their replacements which often suffered the same fate.

Some towns, however, were largely composed of towers, if not quite in the manner of San Gimignano or of Bologna, a little in that of Santillana in Northern Spain, the home town of Gil Blas. Such 'towns of towers' survive in part at Ardglass, Carlingford and Dalkey, and Carrickfergus is known to have had several towers. Both Galway and Kilmallock were formerly renowned for consisting largely—and this was probably always an exaggeration—of merchants' secure dwellings, of stone, with storage space in their vaulted basements. There is little enough of this kind of thing to be seen today in Galway, still less in Kilmallock. Kilkenny and Limerick can still show fragments of stone town-dwellings of sub-mediaeval date and mediaeval type. In Kilkenny the Rothe House[1] which dates in fact from 1594-1604 is not a tower but a stone house of sub-mediaeval type with two courtyards in a plan of considerable depth, apparently containing two lesser houses also of stone.

Neither the Rothe House nor the Lynch House in Galway, the two best-known examples of pre-Renaissance urban architecture, is now in any state from which confident assertions about its original form and function can be deduced.

A better example, in some ways, than any of these is the small walled town of Fethard in Co Tipperary (fig. 69) which, not having been blest with prosperity nor suffered the misfortune of frequent burning, still has a mediaeval church, part of an Augustinian priory, three or four late-mediaeval houses all in ruins, and a town-house or tholsel by the church gate, altered and adapted but still extant and carrying armorial decorations, not to mention a fair amount of town wall and even a modest gateway. The visitor to Fethard must not expect to find anything comparable to even a modest example in France or England: its interest is, truth to tell, rather antiquarian than architectural. But the stepped battlements of the West tower of the church are perhaps the best in the whole of Ireland.

Fethard is a comparative latecomer among walled towns. Though it received a murage grant from Edward III in 1376, the effective date seems to be much later, when Richard Duke of York's council in 1449 confirmed the licence. This did not save it from being burnt, perhaps rather perfunctorily, by Garret of Desmond some 20 years later.[2] The walls are not very impressive, but they are still there in part, and like those of Athenry (which are earlier) they give in places (and especially to the South) a tolerably convincing idea of what such a town must have looked like.

Among the very few unfortified town-dwellings which survive in any sense, are two episcopal palaces. That of St Sepulchre to the South-East of St Patrick's Cathedral in Dublin (fig. 70), though much cut about and in use for well over a century and a

69

70

half as a police-barracks, still looks like a mediaeval house, surrounding three sides of a deep courtyard, and with some diagonal buttresses, some stone vaults, and a fragment of a mediaeval roof-truss. It has not yet been subjected to close scrutiny, and is at present chiefly remarkable for its stately pair of seventeenth-century gate-piers.

The Bishop's palace in Irishtown, Kilkenny, by contrast, looks from the outside like a substantial house of the early to mid-eighteenth century, mainly in the shape given to it by Bishop Este in 1735-6. But the North-East part of it is a fourteenth-century tower probably built by that Bishop de Ledrede whom we have already met, and to the South and West of this are further apartments, vaulted, like the tower, with central piers, which may well be of the same date or a very little later. Standing as it did within the walls of the small hilltop ecclesiastical borough which adjoined the walled city of Kilkenny, it probably had little need of defences of its own, and is consequently more horizontally disposed than most other surviving buildings of its time. It would repay closer investigation, but is probably not typical.[3]

During the last quarter of the fifteenth century the English kings found it necessary to make a series of arrangements with the great Anglo-Irish families, for the governance of the country. Having their own troubles at home they could not afford to send armies to Ireland: indeed the traffic was sometimes the other way about. From time to time they sent personal representatives: Tiptoft, Grey, Edgecombe, Poynings, Kite, Surrey; but more often they allowed one of the great lords of Ireland to represent them, and most often it was one of the Fitzgerald house of Kildare. The 'Kildare Ascendancy' as historians call it lasted from 1470 till 1534.[4] Warfare had become a kind of stylised and seasonal sport, and accommodations between the Anglo-Irish and the Gael were frequent. The Pale was at its smallest: a rather narrow strip from Ballymore-Eustace to Dundalk. Outside it lay the great earldoms of Kildare and Desmond (both Geraldines) and of Ormonde (Butler). The principal seats of the Kildare family were at Maynooth Castle and Kilkea Castle. The former has long been fragmentary and difficult to interpret, while the latter, said to have been largely rebuilt by the sixth Earl in 1426, suffered a fire in the 1840s and further drastic alteration.

The Butler Earls of Ormonde, whose earldom lay originally to the West in Co Tipperary, moved into Ossory and in 1391 bought the great castle of William the Marshal in Kilkenny. In origin this was a trapezium with massive cylindrical towers at the four corners: three of these survive but they have been much altered and the building as a whole is now of the late seventeenth and early nineteenth centuries, so far as can be determined, though it has never been properly studied (fig. 41).[5]

Although to the political historian the death of the Great Earl of Kildare in 1513 may signify the end of the Middle Ages, from the viewpoint of the historian of architecture they had still a clear century and a half to run. The span of the Tudor re-conquest of Ireland, which may be taken as beginning in 1534 with the death of the ninth Earl of Kildare, the rebellion and execution of his son Silken Thomas, followed almost immediately by the 'Reformation Parliament' of 1536-7, and as being complete by the Flight of the Earls in 1607, was a 'warlike and tragicall' age, the span of a man's life, and by no means propitious for building. As we have already seen, the tower-house as a well-established architectural form lasted till the mid-seventeenth century. The latest of the friaries, Creevelea near Dromahair in Co Leitrim,[6] was reconstructed after a fire in 1536: but ecclesiastical architecture of the sixteenth century is almost non-existent. This is not surprising since it is virtually absent from England also, where Elizabethan churches are a great rarity.

69 Fethard, Co Tipperary: the tower of the church, with typical Irish stepped battlements, and part of the town wall

70 Dublin, St Sepulchre's Palace (now and for many years past a police barracks). The East wing is visible between the late seventeenth-century gate-piers

There are records of buildings being repaired and re-edified and even new-built, but hardly a complete building standing in recognisable form. An exception is the so-called Manor House at Carrick-on-Suir, which would be more instructive if only we knew its exact date. Thomas Butler, the tenth or 'Black' Earl of Ormonde, its builder, was the one who came out on top at the downfall of the Kildare Geraldines, and profited still more by that of his own kinsman the last Earl of Desmond. He succeeded to his own (Ormonde) earldom at the age of 14, and was kept at the English court until he was 22. The object was to attach him by sentiment to the throne and crown of England, but an incidental result must have been to familiarise him with English architecture. From 1554 to 1565 he was in Ireland: from 1565 to 1569 again at the English court, apparently occupied in flirting with the queen. A chimneypiece in the Carrick-on-Suir building bears the date 1565, and Mr Waterman accepts this date for the 'house',[7] while Leask considered it to date from 1600 or even a little later.[8] Ormonde paid another visit to London in 1572. On the assumption that he built it soon after a return from England the likeliest dates are about 1565 or 1570. On the other hand it is possible that he built it to celebrate his large grant of Desmond lands in 1602, but by then he was 70 and the queen of whose friendship he was so proud was 69 and had not long to live.

In style Carrick-on-Suir is exactly like hundreds of buildings in Northamptonshire or the Cotswolds but like no other in Ireland. In plan it is altogether anomalous, being a rather low and wide-spreading addition to the existing castle which consisted of two massive towers set rather close together. In front of and below these the new building has an elevation a little longer than the spread of the towers themselves, to which it is connected by a return at each side, making an enclosed courtyard. The façade is of two storeys, with three gables and a central porch and oriel. It is almost completely symmetrical, but only one room thick. It is also virtually unfortified, having no basement, windows only three feet from the ground, and a few shot-holes for defence by hand-guns.* The whole of the first floor of the front (which faces North) is taken up with a long gallery in which is some of the earliest plaster decoration in Ireland, glorifying Queen Elizabeth and the Earl's association with her.

Functionally the building is not really a house, or rather it is as much and as little of a house as Burlington's 'villa' at Chiswick: another pleasure-building attached to a house which was already there. As for the details of windows and doors, they are such as may be found in countless Irish tower-houses of similar date. The windows are of two elliptically-headed lights on the ground floor, but on the upper floor of three: a minor concession to defensibility which is found in some later buildings as well. The rather marked batter of the central porch as against the plumb corners at the ends, seems to owe more to English models than to Irish. The finished effect of the whole, with the low two-storeyed gabled range spread out like an apron below and in front of the twin mediaeval towers, is not very like anything else and, with its intimately-scaled courtyard, is architecturally very satisfying.†

Within a very few years of the Ormonde building, a structure went up in South Co Dublin which was to be the first of a very significant group. It is called a 'castle' and such, in some sense, it is (figs. 72 and 73). But it is also the first, or apparently the

---

* Mr le Clerc suggests that the ground-floor windows may possibly have been widened. Inspection bears this out, though the work was very carefully done.

† The stacks are of brick and have moulded brick bases: if original as seems possible, the earliest in Ireland?

71

71   Ballyannan, Midleton,
Co Cork: a 'Z-plan' house
with additions, built
probably by Sir John
Broderick in about 1641

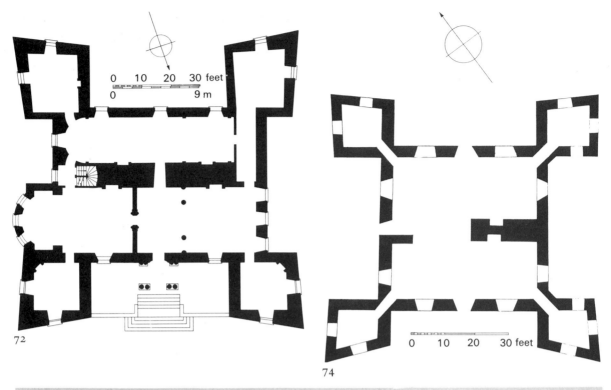

72

0   10   20   30 feet
0   9 m

74

0   10   20   30 feet

73

first, of a series which have an increasing claim to the title 'house'. Adam Loftus, its builder, came to Ireland with the Earl of Sussex in 1560 at the age of about 27, and was very soon made Archbishop of Armagh, an empty honour since the city was then virtually non existent, the see lands laid waste and its revenues much diminished. But Loftus was nothing if not buoyant: he held successively (and sometimes simultaneously) the offices of Dean of St Patrick's, Archbishop of Dublin, Lord Chancellor of Ireland and Provost of Trinity College: an achievement unlikely to be repeated. Very much the political prelate, he joined issue with the Lord Deputy Perrott (reputed natural son of Henry VIII) who was recalled to England and accused of treason. Loftus himself lived on till 1605 when he died in the old Palace of St Sepulchre beside St Patrick's Cathedral. Early on in his tenure of the see of Dublin, in 1573, he had suffered the mortification of having his archiepiscopal castle-palace of Tallaght, only five miles from Dublin, sacked by the O'Byrnes and O'Tooles from the Wicklow mountains.[9] This was a common occurrence but it had never happened to him before, so in 1589 or so, when he bought the lands of Rathfarnham, only three miles from Dublin, he built there a massive rectangular semi-fortified but very habitable house of three storeys over a basement. It still stands and, unusually among its fellows, has always been roofed, though it was drastically remodelled inside in the eighteenth century.

It is clear from the plan that the four flankers, which correspond to the four flankers of Dunsoghly or Bunratty, are at Rathfarnham spear-shaped, which has defensive advantages and which is a form found both in multi-storey buildings such as this and in artillery-fortifications of large area and low profile.

Though the other houses which go with Rathfarnham were built over a period of 50 years or more they are best considered together as a group. They are, in chronological order:

Rathfarnham	Adam Loftus the elder	*c.* 1590
Kanturk	MacDonagh MacCarthy	before 1609
Portumna	Earl of Clanrickarde	before 1618
Manorhamilton	Sir Frederick Hamilton	(probably about 1634)
Raphoe	Bishop John Leslie	dated 1636
Burntcourt	Sir Richard Everard	before 1650

The geographical spread of these six examples is remarkable, from Co Cork to Co Donegal via Tipperary, East Galway, Dublin and Leitrim. One was built by a very political bishop, another by a military bishop who lived to be 100 and was at least as remarkable as his brother in God, another by a native chieftain (MacCarthy of Duhallow). Two of the builders were Old English (Everard and Clanrickarde) and one (Hamilton) was a Scotch adventurer. Rathfarnham, Raphoe (fig. 74) and Manorhamilton have in common the spear-shape of their flankers. Rathfarnham and Raphoe have in common the thick wall down the middle, more complete at Rathfarnham than at Raphoe, while at Portumna there are two such walls forming between them a corridor. Kanturk (fig. 75), Burntcourt and Manorhamilton had only timber partitions subdividing the same space. Manorhamilton has, exceptionally, an indentation in the middle of one wall,[10] probably containing the principal door: a feature which we shall meet again at Glinsk.

From Raphoe which is virtually square to Burntcourt which is more than three times long as it is wide, they vary considerably in shape, but they are all identifiably of the one family. To them may be added, at a pinch, those large houses which were brought into being by adding a spacious large-windowed block to an already existing

72 Rathfarnham Castle, Co Dublin: plan of ground floor as existing

73 Rathfarnham Castle from the North: the bow-windowed projection adjoining the North-East flanker is an eighteenth-century addition, as is the porch, and the buildings to the right are of the twentieth century

74 Raphoe Palace, Co Donegal: plan by William Garner. The spine wall may once have extended right across the building, which was altered in the mid-eighteenth century, when it received an extra storey. The resemblance to Rathfarnham is very close indeed

tower, as at Donegal Castle, Loughmoe Castle Co Tipperary, Leamaneagh Castle Co Clare and Courtstown Castle Co Kilkenny, of which the first three[11] survive but the last, at least their equal, has gone. Donegal was enlarged by an English planter, Loughmoe by the Purcell family who were gaelicised Anglo-Normans, Leamaneagh by Conor O'Brien and his celebrated wife Maire Ruadh (Ni Mahon), and Courstown[12] by the Old English family of Grace.

In silhouette these houses vary a good deal. Rathfarnham has and probably always had a flat-topped appearance, battlemented but with low-pitched hip-roofs. Kanturk is crowned with a continuous row of massive stone corbels but was unfinished and perhaps originally intended to be gabled. Portumna has a system of curvilinear gables★ alternating with gablets and round-topped merlons. Raphoe has been altered by the addition of an upper storey in the eighteenth century, and Burntcourt has 24 gables, even though it was burnt in 1630 to save it from falling into the hands of the Cromwellians.

It is certain that Portumna (figs. 77 and 78) had the classic English sub-mediaeval arrangement of a hall entered by the front door at one end of it, and the existing arrangement at Rathfarnham, though now in eighteenth-century guise, no doubt perpetuates a similar hall-and-screens entrance. The fact that the front door at Burntcourt is markedly displaced to the right in an otherwise symmetrical façade makes a similar arrangement there more than probable. The main block of Burntcourt (figs. 79 and 80) was only one room thick, but Kanturk, though it shares with Burntcourt the long and narrow proportions, seems, on the evidence of the fire places, to have had four rooms on the principal floor.[13]

Efforts have been made to tie this group in with English semi-fortified houses such as Lulworth and Mount Edgcumbe and even Bolsover. But they resemble each other more than any of them resembles anything else. They are quite different from those houses of purely English inspiration erected at the same time or soon afterwards, of which the house inside the Charlemont Fort, Joymount near Carrickfergus, Myrtle Grove at Youghal and Oldbawn in South Co Dublin are known examples out of many more which must once have existed.

The origins and fates of their builders are, as has already been hinted, curiously diverse. Besides the two bishops there was Richard Burke, fourth Earl of Clanrickarde. Like Ormonde of Carrick-on-Suir, Clanrickarde of Portumna had been brought up at the English court. It is in fact unlikely that he ever saw Portumna after its erection.[14] MacCarthy of Kanturk was never allowed to finish his house, so intense was the jealousy of his planter neighbours. Sir Richard Everard of Burntcourt was high in the councils of the Kilkenny Confederation. His wife burned the house on the approach of the Cromwellian army in 1650, and in the following year Sir Richard was one of those hanged by Ireton after the capture of Limerick. It is comforting to recall that the vengeance of heaven upon Ireton was not long delayed, though leisurely in its effect. As for Hamilton the builder of Manorhamilton, he was an unusually disagreeable character in an age notable for nastiness,[15] and though he died, most undeservedly, in his bed in Scotland in 1647, his house was destroyed five years later by the followers of the fifth Earl of Clanrickarde, son to the builder of Portumna.

In one respect Kanturk differs from the rest of the group (so far as present knowledge goes): the position of the staircase. At Kanturk this occupies one of the

---

★ This type of finish is very widespread: for example, Galgorm Co Antrim, Loughmoe Co Tipperary, Dunganstown Co Wicklow, Balrothery Co Dublin etc.

OVERLEAF

78 Portumna Castle from the air, showing the two courtyards and the outer and inner gatehouses

79 Burntcourt, Co Tipperary: view from the West. The deep corbels above the first-floor windows were to carry a timber alure or defensive gallery. The house was new when it was burnt in 1650 by its owner's wife, to deny it to the approaching Cromwellians

75 Kanturk Castle, Co Cork: two of the flankers and one of the end walls

76 Leamaneagh Castle, Co Clare: the early-seventeenth-century addition made by Máire Rúa Ní Mahon to the late-fifteenth-century O'Brien tower-house (to the right). The bartizan hanging on the corner is typically Western. Other such composite buildings are at Loughmoe Co Tipperary, Donegal, and formerly at Inchmore Co Kilkenny

77 Portumna Castle, Co Galway: plans of ground and first floors. The circular extension at the back (South) is of the late eighteenth century. The exact disposition of the rooms before the fire of 1826 is uncertain, but it is known that the Hall was entered across one end in the mediaeval manner (as at Rathfarnham, see p. 116) and it probably extended to the right (West) of the front door

75

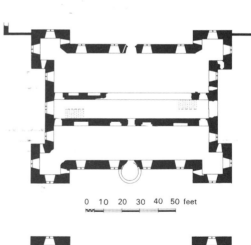

0 10 20 30 40 50 feet

76

77

78

79

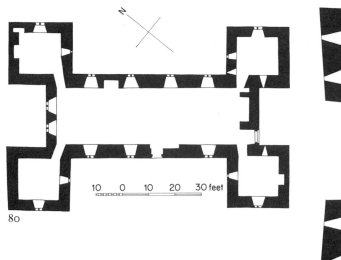

80

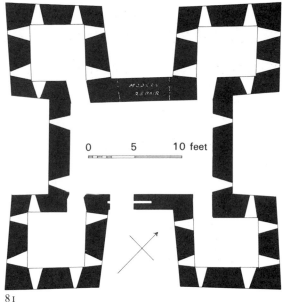

MODERN
REPAIR

0   5   10 feet

81

82

flanker-towers:[16] in most of the others probably, and in some certainly, it is within the main rectangle. In these transitional buildings one criterion serving to distinguish 'castle' from 'house' is that in the former the stairs are narrow, of stone, and spiral or mural, while in the latter they are (or more often were) four feet or more wide, of timber, and open-well, dog-leg or newel in form. The group we have been considering is very advanced in that they are essentially rectangular in plan: they would be complete without their flankers, which are generally entered diagonally or at least at their corners.

It may seem that we have passed rather swiftly from the mid-sixteenth century to the mid-seventeenth. So we have, and in part this is because substantively sixteenth-century buildings are hard to find. Let Dunmoe Castle, Co Meath, stand as an example. It is, or rather it was, a rectangular building with four rather tall and rather slender corner towers of circular plan, two of which survive. In short, it is like a tall thin version of the Carlow-Ferns type of the thirteenth century.[*][17] The modern authorities are all at sea with it. One calls it sixteenth century, another fifteenth or sixteenth, another plumps for 'thirteenth century in style, probably built in the sixteenth', Leask is silent on the topic, Wilde a century ago called it sixteenth century, while Grose in 1797 says it 'was in a great measure new built' in the time of James II. Segmental brick rear-arches support this assertion, but for the rest it lies wide open: anybody's guess.

There are other buildings of about the same time which have points of resemblance to these. Thus the plan of Mountjoy Fort (fig. 81) built in Co Tyrone during the campaign of 1600–05 is startlingly similar to that of the episcopal buildings at Rathfarnham and Raphoe. But though it is a three-storey building of brick—among the earliest brick in Ireland—it was of purely military purpose. The house at Killenure (fig. 82) Co Tipperary, on the other hand, though somewhat smaller than Kanturk (the smallest of the group considered above) differs from the rest only in having cylindrical flankers,† and shows very clearly, from the smallness of the ground-floor windows, that though the door was at this level the lowest storey was treated purely as a basement, and formal living began only at the floor above.

Luckily for us, the antiquary Austin Cooper lived at Killenure and his drawing[18] of it done in 1793 shows that the old house was by then already unroofed (though not much more complete than it is today) and shows us also the unpretentious little residence in which, apparently, his family then lived.

Extremely like Killenure, though perhaps a little smaller, were two of the houses put up by the London companies on their plantations in Co Derry, before 1622: those of the Ironmongers at Agivey and of the Mercers at Movanagher.[19] But these, like the buildings of the other London companies which were in purely English style, seem to have been rather poorly constructed and hardly a vestige of them now remains. Other, more substantial planters' buildings have survived, such as the two habitable (and inhabited) cylindrical flankers of Dalway's Bawn in Co Antrim, and a similar structure at Bellaghy (of the Vintners).

Like the four-flanker-system, the frugal Scotch so-called Z-plan was used both for whole layouts (bawns or forts) and for individual buildings more vertical in character.

---

* Enniscorthy is another case of a castle rebuilt to an indeterminate degree at an indeterminate date. It is still roofed and now in use as a museum.

† Derrinlaur Co Waterford had apparently also cylindrical flankers (*Studies in Building History*, p. 265 n9, and see also *JRSAI* 1909 p. 269). With walls 8 feet 6 inches thick it may have been mediaeval in origin.

PREVIOUS PAGES

80 Burntcourt (Clogheen): plan (OPW). The asymmetrical position of the front door is unusual in a house of this type

81 Mountjoy Fort, Co Tyrone: plan after Jope. It was built by Sir Francis Roe in 1605, of brick, over a stone basement (compare Jigginstown). Very un-domestic in character—note the absence of fireplaces, the profusion of loops, and the spear-shaped bastions—it nevertheless closely resembles Monkstown Co Cork (p. 127) and Raphoe Palace (p. 116)

82 Killenure, Dundrum, Co Tipperary: the seventeenth-century semi-fortified house and its early nineteenth-century successor. Killenure differs from the Kanturk-Portumna family only in having round flankers instead of square. Though entered on the ground floor it has slit windows only at that level: as in the tower-houses, living begins at the first floor. It was the home of Austin Cooper but already roofless in his time, and the family lived in a single-storey house not without formality, illustrated in *An Eighteenth Century Antiquary*, edited by Liam Price, Dublin 1942, plate 19

In this plan, which does not really resemble a Z at all, there are flankers only at one opposed pair of corners, which serve to command the whole length of all four walls. It is found as far South as the bawn of Knockkelly Castle Co Tipperary, probably in the sixteenth century, and the main block of Ballyannan Co Cork.

A number of the planters' bawns in mid-Ulster, such as Crossalt (Brackfield) and Salterstown, both in Co Derry,[20] show this plan, though built under English auspices. More remarkably still, some buildings of very Scotch character, early date and Irish patronage are to be found in West Ulster. Burt Castle seven miles West of Derry in Co Donegal was built by the O'Dochertys before the end of the sixteenth century to the Scotch 'Z' plan,[21] while the watergate at Enniskillen, built by the McGuires* also before the end of the century, has twin corbelled-out angle-turrets with conical roofs which have a strong flavour of Scotland about them.

An equally Scotch-looking building, also in Fermanagh, is Monea Castle, built by one Hamilton, a settler, in 1618-19, an oblong with twin cylindrical towers at one end, a high arch between almost in the Kilclief manner, and square turrets obliquely corbelled-out at the top, as at (for example) Claypotts. Ballygally Castle Co Antrim, and Killyleagh Castle Co Down are both virtually Scotch buildings built by individuals from Scotland in non-planted counties, in both cases in about 1625. Both are still occupied, and Ballygally has suffered little alteration.

The so-called 'Z' plan occurs also at Knocklyon Co Dublin, an originally semi-fortified house not far from Rathfarnham, but here the builders seem not to have fully understood the implications of the diagonally-opposed flankers, for one wall is left virtually without protection. Unfortunately this building cannot be precisely dated, but it is almost certainly of the early seventeenth century.

Efforts have been made, without conspicuous success, to find buildings corresponding to the earlier plantations, notably those of Leix-Offaly in 1556 onwards, and the Munster Plantation of 1586 onwards. There are plenty of buildings in Munster generally, and in Leix and Offaly, and elsewhere, but few are securely datable and they seem for the most part to be from after 1600.

For this and other reasons it seems more profitable to attempt a typological resumé of the whole field of emergent domestic building during this period. For town architecture the materials are, as yet, too scanty to warrant such a treatment: our concern is with the 'castle' in the process of turning into the 'country house'. It was a period during which the claims of defence gradually yielded to those of comfort and convenience, in which rationality and order prevailed over atavistic fantasy, in which, by the simple but inevitable operation of quantifiable factors, the style sometimes miscalled 'Georgian' came into being. There can be no arguing over the fact that a shape approximating to the cube provides the largest quantity of usable space for a given cost, both in original outlay and in recurring expense. But it took quite a long time for this truth to sink in, and there were numerous diversions on the way.

One widely diffused plan-form is represented, and was perhaps initiated, so far as Ireland is concerned, by Sir Thomas Norris, the younger of two brothers who succeeded one another as Lord President of Munster. Sir Thomas, a promoter of the not very successful plantation of Munster, received in 1588 a grant of 6,000 acres in and about the town of Mallow in Co Cork. How soon after this he built the house

---

* H. Dixon, *Enniskillen*, UAHS list, 1973, p. 35, shows good reason for believing that the Watergate was not built until after 1594, and probably not till after 1607, and is therefore settlers' work, possibly by the same masons as the neighbouring Castle Balfour of 1618.

called Mallow Castle is not known: very possibly not till about 1593. It is an oblong one room thick, with four polygonal projections: two set obliquely at the front corners, one in the middle as a porch, with a sideways entrance, and one centrally at the back containing the staircase (fig. 85). Though elevationally they are sharply contrasted with one another, Mallow has a close counterpart in Ardtarmon Co Sligo (fig. 86), built early in the seventeenth century by one of the Gore family (later Gore-Booth of Lissadell). The relationship of Ardtarmon to its bawn is reminiscent of some of the Ulster plantation layouts, but larger and more substantial. The house itself is a storey lower than Mallow, and its windows fewer and somewhat smaller, but, with the substitution of three circular and one square projection, the plan is virtually the same.[22] The same plan minus the porch on a much smaller scale (80 feet overall as against 115 at Ardtarmon) appears in the fairly ruinous remains of another seventeenth-century house at White House on the North-West shore of Belfast Lough.[23]

It is possible to regard these houses as slightly more economical and less secure versions of the four-flanker type, but I think it makes better sense to keep our attention on the fact that the staircase is in a separate tower projecting at the back. This an almost universal feature of seventeenth-century houses and persists well into the eighteenth. Another characteristic of the seventeenth century which did *not* survive into the eighteenth was the practice of making the room-divisions inside the main rectangle of timber stud-work.[24] As a result, nearly all these seventeenth-century ruins are now quite unobstructed, though the 'ghosts' of original partitions may often be traced. The exceptions among the large four-flankers have already been noted: an exception among the smaller houses is the house variously called Wray or Faugher in Co Donegal, which has substantial stone cross-walls in two directions, like an eighteenth-century house.

The splendid semi-fortified house put up at Ballyvireen near Rosscarbery in Co Cork by Sir Walter Coppinger may be regarded as a rectilinear variant of the Mallow-Ardtarmon plan, adapted for even more effective defence. Sir Walter was 'Old English' by origin, but had 'for some years led the Irish of Carbery in an unremitting assault, both legal and physical, upon [the English settlement at] Baltimore' in the decade 1615-25.[25] He was not untypical in that besides having extensive holdings in land he was a leading merchant in the city of Cork. Ballyvireen is over 30 miles from Cork, so that it is not easy to envisage how, in the conditions of the time, he was able to supervise his various concerns, let alone that of molesting Baltimore which lay another 16 miles further on, across difficult country.

Nor is it possible to determine the exact date at which he built the house, now and for long since known as Coppinger's Court (figs. 87 and 88). Certainly before 1641, because the disturbances of that year frustrated his intention to build a market-town there. The giant pyramidal corbels supporting a continuous machicoulis which leaps the wider intervals by shallow arches, are merely the last and most splendid examples of a long and well-established line.* Whether the house dates from the 1620s or the 1630s, its plan appears again, in almost identical form, at Richhill (fig. 89) in Co Armagh in the 1660s or even, perhaps, the following decade. For at Richhill, as at Coppinger's Court, the exact date of building is uncertain.

---

* The staircase-block has no string-course unlike the rest of the building, and has a straight joint in a perplexing place (see the plan). Some recent opinion inclines to the view that Richhill is possibly earlier than was hitherto thought. If so, it is likely to have been more defensible in its original form, particularly where the walls meet the roof.

83 Killilea Castle, Borrisokane, Co Tipperary, which is on an unusual plan consisting of two overlapping rectangles, with a stone newel-staircase of square plan. Early seventeenth century, but now with brick vaulting inserted in the nineteenth century. The entrance-door (seen here) is on the South

84 Ardtarmon, Co Sligo: plan (after Waterman)

85 Mallow Castle, Co Cork: plan. Built probably in the early years of the seventeenth century, Mallow has a plan essentially similar to that of Ardtarmon or White House Co Antrim (*UJA* 1966 p. 111), except for being taller and more openly fenestrated. The rear staircase-tower contained also privies. The kitchen lay, rather surprisingly, outside the main walls, on the South-West side

83

85

84

86

87

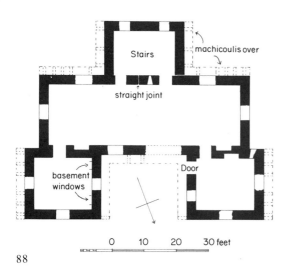

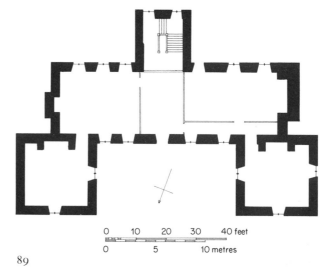

88

89

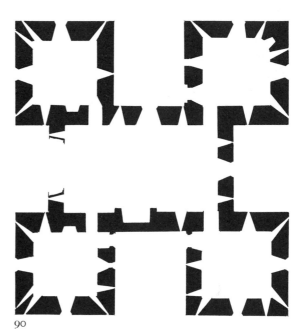

86 Ardtarmon, Co Sligo: the back elevation, with remnants of the bawn and barn in the foreground, and the staircase-tower in the centre. Built by the Gore (later Gore-Booth) family

87 Coppinger's Court from the South-West

88 Coppinger's Court: plan

89 Richhill 'Castle', Richhill, Co Armagh: plan, after the Co Down archaeological survey. The house, which now has curvilinear gables and a totally undefended aspect, is supposed to have been built after 1655, but the extraordinarily close

resemblance between its plan and that of Coppinger's Court cannot pass unremarked

90 Monkstown Castle, Co Cork. Built in 1636 by the Archdekin family, this is essentially a scaled-down Kanturk or Portumna type, with very lavish provision for defence. At 60 odd feet square it is not much bigger than the Mountjoy Fort (p. 121) which it much resembles in plan though not in function. After OPW.

The contemporary gatehouse at Lismore Castle Co Waterford has some points of similarity to Monkstown

90

There are, also in Co Cork, two houses which, appearances and dimensions notwithstanding, seem to belong to the family of Kanturk and Burntcourt. Monkstown (fig. 90) and Mountlong are only ten miles apart, and so close in date (1636 and 1631 respectively) that they must be by the same designers and craftsmen.[26] Monkstown is still, or more probably again, roofed, though empty and unused. Mountlong atones for its fragmentary and ruined state by showing less evidence of later interference and adaptation.

Both houses present the appearance of consisting of four tall gabled towers arranged rather close together in a square figure, with a solid in the centre, not unlike Mountjoy Fort which, as we have already seen, has such remarkable similarities to the episcopal constructions of Rathfarnham and Raphoe. But this is deceptive: as their plans show, Monkstown and Mountlong have rectangular bodies (38 feet by 20 feet at Monkstown: slightly less at Mountlong), and the flankers overlap their long sides.

The Longs who built Mountlong and the Archdekins who built Monkstown were both Old English families, and in what is by now a depressingly familiar pattern, John Long was executed on Cromwell's orders after 1649. Monkstown has bold bartizans on the outer corners of its flankers, which Mountlong seems never to have had, having instead little finials at the haunches of the gables. Mountlong, on the other hand, is recorded as having had an historiated plaster cornice in its principal room, representing 'spiritual subjects and field sports'.

Another pair of Co Cork houses of slightly later date are almost equally similar to one another, though about 36 miles apart. Both, again, were built by old English, Ightermurragh in South-East Cork by the Supples who were intermarried with the Imokilly FitzGeralds, and Kilmaclenine near Buttevant in the North of the county by the ubiquitous family of Barry. Ightermurragh is very much the better-preserved of the two, standing to its full height and lacking little but its floors and roof (figs. 91 and 92).[27]

Though cruciform in outline, Ightermurragh is really a long, narrow, rectangle, partitioned into two spaces on the principal floor and on the upper floors into more and smaller spaces, with a full-height staircase-tower at the back and a full-height porch-projection on the front. Its defensive posture is still very evident: in the few and small, though regular, windows, in the machicoulis over the door to which no permanent steps seem to have been provided, and in the continuous wall-walk which passes between the stacks and the gables. Another Munster house, Ballyduff on the Blackwater West of Lismore, has full-height fore-and-aft projections serving similar purposes, but though its one surviving window is stone-mullioned, the main block is relatively much deeper and the house seems to be 20 or 30 years later.

Another category of house on the rectangle-plus-flankers principle is represented by yet another pair of buildings, close together and clearly by the same builders. Gort, Co Roscommon and Athleague in the same county can be considered as reduced versions of the Burntcourt type, with the two flankers at the 'back' omitted. (It is not certain in either case, such is their state of ruin, that there was not, in the 'back' wall as we presume it to be, a staircase tower now vanished. Only excavation can determine this. If there was such a tower, they should be considered as part of the family of Coppinger's Court. At Dunganstown Co Wicklow it is the staircase-tower which has principally survived; but in complete state it must have resembled Coppinger's.) Gort is said to have been built by the Dowell family, and Athleague by that of Lyster. They are less obviously defensible than those we have just been considering, but there are still some defensive features such as loops, and there may

OVERLEAF

91 Ightermurragh, Imokilly, Co Cork, from the South-West. Built in 1641 by the Supple family, it has a very close parallel at Kilmaclenine, also in Co Cork

92 Ightermurragh: isometric view. Access to the doorway was no doubt by some temporary and removable steps or bridge, though here, again, the door at the rere, at basement level, is much less strongly defended. It is noteworthy how the wall-walk passes between the chimneys and the gable-ends

93 Glenbeg, Ballyduff, Co Waterford: the rere view, from the North-East, with massive stacks and other archaic features, invites the supposition that this was a late seventeenth-century house of which the central block has been refenestrated and made less defensible in the eighteenth

have been machicoulis on the now-vanished wall-tops. Outer defence by a bawn may, as always, be presumed. Both houses are notable for having forward-facing gables entirely devoid of windows, a feature found also in Sir William Villiers's large house at Dromahair,[28] of 1626, and again in later houses perhaps even of the eighteenth century such as Glenbeg Co Waterford (fig. 93).

Dromahair is still very impressive, especially in silhouette, with its seven lofty and contrasted stacks set at right-angles to one another like an elaborated version of Gort or Athleague. It has in fact the U-plan so common in England, yet never common (though sporadically found) in Ireland, and in the corners of its forecourt are a pair of curiously sloping corbelled stone porches one of which apparently contains the main entrance. The whole back wall is missing, and the whereabouts of the staircase is unknown, so that, once again, only excavation could show whether there was a projecting staircase-tower or not. And if there was, Dromahair too would have to be classified with Mallow and Coppinger's Court.

There are a few medium-sized castle-houses of irregular outline which are not easy to classify but which seem to form a link between the elaborate types we have been considering and the much more numerous and simpler L and T plans. Such, for example, is Killilea in North Co Tipperary (fig. 83), an O'Connor house perhaps built in about 1601 (though the dubious evidence of a date-stone is hardly, taken by itself, adequate evidence). It consists of two unequal rectangles overlapping corner-to-corner, and in the overlap is a rather spacious stone newel-stair, something we have not met before in Ireland. Killilea stands to its full height with an imposing array of bartizans, gables and stacks, and has its original, rather small windows, though someone in the last century who intended to found a religious establishment in it filled it up with brick vaulting of good quality and of some interest in its own right.

Not far away Kilcolgan, barbarously destroyed in recent years by the Electricity Supply Board, appears to have been somewhat similar, and a little further again to the East, beside the Grand Canal, is Ballycowan, three miles West of Tullamore (figs. 95, 96 and 97). This house, built by Jasper Herbert in 1626, is virtually an L-plan, with the entrance-door and a wide open-well stone staircase in the minor arm of the L,[29] and large well-lit rooms over vaults in the major arm. There are as many stacks on the minor arm as on the major, no doubt because the staircase, like those in later houses, goes only from ground (basement) to principal floor, and castle-like mural stairs gave access to the higher levels which, in the minor arm as well as the major, contained rooms.

Another, rather smaller, L-plan house in South Co Carlow, Tinnehinch on the outskirts of Graignamanagh, had its entrance (protected as at Ballycowan by a machicoulis) in the re-entrant corner between the staircase-tower and the main block, while in the opposite wall of the main block there are three storeys of perfectly regular windows, three to each floor: small and square at basement level, for security; large and square on the floors above, for comfort: as orderly as a house in Merrion Square.

Order and grandeur are the notes struck by another house which does not fit very readily into the typological series now being attempted. Glinsk, a seat of the Burkes in North-East Galway near the Roscommon border (figs. 98 and 99), would be a simple block but for having a bite only 11 feet square taken out of the middle of its principal entrance-front. This is much too small to be called a fore-court, and its clear purpose is to bring the intending visitor into a confined space where he could be kept in sight, and in the sights of the garrison's hand-guns, before he turned left

91

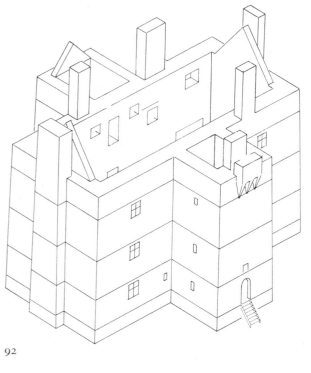

92

93

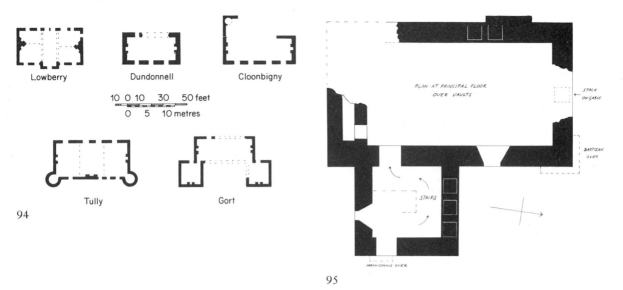

Lowberry Dundonnell Cloonbigny

10 0 10 30 50 feet

0 5 10 metres

Tully Gort

94

PLAN AT PRINCIPAL FLOOR
OVER VAULTS

STACK
ON GABLE

BARTIZAN
OVER

STAIRS

MACHICOLIS OVER.

95

94 Five seventeenth-century houses in Co Roscommon, all ruined. Dundonnell, Cloonbigny and Tully are all quite close together in the South of the county. Dundonnell stands within an earlier circular earthwork. Gort is in the East of the county, near Lough Ree, and has a virtual twin at Athleague nearby, while Lowberry, in the extreme West of the county, is probably somewhat later than Gort and may well be after 1660 or even 1680

95 Ballycowan Castle, Co Offaly: built in 1626 by the Herbert family. The lower part of the main stairs is contained in the entrance projection, with rooms above it (hence the stacks of which the outlines are shown in white). Further ascent was probably by a mural stair in the thickness of the South wall

96 Ballycowan: view from the South-West

96

97

98

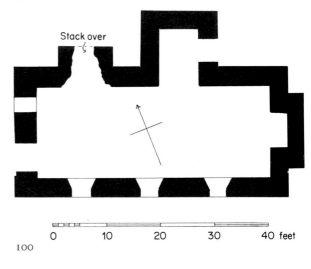

Stack over

0   10   20   30   40 feet

0   5   10 metres

100

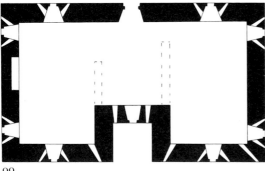

0   10   20   30   40 feet

99

at first floor-level to enter the principal floor. As at Kanturk, there is a doorway in the back wall at basement-level, and indeed the rere elevation is of comparable nobility to the front. The end-walls are crowned with massive quintuple batteries of diagonal stacks, and there were originally two gables on each of the main fronts set behind parapets with wall-walks. The small windows of the basement storey are each furnished with a pair of angled loops as in late tower-house practice.

Glinsk was probably built by Sir Ulick Burke, created a baronet in 1628. Sir Jonah Barrington tells an entertaining if somewhat long-winded story of the tenth baronet courting the rich Miss Ball and regaling her with the glories of Glinsk until, having married him, she wanted to see the place, whereupon, since it was by then a virtual ruin, Sir John had to arrange for her to hear stories of its being haunted and so successfully head her off.[30]

The position of the staircase at Glinsk is uncertain: we know only that it was inside the main block. But at this time and for long afterwards it was more usual for it to be in a separate tower at the back, either at one end making the L-plan, or, more commonly, in the middle resulting in a T. The total number of houses, including fragments, dating from the semi-fortified period is of the order of 200, of which the majority, certainly among those of modest size, are of the T-plan. Virtually all are in ruins. Here and there are fragments which have clearly been houses of some size, such as Castle Lyons in Co Cork, Ardmayle in Co Tipperary, or Lough Mask Castle in Co Mayo (which has a date-stone of 1618), but are no longer decipherable.

The distribution of the surviving remains is fairly random, though there appear to be some empty patches, notably Cavan and Monaghan, and a more or less continuous belt in the Shannon basin, taking in North-East Galway, South Roscommon and the adjoining parts of Longford, Westmeath and Offaly. Tipperary is rich, in this as in almost every other respect, and there are significant concentrations in Co Cork, along the Blackwater valley and along the South coast. Much of the land in Galway, Roscommon and Longford on which such ruins now stand is rather poor, suggesting that the parcels could not really support houses of this kind, which after falling into ruin were not even much used as sources of stone for their successors. By contrast, though there is a respectable spread in Fingall, many more such houses in that rich territory must have been replaced by eighteenth-century ones, not to mention the large number, here and elsewhere, of which the fabric must lie hidden in a later construction, such as (to take a known and large example) Birr Castle.

Cut-stone detail, the best and often the only available criterion of style and date, is generally missing, and timber lintels have all too often been looted or have rotted away.[*] A T-plan house, rather larger than most, Ballincar Co Sligo, is virtually undatable.[31] Its proportions are almost those of the eighteenth century, and in its rere wing it has three floors occupying the same height as two, but its massiveness, its diagonal stacks, and the asymmetry of its main elevation put it clearly in the century preceding.

Details, when they are available, range from the mediaeval-style pointed doorways of Ballintemple, a T-plan house near Cloghjordan (fig. 100) which has one door at the side and one at the back but three windows very neatly arranged on each of two floors on the main front, to Ballyloughan, also a T-plan house near Bagenalstown, which by chance still has one piece of classical cavetto cornice which, as Mr Waterman observes,[32] suggests a date in the second half of the century. Yet it is very evident that this class of building spans the century and is little if at all affected by the great

97 Ballycowan: view from the East. Over the front door is an armorial tablet

98 Glinsk, Co Galway: the South (entrance) front. The door is on the main floor on the left in the central recess, no doubt for defence, though the door at the back (compare Kanturk) is at basement level. It was probably built by Sir Ulick Burke created first baronet in 1628

99 Glinsk: plans of basement and principal floors. The principal entrance is in the West wall of the 'bay' in the middle of the South wall, at principal floor level

100 Ballintemple, (Cloghjordan) Co Offaly: plan. An enigmatic ruin, its thick walls and pointed doorways making it archaic even in the seventeenth century, while the regular fenestration of the South front looks forward to the eighteenth

---

[*] But flat arches in rough stone are often found.

political divide of 1641–60. Whether accidentally or otherwise, most of the buildings with dates attached come before 1641. But what are we to make of, for example, Derrin near Borris-in-Ossory, a little house only 40 feet long (figs. 101 and 102), with its massive diagonal stacks at each end, its staircase-tower at the back, and its door exactly between its two windows as primly as any villa in the Dublin suburbs?

Derrin stands now abruptly in the middle of a large field, but only three miles away to the West Cloncourse, a similar house, stands in the middle of a small bawn with pistol-loops. It had formerly a date-stone recording its building by John O'Duigan in 1636. Another such is Old Court, four miles South of Kinnity Co Offaly. Other similar houses were sometimes built inside existing earthworks, as at Dundonnell in Co Roscommon and Ballyduagh in Co Tipperary.[33] Just the other side of Roscrea from Cloncourse, high on a hillside, looking from the distance like a Tuareg fort in an early film about the French Foreign Legion, is Ballynakill (fig. 103), standing in the middle of an enormous bawn some 450 feet by 250 feet. The house, a tower-house expanded into an H-plan and refenestrated, is of three storeys surmounted by a deep blind attic, and is chiefly remarkable for the ornamentation of the latter by a series of alternating oval and diamond-shaped sunk panels edged in brick.

Finally, the simple rectangle. This is not very common, but it is known. In the following century it was to become the norm. Galgorm in Co Antrim and Huntington in Co Carlow are each three storeys high and date from the second quarter of the seventeenth century. Both have been considerably altered, but Galgorm at least still has its Portumna-Loughmoe-Dunganstown type battlements which it had in 1833,[34] even if they were worked over in about 1850, and its original oak staircase.

A very much humbler type is extant in a few examples which seem to foreshadow, if they are not early examples of, the simple stone-built farmhouse of the last two hundred years. Ballynamire Co Offaly is a simple rectangle 57 feet by 23, regularly fenestrated, with a projecting stack at each gable-end and a stack in the middle, in way of the front door. The shafts of the end-stacks are of brick, no doubt a replacement, but the central stack has two diagonal shafts. The house had low eaves, was doubtless thatched, and was of one-and-a-half storeys. Lissyconnor in East Galway is more fragmentary, but the end-stacks, of stone, still stand to their full height, and served pairs of corner-fireplaces in the end-walls, exactly as at Lowberry, a much grander house only three miles away to the North.[35] Lissyconnor also was of one-and-a-half storeys. Ballyspurge, near Whitehouse in Co Down (on the Ards peninsula) is also very fragmentary but appears to have been rather similar, though with more obvious defence both by pistol-loops and a bawn with a small gatehouse.[36]

These are all in ruin, and many more, we cannot doubt, remain to be identified. But for some idea of what such houses may have looked like we should go to Tinnycross (fig. 104) or Hollow House, near Tullamore, which is still thatched, still occupied, and has two detached cylindrical towers set in the field in front, the remains of the bawn which originally protected it, another at one corner of the back and remains of a fourth to complete the rectangle. It was measured by Dr Loeber in 1978 and had become derelict by 1985.

101

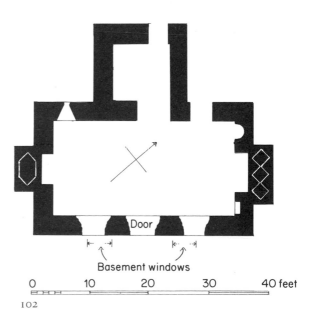

101 Derrin, Co Leix:
South East front. Such
prim symmetry is notable
at so early a date. There is
no brick in the structure,
and the missing lintels were
of timber

102 Derrin: plan of the
small seventeenth-century
house. The outlines of the
upper parts of the stacks are
shown in white. The stairs
were doubtless in the rere
wing, and an oven in the
North corner

Door

Basement windows

0   10   20   30   40 feet

102

103

104

CHAPTER NINE

The Restoration

The last third of the seventeenth century is one of the antechambers of history. Confused and confusing in its political aspect (and nowhere more so than in Ireland), it is full of discontinuities on other planes. The gulf that separates the prose of Milton and Jeremy Taylor from that of Defoe and Swift is at least as great as that between either and Burton or Donne. In architecture it is, even in England, a period of anticipations and retrogressions, bewilderingly intermixed.

The life histories of two Irish-born men,[1] one from Ulster and one from Munster, may serve to illustrate the chequered background. Both were important but neither of the first importance, and both were, ultimately, involved with architecture.

Daniel O'Neill was born in about 1612, nephew of Owen Roe who was in turn nephew to the even more celebrated Hugh, the 'Great' O'Neill, Earl of Tyrone. Daniel was brought up as a protestant at the court of Charles I, and though much of his time was spent in the Low Countries and on various missions he managed to get on the wrong side of Strafford in Dublin in 1635 about lands which his kinsmen had sequestered. Though taken prisoner by the Scots in 1640, he was released, only to be imprisoned by the English Parliament in the Tower of London, whence he escaped in women's clothes to serve in the Royalist army. He was on a mission to Ormonde in Kilkenny in 1644, then negotiating with his uncle Owen Roe the general of the Irish army, thence to St Germain, then back to command his uncle's army during the latter's fatal illness. He arranged with Ireton to be allowed to take 5,000 Irish troops for service on the Continent, rejoined Charles II, was expelled from Scotland, journeyed all over North-West Europe, went spying in Commonwealth England, was expelled from France, accompanied Charles again as far as the Pyrenees, and was richly rewarded at the Restoration with lands, and jobs, among them that of post-master-general, and died in 1664.

Roger Boyle, usually called Lord Broghill, and after 1660 Earl of Orrery, the third son of the 'Great' Earl of Cork, was born at Lismore in 1621, educated at Oxford,[2] and travelled in France and Italy. He served in the same expedition against Scotland as Daniel O'Neill, married Lady Margaret Howard and returned to Ireland, where he won the battle of Liscarrol in 1642, serving under the Parliamentary Commissioners until 1649, when he passed through London on his way to join Charles II. Here he was unexpectedly called upon by Cromwell, who offered him a command in the war against the Irish. He joined Cromwell at Wexford, and at the battle of Macroom defeated the Catholic Bishop of Ross whom he subsequently hanged. Though based mainly at Youghal, he held also Blarney Castle. He was member for Cork and also for Edinburgh in Cromwell's parliament, and spent a year in Scotland as Lord President of the council there. As a member of Cromwell's House of Lords he was one of those who urged the Lord Protector to make himself king, and even suggested that Charles II should marry Cromwell's daughter. As Governor of Munster he conspired with Coote to manage the Irish end of the Restoration, and was rewarded with the Earldom of Orrery. Though disagreements with Ormonde

103 Ballynakill, Roscrea, Co Tipperary: the house and bawn from the West. The left-hand third of the house is an earlier tower-house, and the bawn is unusually large and complete

104 Tinnycross or The Hollow, Tullamore, Co Offaly: single-storey, thatched, and in its present form of about 1800, it stands within a quadrilateral of cylindrical stone towers, one of which is visible on the left, and represents a semi-fortified bawn-type dwelling of the seventeenth century

caused him to resign the presidency of Munster, he lived much in Ireland and, dying in 1679, was buried at Youghal. He also found time to produce a copious literary output, including a dramatic allegory of his own career which was actually staged in Dublin.

The factor common to these curiously contrasting histories is that both these adventurous gentlemen, as soon as they had the leisure and the money to do so, built themselves stately houses. O'Neill's grand residence, just outside London, was called Belsize Park, and its name liveth for evermore. During the same years, following 1661, Orrery was building in North Co Cork, and wrote to Ormonde: 'I am now building a house for myself in Munster, of which I am the architect, and therefore pretend something to engineership. . . .' This house, at Charleville, was regarded as the most magnificent of its period in Ireland, but was burned by the bastard Duke of Berwick after he had spent a night in it in 1690. Little is known of its appearance other than that it occupied one side of a walled court and could be defended with 16 guns. Orrery's claim to be its architect is probably to be taken seriously, especially as, in his letter to Ormonde, he goes on to propose himself as designer for a new wing to the official viceregal residence.[3]

In England, one of the main links providing architectural continuity during this fragmented period was the Royal Works. Neither Inigo Jones, the architect-royal *par excellence*, nor his 'nephew' and successor John Webb, lacked employment during the Commonwealth period, nor did another equally accomplished architect of their school, Sir Roger Pratt.

Ireland had no Inigo and, as we have seen, English kings had concerned themselves very little with building of any kind in Ireland since the thirteenth century. From time to time a more than usually active Lord Deputy would exert himself to do something about Dublin Castle:[4] Sir Henry Sidney, for example, in 1566-78 and Sir Henry Cary, Lord Falkland, who in 1622 built a gallery carried on arches and leading from the chamber of presence to the council chamber. Though later described by an English visitor as 'built . . . very gracefully' it had a short life of only sixty years because it was blown up by Ormonde's son Lord Arran in 1684 to prevent a fire from reaching the powder-magazine. On this same occasion perished also 'the new building built by the Earl of Essex' (not Elizabeth's Essex but the Capel Earl).

Strafford, too, did something to the castle but we do not know what. But the lack of a court tradition in architecture is most clearly exemplified by the extraordinary structure which Strafford built near Naas, some 20 miles from Dublin, in 1637. It still survives, in ruins, all 380 feet of it, close beside the main road to Limerick and Cork. The ambiguity of its plan is matched only by its bizarre detail, an amalgam of gothic and of artisan mannerism. Long and thin and quite unlike the Rathfarnham-Portumna group of houses, it has no discernible shape and simply goes on until it stops, like one of the obscurer English cathedrals.

Cathedral-like indeed is the splendidly-executed brick rib-vaulting, 14 consecutive bays of it, two bays wide, which supports much of it, the rest being carried for the most part on a solid basement. It is the first employment of brick on a large scale in the whole country, and in its technical perfection must be the work of immigrant craftsmen. There are four separate kinds of brick in it, assigned to separate roles, and of these one at least is probably also an importation.[5]

Having neither ancestors nor offspring, Jigginstown (for such, in various protean guises—Sigginstown, Gigginstown, Zinckinstown, Smokingstown, Jinglestown,[6] Xigginstown[7]— is its singular name) cannot be fitted into the canon of Irish architecture and must be regarded as a freak (fig. 106). Its architect is alleged to have been a

105 Castle Ffrench, Co Galway: a seventeenth-century chimney-piece now built into the outside back wall of the eighteenth-century house. Besides the low-relief 'drawing' of a window, there are scribed mock-voussoirs on the lintel or arch of the fireplace itself

106 Jigginstown, Naas, Co Kildare: plan of basement and principal floors, the basement plan reduced from the survey by the late Dudley Waterman

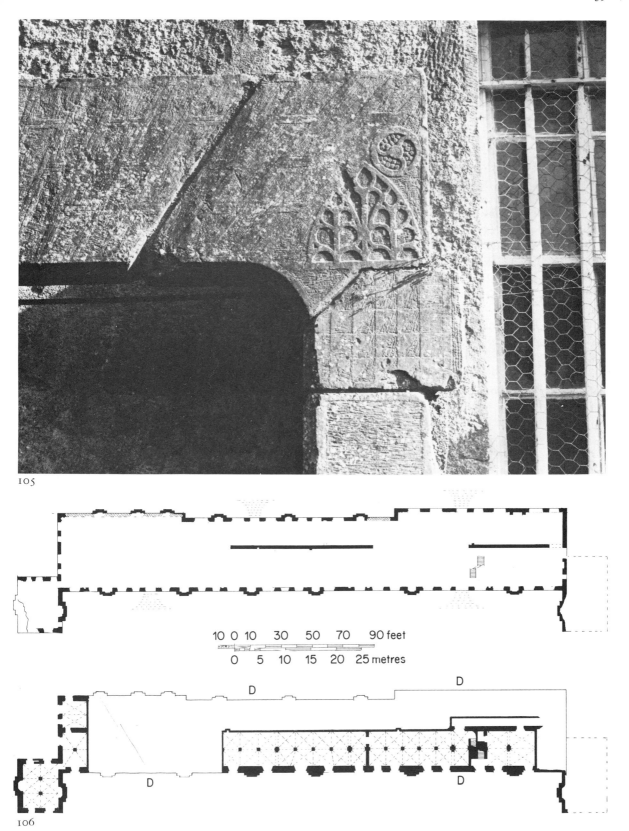

105

106

10 0 10   30   50   70   90 feet

0   5   10   15   20   25 metres

Dutchman called John Allen, but this lacks confirmation and the name of the Rev. Mr Johnson is mentioned as having supervised it.[8]

The viceregal house called the Phoenix, in what is now the Phoenix Park, acquired in 1618, was enlarged by the addition of a wing by Henry Cromwell who acted in Ireland as his father's deputy in the years 1657-9. We would give much to know what this building was like. Sir William Petty describes it as 'A very stately house'. In 1661, as we have seen, Lord Broghill further enlarged it. 'I proposed to the Council', he writes, 'that to make the house uniform, the hall should be built as a room answerable to the new building Co. Harry Cromwell made; and that to make it of even length thereunto a chapel should be added. . . .'[9] We can hardly doubt that this building, almost the first purely domestic non-military structure of any pretension of which we know, deeply influenced the designs of such Dublin mansions as those of Lord Longford, Lord Conway and Sir Maurice Eustace, which were presently to be built.

In default of a court, the intermittent presence of the Duke of Ormonde, and particularly his return as Viceroy in 1662, supplied the lack. But most of the building done on his own account was at his seat of Kilkenny, and a few miles away at Dunmore his Duchess was also busily building in the grandest manner. Dunmore has gone entirely, and the question of the Duke's work at Kilkenny must be left for later consideration. In about 1665 Sir Maurice Eustace's house at Chapelizod, henceforth known as the 'King's House', supplanted the Phoenix; but we know nothing of this either.

No doubt these buildings embodied overtly classical features in the form of the orders. As usual, the orders showed themselves first on a small scale in such things as tombs and doorcases.★ A number of Jacobean tombs formerly existed in Dublin and drawings of them survive: besides the two small examples in St Audoen's there is the gigantic Boyle monument of 1631 in St Patrick's, the Earl's own tomb in Youghal, the Jones monument also in St Patrick's and the Chichester monument in Carrick-fergus. Most if not all of these were probably imported from England.[10] But far inland there are classical monuments of which some were certainly locally produced: the group, for example, by Nicholas Cowli and Patrick Kerin, for purely Irish clients, some of which, such as those at Lorrha in North Tipperary, are signed, and the classical tomb of Sir Nathaniel Fox in the early classical mausoleum-church of Rathreagh Co Longford, dated 1634.[11]

The main doorcase of Kanturk would be classical if it knew how: but it is very early (before 1609) and very far away from the centres of taste, so, not surprisingly, it is a shade barbarous. The gateway to Portumna, and the front door of the house itself, which are perhaps ten years later, would pass unnoticed as Jacobean work in England. Much the same may be said of the piled-up frontispiece, rather like the Boyle tomb, which Sir Hugh Clotworthy built at Antrim Castle in 1613. The very grand chimneypiece at Donegal Castle put up by the Brookes soon after 1610, is both well proportioned and elaborately enriched. But a door in the same building is hardly more advanced than that of Kanturk. The remains of a colonnade at Dunluce Castle Co Antrim, appear to date from the end of the sixteenth century.

The cathedral at Raphoe, and the church of Donaghmore at Castlecaulfeild Co

---

★ First of all, perhaps, in the chimney-piece at Carrick-on-Suir which is dated 1565. The Barnewall tomb at Lusk is dated 1589 (*Austin Cooper*, p. 76). There are what appear to be early classical fragments at Kilkea Castle and Moore Abbey, both in Co Kildare.

107

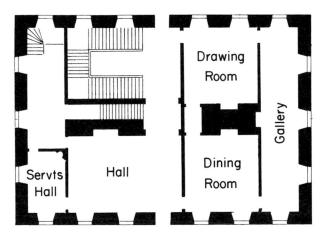

Drawing Room

Gallery

Servts Hall

Hall

Dining Room

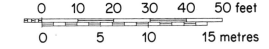

| 0 | 10 | 20 | 30 | 40 | 50 feet |

| 0 | | 5 | | 10 | | 15 metres |

108

107 Drimnagh Castle, Co Dublin, from the South-West. Surrounded by a rectangular moat still containing water, the late-mediaeval tower has seventeenth-century additions with 'artisan-mannerist' detail probably by the Loftus family

108 Burton, Co Cork: plan re-drawn from the drawing in BM Add MSS 47857 'as it was before it was burnt at the Revolution by the Irish'. There is also, in the same Egmont papers, a later plan of a more centralised and formal kind but to the same outside dimensions. This plan has many archaic features such as the long gallery and the shape of the hall, and it appears that the bay on the left probably had a mezzanine floor reached by the minor staircase in the corner

Tyrone, have porches of a would-be classical kind: the latter is dated 1685, while the former, though perhaps not much earlier, is frankly a mediaeval hybrid.

There is some very presentable artisan-mannerist work to be seen at Drimnagh Castle in South Co Dublin (fig. 107), a moated seat of the Barnewall ('Old English') family, modernised, probably by one of the Loftus family, who leased it from the Barnewalls early in the seventeenth century. In the later part of the century there were ripe specimens of the artisan-mannerist style to be seen in the interior of Eyrecourt (for which see page 146) as old photographs[12] testify, and we can hardly doubt that it was once widely diffused.

There is scanty evidence of the plan-forms of most of the houses built by magnates, Cromwellian and other, during the middle years of the century. Even so, it is clear that the four-square plan was coming into its own. At Burton near Buttevant in North Co Cork, Sir John Perceval built a house of which ground and site plans are extant, showing it to have been a double-pile with a massive row of stacks set transversely on two great piers rather than a continuous wall, a very large staircase to one side of the plan, behind a hall which is still sub-mediaeval in form and function, being the largest room on the entrance-floor, and a long gallery communicating with both the drawing-room and the dining-room. It was set symmetrically within a great system of courtyards, walled gardens and subsidiary buildings, with six spur-footed defensive turrets, the whole 496 feet by 248 feet exclusive of the flankers, totalling nearly three acres. In aspect the house was a typical Carolean wide-eaved platform-roofed block with a domed gazebo on top like Ashdown or Coleshill. Its life was short, for like its neighbour Charleville it was burned by the retreating Jacobites in 1690 (plan, fig. 108).[13]

Carton, built at about the same time by the Talbot family of Palesmen, was somewhat larger, with the addition of four towers attached to the flanks near the corners and rising above the eaves. Lord Conway's house at Portmore was probably larger still, but has vanished utterly while Carton has been swallowed up in the present mansion. Thomastown Co Tipperary, built by the Duke of Ormonde's half-brother George Mathew seems also to have been large, and now lurks within the shell of the vast mock-castle which enveloped it in the early nineteenth century. It probably resembled the Duchess of Ormonde's Dunmore of which no trace now remains.

Some of the houses of the mid-century magnates were not very large. Sir William Petty was a not inconsiderable landowner yet his house near Kenmare was only 44 feet square. It sat inside a clay fortress with walls 12 feet thick and 14 feet high with pentagonal flankers; yet none of this saved it from being wiped out by the dispossessed Irish in 1687.

This was an exceptional occurrence at so late a date. When we explain a bout of building fever by the advent of a stable regime we are apt to forget that stable regimes have sometimes been thought unstable at the time, and vice versa. The clearest expression which a building-owner can give to his estimate of danger and security is not to be found in plan-form, but in the treatment of that most critical region where the walls of his house meet the roof. We have already noted that the plan of Coppinger's Court was used again some time after 1660 at Richhill Co Armagh.[14] But where Coppinger's has a formidable parade of stone machicolations, Richhill has Dutch-inspired curvilinear gables alternating with plain eaves: in other words, no possible provision for defence. Waringstown in the neighbouring county of Down is now three storeys high, but when first built was of two like Richhill, and still has Dutch gables on its flank-walls, so that the original termination is conjectural,

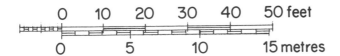

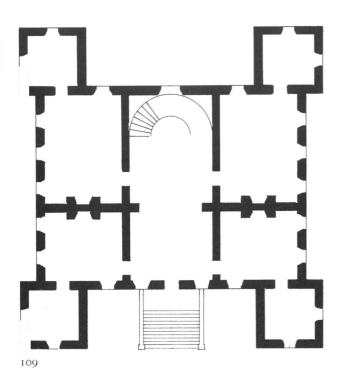

109

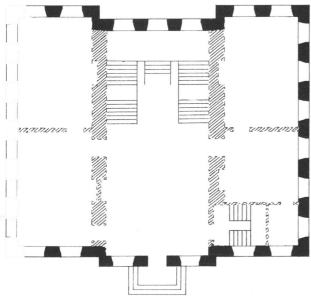

110

109 Annegrove, Carrigtohill, Co Cork: sketch-plan based on information supplied by Jeremy Williams and on a surviving photograph. The influence of the four-flanker Portumna or Kanturk type is still visible in this essentially non-defensible house

110 Eyrecourt, Co Galway: plan, after John O'Connell. The interior walls (shown hatched) are inaccessible because of fallen debris, undergrowth, missing floors, etc.

111

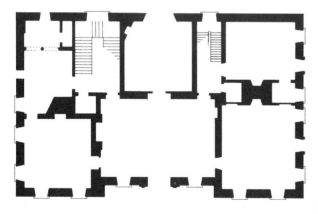

112

113

but certainly did not give even such provision for defence as is afforded by a plain parapet.[15] The plan of Waringstown has a deep indentation in the back:* deeper and wider even than at Glinsk, and the stacks are all in the outer walls as they are at Glinsk and Waringstown and nearly every other house before them except Rathfarnham, Portumna and Raphoe.

The timber eaves cornice with dormers above it is the *ne plus ultra* of indefensibility, and it, like the curvilinear gables, is of Dutch derivation, from van Campen by way of Hugh May and Sir Roger Pratt. Both ran their course at the same time, in the town as well as in the country, and both in the end yielded to the parapet. A little after 1660 they were both very up-to-date.

Eyrecourt Co Galway (figs. 110 and 111), is of exceptional interest, not least because its state of advanced dereliction casts light (in both senses of that phrase) on its construction without, as yet, totally obscuring its form. Its plan is strongly suggestive of the Mauritshuis, save that the four stacks stand on fore-and-aft walls instead of being set transversely. The walls are made of bright red brick, laced horizontally with massive bond-timbers at the level of, and forming, the lintels of the windows. Outside this a rubble masonry facing is coated with fine lime plaster, brought to a finer surface still for the false coigns.[16]

Very curiously, there exists a description of building methods in Ireland published a little earlier than the building of Eyrecourt which can neither be ignored nor easily made sense of. The *Natural History of Ireland* was assembled by Gerald Boate and his brother Arnold before 1649, and published by the latter over the former's name in 1652. He speaks of the 'freestones' (i.e. limestones) of Ireland 'both gray and blew' and tells us that they were first used by the English and not previously by the Irish, which we know to be true as regards the carved work before the Anglo-Norman invasion. 'The gray free stone', he says, 'draweth in the moisture of the air continually to it, and so becometh dank and wet both in and out-side, especially in times of much rain. To mend this inconvenience the English did wainscoat those walls with oak or other boards, or line them with a thin coat of brick.' He later describes the making of bricks in Ireland, the burning of them in large clamps of 2–3,000,000 at a time, so that about one-third are correctly fired and serviceable. Brick, he says, has not been very common until recently, especially in Dublin, and the Irish bricks are inferior to those imported.

So far as I know, no houses earlier than 1649 have thin (or thick) brick linings to their walls. But after Eyrecourt (which is some time later than 1660) many instances are known of houses entirely lined with brick, with their dividing-walls of brick also, but finished externally with rubble masonry rendered with lime-plaster. Two examples, almost at random, are Whitesfort in Co Waterford near Clonmel, and Ledwithstown in Co Longford.† It is awkward, to say the least, that Boate's description does not quite fit any known building very closely and was in print about 15 years too early to fit most of the known material evidence.

The interior of Eyrecourt (which survived long enough to be photographed) was darkly opulent, with doorcases in an artisan-mannerist style recalling Thorpe Hall, Northamptonshire. The staircase survived to be shipped off to America: it had continuous pierced decoration of a kind not uncommon in England but in Ireland paralleled only by Desart Court (where it is either 50 years later or taken from an earlier house), and ceiling plasterwork to match. The splendidly robust late

111 Eyrecourt: the house as it stood in 1957. Much less of it is now standing

112 Beaulieu, Co Louth: plan. The large entrance-hall is two storeys high, and the North-East staircase appears to be early-to-mid-eighteenth century, though the house as a whole is from soon after 1660. The plan shows strong English influence (for example in the closets flanking the stacks)

113 Kilkenny: the main (West) gateway to the Castle, probably designed by William Robinson, either for the first Duke of Ormonde in about 1685, or for the second Duke, his grandson, after 1698. In either case it was largely reconstructed by William Robertson in 1830-40, and how much of the rather uncertain proportions (e.g. of the keystones in the flanking niches) is attributable to the original design and how much to the reconstruction cannot now be determined

* Compare the plan of Cuba Court Co Offaly in Craig, *Classic Irish Houses* 1976 p. 83.

† Castlestrange Co Roscommon is another.

seventeenth-century staircase at Birr Castle is quite different and much simpler in character: boldly turned balusters and a broad ramping rail.

The last of the richly carved consoles of the Eyrecourt eaves-cornice has dropped, or will have dropped by the time these words are read. Beaulieu in Co Louth (fig. 112) has fared better and is in fact the only wide-eaved hip-roofed house of Restoration date now surviving in Ireland. Somewhat smaller than Eyrecourt, it contrives to look larger. Nobody knows what its walls are made of, but all the dressings including a string-course and the main architrave and frieze, are of bright red rubbed brick of a kind otherwise virtually unknown in Ireland. Beaulieu is at the mouth of the river Boyne and no doubt both bricks and the skill to work them were imported. The hall at Beaulieu rises through two storeys, and its rich carvings, together with the staircase, belong to the early years of the next century.

These wide-eaved houses must have been tolerably common before 1700, being the prevailing mode of most of the new constructions of the age of Ormonde. Another which survived long enough to be photographed was Ardfert Abbey Co Kerry. Another which must have been among the very finest was the Boyle mansion at Blessington built by the Earl of Cork's kinsman who was Archbishop of Dublin and, like his predecessor Loftus, Archbishop of Armagh and Lord Chancellor. He went so far as to build lodgings for the 'six clerks' at Blessington, and there hold his Chancery court, though it is 17 miles from the capital. Mediaeval habits die hard. Blessington House was burnt at the end of the eighteenth century, but its appearance is known from an engraving, which shows that its slightly recessed centre of five bays had, like George Mathew's house at Thomastown, an open arcade on the ground floor, an unusual feature in this type of house.

The plans of these houses are all more or less rectangular. Some of the exceptions such as Richhill have been noted. Another is Finnebrogue in Co Down which has a U-plan and survives in a manner of speaking.[17] A house of the utmost interest, said to be of the late seventeenth century, which survived till about a quarter of a century ago, apparently intact, seems to have been a late embodiment of the block-and-four-flankers type, unless indeed its inspiration is, as has been suggested, from further afield. This house was Annegrove, otherwise Ballinsperrig, near Carrigtohil in Co Cork, built by Sir James Cotter, of an old Catholic family, who succeeded in 1660 and died in 1705. It is more likely to date from the beginning of that period than from the end.[18] A sketch-plan is given, based on the recollections of Mr Jeremy Williams. The flankers are known to have been 12 feet square internally, which is about the same as those at Portumna, though smaller than those at Monkstown and Mountlong, and they had moderately steep pyramidal roofs above a cornice ranging with the cornice of the main block. From a surviving photograph the house seems to have been one of great elegance and charm. Like most Irish houses, it was of two storeys over a high basement, with a broad flight of steps up to the front door.

Stylistically neither 1690, nor 1700, nor for that matter 1714 marks any particular change. Kenmare House, Killarney (which has gone) or Boyne House, Stackallen (which still survives) or Castle Durrow, Leix (which survives more or less) could all be of the seventeenth century though they are in fact of the eighteenth*—1716 for Boyne House, 1713–32 for Castle Durrow, which as we shall see in the next chapter, is precisely contemporary with Trinity Library.

Castle Durrow has a giant order of Doric pilasters, but this is not the first

---

* Similarly, the drawing by John Curld [sic] for old Castle Coole Co Fermanagh (*I. Arch. Drgs.* no. 33), though of 1709, could just as easily date from 1665.

appearance of such a feature in a house in Ireland. That honour is probably to be awarded to the three-bay frontispiece of Kilkenny Castle (fig. 113), which may still be seen though in a re-worked version from the early nineteenth century. Unfortunately we do not even know for certain whether this was done for the first Duke who died in 1688, or for his son who was attainted and fled abroad in 1715. Dr Loeber accepts[19] the attribution to William Robinson which seems to make an early date, perhaps in the 1680s, more likely than a late one, because both Ormonde and Robinson were active about the Royal Hospital (also with a giant order of Corinthian pilasters) at that time, whereas after 1702 Robinson was in more or less permanent disgrace. The heavy swags between the capitals are unmistakably late seventeenth century in feeling, even if re-cut in the nineteenth.

Not far from Kilkenny is Swiftsheath, a curious and ungainly house which has a wide steep pediment and is set about with giant Corinthian pilasters. It also has a date-stone, immediately above one of the capitals, saying 'AD 1657'. It has obviously been much altered, and it is even nearer to the Duchess of Ormonde's vanished house at Dunmore than to the Duke's castle.

We have now reached the period when the names of artificers and designers begin to be heard: faintly at first, and often in equivocal contexts. Such men as Daniel Thomas, William Kenn, Thomas Smith, John Mills, William Hurlbutt, William Dodson, James Archer, Thomas Lucas and Dr John Westley are mentioned as 'contrivers' or as producing estimates for the building or repair of forts or bridges, or as furnishing 'plots' or 'models'. They were mostly if not all English, yet only two of them have known English careers. They are all shadowy figures: none of them has a known life history at all comparable to those of the two magnificoes sketched in at the beginning of this chapter.[20]

Nor has it yet been possible to reconstruct architectural personalities for them either. To take an example: both Thomas Smith and William Kenn were[21] involved in preparing designs for Burton, Co Cork. The plan, which survives (fig. 108) is very competent, with some archaic features such as a hall entered at one end as at Portumna, and a long gallery. But it is more than likely that Perceval's own part in this was at least as important as those of Smith or Kenn. The very grand stables which William Hurlbutt designed for Lord Conway at Portmore have disappeared utterly: we know only that, not for the last time in Ireland, they outshone the house. James Archer built, most appropriately, a bridge at Carrick-on-Suir which at least in part survives, though endangered (fig. 239).

If we had any idea at all of the appearance of the Phoenix House we might be able to hazard an opinion about the respective contributions of Henry Cromwell and Roger Lord Broghill, or Randolph Beckett and John Mills who worked on it during the Commonwealth, and of Dr John Westley and William Dodson who had a go at it in Ormonde's time. Most of what we know of Dodson relates, all too typically, to his defalcations in the matter of the Phoenix Park wall: when things of this kind go wrong they are apt to show up in the records.

The surviving remains scattered through the countryside display, perhaps, more consistency than we might expect from an age of such political and social fragmentation. The taste and ideals of the period did not radiate from a single centre: rather they reflected the experience and preferences of a number of individuals of very varied background: McCarthy of Kanturk, Loftus of Rathfarnham, Clanrickarde of Portumna, Perceval of Burton and of Egmont.

Inevitably the question has been asked, whether the buildings of the Gaelic and old English families differed stylistically from those of the more recent settlers. Apart from the occurrence of a few, mostly rather superficial, scotticisms in some of the Ulster plantation buildings, the surviving material evidence suggests that they did not, or not very much. The Irish and old English were doubtless just as keen to go after the latest English fashion, or what they believed to be the latest English fashion, as their descendants observably are today.

One factor in the situation must have made for stability while the musical chairs went on. The testimony to this factor comes from a rather unexpected quarter. Vincent Gookin, brother of the better-known Robert Gookin, wrote in a pamphlet of 1655 that of every hundred Irishmen five or six were carpenters or masons 'more handy and ready in building ordinary houses and much more prudent in supplying the defects of instruments and materials than English artificers.'[22] National character does not seem to have changed very much.

As Dr MacLysaght remarks, the Gaelic poems in which such poets as O'Bruadair and O'Rahilly praise the houses of their patrons, are full of superlatives but display no eye for detail:[23] we remember that centuries later James Joyce was to describe one of his characters as sitting on a 'pediment'. The accomplishments of the man of letters do not always include a command of architectural or even topographical terminology. That fine writer Ernie O'Malley's soldierly description of the Four Courts is a masterpiece of confusion.[24] But I digress. Or perhaps I do not digress.

A hitherto little-noticed exception to the general rule of paucity of description of Irish buildings in the late Middle Ages is the account by Edward Wright of 1598 of Dingle or Dingle-i-couch, printed by E. Arber in his *English Garner*, vol III, 1880: page 390ff:

> This Dingleacush is the chief town in all that part of Ireland. It consisteth but of one main street, from whence some smaller do proceed. On either side, it hath had gates, as it seemeth, in times past; at either end, to open and shut as a town of war: and a Castle too. The houses are very strongly built with thick stone walls, and narrow windows like unto castles: for, as they confessed, in time of trouble, by reason of the wild Irish or otherwise, they use their houses for their defence as castles . . .
>
> [all the houses save four 'burnt and ruinated' by the Earl of Desmond, and the town still mostly in ruins]
>
> . . . Commonly, they have no chimneys in their houses, excepting those of the better sort; so that the smoke was very troublesome to us . . . Their fuel is turf, which they have very good; and whinnes or furs [furze]. There groweth little wood thereabouts; which maketh building chargeable there; as also the want of lime, as they reported; which they are fain to fetch from far, when they have need thereof. But of stones, there is store enough: so that, they commonly make their hedges . . . with them.
>
> [there follow further notes on manners and customs]

It should be noticed that Dingle was built by the 'civil Irish' or 'old English', i.e. the adherents of the Fitzgerald Earls of Desmond, but that to Wright it was well-nigh as foreign as the habitations of the 'wild Irish' themselves ('the king's Irish enemies') supposing he had had the chance to see them.

We have said nothing about church architecture since we looked at the friars' building at Creevelea (Dromahair) on the eve of the Reformation. Indeed I have said nothing about the Reformation itself, nor do I intend to, except to observe that it left virtually every ancient ecclesiastical site in the hands of the reformed church, thenceforth by law established. During the sixteenth and seventeenth centuries old churches fell into ruin and few new churches were built. The Catholic church to which the majority adhered was dispossessed, and though it was sometimes tolerated and sometimes persecuted, such building as it did was discreet and small in scale. In 1670 we find Broghill writing to Conway: 'Many convents have in my absence been erected. I am now pulling them down'.[25] Small wonder that his house was burned.

A small number of Protestant churches were built during the seventeenth century. The oldest Protestant church* built as such is said to be Kilbrogan, begun by Henry Becher in 1610 and finished 15 years later by the Earl of Cork. Kilbrogan is part of the town of Bandon, where another new church, that of Ballymodan, was built in 1614, but rebuilt in the 1840s. Kilbrogan is built of rubble stone and has triple lancets but is not very remarkable in other ways.

As might be expected, there was some church-building activity in the North: for example the almost complete rebuilding of Carrickfergus by the Chichesters in 1614, itself recently robbed of virtually all its character by injudicious 'restoration'.[26] The little church, now ruined, of Derrygonnelly in Co Fermanagh has a West door which must, I suppose, be called 'classical' in that its arch-stones are diamond-faceted in a manner deriving remotely from the Mediterranean, no doubt via Scotland whence came Sir John Dunbar who built it in 1623.[27]

A more serious piece of early classicism is the little mortuary church at Rathreagh or Fox Hall, Co Longford, built in 1636 to contain the rather grand Ionic monument of Sir Nathaniel Fox who died in 1634. The West end of the church was pedimented with a doorway framed by engaged Doric columns carrying a sensitively-detailed entablature, and though it has suffered somewhat from rearrangement during a lengthening of the church in 1772, it can still be seen to be one of the very earliest instances of mature classicism in the country. It is now roofless.[28]

With Derry Cathedral, built between 1628 and 1633, we are back again with the gothic: at least with the gothic in its late perpendicular form as understood by the London companies who built it within the recently completed walls, to replace the old cathedral destroyed by the English general Docwra in 1600. It is a modest enough building, its aisles and clerestory lit by segment-headed windows divided into five lights, but the tower has been rebuilt and the East extended beyond the old corner-turrets which consequently now look rather pointless.[29] Still in the North, the parish church of Donaghcloney (Waringstown) built by William Waring in 1679-81 has been much altered and enlarged 'in the manner' but has a noble timber roof of English character (but Irish oak).[30]

Better known, perhaps, than any of these, is the little church built by Bishop Jeremy Taylor near his patron's house of Portmore in Co Antrim and now called Ballinderry Middle Church. In truth it is a rather ordinary little building, moving us more by its illustrious associations and its box-pews and pulpit of oak rather than by much architectural character. The hand of the restorer has been heavy upon it, filling the very late Perpendicular windows with bull's-eye glass. Jeremy Taylor did not live to see it consecrated.[30] Further South, still in Ulster, the churches of Ballyconnell and Belturbet are also in origin seventeenth century, but larger and more elaborate and much more altered, and set within earthen fortifications.

Security of a different kind is represented by the remarkable little church at Hollywood Co Wicklow, built in about 1698. From outside it looks ordinary enough, except that the batter is a little more marked than usual, and the walls unusually thick. The explanation is that it is covered by a continuous stone barrel-

---

* The church at Newry is assigned to 1579 but is no longer recognisable as such. *County Down Survey* pp. 308-9.

vault, harking back to Taghmon and Ardrass. Like those we have just been mentioning, it remains in use (fig. 170).

The (established) Church of Ireland did not have a complete monopoly of building.
At Urney near Strabane in Co Tyrone the Presbyterian church is alleged, no doubt
with truth, to incorporate the fabric of the church of 1654. More moving, perhaps,
is the two-stone doorhead of one of the three little churches at Loughinisland in Co
Down, which bears the false-relief inscription 'PMC 1636' which may denote the
initials of Phelim MacCartan. Traditionally it, or one of its neighbours, was until
early in the eighteenth century used by both Protestants and Catholics, as in Alsace.[32]
Times have changed, and may change again.

The very extensive rebuilding of Lismore Cathedral in Co Waterford by William
Robinson[31] has left its traces: it was done in 1680 and at about the same time or a
little earlier William Dodson built, in Dublin, the elliptical church of St Andrew[34]
which survived* until 1860. But the mention of these two names has brought us
again to the capital, and to the threshold of its flowering time, the eighteenth century.

---

* It was rebuilt, how extensively is not known, by Francis Johnston in 1793–1807. There is
a plan in W. O. Addleshaw and F. Etchells, *The Architectural Setting of Anglican Worship*, 1948.

CHAPTER TEN

Dublin: the Seventeenth Century

The primacy of Dublin in Irish architecture is even now so marked that we must remind ourselves that, however important its role in the Middle Ages, as the capital of the Pale, the end of the Middle Ages left it looking very unlike our idea of a capital city. Whatever the glories of St Mary's Abbey may have been, and they were certainly considerable, they are represented now only by the chapter house. Of the other monastic houses, the Abbey of St Thomas, the Priory of All Hallows (Augustinian), the Priory of St Saviour (Dominican) and the other mendicant houses, no certain particulars have come down to us. The two cathedrals have already been noticed: by the middle of the seventeenth century both were in bad condition. Of the eight parish churches within the walls, and ten without, only one, St Audoen's, retains anything resembling its mediaeval form.

The Castle, at the South-East corner of the walled city, was still, in 1660, substantially in the form first given to it 400 years earlier: that of a rectangle guarded by five towers and a gatehouse. It too was in bad condition: one of its two great halls, the larger of the two, which accommodated Parliament when it sat in Dublin (which it did not always do) was burnt in 1671: much of the rest was burnt in another fire 13 years later.[1]

We know nothing of the appearance of Sir Maurice Eustace's house, or Lord Conway's, or Lord Longford's, or Sir Robert Reading's or the great house called 'The Carbrie' which was the town house of the Earls of Kildare. The great Earl of Cork had built himself a house more or less where the City Hall now stands, which was, not surprisingly, so big that after his death it was largely tenanted by government departments.[2] Something similar happened to the house on College Green built by the Lord President Carew towards the end of the sixteenth century and acquired in the early seventeenth by Sir Arthur Chichester, Lord Deputy from 1604 till 1614. It was known at first as 'Carey's Hospital' but later as 'Chichester House', and the Four Courts sat in it in 1605-6, and so, in 1641, did the Lords Justices and the Privy Council. By the Restoration it had become the seat of Parliament itself. The interior of the Lords' and Commons' houses are known from late and unreliable copies of untraceable originals,[3] but the ground-plan is known.[4] It was a very simple plan: entry through a gate between guardhouses into a courtyard about 50 feet deep and 40 feet wide, from which, nearly in a straight line, a passage or gallery less than 11 feet wide had three spaces endwise on to each side of it. The middle space of those on the right (East) was the House of Lords, 57 feet by 21, and facing it (West) across the gallery the House of Commons of similar dimensions. The whole block, exclusive of gatehouse and courtyard, was about 135 feet by 66 feet: large for a private house but not for a public building, and the longer dimension agreeing pretty well with the 140 odd feet available when the Parliament House came to be rebuilt nearly 70 years later.

More conspicuous than Chichester House, and very close to it, was Trinity College which had been founded in 1592 on the site of All Hallows' Priory, but apparently provided with brand-new purpose-built accommodation in the traditional form of a square of buildings round a courtyard. The tower of the priory seems to have been incorporated in the North range near its East end. Otherwise it was very modest, two storeys high with dormers and recurring stacks in the outer walls, much like a reduced version of a Cambridge or Oxford college of the time, which is just what it was. In front, that is to the West, of it, was a square garden or court almost equal in area to the buildings themselves, and the approach was axially through this court. The hall and chapel were arranged end-on to each other in the North range, which was the first part to be built, along with the West range. In 1594 the South and East ranges were still unbuilt, but by the 1630s a start had already been made on a second square to the North. These early buildings were of brick, and the whole thing about the size of an almshouse in an English country town.[5]

Modest though these buildings were, and especially so when contrasted with their majestic successors, we must remember that never before in Ireland had there been a non-military building with a courtyard 120 feet square. The symmetry of the layout is to be expected: we recall the close involvement of Loftus whose house at Rathfarnham was of equal formality, and approached, there can be little doubt, through a similar forecourt and gateway.

This pristine simplicity did not last for long. By the bequest of Sir Jerome Alexander, who died in 1670, the College was put in a position to begin a West front on a very much larger scale. It lay well to the East of the original front—on the line of the outer wall in fact—and it was designed by Thomas Lucas, carpenter. Nearly half of it was up by the time of Dineley's visit in 1680, and in spite of the drums and tramplings of the next few years, it was finished by the end of the century. It is known from Dineley's drawing[6] and Brooking's map, but in greater detail from an anonymous wash-drawing of about 1750.[7]

It was a five-part composition with a narrow centrepiece connected to curly-gabled wings by ranges of three storeys plus dormers. The English building which it most resembles, in general massing, is Robert Hooke's Bethlem Hospital of 1675:[8] the Irish building which most resembles it is Palace Anne in Co Cork, built in about 1714. Hooke had some connexion with Ireland through the Percevals and Southwells, and may possibly have been more closely involved. The central pavilion at Trinity, *as drawn by Brooking*, seems to derive from that of the inner (courtyard) elevation of Les Invalides, and Hooke's French leanings are known. The other odd thing about the elevation is (if we can trust Brooking) the curious spacing of the windows. But since neither Dinely nor the anonymous artist of 70 years later show this, it was probably not so. All three artists differ in regard to the Flemish-gabled wings, agreeing only in making them two windows wide with a single window on top between the curly consoles. The mid-eighteenth-century artist has made it altogether more classical, perhaps a shade more classical than in fact it was, and the centrepiece lies outside the frame of his picture. No part of it now remains: all was swept away in the great rebuilding of 1752 onwards.

The four courts of Chancery, King's Bench, Exchequer and Common Pleas, which till the turn of the century had sat in the four corners of the Great Hall of Dublin Castle, henceforth for nigh 200 years roosted in makeshift quarters adjoining the South side of the nave of Christ Church. Though rebuilt in 1695 by Robinson, and again tinkered with in 1744, they never seem to have acquired any architectural character.* It is true that Sir William Brereton described them as 'very capacious,

---

* They are known, however, to have had an octagonal dome, which appears in a drawing by Francis Place (*IGSB* Jan-June 1978 p. 12) An early eighteenth-century plan of the Four Courts from the Surveyor-General's office survives (photostat in National Library).

and as useful as the Courts in England': but that was not saying much. The one surviving plan tells us little.

The Trinity College elevation was certainly the most imposing to be seen in central Dublin for some time to come, and, for its date, not unworthy of its purpose and position. Yet, notwithstanding its French affinities, it can hardly rank as architecture in touch with the taste of a court. A much closer connexion with the Invalides was shortly to show itself, under the direct inspiration of the Duke of Ormonde, whose court was, for the first time after a long interregnum, a true court, radiating ideas of civility and style.

The oldest surviving fully classical building in Ireland is the Royal Hospital at Kilmainham (figs 114, 115 and 116), about a mile and a half West of the city. From now on for at least two centuries at least half of the best architecture in the country is to be found in Dublin, which expanded with great rapidity in the quarter-century following 1660, and continued to expand for the next hundred years, from a population of perhaps 20,000 or 30,000 in 1660 (itself marking an increase of perhaps fivefold since 1600) to about 60,000 in 1685, and about 300,000 in 1860.

The Hospital was in a double sense one of the fruits of peace. Not only did settled conditions make building possible, but the cessation of war and the passage of time had thrown a large number of old soldiers on the mercy of the public purse. It had not escaped the notice of Ormonde and other members of his court who had been with Charles II in France, that the government of Louis XIV, being well aware that war would come again, knew that the morale of serving soldiers was powerfully affected by the prospect of what would be their lot should they, by surviving the hazards of war, find themselves facing the more protracted but no less painful prospects of poverty, sickness and old age or, as it was then called, 'impotence'. To meet this problem King Louis had built Les Invalides, one of the most splendid monuments of his reign, between 1670 and 1676.

'It is not to be doubted', says the first historian of the Hospital, 'but from the excellency of that design [i.e. Les Invalides] first sprung the notion of building the like in this kingdom, which was happily entertained at first by the . . . Earl of Granard . . . in or about the year 1675.'[9] The Viceroy Capel (Essex) who had been in Paris in 1667 also interested himself in the project. Two years later Ormonde, again Viceroy, was in a position to make representations to King Charles, and in 1679 the King's letter authorising it arrived, and Ormonde laid the first stone early in 1680. Within four years the building was well advanced. Chelsea followed suit in 1682.

William Robinson the architect had been Surveyor-General since 1670, when his appointment by patent was made under the viceroyalty of Lord Berkeley; but Dr Loeber suggests that he may in effect have come from England in succession to Ormonde's architect Captain John Morton who died in 1669. Dr Loeber has found no evidence of his activity before 1673.[10]

Our complete ignorance of Robinson's life before his appearance in 1670 leaves us guessing how much of the great conception of the Royal Hospital is his and his alone. His known *œuvre* runs to 19 items—many of them routine jobs it is true—and a dozen or so attributions. Three or four of these are of sufficient substance to prove that he was a fully competent architect, but we know already how large a part the desires, experience and knowledge of the client still played in the process of design.

The resemblances to Les Invalides may be stated in descending order of their significance thus:

1. The purpose of the building.
2. The adoption of a closed courtyard plan with arcaded covered walks corresponding to passages on the floors above.
3. The semicircular upwards curve over the chapel window which somewhat resembles the feature in the centre of the main front of Les Invalides.
4. The shaving off of the impost-mouldings of the arcades which occurs in both buildings on the inner faces of the piers.

Of these the first is obvious and need not be dwelt upon. The second is so widespread a practice (though not till then in Ireland except in the friaries) that it does not call for comment: it was the obvious thing to do (though it was not what Wren did at Chelsea). The last, which is a mere detail, could be dismissed as a coincidence and a matter lying within the province of the executant masons, and indeed it occurs again at Dr Steevens' Hospital and in a building 50 years later in Cork. Perhaps the third point of resemblance is, all things considered, the most suggestive.

The planning of the Royal Hospital does not call for comment except in the North range, where the great hall is centrally placed with three lobbies, under the pediment and tower, opening Northwards off one of its longer sides, flanked on the West by the house of the Master (who was later always the Commander-in-Chief) and on the East by the chapel, a little narrower and only a little shorter. The great courtyard is 210 feet square in the clear.

The building committee were by Order in Council of 27 February 1679 ordered to 'send for artists, workmen and other persons, and after receiving proposals from them to treat and agree' and so on, and immediately afterwards they in turn ordered Robinson to view the site (then part of the Phoenix Park), and 'a draught or design' to be prepared. Robinson soon 'returned a model. . . designed to receive . . . 300 men' together with very full proposals for the carrying on of the work.[11]

This account is doubtless foreshortened and in particular it omits any hints or directives which the architect may have been given in respect of the more ceremonious parts of the building. The placing end-to-end of the hall and chapel (not otherwise usual) may be influenced by Trinity College. The Robinsonian style seems to show in the tall hollow-moulded round-headed windows without imposts (deriving from Hugh May's work at Windsor), which are found elsewhere in his work, their heads filled with that curiously Victorian-looking tracery of tangent circles. Much smaller impostless round-headed features appear also at the Kilkenny Castle frontispiece, which like that of Kilmainham has a giant order of Corinthian pilasters: but as we have already seen we cannot be quite sure that the Kilkenny feature is his, nor of the date of its erection.

Two more features of the Royal Hospital call for notice: one looking backwards, the other looking forwards. We are told of 'part of the walls of the chapel [of the priory of the Knights Hospitallers] the stones whereof were taken down and carefully removed to the new Hospital, and wholly used in building the present Chapel of the same'[12] and in particular there is a rumour that the tracery in the upper part of the East window was re-used, and, more particularly still, it is asserted that the glass in the upper part was/is mediaeval. As nobody has seen the glass since it was taken out and crated for safety 40 years ago, we cannot comment on this except to observe that mediaeval Irish stained glass is of the utmost rarity and that in any case the window-head of the priory church is not likely to have been semicircular.

The other curious feature is the tower which shoots up through the roof of the pediment, and after passing through an octagonal stage, ends up as a spire furnished

114 Kilmainham, Co Dublin: the Royal Hospital. The four South windows of the Great Hall are visible. To the left is the house of the Commander-in-Chief, ex-officio Master of the Hospital, and above is the tower and spire added in 1701, but envisaged from the outset. The tracery in the tower windows is original: that in the lower windows probably not

115 Kilmainham: the Royal Hospital, plan. There was probably originally a staircase in the South-West corner similar to that in the South-East. The Master's House occupies the North-West corner, and in the early nineteenth century part of the open arcade was stolen to enlarge the Master's dining-room. To him that hath. . . .

116 Kilmainham: the Royal Hospital from the North-East. The large round-headed window of the chapel rises through the main cornice, and the first four round-headed windows on the North side belong to it also

114

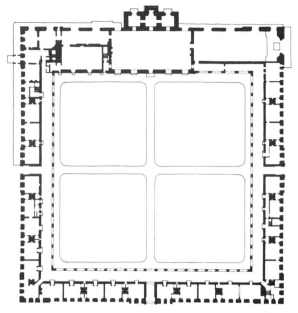

0 ⌊———⌋50 feet

115

116

with curious 'handles' like those on the lid of the mausoleum of Theodoric. James Gibbs is the architect usually thought to have been the first to commit this particular crime, at St Martin-in-the-Fields in London (1722–26), 'an act of insensibility' as Summerson calls it.[13] But here we have Robinson doing it as early as 1701, and the stump of the tower already protruded through the roof in 1698 when it was drawn by Francis Place. The very fine woodwork of the chapel was carved by James Tabary, an immigrant Huguenot craftsman, and will bear comparison with the best work of its time.★

We need not linger long over another institutional building from these years which is known from one of Brooking's little copperplates. This is the King's Hospital or Blew-Coat School, a nondescript and rather rustic building round three sides of a court, with a gate in a high wall and a clock-tower, dating from 1675. More regular, but considerably more gawky because more pretentious, in fact a prime example of *bürgerliches Manierismus*, was the Tholsel, successor to a long line of municipal headquarters, which went up in 1676 and lasted long enough to be engraved by James Malton. As drawn by Thomas Dinely in 1680[14] it had an extravagant top-knot in four stages, which, not surprisingly, had gone by the time Malton made his print in 1793. But it is recognizably the same building, and one of unusual ugliness: the sort of thing to be seen in any one of a dozen English provincial towns, such as, for example, Exeter. It would have looked very odd indeed if it had survived into modern Dublin. No doubt it would still have its admirers, and indeed, had it lasted so long, we would, paradoxically, feel obliged to preserve it for longer still.

★ The restoration of the Royal Hospital at Kilmainham was completed in 1985, since when it has been open to the public.

CHAPTER ELEVEN

Dublin: 1690–1757

There are no houses in Dublin which can be reliably dated to before 1725. On Rocque's map[1] of 1756 we can trace about 16 very large houses, five of them in St Stephen's Green, two in Great Britain Street (Parnell Street), two in Smithfield, and others in such places as Middle Abbey Street, Jervis Street, the Little Green, Crooked Staff (Ardee Street) and Montpelier Hill. Four or five of them have a plan apparently similar to that of 'Schomberg House' in London: with narrow shallow projections at the ends of their fronts. Such were, for example, two on Stephen's Green North, Kerry (Shelburne) House and another to the East of it, and one on Upper Capel Street.

The only house of this date to have survived into modern times was Molyneux House[2] in Peter Street, which I saw both inside and out before its destruction in 1942 or 1943 when I was, alas, too inexperienced to understand all I saw. Unlike the other houses it was free-standing like a country house, and indeed its plan with the large open-well staircase contained in the entrance hall was a common country house plan: and with its armorial doorcase, moulded sills, timber eaves-cornice and dormered mansard (whether original or not) it was just like a smallish country house of its date (1711), though its situation was, from the beginning, completely urban. Needless to say, it could have been and should have been saved. Houses of similar type and date survive at Youghal (the 'Red House') and Cork, where one was destroyed in recent years but another, opposite the School of Art, survives.

Among the larger houses there survived long enough to be recorded three examples of a type which we may conveniently call 'double-dutch billies'. In Stephen's Green West, at 30 Jervis Street and in Mill Street[3] there were houses presenting to the street a pair of curvilinear pedimented gables of the type known to architectural historians as 'Holborn' gables, and traditionally called in Dublin 'dutch billies', but with the front door central or nearly so.

Of the humbler, single-fronted houses, some had simple gables and others the dutch billy proper. The last pair of the latter kind to survive were in Longford Street (figs 117 and 118) and were destroyed in about 1960. The type was common in the Liberties until very recently, but not restricted to Dublin, since examples are known from Cork and Waterford, from Limerick where there was a whole street of them in 1845, and from Newry where some survived until very recently indeed.[4] The roofs were cruciform with purlins running at right-angles to the street and halved over the purlins of the intersecting roofs. The houses were cheaply built and tended to prop each other up, and generally shared one massive stack to each pair. Corner fireplaces were the rule. On the strength of a remark by the English visitor Charles Dibdin the younger in 1797[5] it has been suggested that corner fireplaces are specially Irish. But even a casual glance at London material of similar date shows that this is not so, though it is true that the corner fireplace had already appeared in late Irish tower-houses and their immediate successors.*

---

* e.g. Dungory (fig. 60) or the flankers of Kanturk.

117

117 and **118** Dublin: gable-fronted houses in Longford Street. The last such pair in Dublin, they were demolished in about 1955

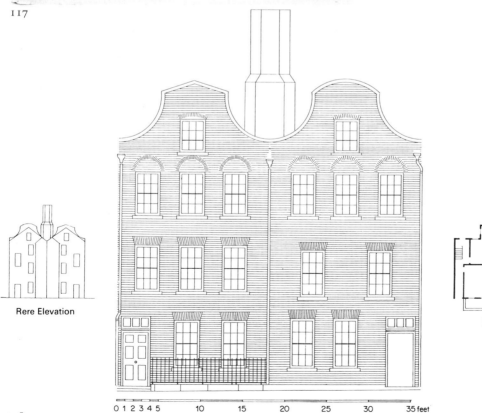

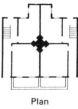

Rere Elevation

Plan

0 1 2 3 4 5   10   15   20   25   30   35 feet

118

119 Dublin: houses in Marrowbone Lane (nos. 73–78) as in 1948, now demolished. They, or some of them, may well have been of the late seventeenth century

120 Dublin: Poole Street, looking towards Braithwaite Street. Weavers' houses of the *c.* 1700 period. The cruciform roof-construction, held together by crossed purlins from gable to gable, is clearly seen. They are all now demolished

119

120

121 Dublin: The Brazen Head, sketch-plan. The plan of the left (Southern) half is taken at the ground floor level where there are two public rooms each the size of two bedrooms. The position of the fireplaces on the upper floors is shown dotted. The right (Northern) half of the plan is in principle valid for all three floors, though now much cut about at ground floor level

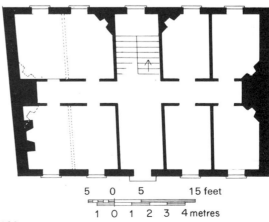

121

122 Charles Fort, Kinsale, Co Cork, from the air. Built from 1671 onwards by William Robinson in collaboration with Lord Ossory and James Archer, most of the barrack etc buildings within the fort are of the eighteenth century

123 Celbridge School, Co Kildare: the gateway from outside the court. The school was built under the will of Speaker William Conolly (ob. 1729) but probably to the design of Thomas Burgh who died in 1730

122

123

These are the houses which Curran had in mind when he wrote of 'the depressing cloud of Anglo-Dutch and Hanoverian taste ... the debased mould into which the town was setting [sic] ... irregular gables stepped or topped with graceless triangles or the feeblest of baroque curves fall[ing] short of the picturesque even in fallacious retrospect'.[6] He goes on to inveigh against what he calls 'the impoverished zone of nordic building stretching from ... Potsdam to Dublin'. These are harsh words, loaded with animus uncharacteristic of their author, who would, I cannot help feeling, wish to soften them now that nothing but a few pitiful fragments remain of something once so characteristic and so common.*

There is another building, neither exactly private nor yet exactly public, which has hitherto escaped serious notice, though a deal of romantic conjecture has been lavished upon it. It would have been, and it was, more profitable to examine the fabric of the Brazen Head in Bridge Street (fig. 121) than to speculate about its age. Its position in the mediaeval town-plan and its situation at the back of a deep forecourt are strongly suggestive of great antiquity. On close scrutiny it proves to be a purpose-built hotel of the very early eighteenth century, with a plan which admits of the ground floor being given up to public rooms while ensuring that all but two of the eight bedrooms on each floor above have their own fireplaces. History does not relate how the less fortunate were warmed: perhaps they merely paid less.

The surviving detail, notably on the staircase, suggests that it may be as early as the first or second decade of the century. The material is brick, and the silhouette, with a stack in each end-gable and two in the back wall, is not unlike that of some small country houses, for example Corbally Co Kildare.[7]

The two great architectural names of the pre-Palladian era are those of Sir William Robinson and Colonel Thomas Burgh, both of whom held the office of Surveyor-General: Robinson from 1671 to 1700 (from 1684 jointly with William Molyneux) and Burgh from 1700 until his death in 1730. Robinson had the more chequered and interesting career, but his buildings, with the signal exception of the Royal Hospital already treated of, are of less interest. Dr Loeber[8] has traced much of the ups and downs of his fortunes, and more doubtless remains to be found out. One of his largest jobs was Charles Fort in Kinsale (fig. 122). Earthen forts are not architecture, but in proportion as they come to be cladded in masonry, as in the era of Vauban and Coehorn they often were, they approach the condition of architecture, and so it was at Kinsale. Robinson also prepared, in 1684, plans for the rebuilding of Dublin Castle, including an 11-bay range with ground-floor arcading to go in the Eastern half of the South range of the yard. This was completed (by Molyneux) in 1688 and set the style for the subsequent treatment of the state apartment side of the courtyard.

Dr Loeber conjectures that Robinson may have had a hand in the Trinity College front already dealt with: if so it would suggest that he had no style of his own but was ready to assume any garment which was fashionable. Before the end of the century he had produced a model for the East window of St Mary's Church and probably designed the church as a whole. The window is a fine rich piece of baroque design with French overtones which remind us that he had travelled on the Continent. The Barracks at Ballyshannon, dated 1700, has been attributed to him and may well have been designed by him in his official capacity: it still survives though changed in use. After 1703 he was in more or less permanent disgrace but his last

---

* So common, indeed, that they appear in virtually every topographical sketch or print set in Dublin or any large town. See below, p. 208n.

work, the charming little Marsh's Library close by St Patrick's Cathedral, dates from that year. He died, apparently in England, in 1712.[9]

Thomas Burgh came of a Co Kildare landed family and was a soldier, like many another architect of his time; and like many another soldier, his father was a bishop. He was born in 1670.[10] His first recorded building is the enormous Royal Barracks (now Collins Barracks) begun in 1701. The middle square which was the earliest has now gone, but the squares to East and West were built during Burgh's lifetime and presumably by him. The Custom House which he designed in 1707 was a conventional enough building[11] of 15 bays with a breakfront, pediment, hipped roof with dormers and a central arcade: it disappeared soon after the building of its illustrious successor in 1781-91. His next building was Trinity Library of which we shall presently treat. He is credited with the design of St Werburgh's, one of four or five new churches put up at about the same time (1715). But Dr Elisabeth Kieven has shown reason[12] to question whether the front at least of this church, which still stands, may not be part of the fruit of the brief visit to Ireland in 1718 of Alessandro Galilei.

Dr Steevens' Hospital, which Burgh planned first in 1713 but which was not begun till five years later and took 12 years to finish, is essentially a scaled-down version of Robinson's Royal Hospital with a façade inspired by Pratt's Clarendon House in London: a building of great charm and still perfectly suitable for its original function, which it continues to discharge. It is more homely than its grander forebear, and its more picturesque feature, the squinches which span the corners of the arcaded courtyard, are late nineteenth-century additions inserted with a sanitary purpose in mind.[13]

Burgh wrote a book on surveying published in 1724, and his posthumous opus, the Collegiate School at Celbridge has, especially in its triple gateway, the boldness and strength typical of his work (fig. 123).

The Library of Trinity College, however, is Burgh's undisputed masterpiece.[14] This library and the Parliament House designed by Pearce are the only buildings of the very first magnitude to be erected in Dublin during the first half of the century. The library is a gigantic conception, and even today, when it is companioned by buildings comparable to it in scale, it strikes a heroic note (fig. 124). How much more so it must have seemed when new we can best judge by the way in which, in Tudor's print of 1753, it towers over the then Provost's House at the end of the South range.

It has been altered since its first building in two principal ways. The open arcade on the ground floor which was designed, following the example of Wren at Trinity College, Cambridge, to insulate the books from damp, was filled in during the late nineteenth century to provide more shelf-space. Before that it was open, both to the square to the North, and to the Fellows' Garden to the South, though in contrast to Trinity, Cambridge, there was a dividing-wall separating the two arcades completely from each other. That to the South must always have been the more attractive, and now that the Fellows' Garden has been replaced by the modern Arts building and Fellows' Square the library is again seen to great advantage, though something has been lost.

The other principal alteration was made when in 1858-60 Deane and Woodward replaced the high flat ceiling with a semicircular tunnel-vault of timber with supporting timber tunnel-vaults over the aisles, quite in the Burgundian manner. Whatever incongruity this may have embodied when new, it has long since been digested as completely as Palladio's work to the Vicenza basilica or Wykeham's work at Winchester.

124 Dublin: the interior of Trinity College Library. The lower part is by Thomas Burgh 1712-32, the upper part by Benjamin Woodward, 1856-61

This library is perhaps the first instance of that passion for the gigantic which, to some people's surprise, shows itself in Ireland from time to time. Though Ireland is a small country, there is plenty of room in most parts of it, and sometimes the labour has been cheap. But though the scale of the whole is grand, one notices with surprise that the channelled ashlar courses of the basement rise a bare ten inches each.

We can hardly doubt that the greatest disappointment of Burgh's architectural career came when, after holding the office of Surveyor-General for 28 years, he was passed over for the design of the new Parliament House. He may already have been ailing, for he died within two years: but whether this was cause or effect we shall probably never know. Initially at least he was in the running, for he was asked to provide a plan, and to the end he remained a member of the building committee.

But suddenly, in February 1727, a new figure appears upon the scene: Edward Lovett Pearce, returned, after a disputed election, as Member for the borough of Ratoath. Little more than a year later his plans had been approved by the King, the Viceroy Carteret and the Parliament itself. Early in 1729 the first stone was laid by Speaker Conolly.

Pearce[15] was a creature of an altogether different kind from any which had till then appeared upon the Irish scene. He was probably only about 30 in 1729, but he had spent about three years travelling in Italy and France, purposefully, as a student of architecture. During his Italian period he was in close touch with Alessandro Galilei, and clearly also acting on behalf of Speaker Conolly, whose great house of Castletown, designed by Galilei, was by 1722 already under construction.

He had many advantages, both natural and acquired. His lineage on his mother's side included a Lord Mayor of Dublin and a clan chief of the O'Mores. His father, General Edward Pearce, was first cousin to Vanbrugh, under whose tutelage Pearce himself came after his father's death in 1715. During the early 1720s he was in close touch with the Burlington circle of architects and leaders of taste. Finally, and not least important, he was related by cousinhood to many of the foremost families who were involved in building, either officially or on their own account, both in Dublin and in the provinces. And, for reasons at which we can only guess, he had the old Speaker in his pocket.

Pearce's career was indeed meteoric. Wherever his childhood and youth were spent (of which we have no knowledge) he is first traceable in Dublin late in 1726, and in December 1733 he died. In those seven short years most of his commissions must have been proceeding simultaneously or nearly so: 12 or 13 which are certain or all-but-certain attributions, and a similar number of attributions ranging from the probable to the possible. By the time of his premature death he had transformed the face of architecture in Ireland.

The Parliament House is a very original building (figs 125 and 126). In part it was the programme which made it so, because never before had a plan been tailored to fit a bicameral legislature. It consists essentially of the houses of Commons and of Lords, placed in an informal relationship to one another, with a corridor surrounding the Commons' chamber on three sides, anterooms protecting both chambers, committee-rooms clustering the periphery, and a grand colonnaded atrium by way of screen and frontispiece. The length of the street façade is 154 feet, but behind this it spreads wider.

There seem to be no grounds for supposing that the asymmetry of the plan was in any way dictated by the limitations of the ground then available. It appears much more likely that the old Speaker was at Pearce's elbow, and that it was his idea to put the Commons with its octagonal dome★ in the centre of the plan and set the Lords in a subordinate position to one side. Conolly was immensely rich and could have bought up a good many lords—indeed he probably had—and his own house was 140 feet long, exclusive of the wings which Pearce was presently to add to it.

Opposed to one another as the Vanbrughian and Palladian schools may have been in England, Pearce's inheritance came from both, and both can be traced in his work. From Vanbrugh comes the use of corridors in the plan (and corridors, especially those consisting of a sequence of domed squares, were to become one of Pearce's trademarks): from Vanbrugh also the bold advance and recession of the front, that play of masses later so much admired by Robert Adam under the name of 'movement'. From Burlington and his Palladian circle comes the great stepped Pantheon dome, like that of Chiswick blown up to eight times the volume, the apse-ended rooms recalling Burlington's studies of the Roman baths and villas, and the delight in a giant order supporting an unbroken entablature.

It is hard to be sure how much the colonnaded front owes to Palladio's Villa Santa Sofia at Pedemonte or to the Palais Bourbon in Paris, both of which Pearce will have had the opportunity to see. His copiously annotated copy of Palladio has no notes on the pages relating to the Villa Santa Sofia. The combined arch and columnar pedimented features at each end† are like gigantic doorcases, and were adopted by Roger Morris a few years later for the Palladian bridge at Wilton, so widely imitated, while the colonnade as a whole was undoubtedly the inspiration for Smirke's forecourt at the British Museum a century afterwards.‡

The House of Lords is the most important of the interiors to survive. Divided into 'narthex', 'nave' and apse, it has a church-like plan not too far removed from that of the chapel at Blenheim or that of St Mary-le-Strand, but of course top-lit owing to its position in the plan. It has a giant order of Corinthian pilasters and a subsidiary Ionic order, in the San Giorgio Maggiore rather than the Redentore relationship (with the giant order on a high pedestal.) Most curiously, the ornaments between the four pairs of pilaster-caps are disposed in a chiasmus: each ornament answering to the one diagonally opposite to it.§

No other official work in Dublin has documentary attribution to Pearce, but it is as certain as anything can be that he designed the South-Eastern range in Upper Castle Yard, replacing Robinson's building from which it borrowed the appearance, though not I think the materials, of the ground-floor arcade. This building now exists in a modern reproduction, having been accidentally burnt in 1941. The most obviously Pearcean parts are the garden front and the central corridor on the first floor, a sequence of domes very similar to those of the Parliament House.

On the opposite (North) side of Upper Castle Yard is a composition of great charm the authorship and date of which remain conjectural. The whole of Upper Castle Yard was rebuilt during the first half of the century, in brick with stone

---

★ Was it a mere coincidence that H. E. Goodridge's competition design for the London Houses of Parliament in 1835 had an octagonal House of Commons (Colvin, 1978, p. 351)? Probably.

† They come from Scamozzi.

‡ Smirke's father drew the figures in the large Malton engraving of the forecourt of the Parliament House (*JRSAI*, XXXV, 1905, pp. 365-6).

§ Dr McParland has pointed out the resemblance between the section of the House of Lords and that of the Temple of Venus and Rome as given in Palladio, *IV Libri* IV Plate XXIII, which is indeed striking. In other ways the House of Lords anticipates the interior of George Dance the younger's All Hallows London Wall.

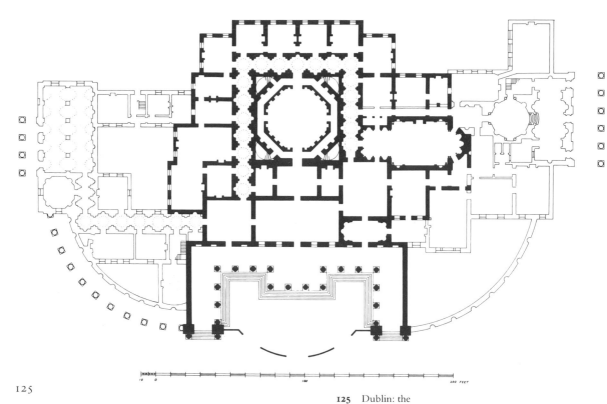

125

126

125 Dublin: the Parliament House as it was before the fire of 1792 which destroyed the House of Commons. The House was rebuilt as a circle within the square contained by the corridor, but demolished as part of the changes consequent on the Union of 1800. The parts to the East (right, Lords) and to the West (left, Commons) were added in the 1780s by Gandon (Lords) and Park and others (Commons). Pearce's work of 1729 is shown in black, the additions in outline. Most of the East and West additions remains much as it is shown here, as does Pearce's corridor, the committee-rooms North of it, and, most splendidly of all, the House of Lords

126 Dublin: the old Parliament House. The House of Lords, the most important interior to survive from Pearce's building of 1729. It later became the Court of Proprietors of the Bank of Ireland

dressings, mostly in a charateristic style marked by segmental-headed windows with keystones, which seem to derive from the East front of the Louvre (by Le Vau, Le Brun and Perrault) and crop up also in many country houses built near Dublin in the first quarter of the century. The centrepiece of the North side, between two handsome baroque gateways, is a composition consisting of a transcription of Lord Pembroke's villa in Whitehall (by Lord Pembroke himself?) with, on top of it, an octagonal tower and cupola taken out of William Kent's *Designs of Inigo Jones* (1727). By a curious coincidence the replacement, in the nineteenth century, of the hipped roof with an attic storey, has made the resemblance to Lord Pembroke's villa more complete than it originally was.

Would Pearce, whom we know to have been an architect capable of original thought, have put up such a building? We must remind ourselves that he was a contemporary of Bach and Handel whose works abound in 'borrowings', and that the Palladian bridge mentioned a few lines back had been copied twice in England alone before the century was out. More to our purpose, he himself built in Henrietta Street Dublin two adjoining houses[16] one of which, No 9, was, and remains, both inside and out, an extremely close transcription of the house built by Lord Burlington in Great Burlington Street, London[17] (later No 30 Old Burlington Street) for Lord Mountrath, only ten years earlier. This house, for Pearce's cousin Thomas Carter the Master of the Rolls, and its neighbour Mountjoy (Blessington) House (which has been altered), are the only houses in Dublin certainly by Pearce, though Drumcondra (All Hallows' College) for Marmaduke Coghill is now, owing to the city's growth, in the suburbs.

In County Dublin his scheme for palladianising Stillorgan House was frustrated by his early death; but the grotto of seven domed chambers which he designed for its garden still survives, and so does the obelisk on a rock-work base, clearly influenced by Bernini, and originally intended as the mausoleum of his friends the Allen family on whose estate he lived (fig. 108).

These topics carry us towards the territory of the country house which belongs to the next chapter. Pearce's only Dublin work which remains to be noted is the theatre in Aungier Street (really in Longford Street) which, like the Parliament House, was unfinished at his death.[18] We know from Rocque's map that it was about 80 feet wide by 96 feet deep, and from a newspaper advertisement of 1767 that in that year it was demolished and the materials of its portico sold.

In both the public and the private sphere Pearce was assisted by Richard Cassels or Castle,[19] who was probably an older man, born in Hesse Kassel and reared in a school of Franco-Dutch Palladianism from which he seems to have passed into the Burlington circle. Whether Pearce, or Sir Gustavus Hume, or both together, brought him to Ireland is uncertain: what is beyond doubt is that he worked with Pearce and was warmly recommended by him, and that as a result of this, and of his own abilities, he inherited Pearce's practice both in public architecture and private. He did not, however, succeed Pearce in the Surveyor-Generalship, which in the hands of Pearce's successors became divorced from the practice of architecture. And, with the exception of work in Trinity College, the public sector became, for the two or three decades after Pearce's death, of less importance than that of building for private clients.

Until about 20 years ago the attributions of Irish buildings of this period to named architects were few, and some were at best uncertain, at worst downright fallacious. It is still the case that research has failed to throw up an architectural personality comparable to Pearce, except Cassels who was already more or less familiar, and who is in any case a less considerable figure. Cassels was the subject of an informative magazine article in 1793, whereas Pearce was rediscovered only in the twentieth century, and that by gradual stages from 1927 to 1964. Pearce is unquestionably the Inigo Jones of Ireland: he is also Ireland's Burlington. To these roles Cassels played, respectively, those of John Webb and Henry Flitcroft. Pearce had more work than he could handle, and Cassels got the benefit of this.

In such a situation, and in the all too common absence of documentary evidence, there is a natural temptation to give all the really first-class buildings to Pearce and distribute the rest to Cassels and a few un-named followers. This temptation is particularly strong in the matter of country houses. The alternative, to postulate an un-named architect of Pearcean attainments who designed only one or two houses in the provinces, may be thought to raise even greater difficulties. So does the concept of 'action at a distance', in which an architect's hand seems to be traceable though his physical presence cannot probably be presumed.

The first independent work of Cassels in Dublin is the Printing House in Trinity College, a little building with a Doric temple-front. It is unlike the rest of Cassels's work in having a true free-standing portico: his other buildings have frontispieces of engaged columns or pilasters planted on to the solid block, and more often than not raised over a basement. For this reason, and for others including the existence of a not dissimilar design by Pearce for a garden-temple, we cannot rule out the possibility that it is in part a work by Pearce, particularly as it was built in the year following his death, and it is probable that the donor of the building, John Stearne, Bishop of Clogher, had consulted Pearce.[20]. Till recently it housed the press, but it has lately been sympathetically adapted for other uses.

Cassels built also a bell-tower of baroque character in the centre of Trinity: it disappeared in the 1780s. Even more short-lived was the dining hall which he began in 1741: by 1744 it was in trouble, by 1747 collapsing, and by 1758 collapsed altogether. (It was, of course, on made ground.) It is all the more surprising that its successor, which vaguely resembles it, incorporates some of its materials, and was contrived in about 1760 by the mason-designer Hugh Darley, shows no sign of settlement whatever.[21] It has been well restored after a fire in 1984.

Cassels's most important Dublin buildings are two large private houses and a hospital. Tyrone House, in Marlborough Street on the North Side, built in about 1740 for Sir Marcus Beresford, Baron and later Earl of Tyrone, still stands, though altered. In a detached situation, it is in effect a country house and, before its entrance-front was remodelled in about 1835, closely resembled several of its author's country mansions, having his sign-manual of a Venetian window surmounted by a circular niche or blind oculus.

Leinster House, on the edge of Molesworth Fields, is even more obviously a country house in town.[22] It was, originally, prefaced by a forecourt closely similar to, and doubtless inspired by, that of Burlington House in London. Both have since been altered. Like Castletown it has a two-storey entrance-hall traversed at its inner end, and on both levels, by the central corridor, with the main staircase in a compartment beside it. The main front is of Ardbraccan limestone, an early use of this stone in Dublin and the plainer but warmer East front of granite. Like Castletown and the Parliament House and some other buildings to come, it is 140 feet long. It dates from 1745–7. Since about 1923 it has housed, not altogether happily, the Irish parliament.*

---

*The North rooms, with their columnar screens and projecting bow, had descendants later in the century at Emo (by Gandon) and later still at Ballyfin (by Richard Morrison). See McParland in *Country Life*, Sept. 13 1973, pp. 703–4, and in vol. CLV.

127

127 Dublin, Upper Castle Yard: buildings of the early eighteenth century based on English Palladian originals (Lord Pembroke's Villa in Whitehall by Roger Morris and a cupola illustrated in William Kent's *Designs of Inigo Jones*, 1727) and possibly by Sir Edward Lovett Pearce, though this attribution lacks documentary support

128 Stillorgan, Co Dublin: the obelisk by Sir Edward Pearce, designed as a mausoleum for the Allen family and built *c.* 1732

128

At the end of his life Cassels built, for Dr Bartholomew Mosse, the Lying-in Hospital colloquially known, for reasons to be given later, as the 'Rotunda'. This design is much like that of Leinster House, save that the whole ground floor is of channelled ashlar, the central intercolumniation is widened to take a Venetian window, and on top of all a slender tower with an octagonal lantern and cupola.

At the back of a low entrance hall is a transverse vaulted corridor, repeated on all floors, and behind this, centrally, the staircase. Over the entrance-hall the chapel, with its magnificent baroque plasterwork, rises through two storeys. With many later additions, the hospital remains in use for its original purpose. Some account of its role in the development and social life of the capital will be found elsewhere.

The Rotunda was still on the drawing-board when Cassels died, at Carton, early in 1751, and the execution was in the hands of his pupil John Ensor. Though Dr Mosse himself died in the year in which the Hospital opened, 1757, the enterprise prospered and we shall hear more of it.[23]

The talents of Cassels lay in consolidation rather than in the breaking of new ground. He was involved with hydraulic matters: he left a manuscript on 'artificial navigation' and a printed work on the Dublin water-supply. Little is known of his music-hall in Fishamble Street in which the first performance of *Messiah* took place, and his small house, No. 85 St Stephen's Green, for Hugh Montgomery, is chiefly remarkable for the splendour of its internal decoration. There is more to be said about his country houses, which make up, by bulk, the greater part of his output.*

If the Rotunda, but for its cupola, looked like a large country house, the slightly earlier St Patrick's Hospital, founded in 1746–8 under the will of Jonathan Swift, looks like a medium-sized house; and this, in part is what it was. Like most schools, hospitals and similar institutions of the time, it consists primarily of a house for the resident head, doubling as the administrative block. But here the front block is only half the depth of that of the Rotunda, the corridor is not medial but at the back, the staircase is contained in a semicircular central bow, and the patients are accommodated in two parallel wings running backwards from the ends.[24]

The architect of Swift's Hospital, George Semple, has another claim to distinction. This was the design and construction, in 1753–5, of Essex Bridge. Semple united practical experience with the readiness to absorb new ways. He consulted Labelye, the Swiss designer of Westminster Bridge, and he both procured the latest technical manuals from Paris and digested their contents. In consequence his bridge, which in its elevations was closely modelled on that of Westminster, was constructed by the use of coffer-dams, instead of the method then and for some time afterwards more usually used, of sinking the piers in caissons. The bridge was a great success, and Semple was so proud of it that he wrote a book[25] about it, and about building in water generally. He or one of his relatives is credited with building the great bridge at Graignamanagh in Co Kilkenny a few years later (fig. 241).

Half a dozen new churches, all for the established (Protestant) church, were built in Dublin during the first half of the century. St Werburgh's we have already noticed briefly. St Ann's was built in 1720 to the design of Isaac Wills, in the new residential quarter of Molesworth Fields. These and others were of the standard Protestant type: rectangles with galleries on three sides and a short sanctuary to the East. The fronts of these two, by contrast, were of strictly Roman derivation, after Vignola's Gesù and its successors with the addition (in intention at least) of towers. The past tense must

---

*The Weavers' Hall in the Coombe, of about 1745 and demolished about 30 years ago, may perhaps have been by Cassels, or perhaps by Joseph Jarratt (see p. 285).

129 Dublin, Leinster House: plan, after the plan in *Georgian Society Records* IV 1912. Essentially a country-house plan, it is closely related to that of Castletown of some 20 years earlier. The bow in the Northern rooms (on both principal floors) is original, but the upper room (now the Senate chamber) was redecorated by James Wyatt

130 Dublin, Trinity College: the Provost's House. The saloon which occupies the whole of the first floor front

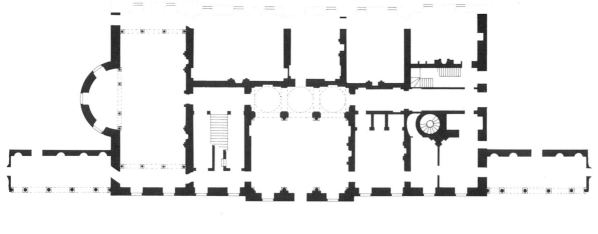

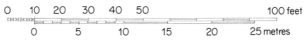

129

130

be used because that of St Ann's was never finished and was replaced in 1868, while of St Werburgh's the lower part only remains. The lower part is all that remains also of St Nicholas Within, an earlier (1707) and simpler version of the same theme.

After a lull in the mid-century, two more Dublin churches were built which call for notice: St Thomas's (begun 1758) and St Catherine's (begun 1769), both by the mysterious John Smyth. They are strangely contrasted: St Catherine's in the old West end of the city, and St Thomas's in the newly-developed and then affluent Eastern sector. Both are (or were because St Thomas's has gone) of the standard aisled and galleried plan with the difference that whereas St Catherine's has a superimposed order of columns carrying a central barrel-vault, St Thomas's had a flat compartmented ceiling spanning from wall to wall. Externally St Thomas's, which stood end-on to the street, displayed (or rather was intended to display because it was never finished) an elevation transcribed from Palladio's Redentore in Venice, whereas St Catherine's stands broadside-on and has a massive elevation which, with its segment-headed lower windows and its undulated aprons hanging from the sills of those above, harks back to the age of Wren or at least to that of Smith of Warwick. St Catherine's was intended to have a West tower, but this never got very far. The completion of churches according to plan was not a matter of very high priority in eighteenth-century Dublin.[26]

It was otherwise with secular buildings, most notably the rebuilding of the West front of Trinity College. In October 1751 the College petitioned Parliament for help in a large-scale reconstruction, and £27,000 had been spent within seven years. The building was, of course, right under the noses of the Parliament-men; and, if the interests of the College and of the Irish Parliament were not completely identical, they were nearly so, more especially as any unexpended revenue was remitted to England. To avoid this they preferred to spend it on their own doorstep.

The result was to house Trinity more grandly than any college in either of the English universities. The design of the West front has long been attributed, on the strength of what seemed adequate evidence, to the English architects Henry Keene and John Sanderson. But Dr McParland has now established[27] that another English architect, the amateur Theodore Jacobsen, must be credited with it. He had already designed the Foundling Hospital in Coram's Fields, Bloomsbury, which does not resemble Trinity in any way. But if at the Founding Hospital Jacobsen leaned on Kent, at Trinity he was clearly indebted to Colen Campbell, and in particular to the third design for Wanstead House, published in *Vitruvius Britannicus* volume III (1725). from which come the end-pavilions with their Venetian windows and attics above the cornice. The one feature which is alien to English Palladianism, the prominent role played by the giant swags over the Venetian windows, harks back to the manner of Wren.*

As first intended, the resemblance to Wanstead (in its third version) was even closer, for both pavilions were to be crowned with cupolas, and that to the North was even erected. Till very recently its 'ghost' was still to be seen from above. But by 1755 Hugh Darley, the master-mason in charge of the work, was reporting that the design had been criticised by 'a gentleman who has lately taken the tour of Europe and is allowed to have made very Judicious observations in the Architectonic way.'[28] This gentleman, whose identity is unknown, objected to the cupolas on the ends and

---

* In a curiously mannerist way, the ashlar of the basement is channelled where recessed and smooth where salient: the opposite of what one would expect. Jacobsen, Keene and Saunderson, or Darley?

also to the much more massive cupola intended for the centre, on the grounds that such features were 'no where to be met with in Italy in such buildings'. He also suggested changes to the central feature of the front, and these apparently were adopted. Though the massive vaulting for the central cupola remains at ground-floor level, its upward continuation had been taken down by 1758 and the fine large room known as the Regent House put in its place.

The weak point of the West front is the indeterminacy of the intervals between the pilasters, and, in the absence of drawings, we cannot be sure whether to blame this on Jacobsen's original design, or on the meddling of the returned traveller. The design was continued in plainer form round the new large court which presently became known as Parliament Square and later in the century was terminated by the pair of Chambers buildings. Parliament Square is, like St Patrick's, and for obvious reasons, a much loved building as well as being one of the key structures in the anatomy of Dublin. Like the Parliament House which it faces, it is of mountain granite with portland stone dressings.

Before it was finished the Provost of the College had set about rehousing himself in suitable style, and in so doing brought into being the most perfect house in Dublin (figs 130, 131 and 132).[29] The progressive refinement of manners towards the second half of the century could hardly be better exemplified than by the succession of Francis Andrews as Provost in 1758. His predecessor Richard Baldwin, who reigned from 1717 for 41 years, was a 'character', autocratic and not conspicuously learned, prepared to lead in person his undergraduates in their traditional and bloody battles against the butchers of the city. The polished Andrews, on the other hand, was a courtier, a parliamentary politician, a friend of dukes (and especially of the Duke of Bedford, Viceroy from 1756 to 1757), and had travelled in Italy. Was he, perhaps, the architectural critic of the West front?

The main elevation of the house is transcribed from Palladio by way of General Wade's house in London which was by Burlington. Wings have been added, which need not detain us. But the internal arrangements bear no resemblance whatever to the Burlington building, and are original and accomplished to the highest degree. Who, then, designed the interior? John Smyth (of St Thomas's and St Catherine's churches) was certainly paid £22 15s. 0d. for a plan for it in 1759. But this does not seem to be enough, nor does Smyth seem otherwise to be quite a good enough architect. Dr McParland has found two further payments both of £108 6s. 8d. Irish, which may, he hints, be one and the same payment (equivalent to £100 British); one of them is to 'the architect' and one of them is to 'Mr Keen'. Dr McParland is too scrupulous a scholar to jump to the obvious conclusion: but we may do so if we wish.

The house is designed with remarkable thoroughness, especially as to its interior. This seems to call for a talent of a higher order than, perhaps unjustly, we imagine Smyth to have had. The progression from the rather low, dark entrance-hall, via the elongated octagonal staircase to the two-tier upstairs lobby, and thence into the magnificent saloon, is difficult to match in any house of the size, in Ireland or in England, and the attention to detail in such parts as the secondary staircase is exceptional also. The balance between disciplined form and decorative fantasy is perfectly struck; and this is rare.

On the other hand two aspects of the house weaken the case for an English architect. One is the extremely conservative, not to say archaic, flavour of the whole. This is perhaps most noticeable in Timothy Turner's ironwork: but it runs right through the building, and if we did not know its date we could easily believe it to be

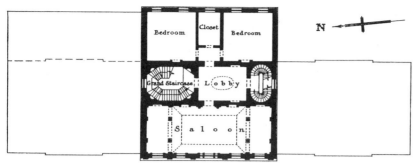

FIRST FLOOR

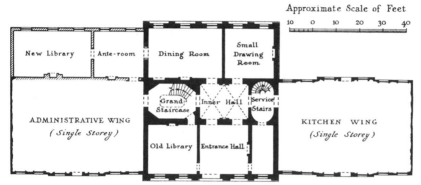

GROVND FLOOR

131

131 Dublin: the Provost's House, Trinity College, plan of ground and first floors. The probable designer of the interior arrangements is Henry Keene, John Smyth probably the executant architect. The very formal treatment of the upper central lobby was already a feature of Irish country houses from Bellamont Forest onwards

132 Dublin: the Provost's House, Trinity College, 1759, the elevation after Lord Burlington, in turn copying a drawing of Palladio in his possession. There were formerly at least three executed versions (none of them in Italy). Those in London and Potsdam have disappeared, and only the Dublin one survives. The interior is of the utmost splendour and still properly used and maintained

132

of 1730. The other is that, as we shall see when we come to consider the country houses of Pearce and Cassels, central upstairs lobbies of strongly architectural character were already an established Irish feature. It may be, of course, that such a feature was already so well established that, as later in Charlemont House and later still at Castle Coole, an English architect would know this and judge it an appropriate feature for an Irish house. If Andrews specified it, his architect would no doubt, whether English or Irish, incorporate it. But here it is so essential to the plan that it is impossible to believe that it was not, in fact, the starting-point of that plan.

The Provost's House is now the only house of its size and splendour in Dublin or any other Irish town still in occupation as a house: a circumstance of unique felicity. It was, of course, always a special case. There were already, as we have seen, a few other houses which were set-pieces, such as Tyrone, Leinster and Clanwilliam, and more were to come, such as Charlemont (begun about 1764), the Whaley house at 86 St Stephen's Green (about 1765), Ely House (1770), Powerscourt (1773), Belvedere (1785) and Aldborough (1796). But the usual Dublin house, including some very large examples built in Henrietta Street in the 1730s and 1740s and in St Stephen's Green, North, in the 1770s, fitted unobtrusively into the street pattern and had no external decoration other than the doorcase and its attendant fittings. They have a family resemblance to London houses of the same period, but differ from them in a number of detailed ways. The great divergence, however, between London and Dublin was to come in the suburban developments of the first half of the following century.

The designers of these Dublin town houses were usually those who risked their money in building them: master-builders, business-men, bankers and the occasional grandee. For example, Nos 2–5 Henrietta Street were built by the banker Nathaniel Clements, No. 5 (now No. 7) for his own use, the rest as speculation. We shall presently meet Clements as a country-house architect: at this stage he was a banker and Member of Parliament. No doubt such men as John and George Ensor were at hand to help with the mechanical parts of the business, as well as building houses on their own account. John Ensor was assistant to Cassels, and to some extent inherited his practice.

There were many possible combinations of interest in the building of a house or small group of houses. If the money-men sometimes turned architect, the master-builders also engaged in speculation, either on their own or in partnership with others including sometimes the ground-landlord. The careers of the two Ensor brothers diverged significantly.[30] George was a clerk of works in the Surveyor-General's office from 1744 till 1751, won a prize for small house designs at the Dublin Society in 1745 (Cassels being the judge), designed the church of St John Fishamble Street, and in 1766 built a couple of houses in Merrion Square. John seems to have been busy earlier on the speculative side, laying out for Dr Mosse what later became Rutland (later still Parnell) Square East, building houses there and in St Stephen's Green and Hume Street, laying out Merrion Square North for Fitzwilliam of Merrion, and Gardiner's Row for Luke Gardiner, and in 1764 building the Rotunda which soon gave its name to the hospital. In 1752 he seems to have overplayed his hand, for we find him being committed to Newgate by the House of Commons for 'gross prevarication' in the matter of the barracks of Carrick-on-Shannon for which he was contractor.[31] None of our present-day speculators has yet landed in jail, though when they fall out with one another they are sometimes found in court.

The names of Darley and Semple have already been mentioned. These were both dynasties well represented in the building and allied trades for several generations:

initially as stonecutters and quarry owners (in the case of the Darleys) and carpenters, bricklayers, plasterers in the case of the Semples, and latterly as full-blown architects. Members of both worked on the Provost's House. There were other similar families of less note. The Ensors retired from trade and set up as country gentry in Co Armagh.[32]

Cavendish Street (later Row) which John Ensor laid out, was not at first designated, nor even perhaps conceived, as part of a square, being called simply the 'New Gardens'. The wide street to the South of it, made by Luke Gardiner in the late 1740s, was a residential mall rather than a street for traffic: a sort of elongated square. On the South side, St Stephen's Green already resembled a 'square', though much larger and somewhat less regular. So the 'square' did not arrive suddenly in Dublin as an innovation, still less an importation, but rather came upon the scene almost by stealth. Merrion Square (1762) is the first of the squares to be planned as such by name.[33]

This semi-conscious planning was done by the estate-proprietors themselves, sometimes in collaboration with one another, and after 1758 with the active participation and guidance of the Wide Streets Commissioners. The planning of the individual houses, which were mostly on a very ample scale, was in general a matter of following common form: it is noticeable, for example, that by the mid-1750s many houses had semi-circular bows at the back, both to improve the lighting and to give interest to the plan. Many, especially at this period, are richly decorated with the rococo plasterwork which in Dublin and in the hands of such masters as Robert West, became an art-form in its own right, and deserves much more space than can here be given to it.[34]

In 1753, three years before Rocque's map and five years before the Wide Streets Commissioners, George Faulkner issued proposals for a work to be entitled *Vitruvius Hibernicus*, to contain 'the plans, elevations and sections of the most regular and elegant buildings, both public and private, in the kingdom of Ireland, with variety of new designs, in large folio plates . . . drawn either from the buildings themselves, or the original designs of the architect, in the same size, paper and manner of *Vitruvius Britannicus*.'[35] It never appeared. Had it done so, we should know much more than we do about the views and purposes of those concerned. Between the death of Cassels in 1751 and the great watershed of the Royal Exchange competition in 1769 a great deal of admirable architecture came into being both in Dublin and in the country at large. But it is an age almost of anonymity. In proportion to the quantity of building there is, or seems so far to be, a dearth of documents and of names. The case of the Provost's House is merely an extreme example of a fairly general rule: ironically, since except for the architect's actual name it is unusually well documented.

CHAPTER TWELVE

Country Houses 1700–80

By the beginning of the eighteenth century building in brick, whether imported or locally burnt, was common for houses in Dublin, Cork and some other coastal towns. While an occasional country house built of brick is reported, such as Castle Bernard Co Cork of 1715 (long since rebuilt), the generality of Irish buildings continued to be of rubble stone, rendered.[1] This did not, as yet, include the vernacular dwellings of the peasantry, which at this stage were still impermanent structures of timber or of sods. The consensus of informed modern opinion is that few of the stone-built or rammed-earth cottages till recently so characteristic of the countryside are as much as 200 years old, and that the majority probably date from the first half of the nineteenth century. The pictorial and literary evidence is clear and consistent.

The smaller 'large' houses were at this period (c. 1700) often T-shaped or L-shaped, and always gable-ended with very massive stacks in their external walls, usually in the gables, the stacks usually flanked by small windows lighting the attics.[2] An early eighteenth-century development was for the stacks above the gables to be made of brick, which is very practical for exposed rectangular structures of small area. Borrisnoe Co Tipperary, Movena (Moyvannin) Co Limerick, Camlagh Co Roscommon, Beaghmore Co Galway, Mount Odell Co Waterford are examples chosen almost at random. They are not usually easy to date, and their time-span extends probably from 1660 or earlier to 1730 or later, and they certainly overlap with the compact cubical hip-roofed type which, in principle, supplanted them.

The Tailors' Hall in Dublin, though a public building with a 'collegiate' internal anatomy of a two-storey hall separated by a passage from smaller single-storey rooms, and built of brick, is a close-relative of the type of country house mentioned above, and shares with them the steeply-pitched roof of its date (1706) with the little attic windows in the haunches of the gables, and, like most of them, it has its staircase in the rearward limb of the 'T'.

We have already seen the appearance of compact eaved houses such as Eyrecourt. By 1700 they had become much more common, though the survivors are now not numerous. One which still stands, though only just, is Kilmacurragh Co Wicklow, of a little after 1700, two storeys high with a wide pediment. Slightly narrower, of almost exactly the same depth, but with much greater vertical emphasis, Shannongrove in North Co Limerick (1709) is also of two storeys, but over a high basement, and with a steep roof culminating in a pair of really tremendous chimney-stacks which are not only visibly of brick but, uniquely in Ireland, have diaper-patterns of headers on their articulated shafts. They excel even those at Beaulieu. Though quite small, the house gives an impression of towering magnificence.[3]

It seems safe to attribute Shannongrove to a member of the Rothery family of whom several are found in the building trades in Dublin in the 1680s, while John, Isaac and James are found in the South-West (Limerick and Clare) a little later. Riddlestown, also in North Limerick, has a similar silhouette, almost as of a tower-house, and must also be by the Rotherys. Their masterpiece is Mount Ievers in Co

Clare, just across the Shannon. Though not begun until 1736, it may conveniently be considered here, not least because in style and spirit there is nothing about it which could not be of 1710.[4]

Allegedly a transcription from Inigo Jones's Chevening which was available in Vol. II (1717) of *Vitruvius Britannicus*, and clearly indebted to it in respect of its plan-form, Mount Ievers transcends its exemplar to become something altogether different. Superlatives have been used about this house, and with good reason. The first sight of Mount Ievers in its improbable setting, up an unimpressive approach from the neat little town of Sixmilebridge, is unforgettable. The rather dumpy proportions of the Jonesian original have been magically transmuted as though by infection from the surrounding towers. By the incorporation of two string-courses at each of which the outline diminishes by a few inches, the profile is given a 'lift' into, as it were, a different key, related to, but distinct from, the traditional Irish batter.

The South front is of silvery limestone, the North front, now the garden front, of a wonderful red brick exquisitely disciplined by the limestone of coigns, strings and cornice. In fact, most exceptionally among such designs, there is a complete entablature with a pulvinated frieze and a noble cornice which itself carries the gutter. The roof is as steep as that of Shannongrove, but the two stacks, though massive, are much less bulky in silhouette.

The plan is very grand (fig. 134) but very, very inconvenient. About one-third of the ground-floor is occupied by a vast space communicating directly with the outer world through the garden-door and with the top of the house via the stair-well, facing North, habitable only in summer and quite impossible to heat. But for the pleasure of living in such a house one would endure much.

By the time Mount Ievers was built there was at least one other important house with one front of stone and one of brick: the Archbishop's Palace at Cashel,[5] designed by Pearce and begun for Archbishop Goodwin before 1729 and finished for Theophilus Bolton. At Cashel the more elaborate entrance-front (which faces South) is of brick, while the plainer garden front is of stone: the reverse of Mount Ievers where both fronts are otherwise alike, the North (brick) front having originally been the entrance-front and again made so by the present owner.

It is difficult to assess the motives of those who used brick for country houses, and still more difficult to relate this to the use of brick for town houses in Dublin. One clue may lie in the fact that right down to the middle of the nineteenth century the inland parts of Ireland had an economy of subsistence and barter, whereas the towns and the coast had a money economy. This would mean that for the building of a country house the brick-burning process described by Boate in the mid-seventeenth century (see page 145) might still be resorted to,[6] whereas not only is there a persistent tradition of brick coming into Dublin and Cork as ballast, but there is evidence from maps of regularly worked brickfields in what is now inner Dublin. Brick sizes, it may be noted, were regulated, in principle at least, by Pearce's act of 1729 (3 Geo. II. XIV) to be not less than $9\frac{1}{2}$ by $4\frac{1}{2}$ by $2\frac{1}{4}$ inches.

Tradition would have the Mount Ievers bricks come from Holland, by way of the oil-mill at Ballintlea a mile to the South, which belonged to Robert Pease of Amsterdam, presumably in exchange or part exchange for the rape-seed oil exported to Holland.[7] However that may be, there were by now some Pearce houses (notably Cashel and Bellamont) so far inland that no such explanation can serve to account for their elevations being of brick.

The ashlar at Mount Ievers is of fine quality: much finer, for example, than that at

133

133 Clonmel: the John Christian house, with decorative slate-hanging incorporating a date '176–': the last digit missing (as, now, are the three preceding digits). Slate-hanging is relatively common in the South-West

134 Mount Ievers, Co Clare: plan. The house was originally entered by the North (now the garden) front, so that the staircase was immediately to the visitor's right, and the present entrance-hall in the South centre was a 'saloon'. In spite of the position of the fireplaces, the flues are drawn together into two great stacks towards the centre of the building

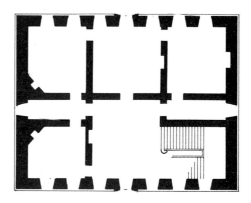

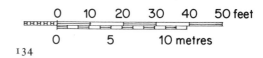

0	10	20	30	40	50 feet

| 0 | | 5 | | 10 metres |

134

Castle Durrow of some 20 years earlier. At this period there was a sudden expansion of building activity, and in particular of fine masons' work, closely comparable to the sudden expansion in the period following 1460, when the friaries and the great cloisters were built. We are apt to assume that a highly-skilled workforce cannot be rapidly expanded, and hence to postulate an influx of craftsmen from somewhere else. But this will not serve, since there was a boom in progress everywhere else as well.

The truth is, surely, that a skill can be diffused much more rapidly than interested parties would sometimes like us to believe. The rather sudden arrival, for example, of the motor-car in the first 14 years of the twentieth century, brought forth a numerous class of mechanics in a remarkably short space of time: some, doubtless, more skilled than others, but many attaining a high standard, still further raised by the present demands of war.

Sir John Summerson has shown that, in England, the great country-house building boom of 1710–60 had its climax during the five years 1720–24, when over twice as many such houses were begun than in any other quinquennium.[8] He rightly regards the dates of beginning as the dates that matter most. The pattern in Ireland is remarkably similar. In the 35 years from Durrow onwards—that is to say from 1716 to 1745—a round two dozen or so sizeable country houses were built or at least begun. They are in general much less well documented than their English counterparts but it is clear that the main movement in country-house building was over by 1750.

Summerson notes that, in England, nearly a quarter of his total were built by new owners on newly-acquired property: a surprisingly high proportion for England where continuity of land-ownership is the rule. In Ireland, where over five-sixths of the land had recently changed hands in circumstances of greater or less violence, nearly all the builders were 'new men': even the Geraldine Earl of Kildare who remodelled Carton had recently bought it,[9] returning, as it were, to the doorstep of his family's mediaeval seat at Maynooth.

Of these two dozen houses the largest number were begun in the the mid-to-late 1730s. In the series as a whole there are two great masterpieces: one still with us, the other now with God.

Castletown (Conolly) Co Kildare (fig. 136) stands almost at the beginning of Irish country-house building, and, as so often happens in the history of art, nothing quite so splendid was ever built again. Its owner, Speaker William Conolly, had risen from being the son of a publican, and through the law and dealings in land, had become one of the richest men in Ireland and an important borough-proprietor. The house was begun between 1719 and 1722. The evidence demonstrating—conclusively as it seems to me—its authorship has been marshalled elsewhere and is of a complexity unsuited to these pages.[10] The sum of it is that in 1719 the Florentine Alessandro Galilei who had been brought to England and to Ireland by John Molesworth of Brackenstown, designed the elevations and perhaps the plan also of the main block, and may have sketched out the general conception of the curved colonnades and wings, and returned to Italy in the same year. The house was still being built in 1722, and though Pearce was already concerned with Conolly and with Galilei, he was still in Italy and seems not to have got back to Dublin until 1726. He certainly designed the entrance-hall and probably most of the rest of the interior except the main staircase. There can be little doubt that he was the effective designer of the colonnades and wings as they were when seen by Loveday in 1732, the year before Pearce died and three years after the death of the Speaker.

135 Roscrea, Co Tipperary: the Damer house in the castle courtyard. It was begun in the second quarter of the eighteenth century and took 20 or 30 years to finish, so that it looks older than it is. It has a fine carved timber staircase but is otherwise mostly plain inside

136 Castletown, Co Kildare, from the (South)-East. The exterior of the central block by Alessandro Galilei, c. 1720; the wings almost certainly by Sir Edward Lovett Pearce, about ten years later. The nearer of the two wings houses the stables and the further the kitchens

135

136

The plan of the main block derives from Coleshill as, 20 years later, that of Leinster House was to do (both houses are 140 feet long and within a foot or two of the same depth). Both fronts (North and South) are completely regular, in the manner of an Italian town palazzo, without breaks of any kind: on the South (entrance) the first-floor windows have pediments, on the North not. The end elevations are both symmetrical, somewhat in the manner of Coleshill. All the flues are gathered together into two mighty stacks which stand on arches over the corridor, at each end of which, round a corner, are secondary staircases. The main staircase was not put in until 1759 but its place was assigned from the beginning, adjoining the two-storey entrance-hall which Pearce designed. In its plan-form this hall set the model for many later Irish houses: Cashel Palace, Castle Dobbs, Castle Ward, Lucan and all its relations, Castletown Cox and many others.* The essence is a columnar screen at the inner end: and because at Castletown the hall is, exceptionally, two storeys high, this screen carries the corridor across at first-floor level, enacting the role of the flying landing at Coleshill.†

The lower order in this hall is Ionic just like that of the colonnades outside, but above, in place of an order, is a series of pedestals diminishing downwards like terms or herms, and with baskets of fruit in the place of capitals.‡ The wings, which join the colonnades in a tangential way which is apparently unique, are each the size of a large house, are works of architecture in their own right, and subtly point up the contrast with the main block by having shallow breakfronts. While the main house is built of a silvery white limestone, very fine in texture and somewhat resembling portland, but so far unidentified, the wings are in a coarser limestone, rich in subtle tints of pink, brown and blue, said to be from Carrickdexter near Navan. The East wing contains the vaulted and palatial stabling, the West the kitchen and allied services.

The building of Castletown was not merely a political act like the building of other such houses: it was also a patriotic action. A much-quoted passage in the correspondence between Berkeley and Perceval expresses the desire that the house should be an epitome of the resources of Ireland. We may call it colonial patriotism if we like, but it was patriotism none the less.

The other great masterpiece of the movement has fared less well. Uncertain as the attribution of Castletown was till recently, that of Summerhill, Co Meath (figs 137-140), remains almost equally obscure. It is credited to Cassels in an article written 60 years later,[11] but not by Bishop Pockocke who wrote much nearer the date of its erection.[12] This is not the place in which to debate the causes which lead me to ascribe it jointly to Pearce and to Cassels, with the rider that in my opinion Pearce's role was probably that of originator and Cassels' that of executant.

The builder of Summerhill, Hercules Rowley, is described as 'a rich presbyterian' which (as someone said about Verdi's calling Mozart a 'quartettista') was probably not intended as a compliment. Through his mother he had acquired the estate and fortune of the Langfords of Summerhill, and he owned land in six Irish counties (including part of what later became Belfast). Still more to our present purpose, he had sat in Parliament since 1703, sharing the representation of the County of Derry

---

* Even as late as Charleville, Co Wicklow, after 1792 (D. Guinness & W. Ryan, *Irish Houses & Castles*, 1971, p. 310).

† There is a somewhat similar arrangement at Blenheim, which may be where Pearce got it from.

‡ Compare St Alphege, Greenwich, by Hawksmoor.

137

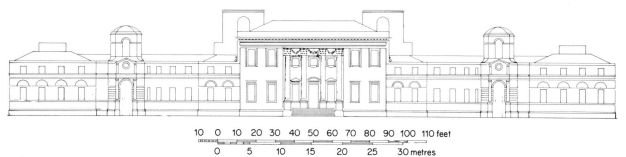

138

137 Summerhill, Co
Meath: the centre of the
North front, and the
Eastern tower, taken in
1950

138 Summerhill: North
(entrance) elevation. The
stone-domed towers are
well advanced from the
plane of the *corps-de-logis*,
and the outer four-bay
pavilions still further

advanced. Not only is the
plan, even of the *corps-de-
logis*, deeper than is usual in
Irish houses, but the general
height of the subsidiary
masses is much greater in
relation to it. The South
(garden) front terminates in
niched features of purely
monumental purpose. All
the foregoing must, alas,
properly be put in the past
tense

139 Summerhill: the East tower and wing from the central steps of the North front

140 Summerhill: plan, drawn by David Griffin from a nineteenth-century survey by McCurdy and Mitchell. Mr Griffin has drawn my attention to the fact that the room marked X is of the same shape and dimensions as the drawing-room at No 12 North Audley Street, London, long suspected of being by Pearce

139

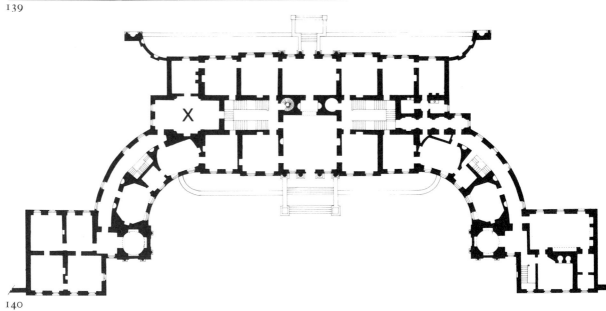

140

with Speaker William Conolly. His son Hercules Langford Rowley made a very advantageous marriage in 1732, and this, within a year or so, is the date given for the house. Pearce was still alive; but since such a house cannot be built in two years or less, Cassels must have finished it.

Unlike Castletown, which you approach sideways from the West so that you do not see the South (entrance) front until it is almost upon you, Summerhill had an axial approach from the North and stood on top of a hill. The central block was comparatively small, two storeys over a basement, with an inset frontispiece of giant Corinthian columns, quarter-engaged. The expected flanking quadrants were here unexpectedly of two storeys, with windows, and were straight for the innermost two bays. They terminated in three-storey towers with octagonal stone domes, beyond which were further massive two-storey pavilions of four bays, with single, large, low central stacks. Beyond these again were pedimented triumphal arches.

In this recital the most salient features of the silhouette have been omitted because they straddle the main block and the wings. These are the two pairs of arcaded chimney stacks which were no doubt the features which caused Bishop Pococke to describe the house as 'in the Vanbrugh style' and which reminded C. R. Cockerell of Blenheim and King's Weston, and with reason, for such Vanbrughian motifs were used by Pearce, though less obtrusively, at Bellamont Forest also. In fact those of Summerhill are more like those of Eastbury than of King's Weston.

The garden front is somewhat more domestic in character, having superimposed orders, Doric and Ionic, slightly recessed in the centre, with some resemblance to the entrance front of Desart Court Co Kilkenny,[13] a house dated 1733 and tentatively attributed to Pearce. The work at Summerhill, however, is of a higher order both of design and of craftsmanship.*

One peculiarity of Summerhill is that the curved corridors and other parts of the ground floor are arched over in brick: as we shall see the use of brick vaulting over ground was an occasional habit of the Pearce-Cassels school, perhaps as a preventative against fire. Summerhill, however, was burned some time in the middle of the nineteenth century, and again during the epidemic of 1922. It stood for many years after that event, if anything more splendid in ruin than in life, for its architecture, and particularly that of the domed towers, had the gift of running grandly to ruin. But year by year the encroaching vegetation obscured a little more of the logic and the rhetoric, until one day in the 1950s came the incredible news that all the cut stone had been sold and taken away. The shapeless mass lingered on for a few more years, until at last the corework was bulldozed into the ground. It is reported that the flanking archways still stand, but, for the rest, it has vanished from the soil of Meath as completely as Coleshill has vanished from the soil of Berkshire, and its place knows it no more.

From the Pearce-Cassels school there came during the period many other houses, inevitably of less distinction. From Pearce himself, Drumcondra, Cashel Palace, and Bellamont Forest, as well as several less firmly attributed, such as Woodlands, Lismore (Co Cavan), Gloster and Cuba Court.[14] Drumcondra is a façade at right angles to someone else's façade: a great puzzle but not much else except that its flat *appliqué* frontispiece reappears in various guises. Cashel Palace is charming, uses the 'Venetian' window on either side of the front door and on the ground floor only,

---

*I doubt whether the rather overdone Gibbsian trim on the windows flanking the centre can be attributed to Pearce: the house must have taken three or four years to build, and someone could not resist the temptation to overdo the orchestration.

and not, as usually in Ireland, as a centre-piece on the first floor. It is also an early example of the 'reflecting staircase' plan.

Bellamont (fig. 141)[15] is altogether more important: a very perfect and complete example of a Palladian villa, very thoroughly designed in every part, as no Irish house had yet been, and as few other houses except the Marino Casino and the Provost's House were ever to be again. Its one great fault is that the portico is visibly an afterthought, but it is so good in itself that we cannot but forgive it. All four fronts were designed to be seen, which was already something new,* and the elaborately columnar lobby on the top floor, out of which the bedrooms open, seems to have been new here also, and became very usual practice in Irish country houses and even one or two in town.

Bellamont is remarkable also for being faced externally entirely in red brick, except for the stone dressings. It is a long way inland, and the bricks must have been locally burnt. Not far away, and in the same county, is Ballyhaise (fig. 142), also built of brick. It is one of Cassels' earliest country houses,† and though ordinary enough at first glance, has two features of very great interest. The entrance front has a stone frontispiece with superimposed pilasters, Doric and Ionic, and end-bays which rather awkwardly are a little lower than the rest. But the centre of the rere elevation is occupied by a semi-elliptical projection, which, after the manner of Vaux-le-Vicomte, contains an elliptical saloon half-in and half-out of the plan-rectangle. This appears to be well in advance of anything of the kind in Britain. The other remarkable thing about Ballyhaise is that both the ground and first floors are completely vaulted over in brick.‡

Ballyhaise is not very large, nor is Belvedere,[16] a somewhat later house by Cassels which also contains innovative elements. Exact dates for these houses are hard to come by, but it seems that Ballyhaise belongs to about 1733 and Belvedere to perhaps ten years later. Unlike Pearce, whose whole Irish career is only seven years long, and most of whose concerns were proceeding at the same time, Cassels would benefit from an established chronology, but this, for most of his country houses, is still to seek.[17]

At Belvedere 'Venetian' windows are used as secondary centres of interest in the façade, in a way which is a hybrid between their use by the English Palladians (for example Campbell at Burlington House) and their use by Pearce at Cashel. But more significant for the future in Ireland was the use of semicircular bows at each end of the house. Numerous minor Irish country houses were to exploit this feature in various guises and combinations, from the middle of the century onwards. It is, and remained, less characteristic of the larger houses. Very close to Belvedere, and built no doubt at the same time and also by Cassels, is the small house called Anneville[18] which has a semicircular front hall projecting in the form of a half-octagon, a feature which had a promising future before it.

Besides building small houses and town houses, Cassels built some medium-large country houses with wings, such as Hazlewood Co Sligo and Bellinter Co Meath: the former with a frontispiece deriving from Pearce's Drumcondra, the latter with

---

* Well, fairly new. Glinsk and Portumna were, after all, a century earlier and designed to be seen from all round. Another feature which Bellamont has and many later Irish houses were to have, is the tunnel leading from the area to the 'offices': it is indicated on Pearce's plan.

† Technically, it is a reworking of another house, but the plan (fig. 142) suggests otherwise.

‡ The contemporary King house at Boyle ('Boyle Barrack') is vaulted up to the second floor.

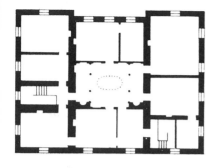

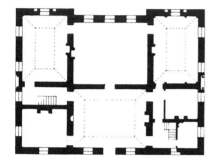

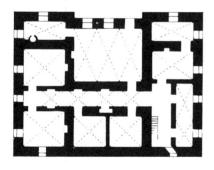

0   10   20   30   40 feet

141

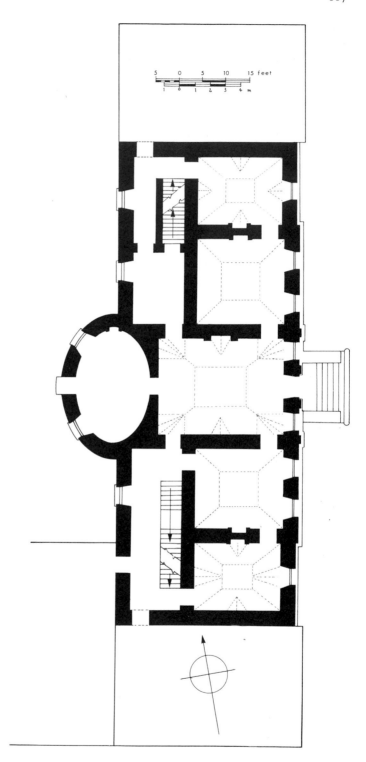

5   0   5   10   15 feet

1   0   1   2   3   4   m

187

141 Bellamont Forest, Co
Cavan: plans of basement,
ground and upper floors,
by Sir Edward Lovett
Pearce, *c.* 1730

142 Ballyhaise, Co
Cavan: plan by William
Garner. The house, by
Richard Cassels, is an
extremely early example
(p. 186) of the plan in
which an oval room is half
in and half out of the main
rectangle, in the manner of
Vaux-le-Vicomte. It is also
remarkable in being
vaulted throughout

142

one based on the flanking walls of Bellamont Forest. His earliest recorded country house, Castle Hume in Co Fermanagh, is the subject of an almost contemporary description: hardly was it built in about 1729 but it was destroyed by fire, whereupon Sir Gustavus Hume immediately rebuilt it 'finer than before'. But it decayed and was pulled down in the early 1830s. Only the stables in part remain; but they are vaulted (like those of Castletown) and of considerable splendour. Of his wingless block-like houses Rochfort Co Westmeath (later renamed Tudenham and now roofless) is perhaps the finest (fig. 143).

Cassels was called in to remodel or enlarge a good many houses: Gill Hall Co Down where he built more vaulted stables, Strokestown Co Roscommon where, in addition to adding curved sweeps and wings, he re-housed the horses in similar state, under brick vaults borne by Doric columns, Rathbeale Co Dublin where again he added sweeps and wings, Dollardstown Co Meath which was almost new-built in about 1735, with detached tower-like wings. Some of his largest and most famous houses are remodellings: notably Powerscourt which he began in 1731 and which was nine years in building. Its entrance (North) front is perhaps his finest achievement in that line: a centre block with a wide pediment over five bays and busts in circular niches, a little reminiscent of Badminton, linked by low four-bay ranges to four-bay wings not unlike those of Summerhill. Beyond these in turn are the finest features of the front: quadrant-walls with blind arcades interrupted by tall pedimented archways of noble scale, and terminating in obelisks upon which triumphal eagles perch.

The interior, apparently fitted within the walls of a U-shaped 'castle' contained, apart from a handsome small octagonal domed room, a strange shell-encrusted entrance-hall above which was the so-called 'Egyptian Hall', almost exactly contemporary with Burlington's 'Egyptian Hall' at York, and like it, closely modelled on the precepts of Vitruvius as filtered through Palladio. It was 40 feet wide and high, and 60 feet long with Corinthian standing over Ionic and supporting a sumptuously coffered ceiling. All this, alas, is in the past tense, for the interior was gutted by an accidental fire in 1975 and is unlikely to be reinstated.[19]

Westport, Co Mayo, is another of Cassels' remodellings but much of his work there was later remodelled by James Wyatt. He also spent many years in remodelling Carton, and indeed died, in 1751, while still at it. But apart from the saloon, of which the principal glory is the Francini ceiling (not to mention other embellishments added later) Carton is a somewhat lacklustre affair: big enough for a duke, but not otherwise very interesting and drained still further of interest by the chill hand of Sir Richard Morrison, who worked it over after 1815.

In his final phase Cassels collaborated with Francis Bindon on two large houses, one of which, Belan, was a remodelling and is now a ruin. The other, Russborough, has been fortunate in the care taken of it and in the contents with which it is enriched.[21]

The client was a rich Dublin brewer, Joseph Leeson, who bought the property in 1741 but was not ennobled until 1756, by which time his vast house had been finished for about three years. Much of the intervening period was occupied in visits to Rome to collect things to put in the house. As at Castletown, the approach is from one side, so that the 700-foot façade is revealed bit by bit. And as at Castletown, the wings rival the centre block in size. No other Irish house is strung out so extravagantly as Russborough (fig. 144): it is a piece of theatrical scenery flung across the Wicklow landscape facing the mountains, and in modern times overlooking a lake as well. Elongated baroque archways topped with cupolas, and pairs of obelisks, lend additional animation. The effect is undeniably splendid, the workmanship admirable, in golden Wicklow granite. Yet there is a touch of the jejune about the detailing of the wings, the colonnades are ambiguous in relation to the centre and barely strong enough to hold their own against the adjoining masses. The façade of the centre block, a 'villa' comparable to Bellamont and with a frontispiece in which the fruity swags of Summerhill, hung between the columns, reappear, seems lacking in surface relief. Like Bellamont, it has an attic storey, which in the nineteenth century was foolishly believed to be an addition.

The plan is simple and effective, the ceilings among the finest of their period and including some by the Francini, and the marble chimneypieces are unequalled for boldness and grandeur.

There are some important smaller houses of the Pearce school of which the authorship is not fully established. The astonishing small centrally-planned Wood-lands (formerly Clinshogh), Co Dublin with its four fronts, Coleshill quotation, vaulted corridor and brick lantern, must surely be by Pearce. At Gloster Co Offaly, where ingenious spatial effects in an adaptation are found with Vanbrughian garden-features, he may be presumed to have participated at a distance. Ledwiths-town Co Longford can with almost equal certainty be given to Cassels.[22]

Many hundreds of minor houses still remain from the eighteenth century, and especially from its second half. Very few can be credited to known architects, though they were all designed by somebody, and there are some fairly well-defined groups. They were for the most part built by minor gentry, whose phase of building activity followed on and outlasted the first frenzy of the larger proprietors.

Having done my best in another book to digest the anatomy of these houses, I find it hard to regurgitate generalisations of a suitable brevity here. The houses are, as might be expected, remarkably consistent in style throughout the four provinces. They are, on the whole, quite remarkably free from provincialisms and lapses in architectural grammar. Their tendency to severity is as marked as their preference for symmetry, and without perceptible departure from the unaffected language in which their functions are expressed, they can, on occasion, deviate so far towards plainness as to deceive the unwary into thinking that they have no style at all. They embody, in short, a totally pervasive vernacular, capable of a suitable response to almost any architectural problem.

A few names float to the surface, or have been dredged up by recent curiosity. The most prominent of these, Francis Bindon,[23] has already been mentioned. A Co Clare gentleman, who was also an amateur painter, he is credited with some 16 houses of which three or four are attested in his obituary or other near-contemporary sources, and a few more are backed up by family connexion as well as evidence of style. He was connected with Pearce by marriage through the Cootes of Bellamont; but we need not attach too much importance to this, considering how small was the Irish ruling class of the time and how endemic was intermarriage amongst them. He seems to have been much of an age with Pearce and Cassels. Two houses of 1730 and 1731 have been given to him for no better reason than that they are not quite good enough to be by Pearce or Cassels, and perhaps this is reason enough. Clermont Co Wicklow is of brick and has no wings, while Furness Co Kildare is of stone and has wings: in other respects they are closely similar. He was concerned at Desart Court, perhaps under Pearce, before 1733, and with Cassels (as we have seen) in two of his late large houses. Bessborough, Co Kilkenny, Woodstock and Castle Morres also in the same county are well authenticated. Bessborough and Woodstock have that air of having been not very skilfully assembled which seems to be the mark of Bindon: Castle

143 Tudenham (formerly Rochfort) Co Westmeath: the shell of the large square house of the 1740s by Richard Cassels, with his typical oculus-over-niche motif in the centre

144 Russborough, Co Wicklow: aerial view drawn by Michael Craig. The West court and wings (nearest to the spectator) accommodate the stables, and the East the kitchens and other out-offices

143

144

Morres, which alone of the three has almost completely disappeared, was simpler and had somewhat more felicity.[24]

It seems likely that he was responsible for the attractive urban development of St John's Square, Limerick, in stone, with oculi, niches and other motifs from the Cassels repertory, of 1751, and two attractive mid-century houses in Co Clare, Carnelly and Newhall, both in Bindon country. Newhall in particular shows derivation from Belvedere and other Cassels houses in its apsidal ends and half-octagon central projection. It is in brick, which continues to be exceptional for country houses until the end of the century.

If Drewstown Co Meath is his, it shows a reversion to his earlier uncertainty of handling, though well built in fine ashlar.

Bindon died in 1765 'in his chariot, on the way to the country', but one more house which may be his must be mentioned. Cooperhill Co Sligo has been given to him because it is so much in the manner of Cassels but much too late to be by him. It is almost too late to be by Bindon either, for it bears the date 1774: but this conceals the fact that it was begun nearly 20 years earlier, and it took eight years to quarry the stone. It has a nobly proportioned façade with grouped windows and the extra-solid corners found in some seventeenth-century Irish houses and spasmodically also through the eighteenth. This reminds us that the building of a house by a minor landowner in the less than affluent North-West could be a very heavy burden.

The very minor architect John Aheron whose activity, like that of Bindon, was partly centred on the Limerick-Clare area, would not be worth mentioning but for the fact that he wrote a book. It is a very large book. Unfortunately it is also a very bad book: but it has the distinction of being the first separate work on architecture to be published in Ireland. It was written by 1751 and published in 1754.[25] Another very minor architect, Michael Wills, produced a book in 1745 which never got beyond the manuscript stage, and was no better than Aheron's.[26] Much more fruitful than either of these was the little book of 12 small house designs by the Rev. John Payne (MS 1753, printed 1757) which I have examined in detail elsewhere.

One of the very finest smaller houses of the mid-century has neither a known architect nor a precise date. Summer Grove near Mountmellick Co Leix, has in unusually perfect form a feature which is found spasmodically in Ireland from about 1640 to about 1840: three storeys at the back taking up the same height as two storeys at the front. It was probably built in about 1755. Another unusually accomplished house of similar size but quite different in feeling, Dysart[27] near Delvin Co Westmeath, is dated 1757 and known to be by George Pentland, though what relation this Pentland was to the John Pentland who designed the ambitious (and for once fully realised) Palladian layout of Wilson's Hospital School in the same county, has not yet been determined.

That is Mr Pentland of Hendrick-street, an eminent Carpenter, Dale-Marchant and Projector, who has executed some of the best Edifices in this Kingdom; a Man who copies after *Castells*, in every Thing but his narrow Windows: *Castells* was out in that Particular, for as we have so little Sun, we require large Windows to let him in—in Italy, indeed, where the Climate is very warm, small Windows may be necessary to exclude his intence [sic] heat. Pentland is deemed by the best Judges, to be singularly happy in fixing upon the best Situation for Prospect and Elevation, and is as honest an Undertaker as any in this Kingdom: He is making a Fortune with an excellent Reputation. He has a son, little Jack, who is a great Genius, and has the Advantage of a genteel Education; great Matters are expected to shine forth in that pretty Lad.

The Public Monitor or New Freeman's Journal, Feb 13–16, 1773.

I owe this quotation to the Knight of Glin. This was Henry Pentland timber-merchant. By 1783 John and Charles Pentland, timber-merchants, are at No. 11 Hendrick Street, and at No. 10 is John Pentland, Architect, the 'Little Jack' of the quotation.

The industry, and the acumen, of the Knight of Glin has filled out the features of two mid-century architects one of whom was indeed already a name, but the other hardly even that. To take the less illustrious first, Nathaniel Clements,[28] whose career as architect runs from *c.* 1751 to perhaps 20 years later or a little more, was primarily a business-man and politician, a close associate of Luke Gardiner whose concerns he seems to have taken over, a member of Parliament and a banker, and Ranger of the Phoenix Park. It was to house himself in this last capacity that he designed and built the house now heavily disguised as Arus an Uachtarain or the Viceregal Lodge, but originally an agreeable modest brick house with L-shaped wings (very common in Ireland) linked by plain quadrant walls to the main block which has a neat and ingenious plan.

It is difficult to be sure how many of the nine or ten houses tentatively assigned to Clements are really his. The group includes very small houses such as Woodville Co Dublin (which certainly belonged to Clements), or Belview Co Meath, and one quite large one, Beauparc, also in Co Meath. They all have in common the use of quadrants leading to subsidiary pavilions, sometimes two and less commonly four, and the use of a Palladian repertoire of tripartite and diocletian windows, niches and oculi. There is no doubt that most of these houses belong together, and no doubt of Clements's association with Cassels, with John Wood of Bath, with Burlington (to whom he lent money) and with William Adam (from whom he borrowed ideas). He was also, we must not forget, probably a mere six years younger than Pearce.

But there is serious doubt whether Colganstown and Newberry can be by the same designer, and some doubt whether Lodge Park Straffan (which seems to be the last of the series and differs a good deal in character) really belongs with the others. Colganstown is perhaps the best of them, bland and harmonious and very typical in the disposition of its 'economic' layout.

Clements is a Dublin figure, and none of his houses (if they be his) are far from the capital. Davis Ducart[29] or Daviso de Arcort, on the other hand, is exclusively a provincial figure. He is, apparently, Clements's exact contemporary, for he is first heard of in 1765 and no buildings are reported after 1771. He is described as a 'Sardinian' which no doubt means a Savoyard or a Piedmontese. Unlike Cassels, who arrived from Germany via England, Ducart seems to have come straight from the Continent to Cork or Limerick, and his architecture is undiluted by English influences.

Like Pearce and Cassels before him, he was concerned with canals, in which he seems to have had some special skills as he is sometimes referred to as an 'engineer'. His canal activity was entirely in the North, while nearly all his houses are in the South. His first recorded building, the Custom House in Limerick, has most of the characteristic attributes which give his work such a distinctive flavour: a frontispiece of *fluted* pilasters, wings made of straight arcades with panelled piers and ornament of a single tangent circle above each arch, concave weatherings to the window-cornices, architraves of the upper windows broken *upwards* over the openings. Some of these, notably the last-mentioned, had been used by other architects, for example Cassels, but together they say Ducart and only Ducart. There is a strong flavour of

145 Dundrum, Co Tipperary: elevation. The house is by one of the Pearce school, perhaps Pearce himself. It was altered in the nineteenth century. In this elevation the dimensions are taken from the house as existing, and the roofs, pediments, etc. supplied from the evidence of a drawing on an eighteenth-century estate map

146 Milltown, Shinrone, Co Offaly: it is relatively sophisticated in being of ashlar and having a cut-stone cornice: relatively primitive in being gable-ended with end-stacks

10   0   10   20   30   40   50 feet

1   0   5   10 metres

145

146

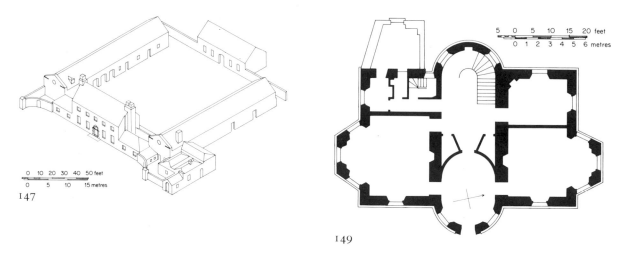

147

148

149

147 Kilcarty, Co Meath, by Thomas Ivory: isometric view

148 Cappagowlan, Co Offaly: a mid-to-late eighteenth-century block added on to the front of a somewhat earlier block. Note the contrast in roofing arrangements and the change of scale between the floors

149 Longfield, Co Tipperary: plan. Built in about 1770, it is a paradigm of the fondness for projecting bows and bays which is a recurrent feature of middle-sized Irish houses from 1745 onwards

the Petit Trianon about the Limerick Custom House, as there is about his finest house, Castletown Cox.

His style is in fact Franco-Italian, and this is why it sometimes looks disconcertingly Victorian. It is, for example, almost impossible to accept the porch of Lota, Co Cork, as an eighteenth-century work until we see it in an eighteenth-century watercolour, exactly as it stands today. Similarly with the ornamented weatherings to the window-cornices at Castletown. The reason is of course that Victorian architects of the Barry school were doing this kind of thing in the 1840s and later, imitatively, whereas Ducart was doing it naturally in the 1760s.

Fired by the example of Limerick, Cork summoned Ducart to build the Mayoralty House, a larger and less successful building, now a hospital. During the five years 1765-70 Ducart was engaged on nearly all his documented works: the four already mentioned, Kilshannig Co Cork (his second-finest house), Lota Co Cork, Brockley Co Leix (now demolished), the Tyrone collieries and the aqueduct at Newmills in the same county. Though he was still alive in 1780 and died probably in about 1785, the attributions of his later career are less certain and of less significance.

Where the Irish Palladians had gone in for quadrant colonnades or at least plain sweep-walls, Ducart's preference was for straight arcades terminating in cubical or octagonal pavilions crowned with domes or lanterns. He had a preference also for extending the wings not merely in an L-plan, but turned once again, inwards, so as partly to enclose a courtyard.

All these traits are seen at their best in Castletown Cox (fig. 150),[30] which is his finest house, partly, no doubt, because it was the most expensive to build. The building-owner, Michael Cox, was a very grand and rich archbishop (of Cashel). The corps-de-logis has four fully-presentable fronts: the end-elevations are even more presentable than those of its great namesake in Kildare, and for a curious reason. The wings are placed corner-to-corner with the main block, which they barely touch. At the ends of the arcades are octagonal slated domes: the only such to survive in Ducart's work, though there was something similar at Kilshannig. The ashlar masonry is of the finest quality, the interior plaster decorations by Patrick Osborne of Waterford, of the greatest splendour. The plan of the house is the by now familiar type deriving from Pearce's Castletown, with the columnar screen at the inner end of the hall and the main staircase in an adjoining compartment.

His other major house, Kilshannig (fig. 151),[30] built for an alderman of Cork, has a more complicated and less successful plan. The general layout resembles that of Castletown except that the arcaded wings are set flush with the entrance-front. The main block has an entrance-front in red brick, a handsome stone Doric centrepiece with blind oculi for bustoes, that most Italian feature, a mezzanine, camber-headed windows (which, perhaps coincidentally, are much commoner in Co Cork than elsewhere) and a circular staircase à la Queen's House Greenwich to the right of the entrance-hall. This latter, with its corner-quadrants supported by composite columns, is not entirely satisfactory; but the plaster decoration of the house, done by the Francini brothers on the second and last of their visits to Ireland, is among the finest in the country.

Having originated the idea that it was Ducart who added the straight arcaded wings to Florencecourt Co Fermanagh, I may perhaps be allowed to cast doubt on it by way of second thoughts. Their detailing, though very different from the chunky overcrowded provincialism of the main block, is almost equally different from Ducart's detailing. Though the terminal pavilions have a superficial resemblance to those at The Island Co Cork (a house of the Ducart school) they are very un-

Ducartian in detail. What the Florencecourt wings *do* resemble is those at Buckland, Berkshire, by John Wood, which was published in *Vitruvius Britannicus* in 1767. It is true that in the following year and at the presumed time of the building of the wings Ducart was working at the Tyrone collieries and canal nearby, and this fact may account for the links being arcaded (which those at Buckland are not). In other words Ducart's contribution, if there was one, may have been little more than a verbal hint.

With Ducart's disappearance there is a natural pause in the history of the country house. His contemporary Ivory (died 1786) had a mind open to neo-classicism, which Ducart had not, and only one country house of his is known: the greatest contrast to those of Ducart that could possibly be imagined (fig. 147).[31]

Not a few of the house builders built also follies: for the usual reasons for which follies elsewhere were built, but sometimes also to provide employment in times of famine and hardship, notably the great frost of the years 1740–41. Follies and mausolea are close kin, and Pearce's obelisk for the Allens (see page 167) was the forerunner of the great obelisk on multiple arches which closes the vista from the North front of Castletown and is credibly assigned to Cassels.

A number of smaller eyecatchers which include minor obelisks also on arches are to be found at Belan and at Dangan, Co Meath and are doubtless also by Cassels. The extremely elegant object in the grounds of Drumcondra, which looks like the top half of an Italian church façade, must be by Galilei or by Pearce and is demonstrably a close relative of Castletown (Conolly).[32] Most of the more extravagant or architecturally notable Irish mausolea date from the neo-classic or the romantic periods: but the fine example, of brick with central 'Venetian' opening, in the graveyard of Castle Lyons Co Cork is of 1747 or a little later.

Besides follies and mausolea, there is another, and perhaps surprising field, into which country-house architecture spilled over. This is the field of industry: the canals, of course, which were furnished with handsome lock-houses and the like, but more impressively, the mills and factories. The most impressive if not the earliest of these is the great flour-mill at Slane on the Boyne. This was built by a partnership consisting of two local landowners, Blaney Townley Balfour, William Burton [Conyngham] later an important patron of architecture, and David Jebb, miller, of Drogheda. It was exceptionally large for its time, even by English standards, and very early for its size, for it was built in 1763–76, and Arthur Young was constrained to describe it as 'a very large and handsome edifice, such as no mill I have seen in England can be compared with.'[33]

It is, (for happily it still stands) a T-plan building 138 feet long and five storeys high, built of ashlar stone, with Gibbsian surrounds to the ground-floor openings, architraves to all the rest, storeys of graduated height, raised coigns and a fine cornice. In other words, whether appropriately or not, it has virtually all the refinements of elevation proper to a country house. The stone was certainly supplied, and the building most probably designed, by one of the Darley family who owned the quarries at Ardbraccan, which is only ten miles away by water and had already furnished the stone for Leinster House.★ The pattern of industrial development by landlords, often in partnership with technical men, had been set in the previous century by the Great Earl of Cork, and there were to be many more large mills after Slane, built under similar auspices, and sometimes, especially the not infrequent

★ Hugh Darley, for example, designed the Palladian Mayoralty House on the North Quay of Drogheda (fig. 157).

150

151

152

150 Castletown Cox, Co Kilkenny: detail of the garden front. Davis Ducart's highly idiosyncratic detailing

151 Kilshannig, Co Cork: the central feature of the entrance front, by Davis Ducart, 1756. The very Italianate mezzanine storey visible on the right is a rarity in Ireland

152 Newtown Hill, Leixlip, Co Kildare: a small mid-eighteenth-century house with an unusual arrangement of wings. The front doorcase is a modern restoration

153

154

155

156

153 Ballynahinch,
Bridget Lough, Co Clare: a
single-storey house,
possibly of the late
eighteenth century and
probably landlord-built,
though of vernacular aspect

154 Slane, Co Meath: one
wing of the Mill of 1763,
probably designed by
Hugh Darley, using a
typically country-house
repertoire

155 Ballyboughlin, Clara,
Co Offaly: a plain and
substantial farmhouse of
about 1800

156 Camp, Co Kerry: the
'Palladian' formula reduced
to perhaps its minimum of
pretension. Compare
Cappagh, Co Down,
illustrated in Alan Gailey,
*Rural Houses of the North of
Ireland*, p. 5, fig. 7.

castellated variety, not without architectural interest. But I know of none upon which quite so much care and expense was lavished as this.

The interest of the landlords was not confined to their rural estates: many of them owned and promoted towns, and it is the architectural character of the eighteenth-century town which must now engage our attention.

CHAPTER THIRTEEN

Provincial Towns and Churches

After the devastation of the Williamite wars, the new proprietors busied themselves with founding new towns, some of which prospered while others did not. New towns had been the handmaidens of colonisation even in Anglo-Norman times, and in the seventeenth century also, so that in the words of Dr J. H. Andrews, 'of the more than 100 corporations existing in 1685, the great majority had been constituted in the course of the seventeenth century.'[1] Prof. Cullen enumerates some 15 dating from the reign of James I, and about twice that number from that of Charles II. At least 150 more foundations date from the eighteenth century, nor did the process come to an end even after 1800; nor even, completely, after the Famine.[2]

Existing towns were as visibly affected by the spirit of improvement as new ones: in some cases more so, especially as the influence of the town's landlord such as the Perys in Limerick or the Chichesters in Belfast was often paramount. Though the walls of towns were still being taken seriously in the 1680s, and some, such as those of Derry and Bandon, were still of rather recent construction, in the middle of the eighteenth century they were in most cases formally abrogated (e.g. Limerick in 1760)[3] and the Middle Ages were at last visibly over.

The preference for open, rational and often symmetrical layouts had shown itself already in the seventeenth century. Even where two landlords were involved, as at Sixmilebridge where the Ievers were on one side of a little river and the O'Briens on the other, they managed to work together as harmoniously as Dr Mosse and the Gardiners were to do in Dublin, and George Street and Frederick Square are still there to prove it. William Conolly, later to become Speaker, seems to have re-planned Limavady soon after his purchase of the town in 1699.[4]

It must be conceded, however, that though the layout of many eighteenth-century Irish towns and villages is often bold and imaginative, the amount of fine architecture now to be seen in them falls far short of the quantity in country-house form. There are several reasons for this. One is that charity begins at home: your typical magnate builds his own house first, and if there is anything left over, it goes into building for the general good: we remember Sir Walter Coppinger at Ballyvireen. (Even Speaker Conolly at Castletown gave himself a nine years' start on the Parliament House).

Another reason is that the pressures of change in towns, even in the relatively stagnant conditions of nineteenth-century Ireland, are greater than they are in the country. For example, the handsome five-by-three arcaded Exchange of 1709 at Cork, much in the manner of Abingdon but with superimposed orders instead of a giant order, had apparently vanished 80 years later.[5] A not dissimilar but pedimented building on the waterfront at Waterford is known from a painting of 1736 but has been gone for a long time. The arcaded Exchange at Limerick survives only as a row of blocked arches.

The public buildings in the older towns are variously known as Tholsels, Exchanges, Town Houses, Guildhalls, Market Houses and Court Houses. The occasional

157

158

159

157 Drogheda, Co Louth: the Mayoralty House (left) and the Custom House (right) both on the North quay and both mid-eighteenth century, the former by Hugh Darley. The Custom House was demolished some years ago, to the great impoverishment of the streetscape, and the Mayoralty House is under-used and unloved

158 Kinsale market and court house

159 Kilkenny: the Tholsel, built in 1761 by Alderman William Colles who owned the marble-works and probably also designed the building. The original lantern, here seen, was of timber and was replaced in about 1960 by one of metal, of similar outline but without the octagonal railing at the base. Dormers were added to the roof

early Custom House, as at Newry (recently demolished) and Cork (incorporated in a later building) was built with at least nominal crown participation and had usually a more domestic appearance, as had the mid-eighteenth century example at Drogheda (fig. 157), which disappeared only about ten years ago.

Among the earliest surviving municipal buildings is the Main Guard at Clonmel, originally the court house of the Ormonde palatinate and probably by Robinson though now much altered, but still dominating the axis of the broad Main Street. The court house at Kinsale (fig. 158), with solid ends but an arcade for markets, has three curvilinear gables and a lantern and stands in an irregular square. It dates from 1706.* The Barracks at Ballyshannon, though of course not a municipal building, could well be such by its position and appearance. It has a decorative keystone and the date 1700 and may be by Robinson who was still Surveyor-General till early in that year. The court house at Antrim dates from 1726 and like Kinsale has solid ends with an open arcade between them but is otherwise very different, larger and especially wider (nine bays), and with a wide timber eaves-cornice which must be nineteenth-century, as is its lantern.[6] Twenty years later comes the court house of Lifford (Co Donegal) by Michael Priestley, of one apparent storey with segment-headed Gibbsian windows and a full-blooded Gibbsian doorcase supporting an armorial centrepiece. The interior has been gutted.[7]

In the same year a court house-cum-market house was built at Loughgall Co Armagh, but not to the design by Pearce which is still extant and which, again, was for a two-storey building with solid ends and a five-bay arcade.[8] Two other Northern court-houses of moderately early date, Portaferry (1752) and the church-like Castle-wellan (1764)† are of moderate interest. In the smaller towns it was usual to combine the two functions in the one building: in the felicitous phrase of Mr Brett 'the scales of commerce frequently came to share a roof with the scales of justice.'[9]

The Kilkenny Tholsel (1761) (fig. 159) was built and possibly also designed by William Colles the originator and owner of the marble works at Maddoxtown from which so many chimneypieces were supplied to Irish (and other) houses. With its five-bay Tuscan arcade projecting right over the pavement, steep roof and three-stage lantern with a pretty conoidal cap, it is unusually attractive both intrinsically and because of its crucial contribution to the townscape of such an important place at Kilkenny. The lantern was of timber, but in a restoration of about 1955 it was renewed in metal, with some aesthetic loss.[10]

The most ambitious of the combined market-and-assembly type buildings is surely that of Newtownards (fig. 160), built by Sir Alexander Steward who employed in 1765 a Bristol canal-engineer called Ferdinando Stratford whose elevation is still extant. The building as carried out differs from this primarily in the fact that the ranges flanking the lofty central feature are in the by now familiar form of an arcade between (relatively) solid ends.[11] The upper part of the building contained Assembly Rooms, and at nearby Belfast there was a building which started life as an open arcaded Market House in 1769, but soon had a grandiose Assembly room built on top of it by another English architect, Sir Robert Taylor, and of this a Malton perspective survives.[12] But the building was twice done over in the following

---

* If the Venetian window in the centre of the front is original it is extraordinarily early for such a feature. See W. Garner, *Kinsale Architectural Heritage* (An Foras Forbartha) Dublin 1980, pp. 14 and 16.

† At Castlewellan it not only looks like a church; it was actually in part-time use as one (P. J. Rankin, *Mourne* UAHS list, 1975, p. 32).

century, first, gently, by Lanyon, then, less gently, by Lynn, and now, though still there, it is to all intents invisible. Possibly the most massive of the arched market houses was that of Longford which has solid vaults over the arcade, but is now a mere shell and embedded, invisibly, in the local military barracks.

At the other end of the country is the very conspicuous building called the Clock Gate at Youghal (fig. 162) which, though it bears the date 1771 follows very closely the form of its seventeenth-century predecessor, no doubt because its designer was told to do so. Who that designer was is not recorded, though I suspect that it may perhaps have been Coltsman of Cork.★ It consists of four massive but diminishing storeys over a wide arch which spans the main street, and above them an octagonal domed lantern. The upper storeys were a prison, which was also the case with both the North Gate and the South Gate in Cork, built in 1715 and 1728-30 respectively, but both now disappeared.

The older guide-books always put jails and almshouses in the same chapter: logical enough since those fortunate enough to escape the one may well find themselves in the other. Almshouses as a building type are of sparse occurrence in Ireland before the middle of the eighteenth century. The oldest surviving set are the Earl of Cork's almshouses at Youghal which are of 1613 or 1634 (the authorities differ) and though said to have been 'rebuilt' before 1837 are most convincingly Jacobean: they take the form of two- and three-storey gabled houses turning the corner of two streets.[13] Those of the Southwell charity at Kinsale, dating from about 1680, are a row of eight little houses of modest architectural pretensions except for the doorcase of the central house: much less ambitious than the same family's foundation at Downpatrick, of which more presently.

The classic almshouse-form of an arcaded building round a courtyard had already appeared, as we have seen, at Kilmainham where the Royal Hospital had been built largely in order to keep discharged soldiers out of jail. Now, on Shandon hill in the rapidly expanding city of Cork, Skiddy's Almshouse (fig. 163), arcaded on two of three sides, went up in 1718-19, and was virtually one building with the Greencoat School (now demolished, but see fig. 163), a U-plan building of 1715.[14] The combination of school and almshouse under one roof was common practice—for example the late seventeenth-century Bluecoat School in Dublin—and it is found again in the Southwell Charity at Downpatrick (fig. 164),[15] a building of such merit and of so suggestive a date (1733) that it has been credited to Pearce himself. A central tower and archway are flanked by two-storey ranges accommodating six aged persons on each side. These terminate each in a schoolroom with tall round windows, and beyond each of these a two-storey house for the teachers: the whole carried out in brickwork with some dressings. The attribution to Pearce is without foundation but derives some colour from the fact that the Southwells' English seat, King's Weston, is by Pearce's cousin Vanbrugh. The beautifully-detailed brick gateway at the back of the Downpatrick building has a strong flavour of Vanbrugh (and therefore also of Pearce) about it. But without more evidence we must remain on our guard against the temptation to attribute every Pearcean-looking building of about 1730 to the master himself.

Returning briefly to court and market houses we may remark that there were formerly more of these than are now to be seen. The original Ordnance Survey

★ William Meade was the builder. For Youghal generally, see C. Beharell in *Country Life*, July 14 and 21, 1977.

160

161

162

163

164

shows one in the middle of the square at Maynooth, while that of Mountrath, which was early eighteenth-century, was destroyed only a few years ago on the usual set of pretexts.* At Ballyhaise (see page 186) the market house was evidently vaulted in brick and described as 'fantastical' and 'of singular appearance':[16] but, alas, neither the building itself nor any known representation of it survives.

The apogee of the small court and market house as the centrepiece of a formal square must surely be that of Dunlavin, built in 1743. This extraordinary building is basically cruciform with a cylindrical tower and fluted dome over the crossing, all made of granite. The spaces at the corners are occupied by rather spindly Doric colonnades making the whole a rectangle. It has been credited to Cassels but it seems to me for all its charm and merit, too clumsy to be the work of an academically accomplished designer.[17]†

The rapid growth of Cork has already been alluded to. This is most vividly illustrated by the rebuilding dates of the churches:

St Mary Shandon	1693
Christchurch	1720
St Nicholas	1720-3
St Ann Shandon	1722
St Paul	1723-6
St Finn Barre	(the cathedral) 1725-35

Since all these are or were largely built of ashlar in the wonderful Cork limestone, they raise in an acute form the question already canvassed (page 180): how did they manage to build so many of them simultaneously? The same applies to the secular public buildings of Cork, six of which have already been mentioned, all falling within the period 1715-30, and more could be added, including several bridges.[18]

Of the churches, three of the six mentioned above still stand while three have been rebuilt. St Ann's, Shandon (fig. 165) is of such importance, especially as a constituent of the image of Cork, that though the subject of churches generally is reserved for another place, something will be said about it here. Reputedly designed by the elusive Coltsman, it conforms to the then current type of country or provincial church in being a simple rectangle with shallow sanctuary and a West tower. This tower, however, is unusually massive and graceful, diminishing by two offsets between three stages, though with four openings on the West face.‡ Both tower and church are built of fine limestone ashlar on their West and South but of red sandstone on the North and East. In about 1749 it was heightened by the most felicitous addition of three more diminishing stages, more elaborately finished and culminating in a small stone dome. The resulting silhouette is so similar to that of the tower of the great mosque at Kairouan in Tunisia that there is a temptation to ask whether it is entirely coincidental. Direct communication between Cork and North African ports was commonplace at the time. The three upper stages are of limestone ashlar on all four faces and surmounting it all is a golden sphere and a large golden weathervane in the form of a salmon.

---

165 Cork: St Ann's Shandon from the West. The church, of 1722, is possibly by Coltsman; the three upper stages of the tower, and the cupola and vane, were added in about 1749

* That at Strabane was much like that of Mountrath, and has also been destroyed. Similarly at Stewartstown Co Tyrone.

† The Charter School at Clontarf is another domed building of similar style and date which has been attributed to Cassels. It was demolished long since.

‡ This not uncommon type of tower is found at, for example, Donaghcloney, Magheranally, Saintfield, and elsewhere. See *Co Down Survey* photos. 114, 116.

The architectural character of Cork is as strikingly different from that of Dublin or Belfast as that of each is from that of the other. The steep contours pressing in upon the site especially to the North contribute to this: so does the division of the Lee into many little channels (as well as two large ones) so that the wide streets which are so conspicuous, such as the quadrant of Patrick Street, the Cornmarket, and even the rectilinear Grand Parade and South Mall, all started life as pairs of quays with a channel between them. (In this respect they resemble High Street Belfast). Even such minor streets as Grattan Street and Sheares Street were once watercourses.[19] Possessing a natural harbour with advantages far exceeding those of the harbours belonging to any other large Irish town, and for most of its history in much closer contact with England and continental Europe than with Dublin, Cork has developed its own architectural personality: much more varied than that of Dublin. The close proximity of the white limestone quarries of which the quays and most of the public buildings are built, and (till the making of the railway) of the red sandstone much intermixed with the limestone for industrial and commercial buildings, together with the availability of imported brick from Holland and elsewhere, as well as of brick locally burnt, has left its mark.

Steep roofs, slate-hanging (as elsewhere in the South-West both of Ireland and of England), bow-fronts (quite unknown in Dublin), camber-headed windows (as elsewhere in Co Cork) and porches shared between adjacent houses are among the features which give Cork its unfamiliar air. It is very miscellaneous: few things in Cork go on for very long before being interrupted by something else: there are no squares and few terraces, and such as there are, are very late.

It is greatly to be regretted that, on the one hand, no serious study of the buildings of Cork as a whole has yet been attempted, and, on the other hand, that so much of its fabric is in a woebegone state, so that, full of wonders and surprises as it is, to walk about in it on a bad day can be a very depressing experience indeed. No doubt the neglect of history is connected with the neglect of the fabrics. No doubt also the splendour and variety of the stones of Cork are partly responsible for the city's having given birth to a literary masterpiece of the artist-craftsman's life: *Stone Mad* by Seamus Murphy. And Cork not only engendered two notable architectural dynasties, the Morrisons and the Deanes: it was also capable, in the early nineteenth century, of containing both the Deanes and their equally eminent rivals, the Pains. But this is to anticipate.

The illustrious Charles Smith, in his description of the city, rather enigmatically describes the new houses 'in the modern taste' as having balcony windows, 'in the Spanish fashion' (whatever that may mean)⋆ and as being built of brick. Some very odd ideas of what is 'Spanish' have been, and still are, current in Ireland (witness the so-called 'Spanish Arch' in Galway) but it is surprising to find the Spanish folly appearing so early. The houses visible in Smith's print of the Exchange are the usual 'Dutch billies' we have come to know so well.†

Individual architects with known names appear first, as we should expect, in Dublin. But we have already met one of the first rank, Davis Ducart, who worked

---

⋆ I suggest it probably means *miradores alla Coruña* such as might be familiar to seafarers and are still to be seen in several Galician towns, that is to say, glazed-in balconies covering the entire fronts of the houses: a protection against the winds of the Atlantic.

† They are also to be seen in the Nathaniel Grogan view of Cork now in the Crawford Municipal Gallery, Cork, and listed in the catalogue *Irish Houses and Landscapes*, Dublin and Belfast 1963 (Cork being neither a house nor a landscape) p. 15, no. 19.

only in the provinces, and the name of John Coltsman has been mentioned. His name, indeed, is almost all that we know about him: his total known *œuvre* consists of two Cork churches (St Anne Shandon and Christ Church) and two Cork bridges (Northgate and Southgate). We do not even know whether he built the structures which accompanied the two bridges: at all events the West side of Southgate bridge is all that now remains. By the time that the top was added to Shandon Tower he may well have been dead. On the other hand, as I have already suggested, he may have lived long enough to design the Clock Gate at Youghal.

John Morrison came, if not from Cork itself, then from the town of Midleton 13 miles to the East, where he enjoyed the patronage of Lord Shannon of Castlemartyr.[20] He is known for three things: for the 'Essay on the Convenience, Strength and Beauty, which should be connected in all private and public Buildings' which accompanied his (unsuccessful) design for a new Mayoralty House for Cork: for having been the father of Sir Richard Morrison (whose baptismal sponsors were Lord Shannon and the Hon. and Rev. Frederick Augustus Hervey, lately appointed Bishop of Cloyne and later to win notoriety as Earl of Bristol and Bishop of Derry): and finally, for having designed Kingston College, the set of almshouses on three sides of a square, built between 1771 and 1775 and forming such a notable part of the formal plan of the town of Mitchelstown (fig. 264).

John Roberts of Waterford, though he lived well on into the neo-classic period and did not die until 1794, was, like Morrison, an unreconstructed Palladian. His practice,[21] based on the town of Waterford, encompassed both the Protestant and Catholic cathedrals there—a unique achievement—the Assembly Rooms (now the Town Hall), a large town house which is now the Chamber of Commerce and where some neo-classic traits, both in the planning and the decoration, have begun to show, and country-house work most notably in the robust and spacious forecourt of Curraghmore (for the Beresford Earl of Tyrone), and as far afield as Tyrone House, Co Galway, of which the name is purely coincidental and the interior in ruins. His Church of Ireland cathedral is a fine essay in the Gibbsian-Wrenish manner (fig. 203), designed to hold a forest of box-pews in ground-floor and gallery, while the Catholic cathedral is five-aisled, similarly treated with columns (in this case Corinthian) carrying each a slice of entablature, but obviously designed to hold a large congregation, standing when they were not kneeling, as was then the universal Catholic custom. The Catholic cathedral never received its entrance-front, while the Protestant one was, almost inevitably, robbed of its galleries. The West end of the nave of the Protestant Cathedral is a little reminiscent of that of St Paul's Cathedral. The tower and spire suffer a little from the relative triviality of their architectural embellishments which emerge incompletely and with difficulty from the over-heavy mass of the tower. But the Doric portico below amply atones for this. Roberts's Assembly Rooms, which still contain a theatre, have some interesting ideas such as the detachment of the round-headed windows from the arched recesses in which they are placed: a complete contrast to the Gibbsian chunkiness of the cathedral. But the three parts of the Assembly Rooms façade are too nearly equal in interest, and the termination on the skyline is indecisively handled.

Michael Priestley of Derry was less distinguished and, so far as is now known, less prolific. He has to his credit the Lifford Court House already described, a very attractive small house, Port Hall near Derry, and the small Palladian church of Clondahorkey or Ballymore near Sheephaven in Co Donegal. No doubt he did other buildings in Derry itself, and Professor Rowan credits him with Prehen, a handsome smallish house of about 1740 a mile to the South of the city.[22]

Priestley was clearly an older man than Roberts. Roger Mulholland of Belfast was certainly younger, and Mr Brett his biographer conjectures that he may have worked under Priestley.[23] Certainly there is little to choose, stylistically, between the First Presbyterian (Unitarian) church at Dunmurry, Co Antrim of 1779 (fig. 167), attributed with some probability to Mulholland, and Clondahorkey, and both are in a pattern-book style which had been current in Ireland for nearly 40 years. It is worth remarking, however, that without its bristling panoply of Gibbsian surrounds (the presence or absence of which is mainly a matter of money) it would be almost indistinguishable from the slightly larger Presbyterian church at Corboy Co Longford (fig. 168), and doubtless others which have now disappeared.

Mulholland was by description a 'carpenter' but as everybody now knows, many a designer was at this time an executant as well and master of one or other of the building trades. His best building is another Non-Subscribing Presbyterian Church, the oval church in Rosemary Street Belfast which has providentially escaped the destruction of its neighbours, 'Second' and 'Third'. Though it has not escaped an injudicious though inoffensive alteration to the front in 1823, and a rather more objectionable modification to its 'East' end in 1907, it remains an exemplar of elegance and a thing of great joy.[24] There had been only two elliptical or 'round' churches in Ireland till then: this one and Dodson's St Andrew's, Dublin, of 1674 as remodelled by Francis Johnston in 1793–1807, which was burned in 1860 and can never have compared in charm with Rosemary Street. Their plans may be compared in Mr Brett's monograph and in Addleshaw and Etchells' *The Architectural Setting of Anglican Worship*, from which it may be seen that while the Dublin church was aligned along its shorter axis, the Belfast one has the longer axis leading from vestibule to pulpit. Ten years after Mulholland the Presbyterians of Randalstown Co Antrim built an elliptical church which, judiciously modernised, still survives.

The old White Linen Hall of Belfast, built in 1785, is also attributed to Mulholland.[25] It was a pleasant, unassuming building round a courtyard, not much adorned except for a parade of Gibbsian surrounds on the entrance-block: the addition of a cupola in 1815 (by which time Mulholland was aged 75) was an improvement: but less than a century later the whole building was swept away to make room for the present City Hall, about which the chronological limitations of this book exempt me from the duty of speaking.

The rather spectacular growth of Belfast which brought it in a short time ahead of every other Irish city except the capital, began perhaps a little before Mulholland's *floruit*: but probably not much earlier. Lord Donegall's spate of new leases was in 1767 and Mulholland married, at the age of 30, three years later. Most of his work, like that of his much more numerous counterparts in Dublin, was speculative building of a rather respectable kind, hardly any of which, in his case, has survived.

There are, in round figures, some 1,400 parishes in Ireland, and in the century and a half between the battle of the Boyne (1690) and the Famine (1847) the great majority of these were provided with churches: one (sometimes more) for the Church of Ireland, three or four (as a rule) by and for the Catholics, and a variable number for such other denominations as the Presbyterians, Moravians, Quakers and Methodists. The civil parishes are virtually coextensive with those of the Church of Ireland (as by law established until 1869), but in most parts of the country several modern Catholic parishes go to each mediaeval or civil parish. Some churches are technically chapels-of-ease but for our purpose this distinction has little relevance.

Very little notice has been taken of this vast volume of building, amounting to several thousand churches and meeting-houses, and indeed most of it was ordinary

166 Cork, Pope's Quay: a five-bay house of about 1700 still retaining its scroll-pedimented doorcase. The extra bay to the left, and the parapet, are additions

167 Dunmurry, Co Antrim: the Non-Subscribing (Unitarian) Presbyterian church of 1779, designer unknown. The general layout may be compared with the Presbyterian church at Corboy (p. 214), with the Moravian church at Gracehill (p. 230), and with the Catholic church at Kildoagh (p. 220). In all the focus of interest is, or was, in the centre of the long back wall, and it is more than likely that the two doors were originally set aside for the two sexes. As recently as 1907 a church was built in Co Offaly with two converging naves so that the men could not see the women. Bogland blood is hot: the Quare Fellow came from the parish in question

166

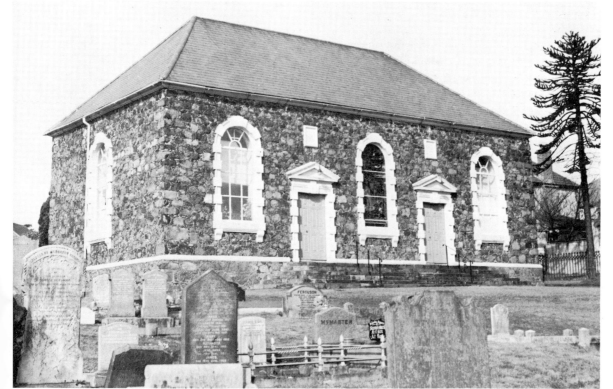

167

enough, as may often still be seen. But in many places the church is the only architecture there is, and more often than many people suppose there is merit to be found there. During this period, as is well known, the Catholic church (and to a much lesser extent the other dissenting groups) was actively discouraged by the Penal Laws, while the building of Church of Ireland churches was promoted by the state, even in places where there were hardly any Protestants, and especially after 1777 and rising to a climax in the 1815 era large quantities of public money were spent in this way.[26] Nevertheless, the well-known survey of 1732 showed nearly 900 'mass-houses' to be in existence, over 200 of them built during the previous five years. Many more were built in the course of the century following, nearly all by the unaided resources of people who were mostly very poor, and though in the 130 years since the Famine many have been replaced by later buildings, enough survive to compel our admiration, though, alas, not always the admiration of their present custodians, so that many are even now in grave danger of destruction or, perhaps worse, of injudicious modernisation.

Some 250 Catholic churches[27] from the period 1750-1845 are still standing. Of these over 20 date (or seem to date) from before 1800, and a further 60 at least from before 1830. Some account of the most interesting of these will presently be given.

The Church of Ireland took delivery from the state, at its disestablishment in 1870, of 1,628 churches, about two-thirds of which are still standing. The great majority of these are of the familiar type built by the Board of First Fruits, mostly (but not exclusively) between 1800 and 1830: and of these some account will also presently be given. But they include also the mediaeval, seventeenth-century and eighteenth-century churches, some of which have already appeared in this narrative.

It is less easy to estimate the numbers of Presbyterian and other such churches surviving from this period, but it must run into some hundreds. The definition of 'survival' presents problems. For instance, the Presbyterian church at Urney Co Tyrone dates from 1654 but we are told that it was reconstructed in 1792 and its present aspect is very much later again.★ Such instances could be multiplied, especially in places where the community has grown richer: for example in Monaghan town where the church of 1827 is still there but almost invisible under the accretions of 1901. By contrast, the Catholic church of Latlurcan nearby, mostly of about 1790, has survived visibly as such though now used as a store: instead of being rebuilt or enlarged it was superseded by McCarthy's cathedral of 1892.[28]

During most of our period the Catholic and Presbyterian churches, especially in rural situations, were apt to resemble one another more nearly than either resembled the churches of the Establishment. The reasons for this were principally practical but to some extent ideological also. The adoption of the T-plan, for instance, is a recognition of the fact that a T-plan church, especially with galleries in each of the three arms, can accommodate more people more conveniently and cheaply, while giving them all a clear view of the altar or pulpit as the case may be, than any other shape. The T-plan is thus even more characteristic of Catholic practice than of Presbyterian. There were, to be sure, differences, the most noticeable of which, at the time, was the fact that Catholics stood up (as they still do on the Continent) while Presbyterians sat down.

Though these denominations had more people than wealth, and the Establishment

---

★ Similarly, Broughshane Presbyterian church is said to be of 1655 and that of Donegore of 1627, rebuilt 1888. In these instances, continuity inheres in the congregation rather than the fabric. But see UAHS *Antrim & Ballymena*, 1969, p. 31.

had for the most part more wealth than people, there were occasional Anglican churches on the T-plan, such as Aghold Co Wicklow of 1716, or St Peter's and St Kevin's in the Southern suburbs of Dublin, both seventeenth to eighteenth century.[29] City churches were almost invariably galleried, and galleries were inserted into cathedrals. The practices of the Irish church were 'lower' as it would now be called than those of the Church of England, and the pulpit was commonly central in the geometrical as well as the moral sense. The very perfect and unaltered little country church of Timogue Co Leix (1736) preserves the arrangement of the 'three-decker' (pulpit, reading-desk and clerk's desk) against the East wall with the Holy table in front and the whole enclosed by a bow-fronted communion-rail.[30] This was the arrangement also at the extremely grand city church of St George's, Hardwicke Place, which is wider than it is long. So are some Presbyterian churches as well as not a few Catholic ones: for example St Malachy's, Belfast (fig. 213).

To avoid confusion it will be best to give some outline of the Church of Ireland's buildings in the Boyne-Famine period, followed by a similar outline of those built by the Catholics during the same period, and some account of those of other communions. I shall adhere to this plan as far as practicable, departing from it as briefly as possible wherever the nature of the subject seems to demand a digression.

A most remarkable survival is the small plain church at Hollywood Co Wicklow (fig. 170), built a little before 1700. With two half-heartedly pointed windows in each long wall, a round-headed East window and a minute bell-cote on the West gable, it would almost escape notice except for the very marked batter of the walls, which suggests—what is indeed the truth—that the church has a stone barrel-vault. It was some 200 years since this had last been done—at Taghmon and Ardrass—and it was not to be done again for more than a century, until the Black Church in Dublin. Among other things, Hollywood indicates how early the Irish church had begun to be tinged by the belief that the pointed arch is essential to salvation:* the nave windows at Aghold, also, are half-heartedly pointed. Gothic survival or gothic revival? Who knows? But for more formal and larger churches the round arch still had many years to run.

There is a small family of single-cell churches in Co Cork all dating from the early years of the century and all with round apses: Templemichael (1707), Ballynamona (1717) and better-known than either because it was Elizabeth Bowen's church, Farahy (1721). Both the inscription and the look of the building suggest that it is a reconditioning of something older.

The building-dates of noteworthy Church of Ireland churches are scattered pretty evenly through the eighteenth century: there are one or two of importance in every decade. In 1737 Cassels built the church of Knockbreda near Belfast, cruciform with semicircular transepts and a spire over its West tower: most notable, however, for the fantastic collection of later mausolea in its graveyard.[31] Moira church, Co Down, of 1723, is a respectable piece of classicism with a segmental-headed West door under a tower and spire.[32] Ballycastle, Co Antrim, of the mid-1750s, is similar but rather more formal: there is a Venetian window with blind side-lights over the door. The clock-face, like that of Shandon, is wildly out of scale: otherwise, as at Shandon, it could not be read at any distance. The local family of Boyd managed to hoist

---

* St Peter's Drogheda, a mid-eighteenth-century town church with rococo plasterwork, has pointed windows with Y-tracery lighting the galleries, while St Mary's Carlow, of similar date, has segment-headed windows with keystones, but filled with perpendicular tracery in granite.

168

169

Ballycastle up, briefly, into being a thriving mining and manufacturing town. Hence the church, built 'at the sole expense of H. Boyd Esq.'[33]

The town churches of St Olaf, Waterford and Holy Trinity, Downpatrick, of the mid-1730s are box-like structures of which the principal interest, at Waterford, lay in the fittings which have recently been dispersed. The finest provincial town church of the mid-century is undoubtedly St Peter's, Drogheda, a galleried rectangle to which the upper part of the tower and a spire were added by Francis Johnston 40 years later. Its interior is strongly reminiscent of both St Mary's and St Anne's, Dublin.[34]

Two or three cathedrals were rebuilt in the period: Waterford we have already met. The new cathedral at Cashel did not, as at Waterford, entail the destruction of its predecessor but merely the unroofing of it. On the other hand the cathedral of 1763 onwards is less interesting than that of Waterford and remained so even after the handsome tower and spire added by Morrison in 1780-88 and depicted on Archbishop Agar's tomb in Westminster Abbey.[35] The little cruciform cathedral of Clogher Co Tyrone, is something of a puzzle. It is alleged to have been built by Bishop Stearne in 1744 'in the ancient English style' and remodelled by Dean Bagwell 'in the Grecian style' in 1818. It is, to all appearance, neither of these things but a mannerly work in mid-eighteenth century classic.[36] In the mid-1770s the town church of St Iberius, Wexford, was rebuilt, probably by John Roberts, in the form of a galleried rectangle with an apse in the middle of one of the long sides containing the altar and screened by a triple arcade carried on a giant Corinthian order.

Fifteen years earlier the church at Hillsborough Co Down, had initiated, as far as Ireland was concerned, the gothic revival properly so called. Like most notable churches of the century, it owed its existence to a single patron, in this case Wills Hill, Earl of Hillsborough.[37] Almost certainly an English architect was involved, and the likeliest of several candidates is perhaps Sanderson Miller. It is still, of course, gothick with a 'k' and in no way constructional. It is rigidly symmetrical, approached by an axial avenue, with a West tower and spire half-detached from the aisleless nave, and narrow towers at the ends of the transepts. It took, apparently, 15 years to build (1760-75). Not the least of its charms is that, apart from some savage ribbon-pointing carried out under another English architect in the present century, it has escaped violation in any way. An even more delightful gothick interior is that of Downpatrick Cathedral, fitted out with undulating joinery some time between 1790 and 1818: Wills Hill was one of the three instigators of the project, and the architect *may* have been Charles Lilly of Dublin.[38]

Magnificent and munificent prelates became conspicuous towards the end of the century: most notably the celebrated Earl-Bishop (Frederick Augustus Hervey) and Richard Robinson, Archbishop of Armagh. Both were Englishmen, which was usual at the time. Hervey built several churches in his diocese of Derry, some of which were designed by his architect Michael Shanahan whom he had brought from Cork. The most striking thing about them is that, though built in the 1770s and 1790s, they pre-figure the model of the typical First Fruits churches of 30 and 40 years later.[39] So does the 1782 church at Moate Co Westmeath.

Richard Robinson came to his see in 1765 and shortly began to live in Armagh: the first archbishop to do so for many centuries. He sent the promising youngster Francis Johnston to work under Thomas Cooley in Dublin, and in his archdiocese of Armagh in the late 1770s and 1780s (Cooley died in 1784) a number of churches— Kells, Ballymakenny, Clonmore, Lisnadill, Grange and others—were built to the designs of Cooley and Johnston (it is not quite certain which). Though more

168 Corboy Presbyterian Church, Co Longford. Dating from the mid-eighteenth century, it is of the same general type as Dunmurry, and had originally its liturgical centre (i.e. the pulpit) in the middle of the back wall

169 Inistioge, Co Kilkenny: the tower of the Augustinian priory church with, behind it, the square-to-octagonal tower (for which compare Askeaton, also Augustinian). To the right is the Church of Ireland parish church of 1824, and to the left the Catholic parish church of 1837

elaborately finished than the Earl-Bishop's churches, they are in the direct line leading to the standard First Fruits type of a simple hall prefaced by a West tower (usually with a stone spire) and often furnished with a small West gallery. At the East end there is commonly a shallow rectangular sanctuary. The general decorative flavour is discreetly Gothic, varying with the amount of money available: pinnacles on the tower, panelling on the gallery-front, elaboration of window-tracery and so on.[40]

Built of rubble stone, the churches were invariably rendered in lime-plaster, though this has all too often been either stripped off or replaced with cement, Ireland's national disease. They seldom if ever had gutters unless they also had parapets. Any heating arrangements now to be seen seem to be afterthoughts: many were cold but few were frozen. Ventilation was often by apertures in the sloping internal sills communicating with the atmosphere a few feet lower down. Many, especially of the smaller churches, had no windows in the North wall, following the example of Rathreagh, and thus practised a primitive form of conservation of solar heat.★

They are, in nearly every case, beautifully sited, and add greatly to the amenity of the countryside, as they were intended to do. In towns and 'villages' they commonly occupy a focal site at the head of the street: for example at Banagher, Mitchelstown, Virginia and countless other places. The principal architect for the Board was in 1813 John Bowden, but by 1830 there was one for each of the ecclesiastical provinces: William Farrell for Armagh, John Semple (and son) for Dublin, James Pain for Cashel and Joseph Welland (the successor of Bowden) for Tuam:[41] but it is on the whole rare for a particular church to be assignable to one or other of these, except that the Pain brothers stand head and shoulders above the rest in architectural accomplishment.

The broom of reform was already at work in the corridors, and in 1834, some 20 years after its peak of activity, the Board of First Fruits gave place to the Commissioners of Ecclesiastical Temporalities, as part of the modest reorganisation which, among other adjustments, provided for two of the four archbishoprics to lapse.

In a vivid passage, that well-informed and fair-minded writer James Godkin, depicts the 'well-endowed rector, ministering to a congregation of twenty or thirty people, while a thousand members of the disinherited Church kneel upon an earthen floor in a rudely constructed chapel'.[42] This is probably not much exaggerated, though the oldest surviving floors of pre-Emancipation Catholic churches are of large clay tiles, not of earth. They are also, sometimes, raked towards the altar like those of a theatre.

The oldest surviving such building in use seems to be the large T-plan church at Grange in the Cooley peninsula in Co Louth, which, except for its tower, dates from 1762.† The arms are very long and the eaves are rather low. It is lovingly cared for. On the other hand, a little church also, as it happens, called Grange, about a mile and a half North of Armagh, though of the utmost charm, has within the past 30 years been allowed, or even encouraged, to fall into total decay.

The oldest, and the best, in any Irish town is beyond any doubt St Patrick's, Waterford (figs 173 and 174), a rectangle with galleries round three sides and an upper gallery at the West end (as in some Dublin Church of Ireland churches), all

170 Hollywood, Co Wicklow: South wall of the Church of Ireland church, late seventeenth century. The very marked batter visible in the window-reveals helped to take the thrust of the barrel-vaulted roof. The wall has been lime-plastered over slate-hanging which can still be discerned

171 Cloghjordan, Co Tipperary: the Church of Ireland church in the main square, perhaps by James Pain who was the First Fruits architect for the province of Cashel at the material time, i.e. before 1834

172 Clonegal, Co Carlow: both the East and West ends of the Catholic church (the East end is shown here) have been very recently destroyed in an ill-considered 'modernisation'

★ This was common in Scotland also. See G. Hay, *The Architecture of Scottish Churches*, 1957, pp. 14, 43, 48.

† So does the oldest part of the Catholic church of Portaferry Co Down, signed by its two builders.

170

171

172

173 and 174   Waterford:
St Patrick's Catholic
Church, a rare and precious
survival of 1764, especially
precious since a similar
church in Cork was
savagely mutilated a few
years back

173   View looking East

174   View looking West

175   Tallanstown, Co
Louth: reredos, in a version
of rococo gothick

174

175

176

177

178

176, 177 and **178**
Kildoagh Catholic Church,
Co Cavan, dated 1796.
Front (North), back
(South) and interior. The
church retains its original
large earthenware floor-
tiles, its galleries and of
course also the twin-door
arrangement as found also
in Presbyterian country
churches. The glazing of
the South wall is probably
original: that of the North
wall apparently early
nineteenth-century

179 Malin, Co Donegal:
the Presbyterian Church, a
little outside the village

180 Templemoyle, Co
Donegal: the Catholic
church, two miles from
Malin and almost
indistinguishable from it

179

180

181

182

183

184

185

intact, together with a fine classical reredos, the whole dating from 1764. Until a few years ago St Finnbarr's South in Cork was of comparable splendour though a little later (1776), with two wide transepts. But it has been brutally gutted and is now totally devoid of interest: a most lamentable loss.

It is worth emphasising that these few survivals stand for a much larger number, probably of equal interest, which once existed but have fallen victim to increased prosperity. The handsome church of Creeslough Co Donegal, for example, of the mid-1780s, has lately been superseded by a fine new church by the most original church-architect of our time, Liam McCormick.

Two churches, taken almost at random from the 1790s, may be described. Cratloe Co Clare,[43] is probably the finest example of an early T-plan barn-church in the country, with low eaves, round-headed sash-windows and a pretty gothick reredos. It incorporates one apparently mediaeval (or seventeenth-century?) doorway. There are three bow-fronted galleries. It has two date-stones, of 1791 and 1806. It is lovingly cared-for. The simple rectangle is represented by Kildoagh church, Co Cavan (figs 176, 177 and 178),[44] which has a date-stone of 1796. The altar is in the middle of one of the long sides, so that most of the congregation sit facing each other across the space in front of it, including those in the two galleries. The floor is of large earthenware tiles. The church stands parallel to the road and a little back from it, and has four windows and two doors, symmetrically arranged, much as at Dunmurry, Corboy, and other Presbyterian examples. The two doors were probably for the two sexes who, in the country, were sometimes segregated in this way. The windows on either side of the altar have more elaborate tracery than those on the road side.

The simple rectangle, of somewhat squarer form, but still with the altar against one of the long sides, is also found, but more rarely. Sometimes there are galleries round three sides. In this form, as at Inniskeen or Lislonan, both in Co Monaghan, they inevitably suggest a comparison with Presbyterian churches. But the commonest type of all is naturally the single-cell longitudinally arranged. Next to it comes the T-plan, perhaps the most characteristic. The beauties of these churches include, though increasingly hard to find, their fenestration, the texture of the lime-plaster rendering, and the carefully graduated slating: all of which are liable, as the saying goes, to alteration without notice.

These buildings are undervalued, I fear, because being simple they are not thought to be beautiful. The very circumstances of their creation, the self-denial and the self-reliance of farming communities in times much harder than anyone alive today can yet imagine—one church bears the inscription 'Anno Famis et Pestis'[45] (1847)—are, by a sad irony, turned against them. Their unity with the farms and dwellings of their time, the essential rightness of their relation to the landscape, the devotion and craftsmanship which they embody, the moving dignity with which they testify to an honourable past, are disregarded and thrown on the rubbish-heap. Literally sometimes.

A few of the T-plan churches have an interesting variation in the treatment of the re-entrant corners, with a kind of 'chamfer' sometimes wide enough to contain a window, as at Ballaghmore, Co Leix (an interesting church in other ways also).★ This is a middle-Western feature, found in South Clare and North Limerick and as far South and East as Ballylaneen in Co Waterford. A quasi-cylindrical sub-variant occurs at Oranmore Co Galway. The dates, where known, are mostly around 1829. The galleries are sometimes (though now rarely) reached by external steps, as at

★ Derived, just possibly, from Soufflot's Sainte Geneviève, Paris (Panthéon).

PREVIOUS PAGES

181 Oranmore, Co Galway: fine carpentry in the roof of the Catholic church of 1803

182 Ballybacon, Co Tipperary: interior of the Catholic church, which, like Kildoagh, still has its earthenware tiled floor, its original roof (partly visible here) and bow-fronted confessionals, as well as the elaborate reredos here shown, ingeniously blended of classical and gothick elements (destroyed 1981-2)

183 Crusheen, Co Clare: this interior of about 1840 is already perceptibly affected by the coming passion for 'archaeological' fidelity

184 Taghmon, Co Westmeath: the Catholic church and presbytery. Built by the Rev. A. McElroy, 1844

185 Ardkeen Catholic Church, Co Down, three miles North of Portaferry. This little early-nineteenth century church close to Strangford Lough could as easily be Presbyterian, except perhaps for the three lancets in the 'East' gable

Rathcabban, Kells-in-Ossory, Lislonan in Co Monaghan, or Kilpedder Co Wicklow, where they are enclosed as at Ardtanagh Presbyterian Church, Co Down which is of much the same date (1826).*

There are places, especially in Co Donegal, where Catholic and Presbyterian churches stand within sight of one another, so similar in their architecture that the stranger cannot tell which is which until he is close enough to see, on the gable of one, the symbol of both. Such, for example, are Lag (Catholic) and Inch (Presbyterian) to the West of Malin, or Templemoyle (Catholic) a mile or two on the other side of Malin, and resembling Inch even more closely (figs 179, 180).

Sometimes the body of the church and the house of the priest or minister form a continuous building with an unbroken roof-ridge. Though visually dissimilar this is no doubt a continuation of the mediaeval tradition of the residential West end as seen, for example, at Taghmon Co Westmeath. As it happens, the modern 1844 Catholic church of Taghmon (fig. 184)[46] is a case in point, with three bays of pointed windows rising to the same height as three storeys of presbytery (in its modern sense). The Moravian church at Ballinderry Lower Co Antrim (fig. 186), and the Methodist church opposite the court house in Castlebar (fig. 188) are just the same, and the Catholic churches at Tullaherin Co Kilkenny, Lisdowney Co Kilkenny and Dunkerrin Co Offaly, both now modernised. The most spectacular example is St Mel's Cathedral Longford (fig. 187), where, if you go round to the back, you will be rewarded with the sight of no less than five storeys of accommodation behind the high altar.

In one respect the Catholic churches necessarily differ greatly from the Presbyterian, and that is in the treatment of the ritual focus which in Catholic churches is the altar. There are still a great many extremely fine reredoses surviving in out-of-the-way churches, though they are being destroyed at a horrifying rate. One of the best and latest to be scrapped was the fine Corinthian one at Tullaherin mentioned in the last paragraph. They are mostly classical in a proportion to gothic of about three to one, with the occasional hybrid. The gothic should mostly be spelt with a terminal 'k' and has often something of a rococo flavour. As a series they are all, with few exceptions, remarkably accomplished and assured: correct yet full of life.

For some reason not fully apparent they have a markedly Southern distribution. Of 58 examples noted, only seven or eight are North of a line from Dublin to Galway, and all except nine lie to the East of Limerick. The greatest concentrations are in Kilkenny and Carlow, with a sprinkling round Limerick and in North and South Tipperary. It may be that this imbalance is the result of recent destruction, but I do not think so. Had I been more assiduous in my church-visiting 30 years ago I should be in a better position to say.

These buildings are nearly all anonymous and vernacular in the truest sense of that word. The name of the parish priest is not infrequently found on a tablet: much less commonly that of an artificer. But there are some:

1800	Slieverue	S Co Kilkenny	Mr Christopher Hill Arch.
1812	Shanballynahagh†	N Co Tipperary	P. Bergin Arch.
1814	Newchapel	N Co Tipperary	built by Patk. Cleary
1831	Buttevant	N Co Cork	Charles Cotterel
1832	Drumquin	W Co Tyrone	Daniel Campbell builder

* Compare Rademon Presbyterian Church, Co Down. Plan in *Co. Down Survey* p. 349.
† Shanballynahagh is clearly, and most exceptionally for its date, modelled on the Romanesque West front of St Cronan's, Roscrea, a few miles away.

186

187

188

189

190

191

192

191 Inch, Inishowen, Co Donegal: the Presbyterian church with domestic accommodation under the same roof

192 Castlequarter, Co Waterford: this Catholic church interior of 1826 shows a spare elegance in its use of classical forms (destroyed 1980)

193 Granard, Co Longford: the nineteenth-century Catholic parish church by John Burke is sited beside the largest Norman mote in Ireland and dominates the street

194

195

194 Banbridge, Co Down: interior of the Presbyterian (Unitarian) Church, 1846

195 Gracehill, Co Antrim: the Moravian church of 1765, dominating the square green of the Moravian settlement. The two doors are believed to have been for the two sexes. Above them are galleries and in the centre an octagonal pulpit. Such an arrangement, with two doors and the liturgical focus in the centre of the long back wall, with, or without galleries, is common to all the 'nonconformist' groups, including the Catholic (compare Kildoagh, Dunmurry and St Malachy's, Belfast)

1833	Carrig	N Co Tipperary	John Hanley architect
1838	Inagh	mid Co Clare	Patto Donoghue builder
1842	Knocklong	E Co Limerick	Samuel Harris Builder
1842	Ballyshannon	SW Co Donegal	Dan Campbell builder
1845	Ballintra	SW Co Donegal	James McKenna builder
1845	Kinvara (tower)	S Co Galway	Michael Linnane Architect
1859	Puckaun	N Co Tipperary	Jacobus Darcy artifex

Needless to say the signed buildings are not always the best. There are no signatures on some of the most splendid examples, such as Cloyne, Templeorum, Sonna, Massmount, Hugginstown or Loughmoe.[47]

Contemporaneously with the later of these buildings some churches were going up which were clearly designed by competent architects, such as Callan in the classic manner or Ardee in the gothick, as well as some, such as Fethard,[48] which seem to display an inspired amateur talent. In many other cases, such as Tallanstown or Kentstown or Nobber,[49] cut-stone frontispieces of considerable charm preface what are essentially barn-churches.

Though much less often than the First-Fruits churches, these Catholic churches are sometimes found in telling and dominant positions in the street-plan of town or village. Some examples are Ballymore-Eustace Co Kildare, Moynalty Co Meath, Ballynacarrigy Co Westmeath, Oughterard Co Galway, and Mitchelstown Co Cork. With the post-Famine revival this became more marked, as, for example, at Granard Co Longford (fig. 193).

The architecture of the remaining denominations can be only briefly touched upon. The Moravians have already been mentioned: they came to Ireland in 1746, and their principal remaining settlement is at Gracehill Co Antrim (fig. 195), where the church of 1765 and other buildings stand round a square. Their church in Dublin, of 1750, between Bishop Street and Kevin Street, survived with its fittings till about 20 years ago.

The Non-Subscribing church at Downpatrick[50] must be among the earliest Presbyterian T-plan churches in the country, of 1729 (though the Down Survey thinks it may have been remodelled later in the same century).* Killinchy, of 1739, is lower and longer. Radémon, of 1787, has external gallery-stairs and an interior of great elegance. Randalstown and Dunmurry have already been mentioned. Outside the heartland of Presbyterianism in the North-East there are good examples at Corboy Co Longford and Mullafarry Co Mayo. Presbyterian churches are sometimes very close together: just outside Ballybay in Co Monaghan there are two almost identical standing cheek-by-jowl in memory of some bygone rift of discipline or of doctrine; not to mention the three in Rosemary Street, Belfast.

By the twenties of the nineteenth century a kind of temple-fronted box had become the norm, sometimes with the columns in antis, Ionic as at Clough,[51] or Doric as at Antrim, both of 1837. Fidelity to the temple-front was observed also at Third Belfast (of 1831, in Rosemary Street) where a Greek tetrastyle portico of cast-iron columns prefixed a massive block, more like a cross between a country house and a court house than a church, and was approached by a massive flight of steps. The architect, John Miller, was the grandson of a local stone-merchant but later went bankrupt and emigrated to the Antipodes. The interior, heavily galleried, with deeply coffered ceiling, was full of mahogany reassurance, but perished by fire in 1941.[52]

---

* For a late example, see No 61, (p. 17) in H. Dixon, *Ulster Architecture 1800–1900*, exhibition catalogue, Belfast 1972.

CHAPTER FOURTEEN

The Neo-Classic

The decade 1758-68 is of crucial importance in the history of Dublin architecture. The arrival of Lord Townshend in 1767, the first viceroy to be committed in advance to the policy of permanent residence in Ireland, was to have far-reaching results especially on the activity of Parliament. But well before that there had been other developments of equal or greater moment. The Wide Streets Commissioners, established by an act of 1757, met first in the following years, and, as Dr McParland has noted, were all, except the Lord Mayor, Members of Parliament.[1] In time they were to exercise an important influence over elevational design as well as over town-planning in the narrower sense. In or about 1759 the (Royal) Dublin Society had started its Drawing School,[2] and by 1764 Thomas Ivory was its drawing master. By 1762, being then 34 years of age, Lord Charlemont had decided that his duty required him to live in Ireland and more particularly in Dublin, where he presently built Charlemont House in the Rotunda Gardens, and the Casino at Clontarf a little distance away, both designed by Sir William Chambers and bringing to Dublin extremely advanced and refined examples of Franco-Roman neo-classic taste.[3]

The Wide Streets Commission, though properly known by its generalizing title, had in fact been first set up to make one particular street, from Capel Street Bridge to Dublin Castle, and by 1762 this had been done. Ideas of how to handle the consequent approach to the castle, whether by a square or otherwise, soon became merged with the project of a new Royal Exchange, which the merchants had been mooting since 1761.[4] By 1766 the 100-feet-square site immediately North of the Castle and axially facing the bridge had been fixed on, and, in emulation of the London Blackfriars Bridge competition of 1758, a competition was organized.

There was, by this time, a perceptible undercurrent of feeling that Irish architects were no longer up to international standards, or that, at best, their experience was provincial and their ideas old-fashioned.[5] Accomplished as it was, the Provost's House was, as we have seen, a very conservative building for its date. Coincidentally with the Royal Exchange Competition an architectural critic, conjecturally identified by Dr McParland as Andrew Caldwell, gave expression to these ideas, nor was he alone.

The resident Irish architects of note included Ducart, Priestley and Roberts, all provincially based, as we have seen, George Semple (who had not yet published his book on the building of Essex Bridge), Robert Mack, a mason-architect who was yet to build Powerscourt House which is robustly, not to say chunkily, Palladian, John Smyth (of the Provost's House) whose two churches we have glanced at: also on the chunky side when left to himself. They included also Ivory, who in performance was to prove open to the neo-classical spirit, though the design with which he had in 1768 won the Oxmantown Green Market House competition appears also to have been of the chunky school, and was never built.

Of these seven men only three entered the Royal Exchange competition, at least under their own names: Ivory, Priestley and Mack. One entrant, Thomas or Joseph

196

196 Marino, Co Dublin: the Casino designed by Sir William Chambers for Lord Charlemont and built in the years following 1758. Now a National Monument and under extensive restoration at the time of writing. Drawing by Michael Craig

197 Dublin: the Royal Exchange (now the City Hall). Plan as originally disposed, based on a plan by Thomas Cooley. Nearly all the space lying outside the central ring of columns was enclosed with later partitions: this plan shows it as it was when all the space, including the two staircases, was essentially one (as may be seen in Patrick Byrne's internal view reproduced in my *Dublin*, plate XIX) and when the relationship of the external and internal orders of pilasters was quite clear. The ground rises steeply towards the South-West (top right)

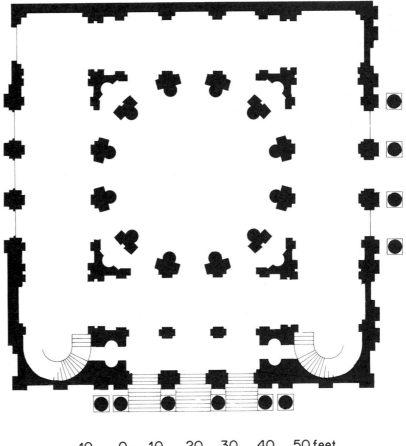

197

Jarratt, was apparently a government architect of some years' standing of whose accomplishments we know nothing.[6] He sent in three designs. There were 25 designs of Irish origin, 18 of which came from 13 named entrants (or 14 if the partnership of Myers and Sproule is counted as two). Seven entered under initials or *noms-de-guerre*. There were 33 entrants from England, and two of unidentified origin.

The most important of the English entries were those of James Gandon, Thomas Sandby, Thomas Cooley and 'J.W.L.' for whom Dr McParland suggests the name of James Wyatt (London).[7]

Nobody seems to have expected the Irish to win. Nor did they. But Ivory, Jarratt and the partnership of Sproule and Myers were given consolation prizes of plate. The winners were, first Thomas Cooley, second James Gandon, third Thomas Sandby, all of London. Gandon and Sandby were close friends and had important allies among a small group of discerning Irish gentlemen who frequented London architectural circles.[8] Cooley, a London carpenter by origin, was the protegé of Robert Mylne and also, as later became very clear, of James Wyatt.

His Royal Exchange (now the City Hall) (fig. 197) is the only domed★ eighteenth-century building in virtually original condition, and since that century set such store by the dome, both symbolically and spatially, this gives it a very special value. Since Cooley, who came to Dublin and stayed till his death in 1784, seems never to have designed any other buildings of comparable merit, the suspicion was early voiced, and has not yet been dispelled, that his design owes more to Mylne, an architect of proven eminence, than to Cooley himself. Since some Cooley drawings anterior to the executed design still exist,[9] there is enough evidence to justify Dr McParland's suggestion that one of the most telling features of the interior, the subsidiary Ionic order which accompanies the main order carrying the dome, was imported from Gandon's premiated design.

The detailing of the Royal Exchange is impeccable, the workmanship of the highest quality, the design suave if not genial. It suffers from facing North and from being, as a building, very evidently almost entirely useless, a defect only partly remedied by the later partial enclosure of the spaces adjoining the rotunda. By comparison with Gandon (to whom it was soon to find itself compared) it may be thought to be, externally at least, a shade too busily textured. By the time it was built Cooley had leapt at a single bound from obscurity into the post of deputy state architect and, *in commendam* with it, that of architect to the Primate at Armagh. We must suppose him to have divided his time between Dublin and Armagh, with excursions to such places as Caledon where one of his sketchbooks is preserved. For the Primate he built in Armagh a library and in the countryside several churches, worked on the palace and the cathedral, and took under his wing and into his office a bright youth named Francis Johnston from near Armagh. In Dublin, as Clerk and Inspector of Civil Buildings (under Christopher Myers) he built Newgate Gaol, an expressive building (now vanished)[10] much influenced by its London namesake, and other minor jobs. But most significantly, as is now known,[11] besides building the record-storage building which still, in a sense, survives as the West wing of the Four Courts, he had much to do with originating the idea of a long building on Inns Quay to house, in the centre, the four courts of Kings Bench, Chancery, Exchequer and

---

★ It set the fashion for copper-covered domes (Custom House, Four Courts, Belfast City Hall etc.), thus linking Ireland with Scandinavia rather than with England or France, where domes are generally covered with lead.

Common Pleas, and even with the idea that they should be set diagonally round a central space. But this is to anticipate.

The effect on Ivory of Cooley's success was immediate.[12] Though some eight years older than Cooley, he was quick to learn not merely from the winner but also, it is clear, from the drawings all of which were exhibited before the adjudication. He soon had his revenge. The Blue-Coat School competition of 1772 brought some of the old rivals again to the lists—Sandys, Omer, Sproule—and others. Cooley was ignominiously routed and actually withdrew under a barrage of contumely, leaving Ivory in possession of the field. Andrew Caldwell, still hankering after the latest English thing, tried to have him ousted in favour of Chambers, but failed.

The Blue-Coat (King's Hospital) scheme was ambitious and, for the usual reasons, only partly carried out. It is essentially a country-house composition (and has its pendant in Ivory's only known country house, Kilcarty), and as Dr McParland has noted, leans a little on the Rotunda Hospital, which was also a country-house composition. But in the delicacy of the ornamentation Ivory had by now little to learn from anybody, as he showed a few years later at Newcomen's Bank in Castle Street. In this building, on a highly sensitive site, facing the main gate into the castle and also facing Cooley's Exchange, Ivory, using a repertoire of shallow arched recesses, a fluted frieze, and delicate swags, paid such respect to Cooley's building as to succeed, in the opinion of one modern critic,[13] in making the Exchange look coarse.

Neither Cooley nor Ivory lived long to enjoy their respective triumphs.[14] When Cooley died in 1784 he was only 43, and in two years Ivory too was dead at the age of 54. By the time of their deaths both had been eclipsed by the major luminary, Gandon: not, we can hardly doubt, without pain and disappointment. For though Cooley was at first (in 1782) asked to prepare plans for the House of Lords extensions, the job was given to Gandon, while though Ivory was Surveyor to the Revenue Commissioners, it was Gandon who built the Custom House.

Cooley, it is true, enjoyed a kind of posthumous prolongation of his existence which was denied to poor Ivory,* for not only were his Public (Record) Offices even more closely entangled with the ultimate achievement of the Four Courts than has till lately been believed, there is also a group of country houses: Mount Kennedy, Lucan, Caledon, Rokeby, Slane and Castle Coole, all inter-related and each with more than one architect. At Mount Kennedy Cooley seems to be acting, with Richard Johnston, as executant for the absent Wyatt.[15] At Caledon he is apparently on his own. At Rokeby Francis Johnston seems to be carrying out the designs of the recently deceased Cooley, and at Castle Coole Wyatt, still *in absentia*, is superseding Richard Johnston.[16] From 1778 onwards Francis Johnston was a pupil in Cooley's office and by 1784 was working semi-independently for the Primate. In this way Cooley's legacy lived on.

The official architects who followed Cooley and Myers, such as Penrose and Gibson, are names of very small note. Gandon, by contrast, never held any official position: there was no need.

The story of Gandon's arrival in Dublin on 26 April 1781, 'smuggled in' as his enemies (not without truth) asserted, has often been told.[17] He had powerful supporters: The Rt. Hon. John Beresford, chairman of the Revenue Board, Lord

---

* Except, of course, insofar as Ivory lives on through his numerous pupils at the Dublin Society's School who included, for example, James Hoban the architect of the White House in Washington.

Carlow, the Earl of Charlemont, Sackville Hamilton, Frederick Trench and, to begin with at least, William Burton Conyngham of Slane. Beresford, Trench and Conyngham were by now active Wide Streets Commissioners, and so was Caldwell who was also well disposed towards Gandon. The powers of the Commissioners were extended by the Act 21–22 Geo. III. c. 17 (1781–2) which empowered them to levy a tax on coal.

Numerous schemes for the improvement of Dublin had been aired. They may be divided into Eastward schemes and Central-West schemes. The nobility and gentry, broadly speaking, were Eastward-minded, and the merchants Central-West in their outlook.[18] For example, there was a parliamentary proposal in 1771 to put the Four Courts in College Green, opposite the Parliament House.[19]

Gandon, in the event, got the best of both worlds. Hardly was the building of the Custom House (an 'Eastward' scheme) well under way when he was embarked on the House of Lords extensions (also 'Eastward') and, very little later, the Four Courts ('Central-West'). All these large undertakings were going on at the same time, and neither Four Courts nor (probably) Custom House were finished when he designed Carlisle (O'Connell) Bridge, the essential link in the Commissioners' Easterly shift of the town's axis from Capel Street to Sackville Street and D'Olier Street.

The political cross-currents of the time were very complex, and Gandon seems to have navigated them with skill, miscalculating (or being outmanoeuvred) only once: in the matter of the Commons extensions of 1786 onwards, where he was served as Cooley had been served by the Lords four years earlier.[20] The main power-groups were the merchants, the parliament, and the executive. To some extent they overlapped in membership, and the lawyers, who may be identified as another group, overlapped both with the parliament and with the executive. The executive (of which John Beresford was a typical member) was not responsible to Parliament as it was in Britain. But since Parliament now sat much more constantly than it had done, its importance, in Dublin, had come to outweigh that of the merchants, at least for the time being.

None of these groups had a monopoly of 'patriotism'. Yet this concept, which was a good deal talked about during the period of 'Grattan's Parliament', was a conscious component of the desire to beautify the city. Men such as Charlemont, Beresford, Caldwell and Conyngham might differ—did indeed differ—in politics, but they were cosmopolitan in taste and determined that Dublin should equal London so far as possible, and even, in some aspects, excel it.[21] This was by no means absurd, as we can see when we reflect that by the close of the century both Parliament and the Courts were housed in incomparably greater splendour than their British analogues which muddled on in their mediaeval way until excoriated by fire.

Two paradoxes flowed from this situation. One was that some of those who had laboured so hard and so successfully to make Dublin into a real capital city were, in the end, supporters of the Union which made it into more or less of a provincial town. The other paradox is that, in their anxiety to procure nothing but the best for Dublin and for Ireland, they were apt to prefer English architects to Irish ones. Twenty years later, after the Union, Irish architects came back into prominence, as though in compensation for the loss of national status.

For the last 20 years of the century the domination of Gandon was well-nigh complete. Not quite: for Trinity College had in 1775 called in Chambers to produce a scheme for the theatre, chapel and East side of Parliament Square. The theatre and chapel only were carried out, between 1777 and 1800 or so, with Graham Myers as executive architect carrying a great deal of the responsibility (for Chambers never

OVERLEAF
198 Dublin: the Custom House. Plan at first-floor level showing the Long Room (actually somewhat wider than it was long) immediately North of the dome. There were open arcades to East and West as well as those still open to the South.

199 Dublin: the Four Courts, Plan from the *Reports from the Commissioners . . . respecting the public records of Ireland, 1813–15*. The impression given here that the great central hall is octagonal is fallacious: it is circular. The main outlines of the plan of the central block were (perforce) preserved in the reconstruction of 1932: the rest of the plan was altered. It is noticeable that the West wing (built by Cooley) consists of separate 'houses' like parts of the contemporary Somerset House in London: the original, primitive, way of building government offices.

came to Ireland, but Lord Charlemont was his eyes and ears) and Michael Stapleton executing, if not also designing, the very neo-classic plaster decoration.[22]

Charlemont's Casino (which deserves a book all to itself) was influential not only on Gandon (at the Custom House) but also on Richard Johnston, who cribbed from it for the wings of his design for Castle Coole. But Charlemont House in Rutland Square had no perceptible influence on the rest of Dublin save in rare cases such as the Commercial Buildings by Edward Park, and Aldborough House by an unknown architect. Dublin street- and square-architecture was by then much too firmly settled in its own identity to adopt anything but decorative trimmings from elsewhere.

Gandon's work outside Dublin is small in quantity: the Waterford court house (see page 267), Coolbanagher church, the Carriglas stables and gateway, the villa called Emsworth,[23] and very little else except Emo, a country house which he did little more than begin. His buildings are interdependent and cast a great deal of light on one another. The same themes are used over and over again, redeployed with subtle resource. Thus the elevation of Waterford court house is very close to one of those proposed for the West (Commons) front of the Parliament House, while its plan is one of the Nottingham designs brought up to date. The end-pavilions of Emo are related to the Commons design.[24] The King's Inns front is (as has recently been established by Dr McParland's most acute analysis)[25] a re-use of his Royal Exchange competition design (thus uniting almost his first with almost his last work). The interiors of Coolbanagher Church and of the Benchers' Dining Hall in the Inns are cousins-german. The circular ground-floor lobby in the House of Lords is a transposition of the first-floor lobby of the Custom House from the octagonal mode to the circular, as well as being a delicate paraphrase on a virtually domestic scale of the Roman grandeur of the Four Courts rotunda. The courtyard gateways of the Four Courts reappear as the central feature of the King's Inns façades, both East and West, and again, dressed in Custom House-style detail, at Carriglas.* The North portico of the Custom House refers again to Waterford and to the Commons front, though primarily of course to Somerset House by his master Chambers.

Gandon's favourite themes were the triumphal arch and the use of a pair of detached columns inset in a plain wall, which owes something to the Pantheon and something to the flanks of St Martin-in-the-Fields, but not very much to either. The latter is seen at its finest in the North and South faces of the corner-pavilions of the Custom House. His relish for subtle dissonances, and his skill in contriving them, can best be seen by looking at the unbroken frieze and cornice which sail serenely across the fronts of these pavilions, and then allowing the eye to descend to ground level to observe how the column-bases find themselves slightly advanced between the flanking slabs of plain wall. A lesser architect would have orchestrated this with respond pilasters and fussy breaks in and out and the point would have been lost.† This device later became a staple of his pupil and successor Richard Morrison as well as being copied by Soane at Baronscourt and by Wyatt at Castle Coole. Another of his favourite devices is the use of plane surfaces shallowly recessed: most notably in the East and West faces of the same corner-pavilions. Surprisingly, the triumphal-arch

---

* The Dublin Gate of Carriglas, in which the mutule-cornice and fluted frieze are mischievously transposed.

† As it is in the elephantine handling of ostensibly similar material by Sir Aston Webb in the College of Science (Government Buildings) in Upper Merrion Street, of 1912.

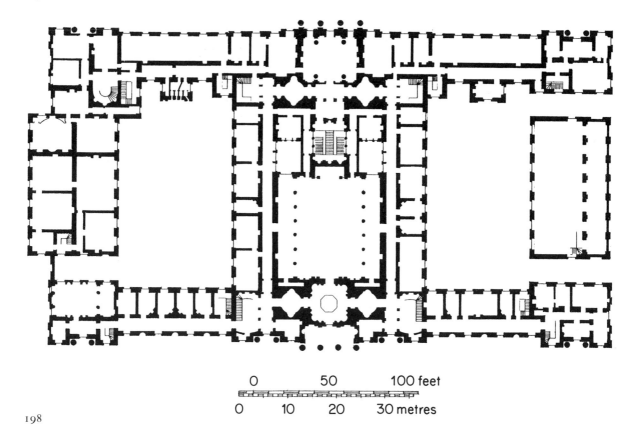

0   50   100 feet

0   10   20   30 metres

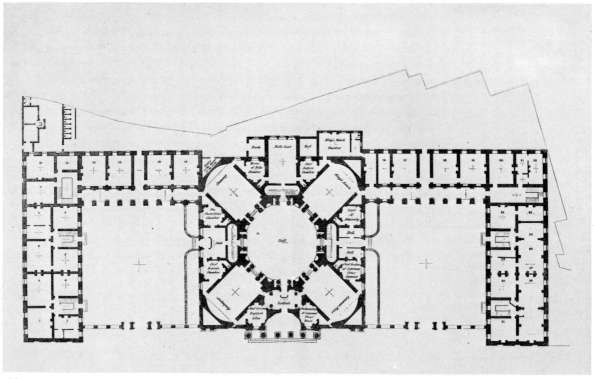

200

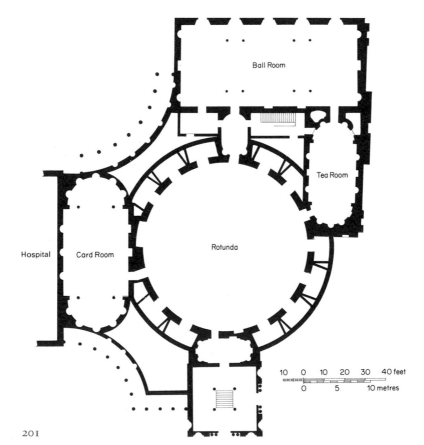

200 Carriglas, Co Longford: the stables by James Gandon, *c. 1795* drawn by Michael Craig from a survey by the author. The nearer (upper) courtyard was for the farm animals and for hay, etc. and the further (lower) courtyard, all in ashlar, for the horses and those who waited upon them. The mannerist role played by the small arches may be seen, and the subtle contrasts of demeanour between the several parts. There is not a single moulding used anywhere in this complex except on the North elevation of the North archway, facing the house but away from the viewer in this reconstruction. The central cupola, now missing, has been supplied by the artist on the author's advice

201

motif appears as an internal wall-treatment at Coolbanagher church, and also very subtly, in the interior of Waterford Court House.

It has already been mentioned that there are indications, chiefly in the Caledon sketchbook, that Cooley had carried matters a little further at the Four Courts before his death and replacement by Gandon than had till recently been thought (fig. 199). But though one sketch-plan[26] does show the traditional four courts plus one (the Rolls Court) disposed round little more than half of an octagon or rotunda (it is difficult to be sure which) this very inconclusive drawing shows no sign of the adroit use to which Gandon put the 45-degree angle at which his courts are set, using the resulting spaces for sound-insulation. We know from Gandon's *Life* that anxiety was felt at the time lest the troops marching daily from their barracks to the castle, with fife and drum, with flam, drag and paradiddle, might disturb the slumbers of the Bench. Most ingeniously he circumvented this, and sound-insulation by plan-form became, as we shall see, a matter to which his successors turned their minds when building the county court houses in the following century.

Like most architects of his time, Gandon was eclectic. But one measure of his greatness is the degree to which he was capable of harmonizing within himself baroque, Palladian and neo-classic elements. The complex ancestry of the Four Courts is a triumphant example. The standard criticism levelled at the Custom House is that there is a break in scale between the river-front and the tower and dome which rises above it. But were it not for the fact that in the restoration of the 1920s Ardbraccan stone was used for the dome structure, and has gradually darkened, this would not be so apparent. Still more does it suffer from the softening of the transition from horizontal to vertical which was originally provided by the statues and the chimneys, none of which were replaced.[27] Comparison of pre-fire photographs with later photographs makes this clear.

There was a mannerist strain in his make-up, which appears in the overlapping symmetries of the Custom House river-front and also in the fact that—as at the West block of Trinity—the salient parts are smooth whereas the recessed parts are rusticated. But it is at Carriglas Co Longford that he gave his mannerism free rein. The main house, an ingenious and very compact villa, was never built but the drawings are extant and show that it would have been of the greatest distinction.[28] The 'office' layout consists of two courtyards with three archways in enfilade. The upper yard, to the South, is for the farm: the lower, to the North and nearer the house, is the stable-yard (fig. 200). They are sharply contrasted in character and in colour. Lime-washed rendering set off by dark grey limestone dressings in the upper yard gives a North Italian flavour to the arcades, lunettes and pediments. The lower yard, entirely in ashlar, with narrow slightly camber-headed openings, is severe of aspect, in fewer and larger units, no doubt, as the Knight of Glin suggests, to point up the special position then—and indeed later—accorded to the horse.

A motif in the upper yard is reminiscent of Palladio's Villa Pojana, and the South entrance-arch, elliptical, deeply recessed and rusticated and with its outer wall on the skew, has a flavour of Ledoux about it. But the real surprises are reserved for the relationships between the various blocks. They are free-standing but linked by little arches no wider than doorways. Axes are displaced to right or left in unexpected ways; blocks disappear behind one another as though by accident. He must have enjoyed himself enormously. The whole thing is done without using any mouldings at all, except on the outer face of the North gateway.

At the Dublin Gate of Carriglas he had more fun in similar vein. It is a miniature triumphal arch of the same family as those to the two courtyards of the Four Courts.

PREVIOUS PAGE

201 Dublin: the Rotunda complex. Plan based partly on that published in the Sedan-Chair List of 1787, partly on the MS plan in the records of the Wide Streets Commissioners (*Bulletin of Irish Georgian Society* XV, 1. Pl 15 1972) and partly on a modern survey by Michael Scott and Partners. The various plans cannot easily be made to agree: that offered here is an attempt to combine reliable data into a credible whole. The Hospital itself lies to the West (left) and only its East wall is here shown. The Card Room disappeared many years ago, but all the remaining major spaces survive. The land rises steeply from the South to the North, so that the Tea Room is in effect underground, and the entrance to the present Gate Theatre is in the upper half of its Northern apse. The Southern porch, with steps going *down*, is by Gandon and survives, more or less. The Rotunda proper is a cinema. The North-East part is by Michael Frederick Trench and Richard Johnston, the elevation to East derived from Adam's published design for Kenwood. Over the Ball Room is the Great Supper Room (now the Gate Theatre), and over the Tea Room the Lesser Supper Room (now split up into dressing-rooms, etc.). Both the curved colonnades are still *in situ*

But in place of the impost moulding there is a bold mutulated cornice like that of the Custom House, and in place of the cornice we are given the dentilled platband which, at the Custom House, marks the level of the first floor.

Gandon's reliance on a small number of basic ideas is one measure of his greatness. To make much out of what seems to be barren or empty is what a great composer can do with a trifling waltz, and as for turning the theme upside-down, that is, after all, a familiar device. Almost the only thing the architect cannot, in the nature of things, do, is to play it backwards.

To return to Dublin. Gandon was concerned, though peripherally, in the enlargement and embellishment of the Assembly Rooms attached to the Lying-in Hospital. The Rotunda (fig. 201), a rather plain but very large (80 feet in diameter) room with a flat ceiling and no central supports, had been built, to the East of the Hospital, by John Ensor in 1764.[29] Between it and the hospital there was a large (77 feet by 32 feet) card room, columnar and with round ends, which has now completely disappeared. From 1784 onwards additional assembly rooms were added to the North-East, up the side of what was shortly to be renamed Rutland (and is now Parnell) Square. The amateur architect Frederick Trench at first supplied the ground-plan and an elevation to Cavendish Row with three Venetian windows in arches, rather like an astylar version of one of the wings of Stowe. Under Gandon's supervision this was redesigned by Richard Johnston, on a larger scale and, it must be confessed, to a more conventional pattern imitated from Adam's Kenwood, with a broken-out portico over a mock entrance in the middle and terminations with coupled pilasters. (The mock entrance now, by an ingenious piece of twentieth-century jugglery, gives access to the Gate Theatre). Behind this two storeys of rooms are placed at right-angles to one another, or rather more or less at right-angles because the 'square' is not square. Owing to the slope of the land the Northerly rooms of the ground-floor are in effect underground. The ballroom, with eight columns in pairs supporting a system of shallow groined-vaults, must have been very handsome but has fallen on evil days. It has since been restored (1987).

Entrance to the Rotunda was originally by one of the rather low pavilions which flanked the hospital as terminations to its very country-house-like pair of quadrant colonnades. This was now replaced by a much larger and very elegant pavilion by Gandon, all three faces of which were (and are) versions of his triumphal arch theme, this time diversified by having inset *coupled* columns, and on top of the middle of each elevation a typical Custom House urn. Most of this is at present invisible behind hoardings and neon-lights, but it is still there. At the same time, in about 1786, he made the dull exterior of Ensor's rotunda more acceptable by raising the circular wall and tricking it out with Coade-stone panels and an ox-head frieze by Edward Smyth.

By this time the Cavendish Row houses, which are among the most splendid in Dublin,[30] were beginning to seem a little old-fashioned. All over Dublin four-storey houses were springing up with unprecedented rapidity, street after street and square after square: externally (as a general rule) somewhat plainer than their predecessors, but none the worse for that. They differed from them, however, in two important ways: in plan-form and in decoration. By this time, with the exception of a few very large houses in dominant situations, such as Belvedere House at the head of North Great George's Street, or Ely House facing down Hume Street, they had become standardised as three windows wide, the doorcase set back within a wide arch, the hall relatively narrow and no longer in any sense a waiting-room but now simply a passage, the main stairs going, as before, to the first floor only, continuing upwards in smaller, secondary form. Increasingly the return projecting rearwards from the half-landings is used for extra accommodation. The interesting developments of this standard plan are reserved for the following century and for the suburbs.

The typical Dublin contrast between a plain exterior and lavish internal decoration still held good. But of two virtually identical houses one will be decorated and the other not, according to the circumstances of their original construction or disposal. And whereas down to 1770 the decoration had been of the utmost vigour and freedom, hardly ever the same twice running and nearly all done by hand, now the advent of mass-production and neo-classic repetition brought with it an element of the perfunctory, inducing a certain weariness. These houses were not always as well built as their predecessors. There was, perhaps, something febrile about the building boom as though the curtain were about to fall, which indeed it was. The end of the century was in sight, and so was the end of the Irish Parliament. Though the effect of the Union on Dublin has sometimes been exaggerated and was in some respects not immediate, the year 1800 is still a good deal more than a chronological convenience. Gandon survived in practice until 1808, but built little, and lived on until 1823. Though the whole of his active career was run during the ascendancy of neo-classicism, he took from that movement only what would strengthen him and could be blended with the other and earlier strains from which his main strength had come: Wren, the Palladians and his master Chambers.

'Few subjects would be more rewarding or more valuable for the history of Dublin than a full account of the Wide Streets Commissioners' wrote Dr McParland, and went on to supply to some extent, in an important 30-page paper,[31] the want to which he had drawn attention. In particular he makes it clear how far, in the mid-1780s, the membership of the commission coincided with that of the parliamentary group who were actively promoting splendour and were, almost to a man, supporters of Gandon. In advancing the grandeur of the capital they had on one flank the country members and on the other the London-appointed executive. From both, opposition might be expected. But, for these few years at least, the country gentry spent more money on their Dublin houses than on their country seats, while the constitutional developments of 1782 had, for the time being, clipped the wings of the Viceroy and his London-appointed staff. Never before had the commissioners disposed of so much money, numbered among their membership so many men of taste and influence, nor taken such a minute interest in the details of designs submitted to their scrutiny. In 1783 they were censuring the windows of Mr Colles's house for being 'too high by four Inches and an Half' *and* obliging him to alter them. By 1792, however, they were being chided by the Chief Secretary for spending too much money, and though they recovered enough in 1799-1800 to initiate, irreversibly, the great Westmoreland Street-D'Olier Street scheme and the Beresford Place layout behind the Custom House, they were being rapped over the knuckles by the London Treasury in 1802, and the days of their glory were numbered. In 1826 London cut off their annual grant, and in 1846 abolished them. One is reminded that in 1843 Nicholas I, by edict, allowed private persons to build as they liked in Petersburgh: '*liberté néfaste, qui installe l'anarchie à la place de l'ordre.*'[32] Luckily, the effects were not immediate, in either city.

The commissioners kept their eyes on London, as Dublin people do, with a mixture of adulation and distrust. They flirted with James Wyatt, they took a look at George Dance. They had, it seems no regular architect of their own, employing, at various times, Samuel Sproule, Gandon himself, and most significantly, Henry Aaron Baker, Gandon's pupil, partner and successor.

Though they entertained the idea of composing whole streets, or sides of squares, as formal centre-and-ends elevations such as were initiated 60 years earlier by Shepherd and Wood[32] and by now carried out in Bath, London and Edinburgh, none of this, probably for economic reasons, actually happened. The same applies to the phantom elliptical Circus at the top of Eccles Street which for so long haunted the maps. They did, on the other hand, succeed in imposing uniform elevations on Westmoreland Street and D'Olier Street, as well as elsewhere, and these elevations are by Baker. At one stage it was proposed that the ground floors should be colonnaded, an idea taken from Paris or Bologna, but this did not happen. But what did happen was just as significant. As early as 1787 they had before them a scheme for a street-front with shops integral to the architecture, as 'has long been in use on the Continent'.[34] Westmoreland and D'Olier Streets, as built in 1799–1801, incorporated shops as part of the design: something which was not to happen in London till very much later. Though most have since been destroyed or altered, one or two still remain, and so do some of the commissioners' arcaded elevations, on Burgh Quay and Eden Quay. Nothing now survives of either side of Lower Sackville (O'Connell) Street, another of the commissioners' achievements, of similar character to the surviving quayside elevations, and also incorporating shops. Their authorship is unknown, but they were drawn out by the surveyor to the commissioners, Thomas Sherrard. The scheme which Gandon is known to have prepared for this street is lost, but his bridge survives in a form which can best be called a paraphrase.[35]

CHAPTER FIFTEEN

Neo-Classic to Romantic

If the last 20 years of the eighteenth century were a period of domination by English architects, they were mainly architects who had, like Myers, Cooley, Penrose and Gandon, become permanent Irish residents and whose careers were thenceforth entirely Irish.★ Neither Chambers nor Adam ever came to Ireland. There are, as we have seen, significant buildings by Chambers here, but those of Adam are of less account: the elegant mausoleum at Castle Upton, a handful of fine rooms at Head-ford, some interiors (now gone) at Langford House in Mary Street, the Castle Upton stables and his work on the castle itself which has virtually vanished.

The exception is James Wyatt, whose Irish operations were prolonged and wide-spread, and exercised, except for a single visit in 1785, through agents on the spot: Cooley, Thomas Penrose, Richard Johnston and perhaps others.

They seem to have arisen through his involvement with Mount Kennedy for which he prepared designs as early as 1772 (June). In May of 1773 Chambers was writing to Mr Vesey of Lucan about plans for the house which we know as Lucan House.[1] Mount Kennedy was not in fact built until about 1783-4, by which time Lucan was finished. These two houses are almost identical in plan, and the same plan, with little variation, is found at Caledon (1779) by Cooley, and at Castle Coole, in a plan signed and dated by Richard Johnston in 1789, and adopted when the house was built to improved elevations by Wyatt in the ensuing ten years. Closely related plans are found at Slane (1786, presumably by Wyatt who had been consulted eleven years earlier)† and at Rokeby, Co Louth, built between 1785 and 1794 to Cooley's designs but under the supervision of Francis Johnston. To add to the confusion—or to confirm the impression of an interlocking cartel of Wyatt-directed architects—Cooley was the executant at Mount Kennedy, while at Lucan the owner Mr Vesey was taken seriously as an architect, and the name of Wyatt is coupled with that of Chambers, not to mention the name of Michael Stapleton, known principally as a plasterworker but sometimes invoked as a designer as well.[2]

These are neo-classic houses, but is their plan neo-classical? They have all three features in common: an end-on entrance-hall with a columnar screen across its inner end, a staircase or staircases in a compartment to the right or left of this *but not both*, and most have an elliptical saloon end-on to the hall and projecting to the rear in the form of a bow. Only Rokeby lacks this last feature, which at Slane is circular and at Caledon on its long axis, like that of Ballyhaise. The entrance-hall comes straight

---

★ Some architects became quite deeply involved in Ireland without coming here, certainly not settling, and even leaving nothing identifiable behind to last to our time. One such was James Lewis, whose book of *Original Designs* (1779-80) contains five Irish designs including a fine theatre for Limerick. All were to have been in the South-West but none, it seems, was executed. Colvin, ed of 1976, p. 518.

† Slane was built on the foundations of an earlier house but this does not affect the particular point at issue.

from Pearce: from Castletown, from Cashel and from his villa-designs, and was used in identical form by Ducart at Castletown Cox and by the unknown designer of Castle Ward in 1763. As for the elliptical saloon projecting through the back wall, what is it but the Ballyhaise saloon with its axis turned (except at Caledon) through a right-angle? Yet both Chambers and Wyatt, neither of whom had ever set foot in Ireland, come up with this plan at exactly the same time.

Wyatt did other work in Ireland, at Abbeyleix, Curraghmore, Westport, perhaps Farnham, and, just possibly, Ardbraccan and Avondale. But his masterpiece in the country-house field, not merely in Ireland but anywhere, is beyond doubt Castle Coole.[3] It is much larger than the other members of the family just described (112 feet by 85 feet as against the 86 feet by 63 feet of Lucan) and in addition it has its colonnaded wings terminating in deep pavilions. It is fully formal all the way round and has no back: communication with the out-offices is by way of that by now well-established Irish device, a tunnel. With an overall length of 275 feet it is comparable in size with the mammoths of the Pearce and Cassels era and as such is alone among its contemporaries. Inside as well as out it is both fully designed and fully crafted: there are no ragged edges or loose ends. It has not altogether the look of an Irish house, and small wonder since all the stone and nearly all the craftsmen were sent over from England. But one feature of the interior, the grand central upstairs lobby, though grander than any other Irish example, is of Irish derivation and may therefore be part of Richard Johnston's contribution.

The only other late-eighteenth century patron to build on such a scale was the Earl-Bishop of Derry, who is in other ways also a special case.[4] He held the see from 1768 till his death in 1803, but was intermittently in Italy and left Ireland for good in 1791. It was all the more astonishing that besides his church-building and bridge-building he contrived to build, or at least begin, two prodigy-houses, both in the diocese and county of Derry. Though in connexion with Downhill the name of Wyatt is, almost inevitably, mentioned, this seems to have been merely in passing. Though the Earl-Bishop brought both Ducart and Soane there, the principal and effective architect seems to have been Michael Shanahan of Cork. Though the Italian Placido Columbani appeared on the scene, his concern was principally with water-closets and such matters. If there is a hidden hand, it may be that—as Mr Peter Rankin has very persuasively shown—of Charles Cameron, for there is in the Hermitage Museum in Leningrad a plan and elevation★ of a house in both respects close enough to Downhill, as built, to make us wonder very much. The house was begun in 1776, and in 1779 Cameron went to Russia. It is quite unlike any other Irish house.

The siting of Downhill can only be described as Ossianic: on top of a cliff facing North across the Atlantic towards the Outer Hebrides, where only a romantic would expect to find a house, and only a lunatic would build one. The Earl-Bishop qualifies on both counts. By a strange paradox, this least cosy of houses seems to have been one of the very first to have one of its principal rooms labelled a 'lounge'.[5] In its present state of roofless ruin it has the same kind of desolate splendour as Sutton Scarsdale, the fruit of a fire in 1851, subsequent re-edification by John Lanyon, and a final gutting about 25 years ago.†

★ There are, however, difficulties: notably the fact that the external facing, including the fluted Corinthian pilasters, was added by James McBlain the Belfast builder, after 1784. Cameron's drawing is dated 1779, the year in which he went to Russia.

† The huge yard gives it a certain resemblance to James Wyatt's Norris Castle, I.O.W. of 1799.

Michael Shanahan was from Cork, where the Earl-Bishop had found him during his brief tenure of the see of Cloyne, and where his best-known work was the predecessor of the present Patrick's Bridge. In the early 1770s the Bishop took him with him to Italy, and in Vicenza he began to produce an architectural book which, like too many Irish projects of the kind, never came to birth.* Besides acting as the Bishop's factotum in many matters, he had a marble-works of his own in Cork, and had the satisfaction of supplying therefrom chimneypieces, sent from Cork by sea to Derry, to replace some from England which were collapsing.

Ballyscullion, Hervey's other Irish house, was in complete contrast but equally striking. Its designer was probably Francis Sandys, from Dublin, son of an architect and brother of a clergyman also in the Bishop's entourage. This cleric acted also, like his mediaeval predecessors, as a clerk of works. Though nothing now survives *in situ* of Ballyscullion we know with some precision what it was like, or at least what it was intended to be like. The plate in Sampson's *Statistical Survey* of 1802 shows an apparently cylindrical porticoed centre connected by forward-curving links to wings which can best be described as each consisting of three blocks of late-seventeenth-century appearance standing at right-angles back-to-back to each other. The craze for circular or elliptical houses was just then (1787) beginning, and Ballyscullion was avowedly[6] modelled on the circular house by John Plaw at Belle Isle on Lake Windermere: dome, portico, central staircase and all. It seems that only the central oval was ever built, perhaps because Shanahan could not, in the end, keep up with or indeed put up with the Earl-Bishop's volatile temperament. The more compliant Placido Columbani seems to have lived up to both halves of his name.

The central staircase was a double-spiral 'occasionally communicating' as in the (much later) London board-schools, to keep the servants apart from the gentry. In its siting, Ballyscullion was in complete contrast to Downhill, being on gently sloping ground between the village of Bellaghy and Lough Beg, a local widening of the Lower Bann a little North of its exit from Lough Neagh. Though its place knoweth it no more, Ballyscullion survives in two senses: first, that a full-size virtual replica of it was built in England and still stands, and second, that its portico and a (still visibly curved) part of its front wall were re-erected in 1816 by John Bowden to form the frontispiece of St George's Church in Belfast, where it has so far survived the many perils of such a situation.[7] The English replica is Ickworth near Bury St Edmunds, begun, in the Earl-Bishop's absence, by Francis Sandys on his return from Rome in 1796: this time with the participation of another Italian architect, Mario Asprucci. It is larger than Ballyscullion, having superimposed orders instead of an order with an attic, and its wings were, ultimately, built. But they are much plainer and more conventional than those intended for Ballyscullion.

Francis Sandys remained in East Anglia, where he designed three or four more buildings, one at least of which shows strong geometric preoccupations, but ultimately came to grief over the building of Durham Gaol, and is heard of no more.[8]

Slane Castle has been mentioned but laid aside, and must now be considered.[9] It is important as forming a link between the Lucan-Caledon-type plan of classical house and the mock-castles which were to become so popular after 1800. Many architects were involved in it, including in 1781 and 1783 Gandon, two of whose drawings for a river-front baroque in conception but gothic in detail, have survived.

---

* To be exact, one copy only of his book on bridges seems to exist, in the RIBA Library. See P. du Prey in *Zeitschrift für Schweizerische Archäologie und Kunstgeschichte*, 36, 1979, pp 51 sqq.

The owner, Colonel William Burton Conyngham, had begun as one of Gandon's supporters but changed over to the Wyatt party.[10] He was a bachelor and had no other occupation but the patronage of the arts and commerce, whether in Parliament, in the Wide Streets Commission, at his projected town of 'Rutland' or Burtonport on his Donegal estates, or at Slane itself.

There had been symmetrical castellated structures before in Ireland, notably the curious gatehouse at Hillsborough Co Down, and there were to be plenty more, such as Killeen, Gormanston and Clongoweswood. Even when a genuine 'castle' was being added to, as at Killyleagh Co Down in 1666, or Johnston's proposals for Killeen Co Meath in about 1800, some effort at an at least approximate symmetry was made.* Perhaps Charleville Castle (or 'Forest') begun by Johnston a little before 1800, is the first deliberately asymmetrical house to be built in Ireland, though even there the asymmetry (as at the Westminster Houses of Parliament a generation later) is still only skin-deep and entirely a matter of how the towers are managed to give a picturesque skyline.[11]

Slane is not like that at all. The only gothic thing about it is a little window-dressing and some superficial trim, and a little, a very little, of the internal decoration. And, of course, the fact that it was built on the foundations of the earlier castle of the Flemings. The close congruity between its plan and that reproduced by Mr Guinness and inscribed 'comme il est actuellement' is a puzzle: but there is no denying its relationship to the other school-of-Wyatt plans, nor the presence, in the 'actuellement' plan, of a staircase obviously left over from a much earlier building.[2] In the plan as carried out, a room in the West corner has a typically neo-classic shallowly curved end such as Johnston used elsewhere, e.g. Rokeby, and the quality throughout is first class.

The motives behind these fancy-dress exercises, which become almost the rule for houses above a certain size after the turn of the century, must have been the same as those which actuated Vanbrugh, and after him Adam, and their clients. Yet in Ireland I dare to suggest that an additional motive was at work. During the latter part of the eighteenth century a handful of houses, all in and near the Pale, were enlarged or re-edified in a gothic or at least castellated manner: Ballinlough Co Westmeath, Malahide Castle, Dunsany and Killeen both in Co Meath, Gormanston on the Dublin-Meath border, Louth Hall and Smarmore in Co Louth, Clongoweswood Co Kildare.[13] All these belonged to noble or landed families who were still Catholic (except for the Talbots of Malahide and the Plunketts of Dunsany who conformed to the established church at about this time). They were naturally mostly inter-related, and Professor Rowan has gone so far as to suggest that the architect of three of these, Ballinlough, Malahide and Clongoweswood, was the owner of the last-named, Wogan Browne, who had a hand also in Killeen.

Nearly all these families, and others like them such as the Barnewalls and Netter-villes, had managed to remain settled on their lands as long as, or longer than, English landed families. The Nugents of Ballinlough, in fact, concealed the true antiquity of their lineage by changing their name from O'Reilly in 1812, thus giving occasion for jibes about 'Old Reillys and New Gents'. (Nugent, an Anglo-Norman name, is today very common in Ireland.) Ballinlough, their house, is a perfectly reasonable two plus three plus two house with a normal plan (though evidently incorporating in one end-wall part of its castle-predecessor) to which was added in about 1780 a

---

* So also at Moore Abbey, Monasterevan, by Christopher Myers in the 1760s.

large out-of-scale wing with round turrets, and the whole embellished with Irish stepped battlements.[14]

Being Catholics, none of these people could take an active part in politics nor sit in the House of Lords, though Lord Fingall (of Killeen) did a little in the way of 'moderate' and 'loyal' lobbying behind the scenes. But the majority of landed proprietors were very differently placed. They had been brutally reminded by Lord Clare in 1782 and in the Catholic Emancipation debates of 1793 that their titles to their estates rested on confiscations and were not of very long standing. And again in the Union debates:

> The whole power and property of the country has been conferred by successive monarchs of England upon an English colony, composed of three sets of English adventurers who poured into this country at the termination of three successive rebellions. Confiscation is their common title; and from their first settlement they have been hemmed in on every side by the old inhabitants of the island, brooding over their discontents in sullen indignation.[15]

This was a gross overstatement, made by a man, who, like Burke, was of Catholic stock but had 'passed over' into the ascendency system. Like many of Burke's utterances, it is very highly charged with emotion; and of course it is also at least a half-truth.

After the Union, I believe that the landed class were haunted by these words and did not want to believe them. By castellating their houses, or adding castellated wings to them, or in extreme cases replacing them by sham castles, they sought—at the sub-conscious level no doubt—to convince themselves and others that they had been there a long time and that their houses, like so many in England, reflected the vicissitudes of centuries. As it happens, the romantic fashion for irregularity was just now hitting European architecture (having affected gardening a couple of generations earlier), so that, once again, if only for a moment, Ireland was bang up to date. This mood lasted down to and beyond the 'tithe war' of the 1830s, but hardly survived the Famine of the 1840s, and for the most part it affected only the larger houses. The smaller ones continued to be unselfconsciously classical.

Some of the results were amusingly ingenuous. The Otways at Castle Otway, Co Tipperary, for example, built themselves a decent house in about 1770 in front of the insignificant ruins of a tower which, however, at some later date they thought fit to re-edify until it rose far above the chimneys of the house, deluding the unwary into thinking that the family had moved from the tower down into the house, instead of the other way about.[16]

Whatever substance there may or may not be in the foregoing speculations, one thing is certain: the architects, in Ireland as elsewhere, were required to hold themselves in readiness to design in classic or in gothic, according to the patron's preferences. There is no clear evidence that either of the two principal practitioners, Morrison and Johnston, had any marked leaning either way. It was understood that gothic was for Protestant churches, especially those in the country or in small towns, and for workhouses, especially after 1834. Classic was for Catholic churches, especially those in the larger towns, and—still for some time to come—for Protestant churches in the larger towns, and for court houses, and for gaols as well as for hospitals. The architecture of industry was classic, and so was that of transport: canals, and the first railway stations (1834 onwards) were classic, though very soon a rough-and-ready rule begun to appear, reserving gothic for small stations and classic for large ones. But this is to anticipate.

202

203

204

202 Kilkenny: a pair of house-doors under a single fanlight. This device became fashionable in Kilkenny in about 1800 and several examples still survive

203 Waterford (Church of Ireland) Cathedral by John Roberts, 1774. The ceiling was renewed after a fire in 1815-18, and the galleries removed by Sir Thomas Drew in about 1893

204 Ballyfin, Co Leix, 1821-6, by Sir Richard Morrison, the South-West corner. The fractured volutes of the Ionic capitals illustrate the folly of executing such work in sandstone. Beyond the apse, which projects from the middle part of the library, the conservatory may be seen

The careers of Johnston and Morrison are instructively contrasted.[17] Johnston, born in 1761, was six years older than Morrison, and Morrison lived to be 82 as against Johnston's 68. Johnston had no son, while Morrison had the grief of outliving his. Both, in a sense, were the heirs of Gandon: Johnston because he got so many public commissions especially in Dublin, and Morrison because so many Gandonian motifs live on in his work. Both were provincials, Johnston moving to Dublin from Armagh in about 1794, and Morrison arriving in Dublin from Cork via Clonmel in about 1800. Morrison's family background was markedly architectural, Johnston's not, though two of his brothers were also architects. In effect, they were contemporaries for about 30 years, from about 1795 to about 1825. Not surprisingly, most of Johnston's buildings lie North of Dublin and most of Morrison's South of it.

Johnston matured late: he began to design Townley Hall, his first major independent job, in 1793 when he was 32, by which time Morrison had already published his book (1793: preface February) which is admittedly not very mature, but creditable for a young man of 27. Townley is, in fact, Johnston's only major classical house. Morrison, also, did only one major classical house (Ballyfin) but it is nearly 30 years later.

Townley is essentially a geometric house of the John Plaw–Francis Sandys schools:* of almost incredible external severity, its flawless and featureless ashlar relieved only by the Greek Doric porch, it holds all its eloquence in reserve for the breathtaking central rotunda round which, asymmetrically like the sash of an order, winds the cantilever stair. The detailing is carefully studied but very eclectic, including some motifs which he never used again, suggesting that his internal decorative style was still unformed, which was indeed the case. In some respects, for example the conjunction of rosette-coffered ceiling with frieze in finicky relief, it looks back to the Primate's Chapel at Armagh, where Cooley had done the outside and Johnston the inside in 1785.

Like Castle Coole, but few other Irish houses, Townley had some furniture evidently made for the house and presumably designed by Johnston; but most of this was dispersed at the sale about 20 years ago.

Morrison's book[18] (coeval with Townley) contains also a design for a house with a central rotunda: but this is in complete contrast to Johnston's. The rotunda (a little smaller than Townley's, as is everything else in the design) is treated as a monumental space in the manner of the Great Hall of the Four Courts, with the various rooms and staircases grouped round it in a way which, while not yet very imaginative, can clearly be seen to point forward to the subtleties of Morrison's series of executed villa-designs: Bear Forest, Castlegar, Issercleran (St Cleran's), Hyde Park (Tara Hill), Kilpeacon, Cangort Park and Bellair. Widely spread but with a strong family resemblance, they seem all to have been built in the first decade of the new century.† In nearly every case they are new structures untrammelled by a pre-existing house. Top-lighting, enfilade vistas and an elegant variation in room-shapes are common to all, and allusions to the work of Gandon and of Pearce and Cassels are easily recognisable. He shows evidence of a debt to Soane, and probably also to Henry

---

* The centralised plan derives of course from Palladio and Gibbs. There is possibly also a touch of James Playfair about the finished article, for Playfair furnished in 1792 drawings some of which are in the National Library of Ireland.

† A teasing question is whether the brick arches now to be seen in Morrison's rubble-stone facades, e.g. at Kilpeacon, were intended to be seen as such, or were concealed by rendering. Exposed brick in such situations was not unknown early in the eighteenth century.

205

206

207

208

208 Armagh: the Dobbin House (until lately the Bank of Ireland). Early nineteenth century, believed to be by Francis Johnston. Set back from Scotch Street, it is flanked by houses which display an approximate uniformity much like that of those which flank Charlemont House in Dublin

209 Carlow: the County Infirmary of about 1830. It is very similar to the Lunatic Asylum at Maryborough (Portlaoise) and of the School of Francis Johnston, who designed the asylum (demolished 1924) at Belfast, from which Armagh, Maryborough and Carlow clearly derive. Armagh was built in 1825, Belfast in 1829, and Carlow in 1832. Maryborough followed in 1833. Johnston had died in 1829

210 Navan, Co Meath: the former Classical School. An enigmatic building, apparently of the early nineteenth century, with an elliptical plan and tapering buttresses with classical niches in them. The eaves have paired brackets so that there was probably never a regular cornice. Would that more were known of its genesis

209

210

Holland. He was in short, a very well educated architect, and small wonder, since he entered the Dublin Society's school under Baker in 1786, while the Four Courts, Custom House and House of Lords were a-building. An unsupported tradition says he spent some time in Gandon's office.

He was better at insides than outsides, at least at this stage of his career. Externally St Cleran's, Kilpeacon and Bear Forest are at least presentable, if unexciting. But Cangort Park and Bellair (which are almost identical) are ungainly and give little promise of the elegance within.

At about the same time he was enlarging Lyons, a house by an architect called Grace. Characteristically, he straightened the curved Palladian colonnades (as he was later to do at Carton), using baseless but unfluted Doric columns. Why he should have had so strong a preference for curves indoors and straight lines outside, when the Palladians were of precisely the contrary persuasion, is by no means clear: yet so it was. Before building the modestly-sized Castlegar Morrison had sent its owner plans for a much larger house with alternative 'modern' and 'monastic' elevations: this was as far back as 1801; the year in which Charleville had been begun, of which its owner, Lord Charleville, wrote: 'In truth I did not mean to make my House so Gothic as to exclude convenience and modern refinements in luxury. The design of the inside and outside are strictly ancient, but the decorations are modern.'[19]

There exist two similar but distinct drawings by Johnston showing half the elevation of Headfort left classical and the other half gothicised, one a little more radical than the other, both unexecuted.[20] The appearance is comical, unless taken in the spirit of those drawings in which a chimney-piece or window-case is frugally drawn in two alternative styles, one on each side of the centre-line.

More importantly, perhaps, both Townley and Charleville have original piped water systems including water-closets to the first floor at least, an ingredient which would certainly have been thought of as 'modern'.[21]

Johnston was never again to achieve an interior comparable to the Townley rotunda, though both the Bank of Ireland Cash Office and St George's Church, and especially the former,[22] are in the grand manner. Morrison was a versatile imitator, and it was probably he who at Woodlands (Luttrellstown) Co Dublin created a large room whose spatial qualities clearly derive from a study of Soane. As Dr McParland has discerned, direct quotations or paraphrases from Gandon, Soane, Cassels, Ducart, James Cavanah Murphy and even Sir Roger Pratt[23] are to be found in his work, and this becomes even more evident in the later phase when he was collaborating with his aptly named son, William Vitruvius, who was perhaps even more gifted than his father.

Minor country house architects of the Johnston-Morrison school include Whitmore Davis, James Sheil, William Farrell, William Robertson of Kilkenny and Daniel Robertson formerly of London and Oxford but from 1829 rusticated in disgrace[24] to Ireland where his practice lay mainly in Co Wexford. Though communications were by now better than they had been in the eighteenth century, some even of the more distinguished architects tended still to have a local sphere of activity. Among the most notable were the brothers James and George Richard Pain, sons of an English architectural pattern-book maker, who had come over to work for Nash at Lough Cutra in 1811.[25] Their extensive country-house practice lay almost entirely in the counties of Cork and Limerick, and—so far as domestic work was concerned— almost entirely in the gothic or castellated style. Their public work, as we shall see, was another matter. Dromoland Co Clare, the large castellated mansion which they built in 1826 for Sir Edward O'Brien to succeed a Palladian house by Aheron or

Roberts, is typical in having been offered to the patron in a number of guises which survive in an album:[26] Palladian, Italian and the baronial which was chosen. The Pains' chief rival in Cork, Sir Thomas Deane, built, at Dromore near Kenmare, at least one castellated house which it would be difficult to tell apart from the work of the Pains, but for the fact that it, too, is unusually well documented.[27]

Another Cork architectural family, the Hargraves, who were probably, like the Pains, immigrants from England, began by being close followers of Davis Ducart. The houses of Abraham Hargrave the elder, such as The Island, Dunkettle and Castle Hyde, all in Co Cork, are markedly less vigorous than those of Ducart but have often a Ducartian flavour, especially in the sphere of planning, diluted with neo-classicism, especially in that of detail. There was a younger Abraham, and a John whose relationships have not yet been sorted out, but who had a practice including minor public buildings in the North.

Though John Bowden is probably best known for his neo-grec St Stephen's church in Dublin, and appears to have lived in the capital, he practised largely in the North and though, as architect to the Board of First Fruits he must have been concerned with many glebe houses, he is not yet credited with any larger country houses. Thomas Duff of Newry, a more significant figure, did a little country-house work which is known, and probably much more which is not known. He may well have been trained in London, though born in Newry, and subscribed to a number of architectural publications, but his reputation rests mainly on churches and public buildings and on his professional position in North-East Ulster.[28]

The classical line of country-house building did not peter out all at once. Emo, Co Leix, which was intended to be Gandon's answer to Wyatt's Castle Coole, though begun as early as 1791, was interrupted by its owner's premature death in 1798, and completed only with the participation of some obscure Dublin architects named Williamson, and ultimately of Lewis Vulliamy of London, as late as 1834-6.[29] Yet Morrison's Ballyfin, 1820-25, which is not far away, shows some marked affinities with the Gandon house, especially in the planning and placing of the library (which goes back via Emo to Leinster House) and in the internal domed rotunda.[30]

Lissadell, Co Sligo, begun in 1830, five years after Ballyfin was completed, by the prolific and versatile Francis Goodwin of London, is the only one of his Irish schemes which came to substantial fruition. It is distinguished more by solidity than by suavity, and more by its literary associations than by either. It is entered by one of its shorter sides, a feature which it shares with a smaller but perhaps more elegant house, Dromdihy near Killeagh Co Cork (architect unknown) where the entrance is by way of a Greek Doric portico, always a rarity in Ireland especially in the domestic field.

Castleboro in Co Wexford, by the exiled Englishman Daniel Robertson (who must be distinguished from his contemporary William Robertson who worked at Kilkenny Castle), was a very ambitious house, and remains an impressive ruin. A very deep central block is connected by short straight full-height links to end-pavilions which, like those of Castle Coole, seem, on their entrance sides, to derive from those of the Custom House. But there are too many pilasters about and as a result the order—Corinthian for the centre, Ionic for the wings—is devalued.*

Another even more cubical mansion with a giant order, and typically for its period, an attic above the cornice, is or rather was Kenure in North Co Dublin. It was an enlargement of a mid-eighteenth-century house containing, till it recently became a ruin, excellent plasterwork. It was given its present form at about the same

---

* Castleboro is a burnt-out ruin, but still there.

time as the building of Castleboro, in or about 1840 by George Papworth, the 'Irish' Papworth, who emigrated from London and made his career in Ireland till his death in 1855. The pilasters here are not overdone, and the capitals of the giant hexastyle portico (which has happily been spared from the general ruin) are bravura exercises in Corinthian undercutting, carried out in—of all materials—granite.

By the middle of the century the classical country house was all but extinct. One of its latest embodiments must have been the mansion for which the overworked word 'palatial' is for once not too strong: St Anne's, Clontarf, which J. F. Fuller was building for Sir Arthur Guinness from 1873 onwards (Lord Ardilaun after 1880) at the same time as a vast castellated seat for the same client at Cong on the Galway-Mayo border.[31] As Mr Bence-Jones justly observes,[32] the affinities of St Anne's are American: the Guinnesses were already millionaires a century ago, and about St Anne's and Ashford there hangs the same air of unreality as tinctures the activities of the Mizener brothers or of Citizen Kane. Even the classical style had, by imperceptible degrees, become a kind of fancy dress.

It was otherwise with the houses of the less affluent. The glebe-house type, which had established itself firmly by 1815 if not earlier, had a long life in farm-house form and houses are still being built which embody the modest and reasonable ideals of the late eighteenth century and can by no stretch be said to be in fancy dress. In the Dublin suburbs a continuous evolution based on the eighteenth-century terrace-house can be traced till at least 1870, developments which will be considered in a later chapter.

CHAPTER SIXTEEN

The Early Nineteenth Century

Contrary to popular belief, which still lingers, the effects of the Catholic Emancipation Act of 1829 were more political than architectural and the act itself was only a stage in the progressive removal of statutory disabilities. We have already noted the existence of richly furnished, though outwardly unobtrusive urban Catholic churches so far back as the mid-eighteenth century. Many others which existed before 1829 and even before 1800 have either been replaced or altered beyond recognition: for example the Carmelite church in Clarendon Street.[1]

The cathedrals are in a somewhat different case. Where the mediaeval see was still a town of convenient size, the new cathedral was sited there, but this was the exception. Save for Dublin and Cork which are anomalous, only six of the 30-odd ancient sites now have modern Catholic cathedrals: Armagh, Derry, Tuam, Kilkenny, Limerick and Waterford; the last of these dating as we have already seen from the end of the eighteenth century. The remainder are in modern centres of population which have arisen since mediaeval times, or at least in towns which, like Ennis, have outstripped their rivals (in this case Killaloe).

The cathedral at Newry was begun by Thomas Duff in 1825, that of Tuam (fig. 212) by Dominick Madden in 1827, of Carlow by Thomas Cobden in 1828,[2] and of Ballina probably also by Madden in the very year of Emancipation. With these can be grouped Ennis, also by Madden, in 1831. It is noteworthy that three of these are in the impoverished but populous West. Though, with the possible exception of Carlow, none of them quite rises to the architectural dignity later expected of a cathedral, they are all respectable buildings in the eclectic and not very exacting gothic which prevailed before Pugin came to terrorise everyone into submission.

It is worthy of remark that the three principal cities of Ireland, Dublin, Belfast and Cork, all lack a Catholic cathedral. (The building at Cork, dating from 1808, much remodelled by G. R. Pain and by later hands, is properly called the 'Pro-Cathedral'[3] like its counterparts in Dublin and Belfast). It is otherwise in Galway. What the self-respect, the piety and the affluence of the mercantile classes of the capital and of Cork failed to achieve in a century and a half, was accomplished in the Western province by the determination of a single septuagenarian bishop, in the space of less than 20 years.

But the building which did, and still does, duty in the metropolitan diocese of Dublin is of exceptional interest. St Mary's Metropolitan Chapel, as it was at first called, is a neo-classic, indeed neo-grec, building of considerable importance. Early accounts say that the design was 'sent to this country by an amateur residing in Paris' and its very evident dependence on Chalgrin's St Philippe-du-Roule in 1774-84 bears this out. In spite of the survival of two original drawings and of the most important architectural model in Ireland (kept, like the St Paul's model, in the building itself), the designer's identity remains conjectural.[4] The amateur may have been John Sweetman, a member of a well-known mercantile family, but it is certain that Richard Morrison was before long employed in the work. The derivation from

211

212

211 Ennis, Co Clare: the interior of the (Catholic) cathedral of 1831, by Dominick Madden

212 Tuam, Co Galway: the Catholic cathedral of 1827 onwards, by Dominick Madden, one of the first of the modern foundations, English Decorated in inspiration

213 Belfast: St Malachy's Catholic Church, by Thomas Jackson, 1844. The spatial qualities are identical with those of a large Presbyterian church of the period, the decorative trimmings appropriately in contrast

214 Dublin: the Pro-Cathedral. Wash-drawing by George Petrie, showing it as it was before alterations (e.g. with the South portico open) but unobstructed as it never was. The portico, though conformable to the original design, was not finished till after 1840.

213

214

215

215 Dublin: St Audoen's
(Catholic) Church of
1841–6 by Patrick Byrne.
On the left is 'Adam and
Eve's' (Franciscan) church,
begun by Byrne in 1830 and
continued by other hands

the Paris church is more obvious in the model than in the church as built, especially in the matter of the lighting by windows between the ribs of the barrel-vault, for which, in the execution, was substituted light from giant lunettes spanning three bays in a pendentive-and-dome arrangement in no way prepared-for by any inflection of the Doric colonnade below. The lighting system of the great model was, however, to be realised in another and even more distinguished Dublin Catholic church, St Audoen's by Patrick Byrne (fig. 215).

Though a writer in 1832[5] was already remarking a preference for gothic on the part of the established church, the great city church of St George,[6] Hardwicke Place, begun after the Union and not finished till 1812, was classic in the Gibbs tradition, and so was the even more conspicuously sited St Stephen's of 1825, though adhering to the neo-grec in all its details.[7] But it was the Catholics who made the running in the matter of classic town churches, having a great deal of leeway to make up, a need for churches of large capacity, and probably also a bias towards architecture which might evoke the spirit of Rome, imperial and papal.

A majestic series of such churches arose in very rapid succession both in Dublin and in Cork: St Francis Xavier, Gardiner Street, by J. B. Keane begun in 1829, 'Adam and Eve's' on (or rather off) Merchant's Quay in the following year, St Andrew's, Westland Row and St Nicholas of Myra in 1832 by James Bolger and John Leeson respectively, St Paul's, Arran Quay in 1834, St Audoen's in 1841. (In each case the foundation date is given: completion usually took a long time.) More splendid perhaps than any of these, St Mary's Dominican church on Pope's Quay, Cork (fig. 216), begun also in 1832, is a building which the humblest worshipper could not enter without being made aware of belonging to an august and enduring empire. As it happens, this Cork church was designed by the Protestant firm of Deane.[8] But the key figure in the Dublin series was Patrick Byrne, who went on to build two classical churches in the suburbs of which one, Rathmines, is very magnificent, besides the church at Arklow and some, less happily, in gothic.[9]

Byrne was a product of the Dublin Society's drawing school and thus steeped in the Gandon tradition as transmitted through Henry Aaron Baker. Faithful to that tradition, he avoided Greek detail almost completely, except at St Paul's, which is exceptional also in not being on the cruciform or T-plan otherwise usual in this group. Instead, it is a simple rectangle diversified at its 'East' end by indirect lighting directly inspired by St Mary Moorfields in London of 1817, itself of French ancestry. Of all Byrne's churches, St Audoen's is perhaps the finest, even though its original dome has been replaced by a flat ceiling. In compensation, his modest dome at Rathmines was replaced, after a fire in the present century, by a dome which, though strictly outside the scope of this book, is one of the grander sights of Dublin.

The Pro-Cathedral does not stand quite alone in representing the Greek revival in Ireland. Major Greek revival buildings are, nevertheless, so rare in comparison with England and, still more, Scotland, as to excite remark. The male prison at Cork (1818–23), of which the massive Delian portico (fig. 218) and outer wall still remain though the rather Vanbrughian interiors have perished, alas, almost without record,[10] is by George Richard Pain and his brother James, while to the former alone is credited the surviving entrance-front of the otherwise rebuilt St Patrick's Catholic church in the same city. The court house at Dundalk (of which more will presently be said) seems to owe the purity of its grecianism to the vigilance and perhaps also the participation of the patron John Leslie Foster as well as to the experience of Bowden.[11] Not surprisingly, the economy of the Doric order appealed to the Presbyterians, not only in Belfast (where Third Rosemary Street looked more like a house than a church) and in the remarkable building at Portaferry Co Down, but as far South as Gloucester Street in Dublin. In Clonmel, William Tinsley was deploying the Greek Ionic for Unitarians and Wesleyans alike (1838 and 1843).[12] Here, as in W. V. Morrison's court houses, the cheaper, unfluted version of the Ionic was used.

The volume of church-building in the first 40 years of the century is very large, as has already been indicated. Many in the Southern province (Cashel) were by the Pain brothers, who used the gothic style for their Anglican churches, for example Mallow, Buttevant (particularly elegant) (fig. 217) or Carrigaline, and seem also to have purveyed a very workmanlike classic to the Catholics, as at Kinsale, Dunmanway, Bantry, Millstreet, Ovens and the Ursuline convent at Blackrock.[13] Like the Pains, the other First-Fruits architects did secular work as well, especially country houses and court houses. But John Semple, the architect for the Eastern province (Dublin) was almost exclusively ecclesiastical, and so remarkable that he must have a paragraph to himself.

Born of a family prominent in the building trades, he showed his originality in two ways: constructionally, in his use of barrel-vaulting in three of his churches, two of which, however, began to fail and had their vaults removed; and stylistically in his rejection of all conventional mouldings for which he substituted an abstract system of related planes of his own devising. He built some 17 churches, all in Leinster, all of which survive to some degree. The two most remarkable are in Dublin: the 'Black Church' just off Dorset Street, and Monkstown Church which is larger and more ambitious than any of the others, besides occupying a commanding site (fig. 220). He designed also the Round Room beside the Mansion House, more remarkable for its construction than for its appearance. He was still alive to take part in the competition for the rebuilding of St Andrew's in 1860 but was unplaced and was even reproached with having made no stylistic progress in the past 30 years. We know nothing of him as a man and he remains the most enigmatic of architectural personalities.[19]

Many factors combined to change the whole character of architectural activity between 1830 and 1860. The death in 1836 of Henry Aaron Baker, who had been the master of the Dublin Society's architectural school for no less than half a century, was, perhaps significantly, followed by a two-year interval before the appointment of his successor George Papworth, whose elder brother John, it is instructive to note, had held a similar appointment in London since 1836. Before 1830 an architect who had travelled as far even as England was a rarity, and still more so one who had travelled to the Continent. Pearce was of course the great exception. But Gandon's learning was from books and directly from his master Chambers. The travels of James Cavanah Murphy, though influential in other ways, had little effect on his subsequent work in Ireland. Francis Johnston's journey to England in 1796 was undertaken at the age of 36 and served chiefly to widen his experience and understanding of gothic.[15] John Bowden had been to Paris where he acquired a copy of Percier and Fontaine,[16] while the younger Morrison went as far afield as Paestum. A little later Benjamin Woodward was to travel widely—and not merely for reasons of health—and was to reflect it even more directly in his work.

The foundation in 1839 of the Royal Institute of the Architects of Ireland was in line with similar developments elsewhere (the senior Institute in London had preceded it by some four or five years).★ Though there were three generations of Sir Thomas Deanes in succession, this is somewhat misleading since the first was knighted

★ The Institute of [Civil] Engineers in Ireland dates from 1835.

216 Cork, the interior of St Mary's Dominican Church, Pope's Quay. The church was designed in 1832 by Kearns Deane (brother of the first Sir Thomas) but took a great many years to build, the portico (for example) being of 1861. There is some doubt about the date and authorship of the very fine interior, and the name of John Pyne Hurley of Cork is mentioned. The sanctuary was designed by George Goldie, and the high altar by the Dublin firm of P. J. O'Neill and sons is of 1885-8. The baldacchino of 1872 is credited to Scannell of Cork

OVERLEAF
217 Buttevant, Co Cork: the uncommonly elegant First Fruits church of 1826 by the brothers Pain. One of the two diagonally-placed vestries can just be seen on the left

218 Cork: the portico of the Male Prison, by James and George Richard Pain, 1818. The use of the 'mantled' Doric order from the temple of Apollo at Delos (via Stuart and Revett) had the advantage of being cheaper than the use of a fully fluted order

219 Cork, the Savings Bank of 1839, by Kearns Deane (on the right) and the Provincial Bank of 1865 by W. G. Murray, the son of Francis Johnston's nephew and partner William Murray, who had designed the bank's head office in Dublin in the previous year. Both buildings are in the beautiful silver limestone from Ballintemple so widely used in the city of Cork

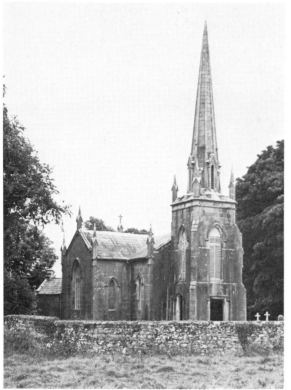

217

218

219

220

221

in 1830 less for his architectural accomplishments than for his involvement in the civic affairs of Cork.[17] But when Richard Morrison was knighted in 1841 it was in his capacity as architect and, no less significantly, as effective head of the Institute during the first four years of its existence.

The character of the corporate client was changing too. The days when the distinction between a grandee such as John Beresford, as an individual, and the various boards and commissions on which he sat, was hardly drawn (as in his dealings with Gandon) were over. The old Board of Works, which had evolved out of the Barrack Board itself, in the mid-eighteenth century, superseding the Surveyor-General's office, was reconstituted in 1831 with three Commissioners, all permanent officials, and so remains to this day.

The municipal reform which began in 1833 was complete by 1840. The Grand Juries were still there, but their scope had already been curtailed, notably by the poor law act of 1834 setting up the Boards of Guardians. The established church had already begun to feel the onset of the process which was to culminate in its disestablishment by Gladstone in 1869. Hardly had these cumulative changes begun to bite when the whole demography of Ireland was irreversibly transformed by the Famine of 1847-8.[18]

A very noticeable change had taken place not so much in architecture itself as in the practice of building. It is much more obvious than many changes brought about by theory or mere fashion. Its social and technical causes remain obscure. We have already seen that an interest in the textural qualities of masonry for its own sake was widespread in the early Christian period but faded in mediaeval times. Such interest in the seventeenth century is still restricted to coigns and openings and other small features. The monolithic lintel, for example, disappears towards the end of the twelfth century and is not seen again until nearly half-way through the nineteenth: but now dressed on its top surface and ends instead of only on its soffit and front face. It is true that in certain highly finished and formal buildings—the first Castletown, the Parliament House, the Royal Exchange, Ducart's Castletown, the Custom House, Townley Hall—unsurpassable standards of masonry were achieved but the command of varied textures: random rubble, reticulated, coursed rubble, irregularly squared ashlar, rock-faced, dragged or hammer-dressed, which spread with great rapidity in the early nineteenth century, is something different. It may have been stimulated by the gathering volume of engineering work from the middle of the eighteenth century onwards: canal-building, bridge-building, the construction of great harbours (the Dublin South Wall 1713-62, Rennie's harbour at Howth 1807-9, his great harbour at Dunleary (Kingstown) 1816 onwards, Nimmo's at Dunmore East of similar date) and the construction of the railways beginning with the Dublin and Kingstown in 1831. It is suggestive that Arthur Champneys, writing in 1910, remarked that the ancient masonry at Dun Aenghus, Rahan and Ardfert had 'a fairly close counterpart' in the retaining-wall of a cutting on the Dublin-Kingstown railway.[19] There is, all over Ireland, an enormous amount of admirable walling of many different types, and the craft tradition is even now not dead. When A. W. N. Pugin, arriving in 1838, demanded masonry of a special quality, he found, as his biographer Professor Stanton is glad to acknowledge, the Irish masons were able for him.

Before these developments were well under way, the old oligarchical system had made its last, and perhaps its finest contribution in the sphere of public buildings: the majestic series of court houses which adorn the provincial towns. These were the responsibility of the Grand Juries, and they were still being built in the 1840s, by which time they were being set up in conscious contrast to those buildings such as

PREVIOUS PAGE
220 Monkstown, Co Dublin: the Church of Ireland church by John Semple, *c.* 1830

221 Dublin: the King's Inns, park wall towards Constitution Hill, early nineteenth century. A deftly managed mixture of grey limestone and common calp

workhouses which emanated, often to standard designs, from centralised boards whose composition and staff had been imported in part from England.[20]

The oldest surviving Irish court house is that of Lifford Co Donegal, which bears the date 1745. It has a handsome if somewhat rustic elevation by Michael Priestley, but its interior has been so altered that the original arrangements are no longer decipherable.[21] The next court house of note is that of Waterford (fig. 230), which has disappeared but has left behind it a numerous progeny. It was designed by Gandon at the request of the Earl of Tyrone, the local magnate, and built, not without difficulties, in 1784-6: that is, a little earlier than the Four Courts.[22]

The internal dispositions of Waterford are known with some precision, from a handsome water-colour (fig. 230) which is either by Gandon himself or less probably, by James Malton, while its exterior survives in a small print which accompanies a reduced version of the water-colour view of the interior. The plan of the interior is closely related to an earlier design of Gandon's, while the elevation is similarly related to one of the designs he produced for the West front of the Parliament House.

Before coming to Ireland, Gandon had prepared two designs for the 'County Hall', i.e. the court house at Nottingham (fig. 229). Both designs are printed in *Vitruvius Britannicus* Vol. V. The cheaper of the two was carried out, but the more ambitious design was not wasted, and at Waterford it was, in essence, put to use. In this design, which has many points of similarity with Sanderson Miller's Warwick Shire Hall (fig. 228) of 1754-8, a wide hall is crossed on its short axis by the judges as they enter in procession on their way to the passage between the two courts, so that they can in due course emerge at what from the spectator's viewpoint is the back of their respective courts.

One feature of the Waterford design which is conspicuous also in the Four Courts and in other early court houses such as Derry is that the 'back' or public end of the court is open and marked off from the main hall only by a colonnade. This undoubtedly reflects the form of the open-ended king's courts at Westminster as they survived down to 1834, and no doubt derives from the idea that justice should be done in public: in a room which, like a theatrical stage, lacks a fourth wall. This appears very clearly indeed in the seventeenth-century court house at Northampton, an L-shaped building in which the two courts are at right-angles to one another, both open-ended towards a common space.

However appropriate in principle, this system has the great disadvantage of leaving the courts open both to the cold draughts and still worse the noises of the public concourse. In the Four Courts the open backs were, it seems, first curtained,* then filled with screens of timber and glass, and finally (after 1922) filled with masonry. Similar expedients were no doubt adopted everywhere else: at Northampton there are glazed screens.

In using the Nottingham design at Waterford, 20 years or so after its inception, Gandon abandoned the Palladianism of his youth and invested the design with a markedly neo-classic quality. The favourite motifs of his mature style are here deployed with great suavity: very clearly evident in the interior, but to be inferred with equal certainty as regards the façade. The building disappeared in or before 1849.

Kilkenny is the most obvious of its immediate progeny. Its authorship and even its date are uncertain and it is in any case a remodelling of an earlier building. If it was

---

*Note that James Malton, in the letterpress to his print of the Four Courts, mentions 'a curtain immediately at the back of the columns'.

222

223

222 A squared random ashlar wall at Carrick-on-Shannon, Co Leitrim

223 Random rock-faced ashlar at the Ordnance Survey Office, Mountjoy Barracks, Phoenix Park, Dublin

224 Ballindaggan, Co Wexford: unusual galleting between the roughly squared blocks of masonry. A somewhat similar technique is observable at Kilpeacon Church of Ireland, Co Limerick

225 A squared random ashlar wall at Ennis, Co Clare

226 Ballyjamesduff, Co Cavan: the market-house of 1813, one of a family of similar structures in Southern Ulster (Newbliss, Ballininagh, etc.) mostly, if not all, by an architect called Arthur McClean who emigrated to Canada

224

226

225

227

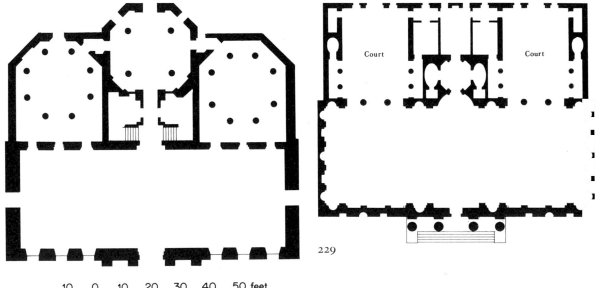

228

229

done as early as 1792 it is perhaps the first adaptation of the Waterford plan. It has since suffered much alteration.[23]

John Bowden's Derry court house of 1817 (fig. 231) may be described as Waterford plus: the additional elements being offices for the Mayor and for the court clerks, and a house for the keeper, which between them provided good sound insulation for the two courts which are embedded in the plan, touching the outer walls only at one corner each: an advance even on the Four Courts. The courts still have open backs, as they have in Gandon's less extravagant Nottingham design: the one which was carried out. This, 'Nottingham II' as we may call it, had less influence in Ireland than 'Nottingham I'. Its plan is the rather obvious one, where economy is a consideration, of three roughly equal spaces side-by-side: a hall flanked by the two courts. Such a plan is found at Armagh (Francis Johnston 1809), at Naas (Richard Morrison 1807) and at Maryborough (Richard Morrison 1812), but with two differences: that the courts lie parallel with the hall instead of at right angles to it as at Nottingham II, and that half the hall is occupied with a grand staircase.

The staircase is usually more important in the Irish court houses than in their English exemplars. This seems to have been because it led to the Grand Jury room on the first floor, and the Grand Jury was not only responsible for building the court-house but was, as well, the effective government of the county.

Maryborough court house has obvious debts to Gandon both in its elevation and in the flying staircase which seems to owe something to the Custom House. Naas was originally similar though with a transverse open-well staircase,[24] and Wexford was probably of the same family. Most of this generation of court houses are in confined and not very prominent street-sites: the same is true of Clonmel, also by Morrison. But Armagh is monumentally placed at the head of the mall then being developed, and was free-standing. Its present internal arrangements are anomalous, no doubt partly because only 25 years after completion it had become very dilapidated, and a 'major reorganisation of the interior' was done in 1859.[25] It has, however, the imposing axial staircase leading to the Grand Jury room.

Premature decay, it may be remarked in parenthesis, has been the lot of several Irish court houses. Since they are among the most solidly constructed buildings in the country, this may cause surprise until we remember that many of them incorporate clever (and therefore complicated) ways of lighting the interiors without exposing them to noise from outside. Complexity usually means trouble, and the admission of light interferes with the disposal of rainwater. So, at the time of writing, two of the most monumental and solidly built of them (Tralee and Waterford) have been allowed to become unfit for public business: a grotesque state of affairs which could have been avoided by a timely attention to the gutters.

Among the very finest of the earlier court houses is Dundalk (fig. 232),[26] by Edward Park and John Bowden, which dominates a small square and is partly free-standing. It is best known for its uncompromisingly archaeological Greek Revival portico taken from the Theseum, but its plan-form is an interesting bridge between earlier and later types. It is in a sense a squashed or widened version of Morrison's Clonmel, with which it shares the characteristic that the width across both courts is somewhat greater than the width of the façade. As at Clonmel, staircases diverge to right and left immediately inside the front wall, while the main one goes up the middle as usual.

The space behind the portico recedes in the centre and there are two further pairs of columns, thus creating a space which is roofed and ceiled yet external. The drama of this device was soon to be exploited by the younger Morrison in his court house

227 Dublin: the Excise Store of 1821 in Mayor Street, by a so far unknown architect

228 Warwick: the Shire Hall, by Sanderson Miller, 1754-8. It was apparently the model for Gandon's Nottingham design and his Waterford court house and their successors

229 Nottingham court house, the grander of the two plans published by Gandon in *Vitruvius Britannicus* Vol 2 (5) 1771: not used for Nottingham but adapted for Waterford in 1784.

designs. The design seems to be essentially Park's, though modified in execution by Bowden. As a sculptural object it is among the most memorable of all (fig. 232).

William Farrell, a competent but somewhat insipid designer, was responsible for a few court houses in the 1820s. Carrick-on-Shannon may serve as an example. As at Derry and elsewhere, the back is smaller in scale than the front, and the axial staircase is prominent. The judges are provided for, but not yet the juries (fig. 235).

The third and last generation of court houses is ushered in by that of Cork, by James and George Richard Pain. But before considering this group we must turn aside to look at the remarkable productions of Sir Richard Morrison's son, William Vitruvius, who lived up to the hopes so evidently placed upon him, but died before his father, at the age of 44.

W. V. Morrison's[27] approach to the design of court houses seems to owe little to his father's example or to any other branch of the Gandon tradition. Gandon and his followers start with a hall out of which open the courts. Morrison starts from the outside and works inwards. As Park had done at Dundalk, he provides a deep portico with dramatically shaped spaces behind it which, though covered, are not part of the interior. He provides two large D-shaped courtrooms, externally expressed as hemicycles (Tralee) or polygons (Carlow). At the back he provides a square or rectangular block of offices. These four elements are disposed in form of a cross.

The whole thing is set upon a great podium: so high that the approach is by two instalments of steps: the outer instalment belongs to the podium—ten steps at Carlow—after which there is a breathing-space or landing, before the steps of the portico itself (nine more at Carlow) are reached.

At the heart of all this there is a square space which is primarily a light-well, since the principal sources of light for the two courtrooms are giant inward-facing lunettes. So, at ground-floor level, the central square is divided up into numerous small rooms, passages, lavatories and small light-shafts. Even the central passage does not, at Carlow, go through to the rooms at the back, while at Tralee an even less orderly arrangement of spaces, including some staircases, occupies this central square. There could not be a greater contrast to the Four Courts, where the whole plan develops outwards from the lofty central rotunda.

Like most of the later court houses, Tralee and Carlow (figs. 233 and 234) are free-standing, though not in grassy parks. Carlow has a dominant position on the Y-junction at the North end of the town, but Tralee is almost tucked away. In both, the external ground-floor windows light the passage which runs round under the galleries.

This feature occurs also in the group of court houses which descend from Cork,[28] with the difference that whereas in W. V. Morrison's court houses the courts themselves are expressed externally, in the post-Cork group they are embedded in the plan. Cork, of 1835 by Nash's pupils and assistants James and George Richard Pain, is extremely grand, as befits what was then the second city in Ireland. It has a gigantic octostyle portico of unfluted Corinthian (the only octostyle portico, except for the Ionic one at Carlow, in the whole of Ireland). The interior was gutted by fire in 1891, but the plan is known from the large-scale Ordnance Survey map, and was clearly much influenced by Smirke's Gloucester Shire Hall of 1816.

The court house at Tullamore (fig. 236) which was new in 1837 and is by John B. Keane, has a plan closely similar to that of Cork. His court house at Nenagh, which dates from 1833, and is in a detached, axial position, is somewhat crude in execution. The plans of Ennis are dated 1838, and it bears a general resemblance to that which he designed for Waterford to replace Gandon's court house in 1849.

230 Waterford: the interior of the court house of 1784 by James Gandon, from a watercolour either by Gandon himself, or (as some suppose) by James Malton. It will be seen that, except for the much refined neo-classic detail, this is essentially the Nottingham plan. This Waterford court house has disappeared but the *salle d'attente* of the present Kilkenny court house is essentially similar

231 Derry: court house, plan, after the original by John Bowden, 1813. The plan derives from Gandon's Waterford/Nottingham design, but the sound insulation of the courts has been improved. The block at the back, smaller in scale, was the keeper's house

232 Dundalk Co Louth: court house, plan and elevation. The spaces between the staircase-hall and the courtrooms now contain lavatories. The side staircases lead to the galleries

OVERLEAF
233 Carlow: the court house of 1830, by William Vitruvius Morrison. Perhaps the finest court house in Ireland, it resembles Tralee by the same architect. The courtrooms at Tralee are semicircular instead of polygonal as here, and the Tralee portico is hexastyle where Carlow is octostyle: the only such portico in the country, except for the court house at Cork

234 Carlow court house

235 Carrick-on-Shannon: the court house, plan redrawn from the original by William Farrell. The grand jury room will have been upstairs in the smaller-scale block at the back. The date is about 1825

230

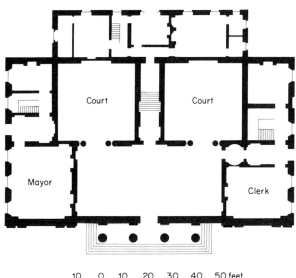

231

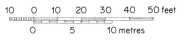

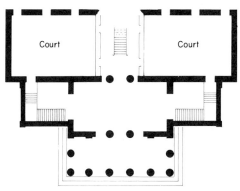

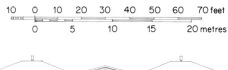

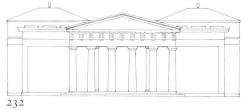

232

233

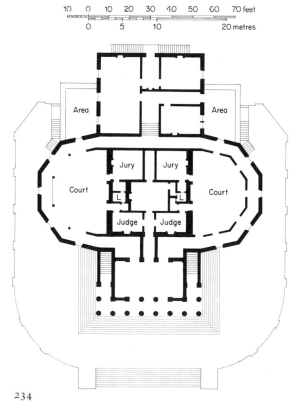

234

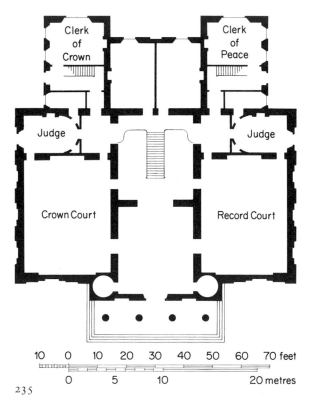

235

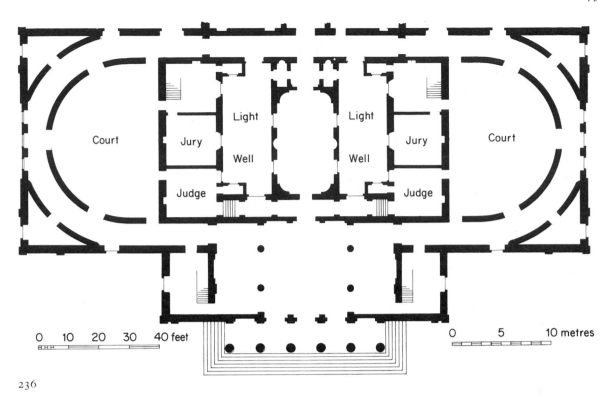

Court   Jury   Light   Light   Jury   Court

Well   Well

Judge   Judge

0 10 20 30 40 feet

0   5   10 metres

236

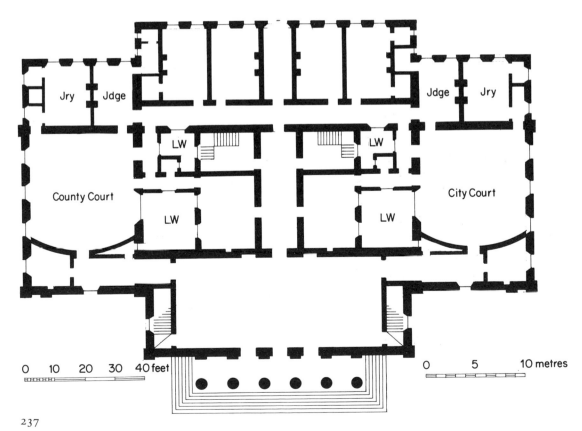

Jry   Jdge   Jdge   Jry

LW   LW

County Court   LW   LW   City Court

0 10 20 30 40 feet

0   5   10 metres

237

Tullamore, Ennis and Waterford are all in park-like surroundings, which encouraged a monumental appearance with three formal fronts, and minimised to some extent the problem of traffic-noise. It had no doubt also advantages from the point of view of security.

Keane was a resourceful planner. Most of his court houses stick to the 'Waterford I' formula of a transverse hall crossed on its shorter axis, but now with staircases to right and left. From there inwards there is great variety: copious and convenient accommodation (including sanitary accommodation) for judges, juries, barristers and witnesses, all beautifully integrated into the plan. By this time, also, there was a considerable demand for office accommodation, and this, too, is satisfied within the overall design, so that to this day many county councils still have their offices in the court house.

The responsibilities of the Grand Juries included also the majority of the country's bridges[29] which are among the most attractive structures of their time. Not many are very old. A few monastic bridges such as those of Athassel and Newtown Trim survive, and the fourteenth-century 'New Bridge' (fig. 238) near Leixlip was well reconstructed in recent years. Some of the many arches of Slane Bridge seem to be mediaeval. Occasionally one sees a bridge so narrow, as for example at Caragh Co Kildare, as to suggest a mediaeval date. Much of the bridge at Carrick-on-Suir is sixteenth century, but many other old bridges were improved out of existence by the engineers, as for example the once celebrated long bridge over the Shannon at Banagher. The six-arched bridge over the Quoile near Downpatrick is believed to be of about 1680.

The oldest of Dublin's bridges, and the most beautiful, is Queen's, built in 1764–8 by Charles Vallancey, a military engineer. But more notice, at the time, was given to Essex Bridge, built in 1753–5 by George Semple, using coffer-dams instead of the more usual caissons, largely because Semple wrote a book[30] about it. The beautiful bridge at Graignamanagh Co Kilkenny[31] is traditionally attributed to a member of the Semple family. It was certainly built in the mid-century, after the great flood of 1764 to which we owe many of the Nore bridges, most notably Green's bridge in Kilkenny (fig. 240) by George Smith, which till early in the present century had a fellow in John's Bridge a little lower down and to a similar design. Graignamanagh Bridge had also a fellow, an almost identical twin at Clarecastle Co Clare, till in very recent years it was destroyed by the road engineers. The fine bridge at Lismore of two arches, by Thomas Ivory (c. 1775) still spans the Blackwater beside the Castle.

A number of wide waterways—the Foyle at Derry, the Slaney at Wexford, the Barrow at New Ross, the Suir at Waterford and the Shannon at Portumna, were bridged towards the close of the eighteenth century, in timber, by the American engineer Lemuel Cox. Timber bridges were of course no novelty in Ireland: a contract for one to be built over the Slaney at Enniscorthy in 1581 survives.[32] The Derry scheme seems to have originated with the Earl-Bishop, who became interested in Swiss timber bridges in the 1760s,[33] while he was still Bishop of Cloyne, and in 1770 onwards set Michael Shanahan the task of measuring and drawing Swiss, Italian and French bridges by the Grubenmann brothers and others, with Derry in mind. He caused to be made also a magnificent large-scale model of the Grubenmann bridge at Schaffhausen which survived in Dublin till a very few years ago when it was ignorantly destroyed 'because it had worm in it'. Already in 1769 Ducart[33] was at work on both a masonry and a timber design for the Derry bridge to be built partly at the Bishop's expense. But for some years nothing happened. By 1788 James Paine junior had done a design[34] for The Irish Society (who owned Derry) and

PREVIOUS PAGE

236 Tullamore, Co Offaly: plan of the court house by J. B. Keane, before 1837. The general arrangement derives from Smirke's Gloucester doubtless via the Pains' Cork (destroyed by fire in 1891). There are further ranges of accommodation behind the rere corridor. The sanitary needs of judges, juries and the public, as well as their separate access to the courts, are well provided for. The interior was burnt in 1922 and altered in reconstruction

237 Waterford court house: plan, by J. B. Keane, 1849. An elaboration of his Tullamore plan, with separate sanitation for judges, bar, jury and witnesses, and an adroit use of lightwells

dedicated it rather surprisingly, to Lord Charlemont who was cool towards the Bishop. In the following year Lemuel Cox of Boston began work and the bridge, entirely of imported American oak, was finished in 13 months. Had it followed the Swiss models it would have been of one or at most two girder-arches made up of short lengths. As built it had 64 spans of 16½ feet, and the four other Cox bridges followed in quick succession and to a similar design. All were by their nature rather short-lived, though the Waterford bridge lasted into the twentieth century.

The handsome bridge at Athy, so proudly inscribed by 'Sir James Delehunty, Knight of the Trowel, Contracter' dates from 1796. A little earlier (1791) is perhaps the most graceful single-arch bridge in Ireland, Sarah Bridge in Dublin by Alexander Stevens from Scotland.[35] The bridge of Lucan is of similar date and design.

The elegant cast-iron footbridge which spans the Liffey at Merchant's Arch is among the earliest (1815) such structures in the world: so it is no surprise to learn that it was made at Coalbrookdale and designed by John Windsor, one of the foremen of that foundry.[36] In complete contrast, the five-arched flat-topped Wellesley (Sarsfield) Bridge at Limerick is among the most admired of masonry bridges, by Alexander Nimmo using Perronet's system of 'bell-mouthing' the openings as at the Pont de Neuilly. It took 11 years to build, from 1824–35.[37] The suspension bridge over Kenmare Sound, by William Bald, was built in 1838 and was the first such bridge in Ireland.[38] Another, of 1845, by James Dredge, survives at Caledon Co Tyrone.

It must be conceded that the picture is predominantly one of designers and technicians from outside, carrying out works in Ireland, and the impression could readily be reinforced by a recital of the Irish activity of such engineers as Jessop, Smeaton, Rennie, especially the harbour works of Rennie at Dunleary and Nimmo at Dunmore East. Yet the nineteenth century was not far advanced when some traffic in the opposite direction began. The Palm House at the Belfast Botanic Garden, designed by Charles Lanyon, the cast-iron structure by Richard Turner of Dublin and the glazing by Walker of Dublin, dates from 1839 and is contemporary with Paxton's similar work at Chatsworth.[39] Before long Turner was collaborating with Decimus Burton on the Regent's Park conservatory and the (still existent) Palm House at Kew in the 1840s, and a little later with William Fairburn at Lime Street Station, Liverpool;[40] and the following decade saw some overseas successes by Irish architects, most notably William Henry Lynn and Benjamin Woodward. The viaduct of Bessbrook Co Armagh, by Sir John McNeill, has 18 arches and was built in 1851–2.

The lighthouses of Ireland have a pedigree as long as that of the bridges.[41] At the beginning stands the tower at Hook Point, Co Wexford at the entrance to Waterford Harbour, a very massive and irregular double concentric cylinder dating from the thirteenth or even the twelfth century and still in use. The Maiden Tower and its companion the Lady's Finger, at Mornington where the Boyne meets the sea, are sixteenth-century sea-marks. A few fragments survive of a primitive and peculiarly Irish kind of lighthouse, the cottage with a vaulted roof on top of which a fire of turf was burned in a brazier or a stone bowl.[42] Much more architectural in character than these, and indeed 'the most grandiose of all lighthouses in the British Isles' (Hague) is the tapering octagonal six-storey tower on Wicklow Head, built in 1778 by John Trail who had been engineer to the Grand Canal Company. With its string-courses, round-headed niches and oculi it does not look like a lighthouse, and, being on a high promontory, does not have to withstand the action of the waves.[43] The South Rock lighthouse off the County Down coast on the other hand, built by Thomas Rogers in 1793, remains in excellent condition though superseded by a lightship.[44]

238

239

240 Kilkenny: Green's Bridge over the river Nore, of 1764, by G. Smith. One of the four or five finest bridges in Ireland, it was complemented, till the early twentieth century, by John's Bridge by the same designer and to a similar design. But John's Bridge has been replaced by a modern bridge, and the North side of Green's bridge (not visible here) has not escaped mutilation. The design is taken straight from Palladio, *IV Libri*, III, pl. VII

241 Graignamanagh bridge, Co Kilkenny, 1764, traditionally attributed to George Semple. The recently-destroyed bridge at Clarecastle Co Clare had five arches but was otherwise the twin of this

240

241

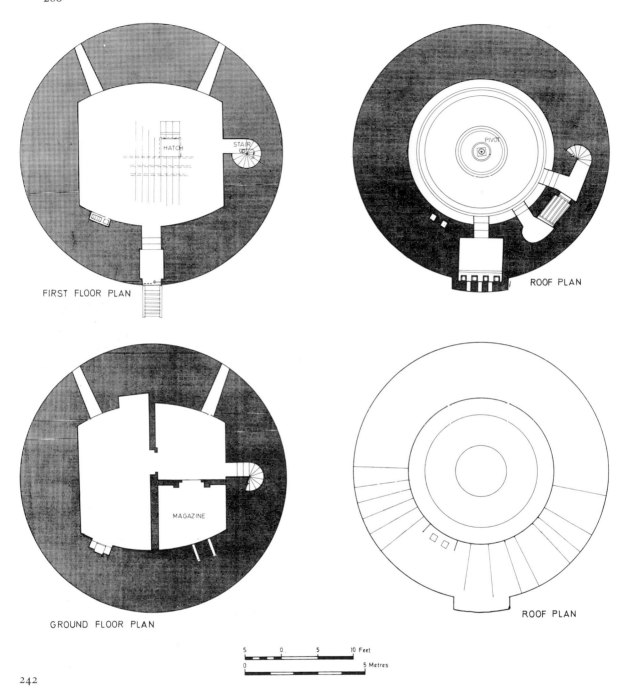

FIRST FLOOR PLAN

ROOF PLAN

GROUND FLOOR PLAN

ROOF PLAN

5   0   5   10 Feet
0   5 Metres

242

242 Bullock harbour,
Dalkey Co Dublin:
Martello tower No 10,
1804–5. The famous Joyce
tower, No 11, is very
similar. Drawn by P.
Kerrigan and R. Stapleton

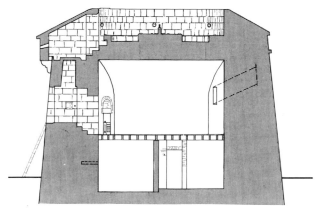

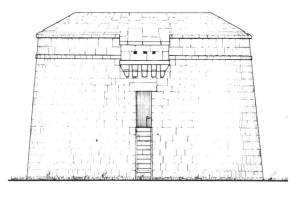

242 B

243

Many of the finest early nineteenth-century lighthouses, such as Inishtrahull (1812) and Tuskar (1815) are by George Halpin the elder, engineer to the Commissioners of Irish Lights. In 1835 he converted the solid stone beacon at Black Rock, Co Sligo[45] into a lighthouse, but because there was insufficient room in the resulting structure his son George Halpin the younger added bedrooms in the form of 'panniers' half-way up the walls and startlingly similar to the bartizans at, for example, Aughnanure Castle. The younger Halpin who succeeded his father in 1849 was less prolific, but the Fastnet lighthouse of 1854 which he built was of cast-iron construction. It gave rise to anxiety and after being tinkered with was replaced in 1904.

The Irish engineer Alexander Mitchell invented the screw-pile which was first used at the Maplin Sands in the Thames Estuary in 1838 and later all over the world including, of course, Ireland.[46]

The subject of Irish lighthouses should not be left without mention of the fluted Greek Doric column with which Alexander Nimmo adorned the end of the pier at Dunmore East in 1814–32.

Both in their situation and in their structure, the martello towers have much in common with the lighthouses. The Irish martellos are anonymous, and about them a certain mystery still lingers.[47] They are slightly earlier than their British counterparts, and cannot therefore have been influenced by them save in so far as both series have a common exemplar. The actions at Cap Mortella in Corsica in 1793 and 1794 undoubtedly much impressed the British military authorities. Yet the fact remains that the tower at Cap Mortella did not much resemble either the British or the Irish martello towers. On the other hand, there are, in the Eastern islands of the Canary archipelago, several towers[48] to which the Irish series bear a quite remarkably close resemblance: at least two on Gran Canaria (at San Cristobal and at Gando), one on Lanzarote (at Las Coloredas near Playa Blanca on the South-West tip of the island), and two on Fuerteventura (at Fustes on the East coast a short distance South of Puerto de Cabras, and at Cotillo on the North-West). The Las Coloredas tower is dated 1769 and one of those on Fuerteventura is said to be of 'about 1740'. Other similar structures in the islands which are not martellos have dates in the reign of Charles III (1759–88). A British force under Nelson invested the Canaries in 1797, and while there is much to be said for Mrs Sutcliffe's suggestion that Lt-Col. Benjamin Fisher designed the Irish towers, the question remains open.

There are about 50 altogether. The largest concentrations are on either side of Dublin, where building began in the middle of 1804. Unlike the English towers which are of brick plastered over, they are as a general rule of the finest ashlar granite. The pronounced batter which they show is found also on the Canary towers and the English series, and cannot therefore be a revival or continuance of the Irish batter. But the workmanship of the towers is of a piece with that in other Irish buildings of the period, and must therefore have been locally contributed. The plans are for the most part simple, without the (literally) eccentric refinement of the English series, though the Meelick tower on the Shannon near Portumna is cam-shaped, struck from six centres, and that at Greencastle in Lough Foyle is elliptical. So is the Banagher tower. The five Cork Harbour towers, exceptionally, have no batter. Being structures entirely in compression, the martellos are incapable of falling down, though a few have been removed, mostly in the course of railway works.

Their general similarity coupled with their lack of uniformity raises interesting questions about how they were built. The Dublin series at least were all constructed in a very short space of time and therefore in many cases simultaneously. Presumably the lieutenant in charge of each gang, or the leading mason, had been briefed in a

PREVIOUS PAGE
243 Shannonbridge, Cos Offaly and Roscommon: the bridge and the fortifications on the Connacht side, from the North. Built in 1804, as a consequence of the initially successful French landing at Killala in 1798, the fortifications consist of a redoubt (extreme right, middle distance) separated from a long slope, possibly an esker artificially shaped, by a dry moat into which projects the caponniere (just visible in the photograph), two barracks (centre) which present a domestic appearance towards the East but a very warlike aspect to the West and, formerly, a defended gateway through which the road from Ballinasloe to Tullamore had to pass. On Lamb Island (left foreground) vestiges of a battery can just be discerned. The Shannon was in flood when this photograph was taken. See Paul Kerrigan in *An Cosantóir*, December 1975. Every important point on the Shannon, from Loop Head to Athlone, was fortified during this period, but Shannonbridge is perhaps the most impressive of the remains, except, of course, the remodelling of the thirteenth-century keep at Athlone

general way as to the model to be followed, while the exact dimensions and details were left vague.

Other fortifications of the Napoleonic period, though differing in form from the martellos, share their architectural character and have, often, great aesthetic appeal. This is especially true of the fortifications along most of the length of the Shannon: for example the battery on Scattery Island near its mouth, and the splendid complex at Shannonbridge some 90 miles further up (fig. 243). Mr Paul Kerrigan has made the study of these structures his peculiar domain, and the reader is referred to his articles, at present scattered in periodicals (see note 46).

CHAPTER SEVENTEEN

The Later Nineteenth Century: Some Miscellaneous Buildings

This account has so far been cast in the form of a continuous narrative, with occasional excursions backwards or forwards to recover matters passed over or to anticipate later developments. The nineteenth century, however, will not tolerate such treatment, for more than one reason. The volume of building, and still more that of surviving building, increases sharply, and so does the amount of available documentation, printed, graphic and photographic. Even more significant is the multiplication of new categories. The four or five primitive classes—ecclesiastical, military, domestic, civic, institutional—are no longer adequate.

On top of this must be added the increasing eclecticism of the period, which leads to fragmentation and makes linear discussion impossible. Communications, in both senses of the word, had so improved (The Irish Mail by Holyhead 1848, the *Dublin* (later *Irish*) *Builder* 1859) that there are times during the second half of the century when Irish architecture seems only to be the out-patients' department of English architecture. Specialisation played its part too: church-architects, for instance, were a new breed of men, prepared to build indifferently in Constantinople or in Cork. Even in the eighteenth century there had been specialists: William Blackburn who designed 15 English prisons and one in Ireland (at Limerick) and hardly anything else, a rarity in his time. Both the Dublin Theatre Royal of 1821[*] and its successor which went up after the fire of 1880 were designed by the leading English theatre-architects of their day: Samuel Beazley and Frank Matcham respectively, and the latter designed also the recently-restored Opera House in Belfast.[1]

It is sometimes impossible to trace the relationship between two Irish buildings directly: the line may pass through a building which is not in Ireland at all, or by way of an architect who practised only elsewhere. For the first time the question poses itself: whether the material is better marshalled round the personalities of the architects or under abstract headings. Neither method is entirely satisfactory, so I have had to fall back on a mixture of both.

These concluding sections, therefore, are in the nature of a round-up, or perhaps more aptly to be likened to the tail of a kite. The notional terminal date is 1880, for no better reason than that it is a century ago. Nothing in particular that I know of came to an end in that year. But the careers of McCarthy, the younger Pugin, Lanyon, Barre and Woodward were over. All the new Protestant cathedrals except Belfast had been built, and all the new Catholic ones except Letterkenny and Galway and Mullingar and Cavan. Most of the institutional buildings which are still so conspicuous were by then in being. Of all the constructional innovations which are so closely associated with the 'modern movement', only the combination of iron and glass for hothouses and exhibition buildings had yet showed itself in Ireland. This

---

[*]It seems, alas, certain that the elegant facade of the Theatre Royal which would have faced Trinity College, and was illustrated by George Petrie in G. N. Wright's *Historical Guide to Dublin*, 1821, p. 269, was never executed. But the interior was by Beazley.

exception is very important, for notwithstanding the fact that exaggerated claims were made on behalf of Richard Turner, his iron-framed glass-houses at Belfast and Glasnevin (1839 and 1842) stand early in the world series of such buildings, as does Sir John Benson's composite iron, timber and glass building for the Dublin Exhibition of 1853,[2] temporary though it was. Ireland has not often been in the vanguard of progress in technology, but it has sometimes been so. The 'Belfast roof' is another instance: appearing a little before 1880 it was a method of constructing long roofing-girders out of short lengths of timber, and spread far beyond the shores of Ireland.[3]

Official Architecture

Official architecture was at first in the domain of the office of the Surveyor-General, who in the late seventeenth[4] and early eighteenth century was a real architect: William Robinson from 1670 (after 1684 jointly with William Molyneux who, like Wren, was a mathematician and astronomer), Thomas Burgh from 1700 to 1730, and overlapping, in effect, with him, Pearce. Arthur Dobbs who succeeded on Pearce's death in 1733 was a politician and economist and resigned his patent after ten years. He was followed by Arthur Jones Nevill, also a politician, who lost both his office and his seat in parliament as a result of a revolt by the 'patriotic party' against the Castle interest in 1753.[5] By this time his principal concern was with the building and maintenance of barracks throughout the country, and in about 1760 we begin to hear of the 'Barrack Board'.

It was composed of the usual assortment of notabilities, though by 1764 we notice among them John Magill ('Buttermilk Jack') who had risen in the world as a building contractor, became Comptroller of the Works under the Board and finally a member of it. It had an 'architect' who appears to have been an absentee, and a 'Clerk and Inspector of Civil Building in Dublin' who seems to have done the work and whose name was Jarrat. The absentee architect was replaced in 1767 by Christopher Myers who came from England, and the Clerk under him was from 1775 onwards Thomas Cooley, also from England and the winner of the Royal Exchange.[6]

This office was by then clearly the official architect's department and ancestor of the present Office of Public Works, and, like it, was familiarly known as the 'Board of Works'.[7] Cooley was suceeded by Gibson, a nonentity best known for having built Gandon's Military Infirmary.[8] Some confusion is caused by the fact that during this period the Surveyor-General *of the Ordnance* (a department concerned with artillery) was Ralph Ward,[9] who is found signing barrack designs in 1770, building houses in Merrion Square, and who seems to have committed suicide following a scandal in 1788. Several of the other government boards of the time did building work on their own, notably of course the powerful Revenue Board under John Beresford, who employed Gandon. The Wide Streets Commissioners, also, were autonomous, and as Dr McParland has made clear[10], they had, before the Union, the complexion of a national authority, and after it that of a municipal one, with all which that implied.

Two years after the Union, in 1802, the Board of Works was reorganised, but in 1811 there were again complaints because the old easy-going eighteenth-century system of personal instructions from the Viceroy and careless estimating by the Board's architect (Francis Johnston) was allowing costs to rise.[11] Though dissolution of the Board was recommended this was not done till 1831, when, as part of the ubiquitous tide of reform, the number of commissioners was cut from seven to three,

244 Dublin, the Phoenix
Park: the Wellington
Testimonial, begun in 1817,
to the design of Sir Robert
Smirke. At 205 feet, it is the
largest obelisk in Europe.
There was a competition
for the design

245 Armagh, Barrack
Street. It dates from the
early nineteenth century,
part of the wholesale
rebuilding under Primate
Richard Robinson (Lord
Rokeby) and his immediate
successors

244

245

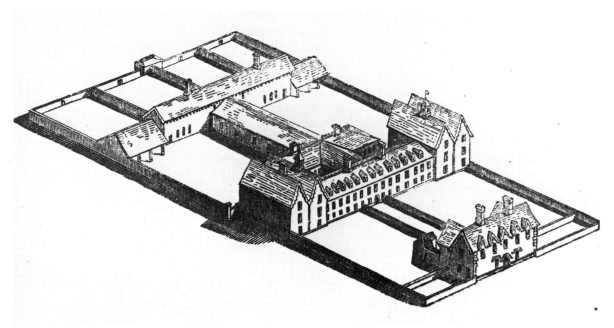

246

246 Isometric view of a typical Irish workhouse, source unknown, mid-nineteenth century. The accompanying letterpress compares the Irish workhouses favourably with their English counterparts. This may be taken as characteristic of George Wilkinson's fairly standard design, of which comparatively few specimens now survive. Bleak as they appear to our eyes, they must have represented a considerable advance in physical shelter if not in human warmth. The disproportionate ratio of chimney-stacks between the inmates' ranges and the master's house seems to tell a tale

Just South of Carlow town there stood until recently a magnificent workhouse in the classical style, presumably also by Wilkinson, with a battery of 11 Venetian windows side-by-side in the main block, and twin Italianate towers, all executed in the finest ashlar

which it has remained ever since. It was given the three state harbours of Kingstown, Howth and Dunmore East (which it still has), and in 1857 a large number of extra and typically modern responsibilities which it still has, such as revenue buildings, constabulary barracks, post-offices and the buildings of the Education Board.

An important branch of official building was handled, from 1712 till 1833, by the Board of First Fruits which built or assisted in the building of churches and glebe-houses for the established church.[12] At first they had no centralised architectural policy, but John Bowden appears as their architect, based in Dublin. At the height of their exertions, not long before their dissolution, they had one architect for each ecclesiastical province: William Farrell for Armagh, John Semple and son for Dublin, James Pain for Cashel, and Joseph Welland the successor of Bowden, for Tuam.[13] All were based in Dublin except for Pain who worked from Limerick.

The Ecclesiastical Commissioners who superseded them in 1833 had a reign of 36 years until disestablishment abolished them in 1869. It is not known whether they took over the same architectural establishment, but Welland was their architect from 1843 till his death in 1860, and later his son's partnership of Welland and Gillespie remained active in church-building. At disestablishment churches became the responsibility of the various denominations of which the Church of Ireland was henceforth only one, but the Board of Works was initially responsible for dwellings for clergy of all faiths. A more enduring concern of the Board's was the care of national monuments. As a result of the Irish Church Act, 14 important ecclesiastical monuments were in 1874 put in the Board's charge: the first state provision for the care of such monuments in these islands.[14] One hundred and five more monuments were added in 1877. The British Act of 1882 confirmed the function which continues to this day. The first inspector was Thomas Newenham Deane. During the nineteenth century the Board acquired functions such as public works loans, light railways, drainage and the management of the Shannon which never came the way of its British counterpart.

The Dublin Suburban House to 1870

As the capital spread out towards and beyond the encircling ring of the canals, appropriate variations of the traditional Dublin house made their appearance. The great height (four storeys over basement) of the town houses was not suitable for districts where land values were lower and the means of the inhabitants more modest. So scaled-down versions of the standard house, of three storeys or two, continued to be built for at least 40 years after the Union with little stylistic change. Sometimes, though not often, the basement was omitted.

At the same time more significant developments were afoot. There had always been single-storey cottages in the poorer parts of Dublin especially South of St Patrick's Cathedral, and some of those which precariously survive may date back to the eighteenth century. They must always have worn the somewhat rustic face which they still show. But before the end of that century a type had appeared which, though perhaps of country origin, was to become widespread in the Dublin suburbs. In this type of house the basement was to increase in importance and at the same time rise out of the ground until it was no longer really a basement save in the academic sense. Such houses as Mount Gordon Co Mayo[15] and Rice Hill Co Cavan seem to be early examples of the type in which there is only one storey above the basement, and the entrance is at the upper level by a flight of steps. In Heytesbury Street and Pleasants

Street (fig. 247) there are terraces of diminutive single-storey houses over basements: the garden at basement floor-level being a few feet below the made-up road level and the principal floor being a few feet above it. This type is widespread in the Dublin suburbs and very attractive: most commonly double-fronted but sometimes single. Houses not unlike these but without basements do occur, especially in the South-Eastern suburbs and by the sea, and are sometimes called, not unfittingly, 'classical cottages'.

On a more ambitious scale the Dublin terrace house was varied by putting the entrance-door and hall, still framed by the Doric or Ionic order and relieved by a fanlight, into a separate compartment to one side of the main block and set a little back from it. Rows of such houses, arranged in pairs so that the doorways also occur in pairs (with or without space between them) have a rhythm anticipated in such purely urban developments as Herbert Street but equally capable of application in semi-detached form (Pembroke Road, Rathgar Road, Belgrave Square Rathmines, Rostrevor Terrace (fig. 249) etc.). The hall-compartment may be only one storey high over the basement, or may run to the full height of the house. In these houses the plan is folded in upon itself so that the return room, at landing-level, which in earlier houses sticks out at the back, is now contained within the main rectangle. Most of these houses are anonymous, but occasionally they are known to be by such people as George Papworth, William Murray, Murray and Denny, or Sandham Symes, known architectural names.[16]

Towards the middle of the century, and especially after 1860, the introduction of fresh details gives these houses a flavour which is increasingly removed from that of the eighteenth century. Polychrome brick, cornices of timber or of notched brick, cable-moulded or otherwise 'Venetian' doorcases, bay-windows whether corbelled out or rising from the ground, and plate-glass are all indications of date, but leave the fundamental disposition of spaces unchanged. Perhaps the latest of such houses, of a rather large size, are to be found in Ailesbury Road, intermixed with houses which could equally well be in the suburbs of any English town. By 1880 the traditional Dublin house was extinct.

Pugin and His Followers

The Irish career of Augustus Welby Northmore Pugin was of comparable significance to his career in England, and began very nearly as early. His first Irish commission, the chapel of St Peter's College Wexford, was afoot by 1837.[17] Like the Anglo-Norman invaders, he first penetrated Ireland via Wexford where his patron the Earl of Shrewsbury (and of Waterford and Wexford) had interests, and where another member of the Talbot family eased his path. As we have already seen, Gothic Revival churches—of a kind—were no novelty. But Duff, Madden and Cobden were no ideologues: the nearest approach to an ideological manifesto was Thomas Bell's *Gothic Architecture … in Ireland* of 1829, an inoffensive document which concludes by holding up Francis Johnston as the exemplar of revived Gothic in Ireland. Pugin was an animal of a very different type: nothing if not polemical. The first edition of *Contrasts* was already out (1836). For Pugin, activity in Ireland was an extension of activity in England, but in a field which he had reason to hope would be even more receptive.

It proved to be so, to the extent that his biographer calls his Irish buildings 'among the best constructed and the largest that he ever produced' and his two Irish cathedrals

247

248

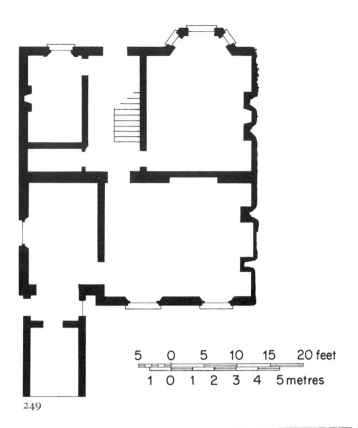

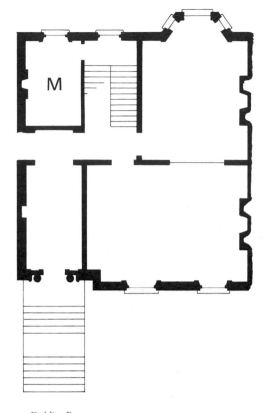

249

250

249 Dublin, Rostrevor Terrace, Rathgar: basement and principal floor plans of a house in a terrace of 1870. The houses are built in pairs, all uniform, with the front door in a smaller block slightly recessed from the main elevation. These doorways consequently appear in pairs and the whole effect is very formal. The bay-windows are original. Note the position of the mezzanine room (the 'return') within the rectangle of the plan

250 Dublin: houses in Orwell Park, some time in the 1870s. The classical form is still intact, but the detailing, e.g. of the doorcases, brick cornice and corbelled-out oriels, has moved on.

'among the best ever produced from his designs[18]. Though generally plainer, his Irish buildings generally score over their English counterparts by being splendidly crafted in stone and in their situations. In all he built 12 or 13 churches and chapels, five convents or similar buildings and some domestic work, all in the space of 13 years or so during which his output in England was even larger.

Pugin's whirlwind visits to Ireland were packed with activity and also, we must conclude, with observation, since his Wexford churches and his Killarney Cathedral show evidence of his having studied Dunbrody Abbey and Kilkenny Cathedral respectively. It may be also that his choice of the round-arched Romanesque for the church at Gorey Co Wexford, contrary to his usual practice, reflects some concern with Irish antiquity. With the exception of Loreto Abbey Rathfarnham, Maynooth College, Birr Convent, Adare and Killarney, all his Irish work is in the South-East. His Presentation Convent at Waterford (1842) is a harmoniously diversified group: later convents, enlarged by other hands, have often been diverse but less often harmonious. Since the ill-advised stripping of the interior of Killarney Cathedral, his best surviving building is probably the cathedral at Enniscorthy: simple, strong and filled with light.

The work which he did at Adare Co Limerick, for the third Earl of Dunraven, a noted antiquary and convert to Catholicism, was continued after Pugin's death by another English architect, Philip Charles Hardwick (best known for his father's Doric work at Euston) who in 1855–65 built the Catholic cathedral in Limerick, a work of Pugin's school.[19]

At Wexford, the epicentre of Pugin's Irish activity, his master-mason Robert Pierce built two churches, the Assumption and the Immaculate Conception, both constructed between 1851 and 1858, very similar to one another, and not unworthy of their situation and their ancestry.

A. W. N. Pugin died, a burnt-out case, in 1852. His Irish practice, however, lived on after him as the partnership of his son E. W. Pugin with George Ashlin, from 1860 to 1870. Ashlin took Thomas A. Colman as his partner and lived on till 1922, so that the Puginian apostolic succession was a reality well within living memory. The best-known Pugin and Ashlin churches are SS Peter and Paul, Cork (1859–66), the Augustinian church in Dublin (1862–78) and Cobh Cathedral (fig. 251) which, though begun in 1867, took half a century to build. In common with other Catholic building of the mid-century and later, they show an increasing dependence on French models. Colour-contrast in the choice of stone is exploited for decorative effect.

The architect who, somewhat ineptly, was nicknamed 'the Irish Pugin', was James Joseph McCarthy,[20] five years Pugin's junior, born in 1817. While Pugin was preaching that only in Gothic could architecture be truly English, McCarthy was proclaiming the indissoluble alliance between Irish nationalism and the pointed arch. In the course of building over 40 churches, nine monasteries, convents and similar institutions, and no less than four cathedrals, he departed from the Gothic on less than half-a-dozen occasions. Between his early church of St Columb, Derry, (1838–41) and his following works he had been converted both by Pugin's writings and by the example of his buildings. McCarthy held, as one would expect, views on church planning and furnishing similar to those of Pugin and the Ecclesiological Societies both British and Irish, reinforced by the specifically 'Catholic' doctrines of the Rev. John Milner whose gospel had already been digested by the classical Catholic architects such as Leeson, Bolger, Keane and, above all, Byrne.[21]

The rising tide of middle-class Catholic prosperity, interrupted but not halted by the disaster of the Famine (1845–8) floated the career of McCarthy on a scale till then

251 Cobh (Queenstown, the Cove of Cork), Co Cork: the cathedral, by E. W. Pugin and G. O. Ashlin, 1868 onwards (roofed 1879, completed 1919). The cathedral of the large and rich diocese of Cloyne, it overlooked the spot from which, during the 50 years it was building, vast numbers of emigrants left Ireland, never to return

without precedent. His first large job was to carry out Armagh Cathedral which had already been begun by Thomas Duff of Newry and had risen some 15 to 18 feet above the ground. Characteristically, he altered the style from Perpendicular to Decorated, so that the spectator must support the absurdity of 'fourteenth-century' work standing on top of 'sixteenth' (except for the tracery which was harmonised); but in most other ways it is a very successful building. The twin-spired West façade was determined by Duff's plan and is unique in McCarthy's work.

McCarthy was a pupil at the Dublin Society's school under Baker, was then apprenticed to, and almost certainly spent the years 1843-6 with Charles Hansom, a prominent English Catholic architect, brother of the better-known J. A. Hansom (of the cab). Though sometimes heavily reliant, as at St Saviour's, Dominick Street, on French models, he laid numerous Irish buildings under tribute: Kilmallock, Ardfert, Gowran, Kilconnell and the Dominican Friary in Kilkenny which he restored. But the round-arched styles on which he drew were not Irish, rather Venetian, Pisan or 'Lombardic', as at Thurles Cathedral, Mount Argus or his rare country house, Cahirmoyle, or nondescript as at Ballitore and Lixnaw.

Six Architects

We have already met William Vitruvius Morrison as the third and last member of an Irish architectural family, and as the designer of the classical court houses at Carlow and Tralee. But most of his output was in country houses, and most of that, in turn, was in the 'Tudor' manner which he is credited with being the first to introduce into Ireland. He was something of an infant prodigy, for we are assured that when his father was clothing Ballyheigue, Co Kerry, in a fashionable mantle so that its owners could re-christen it a 'castle', William Vitruvius—then aged 15 for he was born in 1794—furnished the design. This is by no means incredible.

He worked jointly with his father on Shelton Abbey Co Wicklow, Kilruddery Co Wicklow and Ballyfin. Ill-health, and no doubt also the spirit of enquiry, took him for a long journey to Rome and Paestum in 1821. If his experience of Paestum is reflected in his court houses, it is less easy to account for the finicky pinnacled 'Tudor' with which he tricked out such buildings as Ballygiblin. Though George Petrie acknowledges his help in measuring and sketching early Christian buildings, there is scant trace of this in Morrison's own work, unless we are to count the somewhat absurd Round Tower worked into the gatehouse of Clontarf Castle (1835-7). Like his father, he practised a hybridised classical style seen at its best, perhaps, in Borris Co Carlow. Though he travelled South once more, this time in the vain search for health, he had not long to live and died in 1838 at the age of 44.[22]

Benjamin Woodward, born only 22 years later than Morrison, and similarly short-lived, inhabited a different world and was very much more influential, not only in Ireland.[23] Son of a peripatetic but not pauperised militia captain, he had few of Morrison's initial advantages. But his early apprenticeship to a civil engineer (probably William Stokes) gave him a thorough grounding in construction. His measured survey of Holy Cross Abbey is dated 1842 and by 1846 he is in Cork with Sir Thomas Deane, whose son, later also to be knighted, was by 13 years Woodward's junior. He was engaged on Queen's College Cork, a learned building full of English and particularly Oxford allusions, which occupied the firm from 1846 till 1849, and in 1851 became a partner.

As he died a mere ten years later the whole of his significant career occupies hardly

252 Dublin: Trinity College Museum ('Engineering School'). The central double-domed staircase-hall is by Benjamin Woodward, 1852-7

July 1860.

THE KILDARE ST CLUB.

MESSRS DEANE & WOODWARD ARCHITECTS.

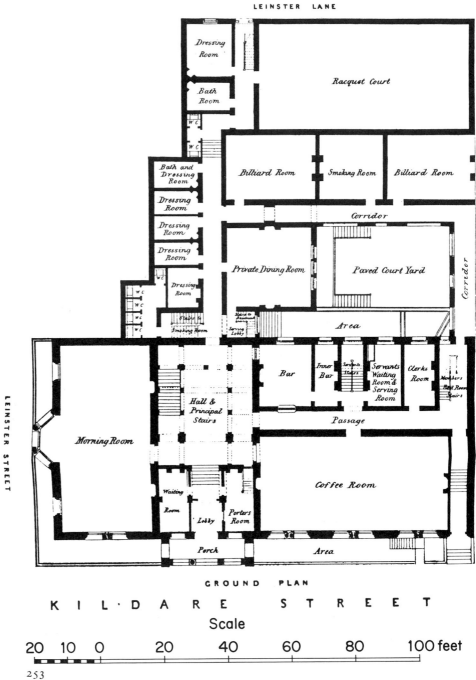

GROUND PLAN

K I L · D A R E   S T R E E T

Scale

20 10 0   20   40   60   80   100 feet

more time than Pearce's, and, as with Pearce, everything was going on all at once: two university museums (one in Dublin and one in Oxford) an insurance office in London, two schools in Dublin (one surviving and one recently destroyed), country houses in Co Kilkenny and South Co Dublin, the Kildare Street Club, not to mention a competition entry for the new Government Offices in Whitehall, an entry initially placed fourth and ultimately third.

It is not surprising that in 1854 the firm moved from Cork to Dublin and that Woodward was soon spending as much time in England as in Ireland, besides long continental visits made necessary as much by his health as by his desire to observe and digest the art of other countries. He is perhaps the most original Irish architect of the nineteenth century. Though most of his work relies on informal groupings of cusp-headed pointed openings, his two best-known, and perhaps best, buildings depart from this formula. At Trinity College Deane and Woodward supplanted John McCurdy who won the competition and whose ground-plan they were bound to follow. The building is rigidly symmetrical, as rigid as Coleshill which in several ways it resembles. The openings are round-headed, though under pointed relieving-arches. The placing of the very prominent stacks recalls another Pratt house, Kingston Lacy, recased and remodelled by Barry in 1838-9, and we know that Woodward was in debt to Barry and in particular to the Travellers' Club (fig. 252).

Ruskin's approval of Woodward's work is well known and must have been based more than anything else on the freedom which he gave to his carvers, the Harrisons, O'Sheas and others, to diversify capitals and enrich strings, all within a very classical framework. At the Kildare Street Club (fig. 253) the framework is less obviously classical though the entrance-hall and stairs and their relationship to the two main rooms are very straightforward. The club's committee rejected pointed and round-headed openings, so that the camber-headed paired colonnetted openings which were in fact built seem a compromise between Woodward's aspirations and the Dublin street style. The glory of the building was the (extremely wasteful) grand staircase which was totally destroyed after the building was divided in recent years.

In brick, like the Club, St Stephen's School at Mount Street Bridge is in every other way a contrast: low but with steep roofs, modest, romantic and charming.

The death of Woodward at Lyon in 1861 at the age of 44 removed the most original of Irish architects. It is clear that in his practice he anticipated as much as he followed the precepts of Ruskin, and in his structural use of exposed ironwork at Oxford he foreshadowed Viollet-le-Duc. In sheer originality (for what that is worth) only John Semple comes near him.

Another short-lived architect of mark was William Joseph Barre who for many years shared with Gandon the distinction of having had a substantial *Life* written and published[24] (W. V. Morrison's is very slim). He had none of Morrison's advantages and few even of Woodward's. Born in Newry in 1830 he worked first with a builder, then, when still not yet 17, with Thomas Duff whom we have already met as the architect of Newry Cathedral, Armagh (before McCarthy) and Dundalk. Although Duff died in 1848 at 56, he was very versatile both in style and scope, from the Greek Revival Old Museum in College Square Belfast (1831) to the King's College Chapel derivative at Dundalk Catholic Church (1835-47), and including a number of country houses both classical and Tudor, as well as court houses and market houses. He left behind him his ex-partner Thomas Jackson who survived till 1890 and is chiefly notable for St Malachy's, Belfast, and for having furnished, in 1871, a design for the Town Hall in Belfast which in the opinion of the burghers was insufficiently decorated.

253 Dublin: the Kildare Street Club, plan from the *Irish Builder* 1860. The elaborate differentiation of rooms for different purposes recalls the planning of country houses of the same period, and is in sharp contrast to the generalised multi-purpose planning of earlier buildings

Few of Barre's designs would have incurred this reproach. On his own from 1850 (having spent the two years since Duff's death with Gribbon, a Dublin architect) he produced in rapid order a great many designs, for competitions (in which he was conspicuously unfortunate), for churches, for memorials, for country houses, warehouses, mills and banks, nearly all in a florid and eclectic style which, while sometimes tending towards the classic and sometimes towards the gothic is best characterised, as by his biographer in 1868, as 'Victorian'.[25]

His work is most conspicuously seen in Belfast: the Albert Memorial Clock of 1866 (a competition winner over which there was a monumental row), the Ulster Hall of 1860 and the Provincial Bank of 1867 which would have been even more highly ornamented than it is, had Barre not died untimely in 1867.

Several of the opulent villas which he built for commercial magnates on the outskirts of Belfast are still extant, notably Danesfort (originally Clanwilliam House) of 1864, off the Malone Road, for a linen tycoon. Like other architects of his time, he designed churches for five different denominations including the Catholic, in well-nigh as many different styles, and he enjoys the credit (if credit it be) for having first steered the nonconformists away from the meeting-house ideal towards greater elaboration of ornament and what we would now call 'churchiness'. But some of his smaller and plainer churches are almost indistinguishable from those of McCarthy or indeed of Pugin, workmanlike, durable and admirably suited to the ethos of their time.

A longer-lived architect than any of these was Sir Charles Lanyon,[26] though his active architectural life ended at the same time as Woodward's and some years before Barre's. Born in England he came early to Dublin and was articled to Jacob Owen of the Board of Works in about 1830. From being County Surveyor of Kildare he moved in 1835 or 1836 to Antrim in the same capacity, where the famous Coast Road and the magnificent Glendun viaduct attest his skill. The Queen's Bridge, Belfast, of 1843, survives though widened, and so do six of the eight or nine prominent public buildings with which he enriched the rapidly expanding town. His re-casing of the old Exchange, or at least the drawing for it, could almost have been done by Pearce, though in the execution it looks, as it is, very much of 1845. His head office for the Northern Bank, of 1852 has a similarly Palladian quality crossed, as usual with Lanyon, with Barry's Italianate. At the Queen's College (treated of elsewhere) the red-brick Tudor cloaked a plan as classical as Barry's at Westminster a decade earlier. He had already used Tudor in the (now demolished) Deaf and Dumb Institution of 1844–5.

Close by the Queen's College his Assembly's College of 1853 (fig. 255) has a Vanbrughian flavour, while his Custom House, finished in 1857, is more purely Italian in feeling. A large 13-bay four-storey warehouse in Bedford Street, also in stone and very Italian, is probably his.

Lanyon was a very pushful character. From the moment when he married Jacob Owen's daughter he never looked back. About 1860, however, he seems to have effectively given up the practice, though not the profit, of architecture. In 1854 he took W. H. Lynn into partnership, joined in 1860 by his own son John. In the following year he opened an office in Dublin, and in 1862 was Mayor of Belfast. Member of Parliament, President of the Royal Institute of the Architects of Ireland, and in 1868 a knight, his cup was overflowing. He died in 1889 aged 76.

William Henry Lynn, who joined Lanyon first in 1846, had equal but complementary gifts.[27] The 16 years' difference in their ages was reflected in a marked difference of sensibility. His (Belfast) Banks in Newtownards and Dungannon of

254 Dunleary (at that time Kingstown): the Royal Irish Yacht Club by J. S. Mulvany. Plan after that given in *The Builder* IX, 418, 1851

255 Belfast: the Assembly's College, by Sir Charles Lanyon, 1853, at the East end of University Square, closing the vista, but nevertheless somewhat retiringly placed behind the Queen's ('godless') College of a few years earlier, by the same architect but in 'Tudor' style

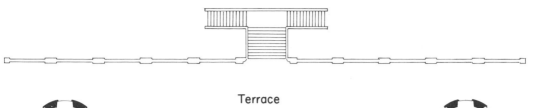

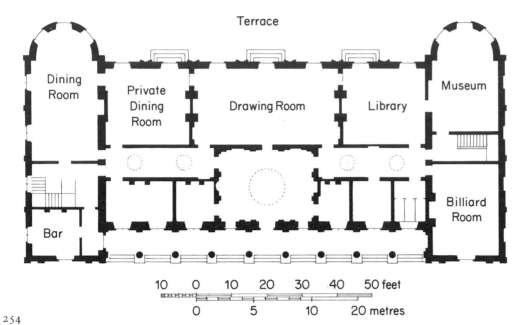

Terrace

Dining Room

Private Dining Room

Drawing Room

Library

Museum

Bar

Billiard Room

| 10 | 0 | 10 | 20 | 30 | 40 | 50 feet |

| 0 | 5 | 10 | 20 metres |

254

255

256

257

256 Belfast: The Diocesan Offices in May Street, by W. H. Lynn, 1867. A very up-to-date and competent essay in the style of Woodward, typical in its compromise between regular and asymmetrical elements, it is related to the Lanyon and Lynn banks in Dungannon and Newtownards. Another competent Woodwardian essay is the combined Custom House and Post Office at Waterford, dated 1876, by E. T. Owen

257 Rathdaire, Co Leix: the Church of Ireland church of c. 1885 by J. F. Fuller, for the Adair family who invented the parish. A West front freely adapted from Roscrea (see p. 43-5) with additional ornament derived from metalwork and manuscripts. A more faithful copy of Roscrea was carried out some 30 years later by James J. McMullen at the Honan Chapel on Cork

1854 and 1855 respectively could pass for Woodward's work and are at least as early. Their qualified symmetry had been abandoned by the time he designed the Diocesan Offices in May Street, Belfast (1865-7) (fig. 256) a building which, in pointed contrast to Woodward's recently-destroyed St Ann's Schools in Dublin, has been adapted for a new use.

Lynn had a very large practice, both before and after his parting from Lanyon in 1872: some 17 churches, a similar number of country houses and some 25 public buildings. He won a startling number of overseas competitions and even crossed the Atlantic in 1875. Much of his later work offends against the maxim of Landor that 'without regularity there is neither strength nor state.' One of his churches is of special note: the Church of Ireland church at Jordanstown Co Antrim.[28] Stimulated no doubt by his task in 'restoring' and rebuilding the nave of St Doulough's in 1863-4, he attempted at Jordanstown a year later to produce a complete church in the Hiberno-Romanesque style, complete with a Round Tower in the same position as that at Teampull Finghín (see page 6). But of course the church is of much more complex plan than any ancient example, and like almost every subsequent imitator of the Irish Romanesque, he gave it a round apse which is unknown in authentic examples though common in English Norman work. He remained innovative to the end of his long life, erecting a steel-framed department-store in 1899, and at the age of 82, in 1910, winning, in an anonymous competition and against 57 other entrants, the competition for the enlargement of the library which he had built for the Queen's College in 1865-7. He lived long enough to see it finished.

An architect even more longevitous than Lynn was James Franklin Fuller. He left a longwinded autobiography written when he was over 80, called, very aptly, *Omniana*, but it is disappointingly thin on the subject of architecture.[29] He was born in Kerry in 1835 and was a schoolfellow of Thomas Newenham Deane, but went to London at the age of 15 and was soon articled to an architect of whom we know only that his name began with P. and that he designed Bodmin Gaol.

Fuller's architectural education was entirely English, in the office first of Alfred Waterhouse and then of M. E. Hadfield. He returned to Ireland at the age of 27 in 1862 to a job with the Ecclesiastical Commissioners, which terminated on their dissolution eight years later. He was to survive for more than half a century more, and to build, among other things, two of the most wholeheartedly Irish Romanesque revival churches in existence. Though he did a good deal of country-house work, including most of the enormous Ashford Castle (with George Ashlin) for Lord Ardilaun in the years following 1870, it is generally lacking in charm.

The Irish Romanesque Revival has a curious history. Though a parish priest in Co Cork, Father Horgan of Ballygibbon, built a revived Round Tower in his churchyard in 1836,[30] and though an obscure country church in North Tipperary is plainly copied from St Cronan's, Roscrea, as early as 1812 (see p. 225), the full revival was a surprisingly late phenomenon. McCarthy, for example, for all his nationalism, is barely touched by it. Among the earliest attempts to apply Hiberno-Romanesque ornament systematically was a commercial building in, of all places, Grafton Street, by an English architect, Matthew Digby Wyatt.[31]

But the Church of Ireland, bereft of its connexion with the state, had forged itself a new destiny as the heir of the supposedly primitive church of St Patrick. Even after disestablishment it still possessed nearly all the historic sites, and the colonels and shopkeepers provided the money for the clergy and architects to spend, at Jordanstown as we have seen under Lynn, at Tuam where a new cathedral was grafted by Sir T. N. Deane on to the ancient Romanesque chancel,[32] and, perhaps most elaborately at Rathdaire Co Leix, by Fuller (fig. 257) Rathdaire is, suitably enough, a phantom parish, summoned into existence in their own honour by a family named Adair, who have since evaporated leaving no trace except the church.

What an extraordinary sight it is, appearing without warning among the lush pastures of Leix! It is a full-size replica of the West front of Roscrea, but improved upon by the application of much more detail and the addition, to the right, of a tower of 'Lombardic' origin.[33] Most startling of all is the enrichment of the door-gable with large-scale zoomorphic interlace surrounding a large 'high cross' without a shaft. Immediately above this—in fact touching its apex—is a wheel-window not related to either of the Irish examples but rather of French or English derivation. The date of Rathdaire is uncertain but probably about 1880. At Clane, consecrated in 1883, Fuller had again the patronage of an enthusiastic and well-to-do family called Cooke-Trench, and the help of the antiquarian Margaret Stokes, so that the interior at least is heavily dependent on Cormac's Chapel, though, as at Rathdaire, interlace ornament is used in a way foreign to that of the ancient builders. The determinedly Irish character of the church is somewhat compromised by the contemporary fittings supplied by various English firms.[34]

The Godless Colleges

The Godless Colleges were so called by O'Connell and the Catholic hierarchy because their begetter Sir Robert Peel, desiring to throw university education open to Catholics and to Presbyterians, did so by founding three colleges free from religious tests and free also from religious endowments.* At the same time (1845) he greatly increased government support for Maynooth and provided money with which Pugin's large-scale work there was built. The three Godless Colleges were sited in the provincial capitals: Belfast, Cork and Galway, and all three are still there though all enlarged and accompanied by many later buildings. But thanks to the fact (fortunate architecturally if not in other ways) that during their first 40 years of existence all three declined almost to extinction,[35] their loss of numbers being inversely proportional to the size of the towns in which they were situated, the original buildings retain their identity and to a large extent even their original setting, and are certainly among the most distinguished examples of public architecture from the middle of the century.

The three architects chosen by the Board of Works were Lanyon for Belfast, Thomas Deane for Cork and Joseph B. Keane for Galway. All three colleges were rapidly built and ready for occupation by 1849.

The Belfast college (Queen's, Belfast, now Queen's University) (fig. 259) is in brick with stone dressings, rigidly symmetrical save for a slender stair-turret serving the entrance-tower which is paraphrased from Magdalen, Oxford, a tranquil building which looks at its best in the afternoon. Deane's building at Cork (also originally the Queen's College, now University College) was in part the work of Woodward, by now aged 30, and in sharp contrast to the Belfast college. On an informal courtyard plan, open to the South with a tower off centre and with the library projecting Northwards from the North range, it fulfilled the programme laid down for all three

*It is comforting to recall that as late as 1908 Cardinal Logue denounced University College, Dublin, as 'a Godless bantling' (J. Meenan, *George O'Brien, a Biographical Memoir*, Dublin 1980, p. 150)

258 Wilson's Hospital, Multyfarnham, Co Westmeath, from the air; designed by John Pentland, c. 1760-70

259 Belfast: the Queen's College of 1849 (now Queen's University) by Sir Charles Lanyon, of red brick with brown sandstone dressings. Taken before 1911, but the scene has fortunately not greatly changed today

258

259

colleges in a more advanced way than either of its fellows. Perhaps because the land was cheaply purchased, there was money for decorative carving, which may be early work by the O'Shea brothers. At Galway Joseph B. Keane, a capable designer of churches, court houses and country houses, chose a closed quadrangle, based, rather remotely, on Christ Church, Oxford. It is very rigidly symmetrical, with the Aula Maxima projecting from the West front on the same axis as the entrance with its Tom Thumb tower. For the rest, it is rather spartan.

All three colleges used up a good deal of their space and expense in providing commodious residences for the President and Vice-President, following the eighteenth-century and earlier practice in schools and almshouses where the master's residence took up about one-third of the accommodation.

There were, and are, needless to say, godly colleges as well, such as St Kieran's College Kilkenny (Catholic) by William Deane Butler (1836-9)[36] or Magee College Derry (Presbyterian) by Edward Gribbon (1856-65),[37] both in the Tudor-collegiate style; the later, as we would expect, somewhat more accomplished than the earlier. The family of such structures is legion, all over Ireland.

The 1860s and 1870s were the great decades for the building of convents and religious institutions generally, with the names of Pugin and Ashlin, William Atkins, J. S. Butler, George Goldie, Alex McAllister and J. J. O'Callaghan prominent. But increasingly such bodies adopted the strategy of the hermit-crab, which moves into premises made vacant by the death or departure of the original owner. Many country houses which might not otherwise have survived were thus preserved until our time, when the whirligig of time has put them again at risk.

Gaols

We, who are accustomed to hutted concentration-camps being hastily reconstructed and rechristened as 'prisons', about which we thereafter think as little as possible, find it difficult to comprehend the complacent frame of mind in which the ruling classes viewed the building of houses of correction. Some of the greatest architecture of the epoch went into gaols. Inspired, taught and encouraged by Piranesi, Ledoux and George Dance, they exploited the mystery of walls without windows, the eloquence of rusticated masonry and the drama of retribution. Nor were they bashful about it. The laying of the foundation-stone of Tullamore Gaol in 1826 was witnessed (if we are to believe Lord Tullamore) by 30,000 people, 'dense, enormous masses of well-dressed orderly good-humoured people [who displayed] such extraordinary enthusiasm . . . wild huzzaing and shouting . . . the town, every single house, was illuminated, many most tastefully . . . a beautiful fire-balloon with my arms etc. was sent up, so constructed as to discharge fireworks' all ending up with dinner for 26 people at the Castle.[38]

Tullamore gaol, as it happens, is in the castellated style, but this is exceptional. Thomas Cooley's vanished Newgate in Dublin (1773) was very clearly imitative of its London namesake, with overtones from Giulio Romano,[39] while Trail's Kilmainham of a little later, though subsequently enlarged, remains among the most explicit.[40] Many others have been demolished, in whole or in part, though Owen's Mountjoy in Dublin and Lanyon's Crumlin in Belfast remain in use. Fine frontispieces survive at Downpatrick (1824) in the Veronese style of Sanmicheli by Robert Reid of Edinburgh,[41] at Carlow[42] by an unknown architect, at Trim[43] by John

Hargrave (1827) magnificently battered and horizontally channelled, and most memorably of all at Cork, as has already been noted, by the Pains (fig. 218).

Schools

Somewhere between the university and the gaol comes the school: less instructive than the one, less restrictive than the other, and as a building-type not identifiable in Ireland before the early seventeenth century. It is true that Cahermacnaghten in Co Clare is known to have housed the law-school of the O'Davorens in the seventeenth century,[44] but it is now much like any other circular stone fort in the West. Dead-letter statutes under Henry VIII and Elizabeth sought to set up a network of 'English' schools all over the country, but the first such effort to leave any permanent trace was the foundation by royal charter of Charles I of the five Royal Schools at Armagh, Dungannon, Enniskillen (Portora), Raphoe and Cavan, all of which survive though rebuilt in the eighteenth and early nineteenth centuries.

The Charter Schools,[45] promoted by the Incorporated Society from 1733 onwards, were architecturally more conspicuous, and some of their buildings are still even now to be seen. Though the conduct of the Society was deservedly branded with infamy, some at least of the motives behind it were by the standards of the times creditable, and their architectural expression often of a noble severity. The school close beside the main road at Monasterevan, which was a 'nursery' or clearing-house for infants, is a finely proportioned block flanked by subsidiary masses, where, in 1761, 20 small corpses were found exposed among the carpenters' shavings behind the school.[46] The Charter School which till recently faced the Rock of Cashel from an adjacent hillside, and which was among the earliest and most monumental, has been demolished; but that at Roscommon, a little to the North of the town, somewhat blander of aspect, looks like a country house and is now in fact just that.

The Clontarf Charter School, domed and approached by a double flight of steps leading to a portico over a basement, was such a remarkable adaptation of the Palladian-Scamozzian villa for other purposes that it has been plausibly attributed to Cassels. It was built in 1748 but stood for little more than a century.[47]

Some of the grander schools looked like country houses: notably Ivory's Blue-Coat School of 1772-3 and John Pentland's Wilson's Hospital School in Westmeath (fig. 258), some ten years earlier. They distinguish themselves, however, by having towers with cupolas, as does Francis Johnston's Hibernian Military School of 1808-13 in the Phoenix Park, a seven-part composition of 21 bays and three storeys.[48] The Hibernian Marine School, probably by Thomas Cooley, was smaller and simpler, without a cupola.

These were all Protestant, and indeed Church of Ireland foundations. Catholic education, theoretically prohibited during the early part of the period, was notoriously short of funds and buildings and was conducted in reach-me-down buildings or even in the open air (the 'hedge-school'). But the remarkable elliptical 'classical school' of early nineteenth-century date at Navan (fig. 210) is symptomatic of resurgence, and so is the school at Kells not far away, elegantly disposed round three sides of a courtyard and dated 1840. The Presbyterians, also, were left to their own devices. By 1808 those of Belfast were prosperous enough, and discriminating enough, to send to Sir John Soane in London for a design for the cumbrously named Royal Belfast Academical Institution, invariably shortened to 'Inst.'. Soane's schemes were pared down with equal ruthlessness. Perhaps through a want of candour on the part of the clients, he continued to churn out grand schemes, at least eight of them, far beyond the means of the projectors. In the end an elevation with a Soanian flavour, 21 bays long, was built: but behind it there is little or nothing to recall Sir John.[49]

A pleasing curiosity is the D'Israeli Endowed School near Rathvilly, Co Carlow, founded under the will of Benjamin D'Israeli of Dublin, lottery promoter, notary public and stockbroker, who was apparently not a relation of his British namesake. The school is a small five-part composition with pedimented wings and a cupola, of 1826, by Joseph Welland.[50] The five-part composition still had plenty of time to run, as witness St Macartan's Seminary in Monaghan by Thomas Duff, built 1840–8, a vigorous specimen of the kind.

But in general the rule in the nineteenth century was for newly-founded schools to move, hermit-crab-wise, into an existing country house and add on to it. Such was St Columba's, Rathfarnham, William Sewell's Anglican foundation of 1842, though it was soon provided with a chapel by William Butterfield. In the same way, such Catholic schools as Clongowes, Rockwell and Glenstal took over existing buildings, and at Clongowes two large blocks were soon built similar in size and style to the original house of the Wogan Brownes.

In urban situations, and especially on the part of the Protestants, who were richer, the second half of the century saw a resumption of *tabula rasa* purpose-building: for example Alexandra College in Earlsfort Terrace of 1866 by Kaye Parry,[51] and the Methodist College in Belfast, by William Fogerty, of 1868.

In parallel with such developments, the government built Model Schools to the number of some 30, under the direct control of the Education Department, of which the most conspicuous is the symmetrical constellation of buildings behind Tyrone House in which lived (and still lives) the Department itself.

Markets and Shops

All early Irish markets were open-air spaces, as most of them continued to be until the day before yesterday, and a few still are. But an early covered market, the Ormond Market behind Ormond Quay, was opened in 1682. It was square in plan until the later eighteenth century, but at some time was rebuilt in circular form and is so found in the early nineteenth century.[52] By the early twentieth it was in ruins and soon afterwards it disappeared. Another circular market of the early nineteenth century, the Butter Market in Cork, was well situated in relation to Shandon church and was largely destroyed by fire in 1980, but since reconstructed.

The linenhalls which normally took the form of an open courtyard surrounded by ranges of buildings were of course markets of a special type. The oldest large one was the Dublin Linenhall of 1728, later extended, but it was soon excelled by those in Belfast, the Brown Linenhall of 1754 and 1773, and the White Linenhall of 1784 which survived almost within living memory.[53] Arcaded or colonnaded markets were common in the early nineteenth century; there are or were good examples at Limerick, Drogheda (by Francis Johnston) and Armagh.

The continental *galleria* or something like it is represented by Home's Royal Arcade and Grand Promenade of 1819 (fig. 262), which was a two-storey gallery with a glass roof and shops opening off both sides at both levels, running from College Green through to Suffolk Street. It had a life of only 18 years and was burnt down in 1837.[54] It was very early in the series, being virtually contemporary with the (vanished) Soho Bazaar and the Burlington and Royal Opera Arcades in London.

These, however, are only single-storey structures. Of equal significance are the shops in D'Olier Street (and formerly also Westmoreland Street) designed by H. A. Baker for the Wide Streets Commissioners, somewhat in advance of anything being done at the time in London, affected by continental and especially French exemplars, and reflecting a concern with the integration of shopfronts with street-elevations which goes back as far as 1786.[55]

Sir John Benson's Princes Street ('English') Market of 1862, in Cork, lately and most lamentably destroyed by fire, was also of the *galleria* family. Fire has also recently gutted his Butter Market beside Shandon Church which dated from about 1852. Though belonging to a single company, Riddel's Warehouse in Ann Street Belfast had much in common with such markets. A polychrome elevation in the Woodward manner was pierced by a carriage-arch leading to a courtyard roofed over with iron and glass. It was designed by T. and A. T. Jackson and built in 1865-7.

The South City Markets in South Great George's Street are the fruit of a competition held in 1878 which was won by the English firm of Lockwood and Mawson. The resulting building, entirely built of blood-red brick and terracotta, bristling with gables, gablets and turrets terminating in candle-snuffer roofs, is the nearest equivalent in Dublin to the Prudential in Holborn. Even so, it was less elaborate than it was intended to be. It was partly reconstructed after a fire in 1892. Long may it remain.[56]

A little later, in the early 1890s (and thus strictly outside the scope of this book) the fish and vegetable markets were built North-East of the Four Courts, on a single-storey layout in brick with attractive illustrative sculpture. These markets are still in use, but the similar markets in Belfast, by J. C. Bretland, of 1890 and 1896, are at the time of writing standing derelict and will soon have vanished.

Town Planning—Dublin and Provinces

It is by now a commonplace that the Act of Union of 1800 did not, as expected, immediately curtail the embellishment and development of Dublin. A change in the social composition of the Wide Streets Commissioners did, it is true, shift the emphasis from magnificence to utility. The King's Inns, for example, tardily begun in 1800, was not finished till 1816, but in view of the unbelievable incompetence and corruption of that body in the preceding years, it is matter for wonder that it got built at all. Yet the same period saw the initiation (1802) and completion (1814) of St George's Church and of the General Post Office, both by Francis Johnston. St George's is an example of a tendency typical of classical urbanism but till then notable in Dublin by its absence: the placing of prominent buildings and especially churches at the terminations of vistas or at their intersections. St Stephen's is another, and so, a little later, is Rathmines church and the Presbyterian church at the head of Earlsfort Terrace (1840).

The general rule was for the churches of the establishment to occupy these places of prominence and honour, and so it was in countless country towns and villages. One need only mention Birr, Fermoy, Carrickmacross, Virginia, Banagher (Offaly), Bailieborough and Mitchelstown. But more often than is generally realised, the Catholic church is similarly placed. At Mitchelstown (fig. 264) it terminates an axis at right-angles to that terminated by the Protestant church. At Ballynacarrigy, Ballymore Eustace and Moynalty it is the Catholic church to which the principal vista leads, and even more dramatically at Granard where the late-nineteenth-century church shares the focus with the large Norman mote. Already, before 1829, the

260

261

262

260 Westport, Co Mayo:
a traditional shop with
house-door and shop-door

261 Westport, Co Mayo:
another traditional shop:
the priorities reversed and a
carriage-way incorporated
as well as the shop- and
house-doors

262 Dublin, College
Green, Home's Royal
Arcade of 1819: views at
ground and first floor levels
from McGregor's *New
Picture of Dublin* of 1821.
The ground floor contained
thirty shops, the Upper
floor a 'bazaar'

263 Killala, Co Mayo:
shop with dwelling over.
Early nineteenth century

263

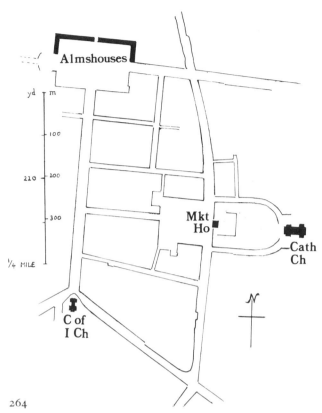

264 Mitchelstown, Co Cork: the road through the square containing the almshouses ('Kingston College' by John Morrison) leads on the West to the gates of Mitchelstown Castle, the seat of the Kings. The old road may be seen wandering from North to South through the town. To the East of it the ground rises steeply, so that the East–West axis passes over the roof of the Market House above which the Catholic church (recently rebuilt) is seen. After a plan in *Irish Geography* II, 107

265 Castlewellan, Co Down, from the air (South–West). Laid out in the 1670s by the Annesley family, it has a broad street linking two open spaces, a half-octagon (Upper Square) and a space with two convex sides (Lower Square, nearer the spectator). Similar layouts, often less completely realised, but sometimes even larger in scale, are found throughout Ireland. On older maps 'Upper Square' appears as 'Old Town' and 'Lower Square' as 'New Town', the latter projected in 1810

264

265

266

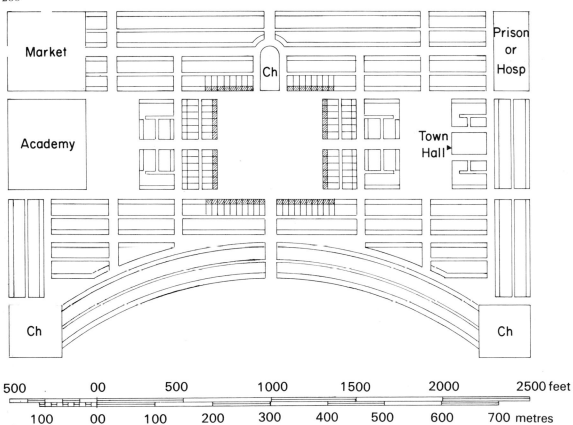

Market		Ch	Prison or Hosp
Academy			Town Hall ▶
Ch			Ch

500	00	500	1000	1500	2000	2500 feet
100	00	100	200	300	400	500	600	700 metres

267

predecessor of St Peter's, Phibsborough, commanded a vista down the North Circular Road, while, in more strictly urban situations, the larger Catholic churches such as Gardiner Street (1829), Westland Row (1832) and Rathmines (1850) are set between domestic buildings which belong to them and pay visible respect to them. St Malachy's, Belfast, closes a vista which, perhaps significantly, seems to have been designed first as a curve, but was in the event laid out as a straight line.[57]

The key building is by no means always a church. It could be an exchange, as in Dublin, or a court house as at New Ross, Armagh or Carlow. It could be a poor house, as in the case of the still existing building of 1774 now called Clifton House, at the head of Donegall Street in Belfast, or the house of someone very rich, such as Belvedere House (now Belvedere College) which looks loftily down North Great George's Street. In some smaller towns the focus of interest is the entrance to the demesne of the local landlord: for example Strokestown or Maynooth or Celbridge.

At Portlaw Co Waterford, three straight avenues converging in the manner of Versailles point towards a building which is neither church nor house nor even strictly a public building: the mill, originally for cotton-spinning; the whole dating from about 1830.[58] Some 40 years earlier another town, founded on cotton and calico, boasted an elaborate layout of streets and squares and was called Stratford-upon-Slaney in honour of its promoter Lord Aldborough. But though substantial remains could still be seen within the author's recollection, they have all gone now. The promoters of Portlaw were a Quaker family called Malcolmson. In County Tyrone, a little later, in about 1835, another godly family, the Herdmans, sought to provide a complete small cosmos similarly based, but this time on linen, and called it Sion Mills. Most of the original buildings have been replaced by late-nineteenth-century buildings in a variety of exotic styles, half-timber, polychrome brick and other un-Irish finishes, mostly by the owner's brother-in-law, an English architect called Unsworth, but including a large mill of 1860 by Lynn and an excellent Catholic church of 1963.[59]

The Richardsons of Bessbrook Co Armagh were, like the Malcolmsons, a family of Quaker factory-owners, who built, from 1846 onwards, a settlement centred on their flax mill and comprising two squares linked by a broad street.[60] Like other such enterprises, it prided itself on what was then thought to be, and perhaps then was, the advantage of having no licensed premises. All these Irish examples, it should be noted, are early instances of their kind: earlier than, for example, Saltaire in Yorkshire.

It would hardly be too much to say that planned towns and 'villages' are the rule rather than the exception, back through Irish history to the early seventeenth century and even beyond. It is true that more often than not the conception outran the execution, and the actual buildings were never built or their sites taken by later, meaner structures. But many were brought to something like completion. Whether they were designed by people whom we should now call architects remains doubtful: in hardly any instance is the name of an architect reliably known. Even in the case of one of the most successful, subtle and resourceful, the layout[61] of the town of Westport in about 1780, the persistent attribution to a prominent English architect lacks foundation.

Among the most interesting of the ideal towns is one which, paradoxically, was no more than barely begun. The settlement of New Geneva, on the West shore of Waterford Harbour, was mooted in 1782 and actively promoted by government, for the reception of Swiss Protestant refugees.[62] Gandon produced a plan (fig. 267) of which the most remarkable feature would have been a segmental terrace nearly half a mile long, facing over the sea. The large central square, called after the Viceroy

PREVIOUS PAGE
266 Belfast: the Poorhouse of 1774, probably by Robert Joy. Like the Southwell foundation at Downpatrick of 40 years earlier, and the contemporary Wilson's Hospital School in Co Westmeath, it exemplifies the close relationship between the architecture of country houses and charitable institutions. But no country house would have had a spire such as we see here. Taking a leaf out of the book of the Rotunda Hospital in Dublin, it incorporated 'a large room where Assemblies and Balls were held to raise funds for the establishment' (Brett). Modern gentility has rechristened it 'Clifton House' but it 'still fulfils something very close to its original function' (Brett again)

267 New Geneva, Waterford Harbour, Co Waterford: plan of the projected town, re-drawn from Gandon's original, in which the houses hatched are described as 'already built'. The present walled enclosure at 'Geneva Barracks' bears little resemblance even to the central square. The vast shallow crescent, 2,750 feet long, would have faced over the harbour and anticipated later and smaller-scale developments on the South coast of England. For the Geneva project as a whole, see Hubert Butler in JRSAI 1947, pp. 150 sqq.

Lord Temple, would have been dominated by a church, though whether Calvinist or of the established faith is not clear. At all events, there was provision for two more churches in places of comparative honour, as well as for an academy. A smaller space was reserved for a 'Prison or Hospital': apparently if one were built the other would not be needed, which sounds more progressive than it probably was. According to Gandon's plan, which has survived, the houses round the central square were built. But this cannot readily be reconciled with the existing remains of 'Geneva Barracks' which attained an unenviable fame in 1798, 14 years after the Genevan settlement had been abandoned.

The expansion of larger towns during the later eighteenth and early nineteenth centuries sometimes, though not always, took regular form. In Cork and Derry both topography and land-ownership were unfavourable to regularity. But in Belfast and Limerick the local proprietors, Chichester Earl of Donegall and Pery Earl of Limerick respectively, embarked at exactly the same time, the very late 1760s, on a policy of improvement. The scheme was in both cases a rectilinear grid: in two separate parts at Belfast, in a single long stretch at Limerick. Both schemes took half a century to fill. Initially Limerick was markedly the more prosperous (in 1831 it still had 66,000 inhabitants against 60,000 in Belfast)[63] but in the second half of the new century Belfast drew rapidly away to challenge, for a time, even Dublin. Both cities are now, for somewhat different reasons, in a woeful state of decay. Though the citizens of Belfast can say, with John Milton, that 'the ghost of a linen decency yet haunts us',[64] the fact is that eighteenth-century Belfast is now to be found only with difficulty, and much of Victorian Belfast has followed it. Some late eighteenth-century street architecture of a rather perfunctory kind may still be seen in Limerick. Neither the Belfast nor Limerick plans were very imaginative: the double crescent at Limerick is almost the only departure from the pattern of the simple grid.

Dublin apart, the greatest successes in visual town-planning were achieved in smaller towns such as Armagh, Birr, Westport, Mitchelstown, Tyrrellspass, Bally-jamesduff, Castlecomer, Dunlavin, Moy, Dungarvan, Strokestown, Gort, Sneem, Ballynacarrigy, Castlewellan (fig. 265). All are compact enough for a coherent scheme to have had some chance of being carried out before some change of ownership, of fashion or of economic circumstances, cut them off.[65]

Cathedrals

Within ten years of the Famine church-building had fully recovered its momentum. In particular the provision of Catholic cathedrals indicated the increased confidence of the Catholic middle class who necessarily bore most of the expense. Work was resumed on those already begun, such as Armagh and Longford, while P. C. Hard-wick, employed by the Catholic convert Earl of Dunraven to follow Pugin at Adare, provided Limerick with a modestly-sized but resourceful cathedral in eclectic gothic, 1855–65. Kilkenny cathedral, by William Deane Butler, was begun before the Famine and finished in 1857: it has a very tall central tower but little to commend it. McCarthy's cathedral for the diocese of Clogher at Monaghan has already been mentioned: it is probably the best and most consistent of his four cathedrals. It was built mostly between 1861 and 1868, but the tower, beside the South transept more or less to McCarthy's design, was added by Hague in 1883 and the dedication of the whole building was delayed till 1892.[66]

At Thurles (archdiocese of Cashel) McCarthy departed from his usual gothic and

268

268 Westport, Co Mayo: a doorcase in the Mall, showing idiosyncratic provincial detailing of considerable charm, especially in the Ionic capitals

269 Carrick-on-Suir, Co Tipperary: the substructure of the eighteenth-century clock-tower is mediaeval. The four-storey slate-hung house with cambered lintels faces straight down the street leading to the mediaeval bridge joining Carrick to Carrickbeg in Co Waterford (fig. 239)

270 Limerick: eighteenth-century street-architecture (now demolished) as different from that of Dublin as were the corresponding houses of Cork or of Belfast

269

270

ventured into a version of Romanesque based mainly on Pisa cathedral but with a detached square campanile close to the North side of the West front and a scaled-down version of the Baptistery in corresponding position on the South. (Since the cathedral, like many Catholic churches of the nineteenth century and after, is orientated 'wrong way round', these are the liturgical bearings only). It was built 1865-72.[67]

Passing briefly over the not very interesting building by Father Jeremiah McAuley (a qualified architect despite his cloth) which does duty as the pro-cathedral of Belfast (begun 1858, completed 1866, spires later)[68] we come to Sligo, cathedral town of the diocese of Elphin. This cathedral, built in 1867-73 and designed by George Goldie, is a work of little-recognised originality.[69] In a curious hybrid round-arched style borrowing from English, German and Irish Romanesque, with a dash of French thrown in, it has, exceptionally for its date, a gallery which flies across the mouths of the transepts, anticipating Pearson at St Augustine Kilburn by a few years. The last of the nineteenth-century cathedrals, Letterkenny, was begun only in 1890 and lies outside the scope of this book.

It might be thought that the Church of Ireland, for which the writing was already on the wall for those who could read it, would have been husbanding its resources. Not so. The universally accepted imperative of the time, 'Build Churches!' was felt to be valid, and especially so where the cathedral bequeathed by the chequered past was felt to be inadequate or unworthy. No less than three cathedrals were built during this period, or, if we include the rebuilding of Kildare, four, or even, if (as is only reasonable) we include the virtual rebuilding of Christchurch, five.

The first of these, Kilmore, designed in 1857, begun in the following year and finished in 1860, was designed by William Slater, yet another English architect. Though of very modest size, just over 100 feet internally, it contrives to possess all the parts then thought necessary for a cathedral, and, like Killaloe, incorporated a twelfth-century Hiberno-Romanesque doorway from another building.[70]

Tuam, the capital of the Western ecclesiastical province, already possessed, as the reader will recall, a magnificent Romanesque chancel-arch and chancel, serving as porch to a modest fourteenth-century building. In 1861 Sir Thomas Deane, the only Irish architect involved in these cathedrals, designed the present building to lead up to the ancient chancel, which it does very well. It is somewhat larger than Kilmore, and chunkier in character.[71]

By far the most ambitious of these gestures of defiance was St Finn Barre's at Cork (fig. 271).[72] This was thrown open to international competition in 1862, and the winner was William Burges. Deane was placed second. There were 63 entries. Burges had already won the competition for Lille Cathedral and that for the English Memorial Church in Constantinople, but in both cases he was frustrated: at Constantinople by G. E. Street. His victory at Cork did not please everybody: it was alleged, probably with truth, that he had not yet kept within the cost limit of £15,000, and W. J. Barre (or at least his biographer) felt specially aggrieved at this. Burges, however, seems to have been quite candid about the cost. Frugally, he adapted his Constantinople plan to his Lille elevations.

The resulting three-spired French-gothic church is one of the wonders of Ireland. Contrary to what usually happens, it was expanded and elaborated during execution, to become one of the richest buildings of its size in Ireland. It is not, in fact, very large: only a little larger than the decent eighteenth-century church which it replaced. It is only 163 feet long, but the central spire rises to 240 feet, nearly one-and-a-half times as much. Like a model railway-train, it has all the expected organs in all the expected places, but the length has been truncated. By 1870 the body of the church was roofed, and eight years later the last of the three spires was complete. Further embellishment followed. Truly may St Finn Barre's be said to have been the first fruits of the loss of the temporal power.

The restoration of St Patrick's, the transformation of Christ Church and the recreation of Kildare—the last two by George Edmund Street, were all roughly contemporary and were undertaken in the same spirit. Kildare was a little later than the rest, begun in 1871 and not complete till 1896.

Five Large Houses

Throughout the nineteenth century there was a constant trickle of large country houses designed by English architects whose connexion with Ireland was otherwise minimal. Some of these houses were very remarkable, and being in Ireland have sometimes escaped the notice of English writers. Five of them deserve something more than a mere mention.

Gosford Castle,[73] near Markethill Co Armagh, designed for the Acheson family, Earls of Gosford, by Thomas Hopper (whose assistant at the time was William Burn) has the distinction of being the earliest Norman revival castle in the three kingdoms and was put in hand just before 1820. It does not, needless to say, look in the least like a Norman castle, but it has a rambling asymmetrical plan, windows which, though too large and too close to the ground, show some effort at correct detail, and is built of good ashlar masonry with extremely thick walls. There is much carving, both inside and out, some of it by John Smyth the son of Edward. A few years later the same architect went on to build Penrhyn Castle in Caernarvonshire on a considerably larger scale.

William Bardwell, who designed Glenstal Castle,[74] Co Limerick, for the Barrington family in 1838-9, has many fewer works to his credit in England than Hopper, though he lived to be 94. As he was 19 years younger than Hooper, he designed his Irish castle at almost exactly the same age, 43. Like Gosford, Glenstal has an entrance between massive drum-towers: both, no doubt, inspired by Rockingham in Northamptonshire. The main doorway in the courtyard is a highly competent copy of the Romanesque doorway in Killaloe Cathedral, carved in 1841 by a local carver called White.

After the interruption caused by the Famine, three notable houses were put in hand at almost the same time. They have also in common the fact that the erection of two of them gave rise to lawsuits, while the architect of the third was sued by his client in respect of the only other house he built in Ireland.

The Puxley family of Dunboy,[75] Castletownbere in West Cork, had been living since about 1730 in a plain square house which by 1838 had been renamed as, and in part made to look like, a 'castle'. The family had grown very rich from their copper-mines nearby and in 1865 commissioned John Christopher, a London architect, to design an addition nearly twice the size of the original house. The addition was on the main axis and its main feature was a vast central hall containing the staircase. This hall is spanned by four transverse stone arches carrying arcades, and between them, at right-angles to them, and as it were in place of purlins, are longitudinal arches carrying clerestory windows at the same level as the arcades, and also all of stone. This astonishing structure is not paralleled elsewhere in Christopher's work, nor readily matched anywhere else. The Puxley who built it was sued by his

271 Cork: St Finn Barre's Cathedral, from the West. Designed by William Burges, begun 1865, consecrated 1870 and virtually finished 1879

builder and settled out of court, then, under grief at the death of his wife, departed for London and never came back. The house remained unfinished but was again occupied at the time of its burning in 1921. What remains, however, is one of the sights of Ireland.

The same may be said of Dromore Castle,[76] designed by that remarkable man Edward Godwin for William Pery, third Earl of Limerick, in 1866. Unlike Christopher, Godwin had studied Irish mediaeval buildings (he had built three churches in Co Donegal) and at Dromore he was very consciously working in an Irish context. The ensemble of the castle, and especially its silhouette, was inspired by the massing of the group of ancient buildings on the Rock of Cashel. It therefore incorporates a Round Tower, and never mind the incongruity of such a feature in a secular context. House and courtyard form a curtilage with an entrance-gatehouse balanced on top of the wall. The construction of the whole is extremely solid, and the workmanship of superlative quality in spite of the rapidity with which it was built. It was noted, even at the time, that it was very defensible. The Fenian rising, we may remind ourselves, took place in 1867, and Dromore was finished in 1873. The interior was intended to be decorated in the Japanese style, but proved to be too damp. It was dismantled, as to its softer parts, about 25 years ago, since when it has remained, as picturesque as ever and additionally poignant, the ultimate in romantic ruins.

The parents of William Wentworth Fitzwilliam Hume Dick must, one feels, have been very anxious to advertise his connexion with the English noble family of Fitzwilliam (who had property in Co Wicklow but are not to be confused with the Fitzwilliams of Merrion who owned about half Dublin). Mr Dick lived mostly in England or France: his Irish property lay near Kiltegan in West Wicklow, and here, in 1866, he decided to build himself a new house. His architect was William White of London. Much more unusually, the builder was English too. Though a large house by Irish standards, Humewood[77] was finished by 1870. But Mr Hume Dick was not finished with White. The builder from Banbury, who claimed to have signed a 72-page contract without reading it, sued owner and architect for £10,000 and, after six years, won and was awarded a similar amount in costs. It was the end of White as a country-house architect.

White was a somewhat unstable character, of considerable abilities. Like many another Victorian architect his head was full of ideas: massing and elevation should express plan which should be controlled by function; colour-harmony should be studied; the equilateral triangle would be found to have special virtues, and so on. At Humewood these ideas found material expression. The building starts at the South-East corner where a large porte-cochère stands corner-to-corner with the staircase-tower which is the tallest part of the building. Everything else slopes away from this, with a variety of incident, in which the 60-degree angle is prominent. The masses and textures are admirably adjusted to make the most of the Wicklow granite of which it is built. Like most Victorian country houses it has a grand end and a less grand end, consisting in this case of the servants' and children's wings which stretch Northwards with a narrow yard between them.★

Gosford is possibly, Glenstal probably, Dromore and Dunboy almost certainly, and Humewood beyond doubt, the most remarkable works by their respective

---

★Subsequently modified by the construction of a large two-storey banqueting-hall over the old nursery wing, and other additions. See Girouard, *The Victorian Country House*, p. 120.

architects. Of the five only Humewood survives virtually unaltered and still in occupation as a country house.

Gate Lodges

Most Irish country houses of any pretension, and some which have none, are provided with gate lodges. In many cases these have survived when the house itself has gone, but the converse has also happened. They are sometimes of considerable merit, in both the classical and the revived styles as one would expect, and do not differ much from their counterparts elsewhere except for one thing. They are very commonly sited not inside the gates of the demesne but opposite them, on the other side of the public road.

One suggested reason for this is that the owners wanted to demonstrate to the world at large that they owned land on both sides of the road. But the practice is too widespread to support (it seems to me) such a frivolous explanation. I think that a combination of practical and aesthetic considerations, among which the simple desire for symmetry ranks high, is much more likely. This habit seems to be peculiar to Ireland.

Among the more noteworthy lodges are the Back Lodge at Castletown Conolly,[78] taken directly out of one of Batty Langley's pattern-books, bedight with ogival gablets and obelisks. Even more exotic is the Hindu-gothick gateway at Dromana, Co Waterford,[79] designed by one Day and built in 1830. But the classical mode is the commonest, from the simple square cottage, with or without columnar trim, up to the triumphal archway-cum-lodge, of which the Dodder Lodge of Rathfarnham Castle is, though a little on the dull side, among the grandest. Follies, of one kind and another, are not uncommon and have been written about and illustrated with the eloquence which they deserve.[80]

Railway Architecture

Being so near to Britain, Ireland was early involved in railways. The earliest line, the Dublin and Kingstown, opened in 1834, but its terminus, Westland Row, was never architecturally very noteworthy. The terminal building of what later became the Great Northern Railway, to Drogheda, Dundalk and Belfast, has an Italianate tower closing a vista. It was designed by William Deane Butler and built in 1844-6, but is not of great distinction. It is otherwise with the terminus of the Midland Great Western which started at Broadstone and served Mullingar, Athlone, Galway and Sligo. This splendid building by John Skipton Mulvany (1841-50) is unhappily no longer in use as a station. But it survives and I have written of it elsewhere with such eloquence as I could then command.[81] Begun later and more quickly finished, Kingsbridge (1845-6) was and is the terminus for Cork, Limerick and the South. It was a competition design by the English architect Sancton Wood and fitly dominates the Western quays.[82]

The termini at Belfast and Cork are markedly less interesting, and the former (1848, designed, like Westland Row, by the company's engineer) has been replaced. Those at Galway and Sligo, by Mulvany and Wilkinson respectively, are better. Though all main termini (including Wilkinson's Dublin Harcourt Street of 1859) were classical, many of the wayside stations were gothic or 'Tudor', whether by

272 Castle Dunboy, Castletownberehaven, Co Cork. The remarkable roof-structure still standing in the centre of the 'castle' was designed for the Puxley family by John Christopher of London and built 1866–7. The house was burnt in 1921 and has remained derelict ever since, but the structure is as robust as it is impressive: (v. Jeremy Williams in *The Architectural Review*, August 1974)

273 Bagenalstown (Muine Bheag), Co Carlow: railway station, *c.* 1850

272

273

Wood, Wilkinson or others such as Joshua Hargrave, W. G. Murray or Sir John McNeill. There are exceptions such as those at Portadown, Armagh and Monaghan, all classical and all probably by McNeill (Portadown (destroyed) certainly), and Bagenalstown of which the designer has so far eluded identification (fig. 273). Stone was the usual material for stations, usually of very good quality. At Thurles station four or five different kinds of masonry may be studied, all admirably carried out. Brick is much less common, and very few stations are rendered in stucco.[83]

Among the most attractive of the smaller stations is Dunlaoire (Kingstown), by J. S. Mulvany, (1842) built, surprisingly, not of Dalkey granite but of granite from the other side of the Wicklow massif at Ballyknockan. It is close neighbour to the same architect's pioneer Royal Irish Yacht Club of 1851 (fig. 254).

Industrial Architecture

The Slane Mill of 1763 (page 196) is the earliest large mill to be built in Ireland, and it was soon joined by others. Some were built for textile spinning and some for grain milling, but not infrequently they were switched from one to the other in the course of their life, sometimes more than once.[84] Many are now derelict, but remain often as conspicuous landmarks. They are generally of rubble-stone rendered, with openings of dressed stone or of brick. The mill at Belmont Co Offaly, still in use, is dated 1769. Henry's Mill at Millbrook Co Meath near Oldcastle, dates from 1777, and Deaves' Cotton Mill at Blarney Co Cork, ten years later, measures 110 feet by 23 feet. The building at Midleton Co Cork, which until recently housed the distillery of that name (now re-housed fourfold in a new building) was erected in 1795 as a worsted spinning mill. The engineering works which occupies both sides of the road at Monasterevan was, most unusually, both a brewery and a distillery. The maltings at Prospect Row, Cork, a group which mass magnificently together in a bend of the river Lee, have lately been taken over and sensitively adapted by University College.

Many towns still have handsome multistorey warehouses, especially along their quays or near water: Ennis, Ballyshannon, Derry, Newry, Drogheda, New Ross and the Jameson's Distillery at Bow Street near Smithfield in Dublin. The buildings of the old DWD whiskey distillery at Jones's Road, Clonliffe, are still worth looking at. A fine set of curved warehouses reputedly by Sir John Rennie, North-East of the Custom House, was demolished in the late 1940s, but neither these nor anything else of the kind in Ireland approached in quality the doomed splendours of London, of Liverpool or even of Hull. During the early and mid-nineteenth century there was a fashion, perhaps peculiar to Ireland, for castellated mills. The Barrow valley is particularly favoured: Moone and Levitstown in Co Kildare, the two enormous mills at Milford Co Carlow, and the one at Barraghcore near Goresbridge in Co Kilkenny. Outliers occur further afield, as at Kilrush Co Clare and Newhaggard near Trim in Co Meath, and perhaps elsewhere.

The still-industrial North-East naturally provides examples of mills which, if not often so early, are more often still in use. The great flour-mill at Caledon Co Tyrone, begun in 1823, is nevertheless as impressive a derelict as any in the South or West. At about the same time (1826) large linen-mills were built in and near Keady Co Armagh. But when Belfast really got going, some of the operations were on a truly awesome scale. The York Street Spinning Mill (1842, destroyed by bombing 1941) was of vast extent, and even vaster the Ropeworks on the other side of the city.

More concentrated in architectural character, perhaps, is Sands's Mill, Newry, of 1876, six storeys high with round-headed attic windows. Bernard Hughes's Hungarian Roller Flour Mills in Divis Street Belfast, by Alex McAllister, (1877–84) was of unusual architectural distinction, eight storeys high with its chimney fully integrated into the design of the whole (fig. 276). It was demolished in 1966.

Two categories of quasi-industrial building call for notice: the lock-keepers' houses on the canals, and the horseshoe-forges. The former seem to derive from a design by Thomas Omer of about 1755, and are small square two-storey gable-ended buildings distinguished by having a large recessed arch, often blind, in one or more faces. They are remarkably uniform and crop up on the Grand Canal, the Lagan Navigation, the Royal Canal, the Shannon and possibly even further afield (figs 274, 275).[85]

The horseshoe-forges are perhaps a century later, and are found mainly in the counties of Kildare, Wicklow and Offaly. They are an expression of the romantic and picturesque spirit and in nearly every case the participation of the landlord may be presumed. The cut-stone arch in the form of a horseshoe, very faithfully reproduced down to the raised swages and the nail-holes, is the only thing common to them all. A well-known and much photographed example is at Enniskerry Co Wicklow.

Coda: Requiescant

Mausolea—that is to say free-standing buildings of funerary purpose, whether in graveyards or elsewhere—are not uncommon in Ireland and are fairly evenly distributed.[86] They are of very uneven interest and architectural merit. The finest is, no doubt, that by Robert Adam at Castle Upton Co Antrim (1789—the only actual Adam building in Ireland), but it is almost equalled by the anonymous Barrymore mausoleum at Castlelyons, Co Cork of about 1747 which is a more likeable building, at least to those who have not the neo-classic taste. Pearce's Stillorgan obelisk counts as a mausoleum, as does the St Rémy monument at Downhill Co Derry (1779 by Michael Shanahan), while that at Coolbanagher Co Leix counts among the minor works of Gandon.

Some of the most interesting later mausolea in revived styles are the neo-grec Bindon Scott mausoleum at Killadysert Co Clare and that of Sir Michael O'Loghlen at Ruan of about 1843 which is in the Egyptian style. The early-Christian mausoleum at Kiltegan Co Wicklow, with steep stone roof, is very whole-hearted, as are two elaborate gothic examples, both apparently by Fuller, at Drumcar Co Louth and Belleek Co Mayo (just outside Ballina). Two examples in Co Galway are notable for the use of cast-iron. At Drumacoo, opposite Tyrone House, the mausoleum of the St Georges, celebrated in a memorable poem by Sir John Betjeman, has cast-iron tracery, while at Clonbern that of the Dennis family dates from about 1865 and is a cylindrical structure entirely in cast-iron[87] with Greek-derived detail, perhaps imported from Scotland.

There are noteworthy constellations of mausolea in one or two places: for example Knockbreda churchyard Co Down (fig. 277), where the very elegant neo-classic specimens, some with a touch of oriental fantasy, date mainly from the last decade of the eighteenth century, and Mount Jerome on the Southern outskirts of Dublin, one of the earliest of the new reforming cemeteries, where the catacombs and above-ground structures, mostly from soon after 1831, are clearly inspired by Père Lachaise in Paris (fig. 278).

274 Shannonbridge: canal house by Thomas Omer, very similar to others on the Grand Canal and Lagan Navigations. Drawing by Jim Horan from *Everyday Buildings of Ireland* by Seán Rothery

275 Grand Canal: Lodge at Miltown Co Dublin

276 Belfast: Bernard Hughes's Hungarian Roller Flour Mills, Divis Street, 1877–84, by Alex McAllister, demolished 1966

274

276

275

277

277 Knockbreda churchyard, Co Down: the Greg mausoleum *c.* 1800

278 Dublin, Mount Jerome Cemetery (founded 1835): catacombs and neo-classic monuments modelled on those of Père Lachaise

278

The most impressive, in many ways, of all Irish mausolea is the enormous concentric circular structure at Woodlawn, Co Galway, adapted for the reception of numerous members of the Trench family. I have seen it only in heavy rain which suited it well.

★　　★　　★

A hundred years of Irish weather have had their way with the latest buildings which have appeared in this narrative. Of all the influences which have moulded them, the climate must seem the most pervasive: its very fickleness a constant to be relied upon. Yet even the weather has seen secular changes in the past three thousand years. Geological time is measurable in vastly longer spans, and the rocks beneath must be counted as even more permanent than the rain and winds above. Yet we have lived to see the relationship between the buildings and the rocks, for the first time in history, ignored and abruptly set at naught. Nearly all the quarries from which these buildings came are now no longer open, and the sites and names of many are forgotten. The order of nature is now no more regarded than are those lesser orders which for so long ruled the art, and it is time that the account be closed.

References

Chapter 1 – Prehistoric (pages 17–24)

1 Harbison, Potterton, Sheehy, p. 18.
2 Moore, *Hail and Farewell*, 1925, ed. I, pp. 12, 17.
3 Harbison, *National Monuments of Ireland*, 1970, p. 71.
4 J. W. Poe, *The Cromlechs of County Dublin* n.d. *c.* 1906, p. 23, quoting W. C. Borlase, 1897.
5 Wm. Stokes, *Life of Petrie*, 1868, p. 381.
6 Dunraven, *Notes*, 1875, I, p. 7.
7 Ibid., p. 20.
8 Raftery, *Prehistoric Ireland*, 1951, p. 32.
9 Evans, *Prehistoric and Early Christian Ireland*, 1966, p. 134.
10 Harbison, op. cit. p. 259.
11 By Liam de Paor, in a newspaper article and in conversation.
12 Hugh Marwick, *Orkney* Official Guide, Edinburgh HMSO, 1952, p. 23.

Chapter 2 – (Early Christian (pages 25–34)

1 At Carnsore Co Wexford, excavation has recently revealed remains of a timber church under a church measuring 31 feet by 15 feet 5 inches. M. J. O'Kelly, *St Vogues Church Carnsore*, Dublin, E.S.B., 1975. At Iniscealtra Co Clare Liam de Paor has recently excavated the remains of an early earthen church.
2 L. de Paor, 'A Survey of Sceilg Mhichíl' in *JRSAI* LXXXV, 1955, pp. 174 sqq.
3 W. F. Wakeman, *Inismurray*, 1893.
4 H. C. Lawlor, *Nendrum*, Belfast, 1925. See also *County Down Survey*, 1965, pp. 292–5.
5 The bee-hive cells are closely paralleled in Quercy: see Pierre Lavedan, *French Architecture*, English ed. 1956, pl. 46 (A), and also Rowland Mainstone, *Developments in Structural Form*, 1975, p. 97 pl. 6.4 'Hut near Gordes, Provence.'
6 Leask, *Churches*, I, 1955, pp. 25, 28.
7 See a recent report on the early church at Derry Co Down in *Ancient Monuments in Northern Ireland Not in State Charge*, 1952, p. 17. Also *County Down Survey*, 1969, p. 290, with plan.
8 Clonmacnois Cathedral 28 feet wide, Kilmacduagh 22 feet 6 inches.
9 Leask, op. cit. p. 56.
10 See also Derry Co. Down, as in note 7 above.
11 Compare also the Eltenberg Reliquary in the Victoria and Albert Museum, London, that of Chur in Switzerland, of Enger in Berlin etc. Dr Harbison thinks the Irish examples were probably inspired by continental models.
12 For example, Garranes Co Cork (Lisnacaher-

agh: see de Paor, *Early Christian Ireland*, ed. of 1978, p. 87).
13 Compare A. C. Champneys, *Irish Ecclesiastical Architecture*, 1910, pl. VI, and also one of the Teampull Breacain doorways on Inismore Aran, Co Galway.
14 K. J. Conant, *Carolingian and Romanesque Architecture*, ed. of 1974, p. 72.
15 It should be observed that the most thorough modern authority G. L. Barrow (*The Round Towers of Ireland*, Dublin, 1979), favours an earlier dating than that generally held by modern scholars. See especially pp. 37, sqq.
16 Among other things they served as libraries. The Devenish tower 'still retains stone hooks from which the leather satchels containing reliquaries could be hung'. *UJA*, Vol. 33, 1970, p. 58. If reliquaries, then also books.
17 Robert Byron, *The Appreciation of Architecture*, 1932, p. 40 with illustration of Clonmacnois.
18 Champneys (loc. cit. p. 59) was misled by the woodcut in Margaret Stokes, *Early Christian Architecture in Ireland*, 1878, fig. 60, into thinking that the Disert Aengus tower doorway had a head formed of stones not laid radially. The photograph in Dunraven, *Notes*, Vol. II, pl. LXXVIII, shows that this is not so.
19 Dunraven, op. cit. II, p. 161. For Egilshay, see also Marwick, op. cit. xiv and pl. 9.
20 K. J. Conant, *Carolingian and Romanesque Architecture*, paperback ed. of 1974, p. 71.

Chapter 3 – Romanesque (pages 35–48)

1 Engraving in Stokes, *Early Christian Art in Ireland*, ed. of 1932, part 2 p. 39.
2 Mr Stalley doubts this.
3 St Flannan's, Killaloe, of which the nave is 36 feet long overall, had a chancel of unknown length, but can hardly have been much short of 60 feet in overall length. The nave vault is 17 feet 6 inches wide which is very wide by Irish twelfth-century standards.
4 Champneys, op. cit. pp. 230–31, contains further discussion of the combination of church and dwelling.
5 Francoise Henry, *Irish Art*, 1940, p. 22 and n. 3.
6 A. T. Lucas in E. Rynne (ed.) *North Munster Studies*, Limerick, 1967, p. 172.
7 Leask, *Churches*, I, p. 37.
8 Leask, op. cit. p. 28.
9 For Semple's churches see below, pp. 262. It seems that the actual crowns of Semple's vaults were laid radially, and the roof-covering laid as

slates are laid, but very close to the extrados of the vault.

10 Mr Stalley, however, thinks this date too early.

11 G. Wilkinson, *Practical Geology and Ancient Architecture of Ireland*, 1845, p. 143.

12 Leask, op. cit. II, pp. 64–5.

13 Reproduced in *The Archaeological Journal*, Clapham Memorial Supplement to Vol. CVI, 1952, pl. X.

14 In *North Munster Studies* (see note 6 above) pp. 133 sqq.

15 Such rosettes are common in West of England work.

16 de Paor, loc. cit. (as note 14) p. 142.

17 The valuable pre-restoration survey of Cormac's Chapel published by Arthur Hill in 1874 should be noted.

18 Lullington, Somerset, is perhaps another parallel.

19 Mr Stalley suggests 1184 for the Tuam arch.

20 Mr Stalley observes that St Saviour's has parallels with the East end of Baltinglass and suggests a date in the 1150s.

21 Helen Hickey, *Images of Stone*, Belfast, 1976, p. 16. Mr de Paor tells me that at St Caimin's Iniscealtra where he has been excavating, there was originally a continuous order of human heads.

Chapter 4 – Cistercian Gothic (pages 49–59)

1 It is curious that the number of bishops in mediaeval England is comparable to the number of (Anglican) bishops in modern Ireland, while the number of bishops in mediaeval Ireland is comparable to the number of (Anglican) Sees in modern England. The explanation is that mediaeval English dioceses were abnormally large, while modern Irish ones are abnormally empty, and especially empty of Protestants.

2 Bernard: Life of Malachy, as quoted by R. Stalley in *The Irish World* (ed. B de Breffny), 1977, p. 82. Too late for citation has appeared R. Stalley, 'Mellifont Abbey: a Study of its Architectural History' in *PRIA*, 80, c. 14, 1980.

3 M. Dolley, *Anglo-Norman Ireland*, Dublin, 1972, p. 88.

4 For Boyle, see Roger Stalley in *Country Life* 6 May 1976, pp. 1176 sqq.

5 A. Gwynn and N. Hadcock, *Mediaeval Religious Houses in Ireland*, 1970, p. 124.

6 R. Stalley, in *The Irish World* (ed. B. de Breffny), 1977, p. 86.

7 Liam de Paor, in a newspaper article *c.* 1978.

8 Stalley, loc. cit. p. 97.

9 R. A. S. Macalister, *The Archaeology of Ireland*, 1927, p. 349.

10 Champneys, op. cit. p. 151.

11 Ibid. p. 198.

12 J. Summerson, *Heavenly Mansions*, 1949, p. 10.

13 Ibid., p. 16.

14 Ibid., p. 26.

15 John Harvey, *The Gothic World*, 1950, p. 2.

16 *The Archaeological Journal*, CVI, 1952, Supplement, p. 29.

17 Stalley: *Christ Church, Dublin, The Late Romanesque Building Campaign*, Ballycotton, 1973.

18 Leask, *Churches*, II, p. 83.

19 The barrel-vault over the presbytery at Jerpoint is, however, fifteenth century (Stalley). Conor O'Brien (*Architectural and Topographical Record*, Westminster, 1908) was mistaken.

20 Stalley in *Country Life*, 6, May 1976, p. 1176.

Chapter 5 – Castles and Churches (pages 60–78)

1 Quoted by Stalley in *The Irish World*, p. 87.

2 See Leask, *Castles*, 1941, pp. 47 sqq.

3 See pp. 119 below.

4 Leask, op. cit. pp. 67 sqq.

5 In effect, they seem to be at least as early as Harlech and Beaumaris, if not marginally earlier.

6 See Stalley in *Architecture and Sculpture in Ireland 1150-1350*, Dublin, 1971, pp. 32 sqq, and P. D. Sweetman. 'Excavations at Trim Castle 1971-74' in *PRIA* 78, C 6, 1978.

7 For Christ Church see William Butler, *Christ Church Cathedral . . . Measured Drawings*, Dublin 1874 (especially valuable for its pre-restoration state), G. E. Street, *Christ Church Cathedral*, Dublin, 1882, William Butler, *Christ Church Cathedral* 1901 (in what later became Bell's Cathedral Series), Leask, *Churches*, Vol II, 1958, Stalley, *Architecture and Sculpture* pp. 58 sqq., *idem. Christ Church . . . The late Romanesque Building Campaign* (Gatherum series), Ballycotton, 1973.

8 *Ulster Journal of Archaeology* 3rd ser. 33, 1970, pp. 63 sqq.

9 For St Patrick's see J. H. Bernard, *The Cathedral Church of St Patrick* (originally in Bell's Cathedral Series), Dublin ed. of 1940, Leask op. cit. as for Christ Church and Stalley op. cit. ditto. Too late for citation has appeared Edwin C. Rae, 'The medieval fabric of the Cathedral church of St Patrick in Dublin in *JRSAI*, 109 (1979) [appeared 1981], pp. 29–73.

10 The most recent examination of St Doulough's is by Dr Peter Harbison, in *Studies* (forthcoming).

11 See Clapham, loc. cit. pp. 17 sqq., and Leask, *Churches*, II, p. 54 sqq.

12 Plan and description in *Archaeological Journal* LXXXVIII, 1931, pp. 363-4.

13 *Journal of the Royal Society of Antiquaries of Ireland* Vol. 78 (1948), pp. 65 sqq. This identification is now doubted by Stalley and Harbison.

14 H. G. Leask, *St Patrick's Rock, Cashel* (official guide) Dublin, Stationery Office, 1940 and later reprints. Also Leask, *Churches*, II, 88 sqq., *Archaeological Journal*, 1931, pp. 386 sqq., Champneys, *Irish Ecclesiastical Architecture*, 1910, pp. 141, 158, 162 etc. and Stalley, op. cit. pp. 84 sqq.

15 Clapham, loc. cit. p. 35-6: Leask *Churches*, II, 118. See also illustration in Craig and Glin, *Ireland Observed*, 1969, p. 33.

16 J. L. Darling, *St Multose Church Kinsale*, Cork, 1895.

17 J. Graves and J. G. A. Prim, *The History, Architecture and Antiquities of the Cathedral Church of St Canice, Kilkenny*, Dublin, 1857. Leask *Churches*, II pp. 103 sqq., Stalley, op. cit. pp. 71 sqq.

18 Stalley, op. cit. pp. 75 sqq.

19 Clapham, loc. cit. pp. 36 sqq. (with plan). Fuller drawings in 78th *Public Works Report*, 1909-10, pp. 18-19.

20 Ibid., pp. 24 sqq., Leask, *Churches*, II, p. 89. See T. M. Fallow, *The Cathedral Churches of Ireland* [1894], pp. 24 sqq. for pre-restoration photographs.

21 M. Dolley, *Anglo-Norman Ireland*, Dublin, 1972, p. 30.

Chapter 6 – Friaries etc (pages 79-94)

1 Otway-Ruthven in *Irish Historical Studies* VII, 25, 1950, p. 14, and ibid. VI, 24, 1949, pp. 261 sqq. M. Dolley, *Anglo-Norman Ireland*, 1972, pp. 160-1.

2 Stalley, op. cit. p. 52.

3 The distinction between 'royal' and 'non-royal' castles is at this period not easy to draw. The fourteenth century Irish Pipe Rolls still remain unpublished. A reasonable working list of royal castles would include Dublin, Limerick, Drogheda, Athlone, Roscommon, Rinndown, Dungarvan, Newcastle Mackinegan (Co Wicklow) Greencastle Co Down, but not, be it noted, Greencastle Co Donegal (Northburgh), nor Carrickfergus, nor, perhaps, Trim.

4 Leask, *Irish Castles*, 1941 p. 73 (plan) and p. 74. It is approximately 140 feet square externally: its courtyard about 77 feet square: much the same size as Quin Co Clare for which see below, p. 90.

5 Leask, *Churches*, II, pp. 131-2. Plan in Clapham, loc. cit. p. 20. Photo ibid., pl. X.

6 Leask in *Journal of the Galway Archaeological and Historical Society*, XVII, 1936, pp. 1-23.

7 For Irish monasteries generally, see A. Gwynn and R. N. Hadcock, *Irish Monasteries and Religious Houses*, 1970. For the earliest phase, Rev. J. Ryan, *Irish Monasticism*, Dublin, 1931.

8 Leask, *Churches*, II, p. 127.

9 Wright, *A Contemporary Narrative of the Proceedings against Dame Alice Kyteler*, Camden Society, 1843 (in Latin). Digested in English in St J. Seymour, *Anglo-Irish Literature*, Cambridge, 1929, pp. 41 sqq. These events found their way, via Seymour, into Yeats's 'Nineteen Hundred and Nineteen', section VI.

10 For the Observant movement, see F. X. Martin, 'The Irish Friars and the Observant Movement in the Fifteenth Century' in *Irish Catholic Historical Committee Proceedings*, 1960.

11 Kilmallock may be as early.

12 For Clontuskert, see D. N. Johnson in B. O'Connell (ed), *Architectural Conservation, an Irish Viewpoint*, Dublin, 1975, pp. 37-54.

13 F. Henry, 'Irish Cistercian Monasteries and their carved decoration' in *Apollo*, October 1966, pp. 260 sqq.

14 A papal protection to preachers collecting for Holy Cross was issued in 1431. *Irish Monastic and Episcopal Deeds*, ed. N. B. White, Dublin, 1936, p. 23.

15 Champneys, op. cit. pp. 172 sqq. Leask, *Churches*, III, pp. 56 sqq and 142-3.

16 Leask, *Churches*, III, pp. 69 sqq. and pl. IX.

17 Champneys, pl. LXXIX, Leask, *Churches* III, pl. IVb and p. 59, also II, pp. 128-9. The Black Abbey in Kilkenny was restored for worship in the early nineteenth century and again in recent years.

18 For the friaries generally, including plans of nine houses, see Leask, *Churches*, III, passim but especially Chapter VI.

19 Leask, *Churches*, III, pls. XXIV and XXV.

20 Leask, *Churches*, II, pp. 124 sqq, III, 113 sqq; Stalley, op. cit. 143, Champneys, op. cit, pp. 171 sqq.

21 *JRSAI*, 86, 1956, p. 125.

22 Ibid., Mooney, loc. cit. 1955, p. 171. Leask, *Churches*, III, pp. 97-8.

23 Ibid., p. 221.

24 Leask, *Churches*, III, 179-80, 184.

25 See Champneys, pp. 230-1.

26 Leask, *Churches*, III, pp. 19-21.

Chapter 7 – Tower-houses (pages 95-110)

1 Leask, *Castles*, pp. 153 sqq.

2 Westropp published numerous papers on the castles, earthworks and stone forts of North Munster (Thomond) in the *Journal of the Royal Society of Antiquaries of Ireland* and elsewhere.

3 J. Lydon, *Ireland in the Later Middle Ages*, Dublin, 1973, p. 8. Cruden, (*The Scottish Castle*, 1960, p. 104), agrees as regards Scotland, while W. D. Simpson (*Studies in Building History*, ed. Jope, 1961, pp. 221 sqq) disagrees.

4 Leask, *Castles*, p. 38.

5 Leask, *Castles*, pp. 76-7.

6 Leask, *Castles*, p. 77 and *Co Down Survey* 1966.

7 Leask, *Castles*, p. 75.

8 Leask at first thought Clara to be of the late sixteenth century (*JRSAI*, LXVII, 1937, p. 284) and later (*Castles* p. 79) revised his view and adopted a late fifteenth-century date.

9 Leask, *Castles*, p. 87 fig. 52.

10 Leask, *Castles*, p. 120 fig. 83.

11 W. Douglas Simpson, loc. cit. (see note 3 above) p. 230.

12 Leask, *Castles*, p. 90 fig. 55, and *JRSAI*, LXXXIII, 1953, p. 37.

13 Rounded corners are reported also from Scotland: for example Drum (Cruden, *The Scottish Castle*, 1960, pl. 15).

14 *Co Down Survey*, pp. 125, 244, 251.

15 Leask, *Castles*, pp. 113 sqq.

16 Leask, *Castles*, pp. 118 sqq.

17 Leask, *Castles*, pp. 116 sqq. J. Hunt and C. Lynch, *Bunratty Castle*, illustrated guide, n.d. c. 1970.

Chapter 8 – The End of the Middle Ages (pages 111-136)

1 K. M. Lanigan and G. Tyler, *Kilkenny, its Architecture and History*, Kilkenny, 1977, pp. 24-5.

The house was restored by W. P. le Clerc in 1962-6.

2 A. J. Otway-Ruthven, *History of Medieval Ireland*, 1968, p. 393.

3 Plan in de Breffny and ffolliott, *Houses of Ireland*, 1975, p. 109.

4 Lydon, op. cit. pp. 153 sqq.

5 *Kilkenny Castle*, official guide, anon. n.d. *c*. 1976, and K. M. Lanigan, *Kilkenny Castle*, n.d. *c*. 1970 (?).

6 R. Cochrane, *Creevelea Abbey*, official guide, 3rd ed. 1934, Dublin, Stationery Office.

7 Waterman in *Studies in Building History*, ed. Jope, 1961, pp. 252-3 (with plan and elevation).

8 Leask, *Castles*, pp. 146-7.

9 W. D. Handcock, *The History and Antiquities of Tallaght*, Dublin, 1877, pp. 26 sqq.

10 Waterman, loc. cit. p. 264, doubts this and thinks the main door was opposite the indentation. The building is now so much overgrown that it cannot be determined. There may have been two doors as at Glinsk.

11 For Loughmoe and Donegal, see Leask, *Castles*, pl. VII and p. 135. For Loughmoe see also de Breffny and ffolliott, op. cit. p. 43 (with plan).

12 Courtstown (called Inchmore in *Dublin Penny Journal*, 15 Dec, 1832) is illustrated in G. N. Wright, *Ireland Illustrated*, 1829-31, pp. 47-8, where it is said to be in process of demolition.

13 Other candidates for membership of this small group of buildings are Castle Coote Co Roscommon (partly visible in a later house) and Moore Abbey Co Kildare (drastically remodelled). Another possibility is the original house on Lambay Island Co Dublin.

14 See Craig in *The Country Seat* (ed. Colvin and Harris), 1970.

15 'Sir Frederick Hamilton' by Fr. Domhnaill Mac an Ghallóglaigh in *Breifne* Vol. III, 1966, pp. 55 sqq., an admirably researched and vivid article. Sir Frederick, in the opinion of Sir William Cole of Enniskillen, was 'extremely distasteful to men of all conditions that lived within twenty or thirty miles of him.'

16 Plan in Leask, *Castles*, p. 128 fig. 90.

17 Grose, *Antiquities of Ireland*, 1797, II, pp. 87-8.

18 L. Price (ed.) *An Eighteenth Century Antiquary . . . Austin Cooper*, Dublin, 1942, pl. 19.

19 See the drawings by Thomas Raven reproduced by Jope in *UJA*, 1966, p. 106. See also, for Dalway's and Movanagher, H. Dixon, *An Introduction to Ulster Architecture*, Belfast, 1975, pp. 19, 20.

20 *Ancient Monuments in Northern Ireland not in State Charge*, Belfast, 1952, p. 34.

21 Leask, *Castles*, p. 109.

22 Waterman in *Studies in Building History*, p. 268 and pl. XXX.

23 The White House building, somewhat remarkably, survives, re-roofed, as a gospel hall, and there is a plan and isometric reconstruction by Jope in *UJA*, 1966, p. 111.

24 See particularly the description by Lord Charleville of 'Redwood', the predecessor of Charleville Castle. 'Near where the Gothic Castle now stands was the original mansion House, built shortly after the year 1641, according to the fashion of that time, with many small and ill-connected apartments, but on the whole not destitute of much comfort and convenience. The interior divisions were uniformly constructed by strong partitions of Oak, probably the growth of the soil, and very liberally supplied; with a ponderous and double roof, also of the same material, and covered with shingles of oak of more ancient date, procured from the adjacent Bogs, which with occasional repairs repelled the beating storms for nearly two Centuries.' *The Marlay Letters*, ed R. Warwick Bond, 1937, p. 113.

25 *Journal of the Cork Historical and Archaeological Society*, 65, 1960, pp. 130 sqq.

26 Monkstown, *JRSAI*, 27, 1897, p. 330, *JCHAS*, 30 p. 17, 37 p. 93. Mountlong, *JCHAS*, 1907, pp. 16 sqq.

27 Waterman in *Studies in Building History*, p. 254 and figs. 14.3 and 14.4. Full description in *JCHAS*, I, 1892, pp. 155-7.

28 Waterman, (loc. cit. p. 264) thinks that Dromahair was entered from what I take to be the 'back' of the house, where the wall has been destroyed. It is, however, just as likely that there was a projecting staircase in this position, in which case the house will have resembled Coppinger's Court and its relations.

29 Compare Ballygally Co Antrim, which has the stairs in a similar position.

30 Barrington, *Personal Recollections*, Vol. III (1832), pp. 92 sqq. Lord Broghill was dining at Castle Lyons with his father Lord Cork and his uncle Lord Barrymore when news of the 1641 rising was brought to them. Among those dining was Lord Muskerry who was to be a rebel general. (Eustace Budgell, *Memoirs of the Boyles*, Dublin, 1754, pp. 30-31).

31 It is illustrated, under the name of 'Cregg', in Waterman, loc. cit. p. 273, where, however, the plan is incorrect as the trace of the staircase is plainly to be seen in the rere wing where the word 'entry' is mistakenly placed.

32 Waterman, loc. cit. p. 262.

33 G. F. Mitchell, *The Irish Landscape*, 1976, p. 172, pl. 23.

34 Girvan, Oram and Rowan, *Antrim and Ballymena*, UAHS list 1969, p. 20 (woodcut from the *Dublin Penny Journal*, 104, p. 409).

35 Craig, *Classic Irish Houses*, 1976, pp. 58-9.

36 Dixon, *Ulster Architecture*, 1975, p. 24.

Chapter 9 - The Restoration (pages 137-150)

1 For O'Neill and Broghill, see their respective entries in *DNB*. For Broghill see also Loeber in *The Irish Sword* XIII, 51, 1977, pp. 106 sqq.

2 Dr Loeber tells me that Broghill learnt his architecture in Geneva.

3 Quoted in C. Litton Falkiner, *Illustrations of Irish History*, 1904, 51n.

4 For Dublin Castle, see C. Litton Falkiner, op. cit. pp. 3 sqq., Leask, *Dublin Castle*, Dublin, Stationery Office n.d. (below this author's usual high standard), J. B. Maguire, *Dublin Castle*,

Stationery Office n.d. [*c.* 1975], (very well re-searched and informative), J. Cornforth in *Country Life*, 30 July and 6 and 20 August 1970, R. Loeber, *IGSB*, Jan–Jun 1973, pp. 9–11, and Loeber, *Studies*, Spring 1980, pp. 45 sqq. Also J. B. Maguire in *JRSAI*, 104, 1974, pp. 5 sqq.

5 Craig, 'New Light on Jigginstown' in *UJA*, 3rd series, 33, 1970 pp. 107 sqq, reprinted in *Journal of Kildare Archaeological Society*, XV, 1971, pp. 50 sqq. Dr Loeber has since drawn my attention to the fact that the drawing catalogued by us in 1964 as No. 8 of the Elton Hall Catalogue, by Pearce, is in fact a detail of Jigginstown. See also F. W. Strath, 'Sigganstown House commonly called 'Jigginstown' in *JKAS*, XII, 1943, pp. 343 sqq.

6 Used by Professor Margaret MacCurtain in *Tudor and Stuart Ireland*, Dublin, 1972, p. 105.

7 Invented by the author for his private use.

8 R. Loeber in *The Irish Sword*, XIII, 1978–9, p. 242.

9 Orrery, *State Letters* (ed. T. Morrice) 1742, p. 31.

10 'Sculptured Memorials to the Dead in Early 17th century Ireland' by R. Loeber [typescript] 1978. Based largely on the MS *Monumenta Eblanae* in the Genealogical Office, Dublin.

11 Craig and O'Connell, 'Rath Reagh Church' in *Irish Midland Studies* (ed. Murtagh) Athlone, 1980, pp. 136 sqq.

12 R. Loeber, 'Early Classicism in Ireland' [typescript] 1978, part published in *Architectural History*, 22, 1979, pp. 49 sqq.

13 For Burton (with reconstruction) see Loeber in *IGSB*, Jan–June 1973, pp. 25 sqq. This article has been much drawn on for this chapter.

14 For Richhill see H. Dixon, *Ulster Architecture* p. 25, which gives view and plan.

15 *Co Down Survey*, pp. 437–8, pls. 138, 141. UAHS list *Craigavon/Moira*, p. 6 and cover picture, ed. of 1970.

16 Eyrecourt: photographs in *IGSB*, April–June 1972, p. 58, Bence-Jones, *Burke's Country Houses Ireland*, 1978, p. 122.

17 *Co Down Survey*, pp. 362–4 and pls. 138, 139.

18 Bence-Jones, op. cit. p. 6 (photograph). See also *JCHAS*, Vol. XLIII, 1938, pp. 28–9. Mr John Lenahan tells me that Castle Cor near Kanturk Co Cork had a similar plan.

19 *IGSB*, Jan–June 1974, p. 8.

20 See Dr Loeber's forthcoming biographical dictionary of Irish architects and engineers to 1730. The engineers in instalments in *The Irish Sword*, XIII, 1977–9, pp. 50–3.

21 William Kenn is described as 'Architect' of Cahernary Co Limerick (*HMC Egmont*, I, 22, for details of contract).

22 Quoted in E. MacLysaght, *Irish Life in the Seventeenth Century*, ed. of 1950, p. 39.

23 MacLysaght, op. cit. pp. 100–101. It is worth noting that the hostile and fantastic description by William Lithgow (1619, quoted by M. J. MacManus in *Irish Cavalcade*, 1939, p. 35) is no more informative.

24 E. O'Malley, *The Singing Flame*, Dublin, 1978,

pp. 70–71, quite impossible to reconcile with the Four Courts as it is or was at any stage of its existence.

25 Quoted by Loeber in *IGSB*, Jan–June 1973, p. 19.

26 Campbell and Crowther, *Carrickfergus*, UAHS list, 1978.

27 *UJA*, 34, 1971, pp. 110–1.

28 M. Craig and J. O'Connell in *Irish Midland Studies*, ed. Murtagh, Athlone, 1980, pp. 136 sqq.

29 T. M. Fallow, *The Cathedral Churches of Ireland*, n.d. [1894?] Ferguson, Rowan, Tracey, *City of Derry*, UAHS list 1970.

30 *County Down Survey*, pp. 336–8, pl. 118.

31 F. J. Bigger and W. J. Fennell in *UJA* 2nd series, III, 1897, pp. 13 sqq. (with drawings).

32 *Ancient Monuments of Northern Ireland in State Charge*, 1928, pp. 18–19 and *County Down Survey*, p. 305. Also *Preliminary Survey ... Northern Ireland*, 1940, pp. 115–6 and pl. 28.

33 Loeber in *IGSB*, Jan–June 1974, p. 8.

34 C. Litton Falkiner, *Illustrations of Irish History*, 1904, pp. 160 sqq. *JRSAI*, LXII, 1932, p. 6, pl. VI (Francis Place).

Chapter 10 – Dublin: the Seventeenth Century (pages 151–156)

1 For a very full publication of the late seventeenth century work in Dublin Castle see Loeber in *Studies*, Spring 1980, pp. 45 sqq.

2 J. T. Gilbert, *History of Dublin*, 1859, II, p. 6.

3 See MacDowel Cosgrave in *JRSAI*, XXXVI, 1907, p. 58 from which it appears that the prints were issued in 1704.

4 Photostat copy in the author's possession of a plan from a collection originating in the Surveyor-General's office (copy also in National Library); a similar plan also reproduced in C. Halliday, *The Scandinavian Kingdom of Dublin*, 1884 (1969), p. 239.

5 See the Hatfield drawing reproduced in C. Maxwell, *A History of Trinity College, Dublin*, Dublin, 1946.

6 Dineley's drawing of 1680 reproduced in ibid.

7 Photostat in author's possession and also in National Library. (As note 4).

8 J. Summerson, *Architecture in Britain*, 1953, pl. 96.

9 R. Colley, *An Account of the Foundation of the Royal Hospital*, Dublin, ed. of 1805, p. 3.

10 Loeber in *IGSB*, Jan–June 1974, p. 3 sqq.

11 Colley, op. cit. pp. 19, 22, 25. It should be noted that Robinson himself owned some of the land to the West of the site (ibid., p. 48).

12 Ibid., p. 38.

13 Summerson, *Georgian London*, ed. of 1947, p. 72.

14 Reproduced in Craig, *Dublin 1660–1860*, pl. VIII.

Chapter 11 – Dublin: 1690–1757 (pages 157–176)

1 Rocque's map is available in an admirable modern reprint on four sheets (together with four sheets of the county and an explanatory booklet

by Prof. J. H. Andrews) published by H. Margary at Lympne, Kent, in 1977.

2 *Georgian Society Records*, II, 1910, p. 5 sqq.

3 *Georgian Society Records*, I, 1909, pl. III, p. 3, II, 1910, p. 101. See also the valuable article 'Dutch Billys in the Liberties' by Peter Walsh in *The Liberties of Dublin*, ed. E. Gillespie, Dublin, 1973.

4 See the Van der Hagen view of Waterford (Crookshank and Glin, *Painters*, pl. 41), the print in Smith's *Cork*, ed. of 1815, I., p. 395, G. Wilkinson, *Practical Geology &c.*, 1845, p. 130 fig. 54, *County Down Survey*, pl. 200.

5 *Georgian Society Records*, I, 1909, p. 6. Sheridan Lefanu, in 'Some Strange Disturbances in Aungier Street' speaks of 'the odd diagonal site of the chimney-pieces' as indicative of antiquity (he was writing in 1853: *Madam Crowl's Ghost*, ed M. R. James, 1923, p. 104); but the corner fireplace, observably, lasted into the nineteenth century.

6 Curran in F. G. Hall *The Bank of Ireland*, 1949, pp. 437-8.

7 Craig, *Classic Irish Houses*, p. 67.

8 Loeber in *IGSB*, Jan-June 1974.

9 Ibid.

10 W. P. Pakenham-Walsh in *Royal Engineers' Journal*, Aug-Sept 1907. Craig, *Dublin*, pp. 94 sqq. Loeber in *The Irish Sword*, XIII, Winter 1977, pp. 110 sqq.

11 Craig, op. cit. pl. VII.

12 In correspondence and conversation with the author.

13 Craig, op. cit. pp. 96-8 and 196.

14 A. O. Crookshank, *The Long Room*, Gatherum series, Dublin, 1976, draws, unlike earlier accounts, on the College muniments.

15 The sources for Pearce's life are:
  (i) T. U. Sadleir in *Journal of the Kildare Archaeological Society*, 1927, X, pp. 231 sqq.
  (ii) C. P. Curran in *The Bank of Ireland* (ed. F. G. Hall) Dublin, 1949.
  (iii) I. Toesca in *English Miscellany* (ed. Praz) Rome, 1952, p. 195 n.
  (iv) H. Colvin and M. Craig. *Architectural Drawings [at] Elton Hall by Sir John Vanbrugh and Sir Edward Lovett Pearce*, Oxford, for the Roxburghe Club, 1964.
  (v) D. Fitz-Gerald (Knight of Glin) in *IGSB*, 1965, VIII, pp. 3 sqq.
  (vi) Craig, Glin and Cornforth in *Country Life*, 27 March, 3 and 10 April, 1969.
  (vii) Craig in *IGSB*, Jan-June 1974, pp. 10 sqq., in which a fuller set of references will be found.
  For the Parliament House, see also J. T. Gilbert, *Parliament House, Dublin*, Dublin, 1896, an expanded and illustrated version of the account in his *History of Dublin*, II, 1859.

16 *Georgian Society Records*, II, 1910, pp. 13-17, pls. XVI-XXVIII.

17 *Survey of London*, XXXII, 1963, pp. 499, 505.

18 J. Bush, *Hibernia Curiosa*, Dublin, 1769, pp. 15-16, relating to 1764, by which time it had been shut for several years. See also *Irish Builder*, 37, 1895, p. 293.

19 The sources for Cassels (Castle) are:
Anthologia Hibernica, October 1793.
T. U. Sadleir in *JRSAI*, XLI, 1911, pp. 241 sqq.
Knight of Glin in *IGSB*, Jan-March 1964.
I have used also the Knight of Glin's unpublished thesis on 'The Irish Palladians'.

20 Stearne had given the money for the building as far back as 1726, which makes it more likely that Pearce was involved.

21 E. McParland in *Country Life*, 13 May, 1976, pp. 1243-5.

22 *Georgian Society Records*, IV, 1912, pp. 43 sqq. and pls. XVIII-XLIX. A large number of drawings relating to Leinster House are in the collection of the Hon. Desmond Guinness at Leixlip Castle Co Kildare.

23 C. P. Curran, *The Rotunda Hospital, its Architects and Craftsmen*, Dublin, 1945.

24 *The Legacy of Swift*, ed. Craig, Dublin, 1948, pp. 31 sqq.

25 G. Semple, *The Art of Building in Water*, Dublin, 1776.

26 H. A. Wheeler and M. J. Craig, *The Dublin City Churches of the Church of Ireland*, Dublin, 1948. Craig, *Dublin*, pp. 107, 111, 179.

27 McParland in *Country Life*, 13 May, 1976, pp. 1244 sqq.

28 McParland, loc. cit.

29 *Georgian Society Records*, III, 1911, pp. 51 sqq. and pls. I-XII. Craig in *The Connoisseur*, April 1960, pp. 148 sqq. Both now superseded by McParland in *Country Life*, 14 and 21 Oct. 1976.

30 George Ensor settled at Ardress Co Armagh, as a country gentleman, in about 1770, and remodelled the house there (R. McKinstry, guide to *Ardress*, 1962). John Ensor is copiously documented in the *Georgian Society Records*: see entry in Vol. V, 1913, p. 113.

31 *Irish Commons Journals*, 17 Jan 1752, Vol. VIII, 1753, p. 416.

32 R. McKinstry, *Ardress, Co Armagh*, 1962, p. 10.

33 Craig, *Dublin*, pp. 104, 187 sqq.

34 See C. P. Curran, *Dublin Plasterwork*, 1967.

35 Gilbert, *History of Dublin*, II, p. 36.

Chapter 12 - Country Houses 1700-1780 (pages 177-199)

1 It must be emphasised that the assertions of Mahaffy (*Georgian Society Records*, V, pp. 9 and 22) about the alleged prevalence of brick in the very early eighteenth century are quite mistaken.

2 Craig, *Classic Irish Houses*, 1976, pp. 54-59.

3 Ibid., pp. 62-65.

4 M. Girouard in *Country Life*, 8 Nov 1962, pp. 1152 sqq.

5 Sadleir and Dickinson, *Georgian Mansions*, 1915, pp. 36 sqq and pls. XX-XXII. Colvin and Craig, op. cit. pp. xliii-xliv and pls. lxv and lxvi. Bishop Pococke (*Tour in Ireland in 1752*) 1891, says it was begun for Goodwin (not for Bolton as was formerly believed and asserted in print by me among others).

6 Professor L. M. Cullen assures me that there is

plenty of evidence for eighteenth-century brick-burning *in situ*, in many places.

7 *Georgian Society Records*, V, p. 26. The Mount levers accounts which were available to the writer of this account in 1913 have since disappeared.

8 Summerson in *Journal of the Royal Society of Arts*, CVII, 1959, pp. 539 sqq.

9 *Georgian Society Records*, V, p. 62.

10 *IGSB*, VIII, 1965, pp. 3 sqq. *Country Life*, 27 March, 3 and 10 April, 1969.

11 *Anthologia Hibernica*, 1793.

12 Pococke, op. cit. Cockerell notebooks in RIBA Drawings Library. For Summerhill generally, see the Knight of Glin in *The Country Seat* (ed Colvin and Harris) 1970, pp. 131 sqq.

13 For Desart Court, see Sadleir and Dickinson, *Georgian Mansions*, pp. 55 sqq. and pl. XXXVIII sqq.

14 Craig, *Classic Irish Houses*, pp. 74-83.

15 For Bellamont, see Craig in *Country Life*, 21 and 28 May, 1964.

16 For Belvedere, see Mark Girouard in *Country Life*, 22 and 29 June, 1961. Plan in Craig, *Classic Irish Houses*, p. 102.

17 A preliminary effort was made by the Knight of Glin in *IGSB* Jan-March 1964.

18 Craig, op. cit. pp. 104-5.

19 For Powerscourt, see Guinness and Ryan, op. cit. pp. 323 sqq.

20 *Georgian Society Records*, V, 1915, pp. 59 sqq and pls. XLI-XLIX; Guinness and Ryan op. cit. pp. 183 sqq.

21 For Russborough, see *Country Life*, LXXXI, pp. 94 and 120; CXXXIV, pp. 1464, 1623, 1686 (1963); *Georgian Society Records*, V, 1913, pp. 68 sqq and pls. L-LXX. Plan in Guinness and Ryan, op. cit. p. 334.

22 For Woodlands, Gloster and Ledwithstown, see my *Classic Irish Houses*.

23 For Bindon, see the Knight of Glin in *IGSB*, April-September 1967, where, however, he claims rather more for his hero than later seemed to him prudent.

24 *Georgian Society Records* V, pls. CV-CVII. The plan of Castle Morres has since been recovered by William Garner.

25 John Aheron, *A General Treatise on Architecture*, Dublin, 1754. The principal interest of the book is the number of artificers and tradesmen who appear in its subscription-list. The book has a complicated bibliography which has never been disentangled. One MS of it is in the British Library, and another in the Metropolitan Museum, New York. See my *Classic Irish Houses*, p. 48.

26 There are two Michael Wills architectural manuscripts: one in the RIBA Library in London and the other in the Chester Beatty Collection in Dublin. The former is the more interesting of the two, but the latter is in a splendid Irish binding.

27 For Summer Grove and Dysart, see my *Classic Irish Houses*, pp. 114 sqq. and 118 respectively.

28 For the career of Clements, see the Knight of Glin in *Apollo*, October 1966, pp. 314 sqq.

29 For the career of Ducart, see the Knight of Glin in *Country Life*, 28 Sep. and 5 Oct., 1967.

30 Both Castletown Cox and Kilshannig are illustrated in Guinness and Ryan, op. cit. pp. 219 and 77 sqq. respectively. The plans given are, however, not to be trusted: for example, the service-stairs at Castletown comes between the entrance-hall and the main stairs.

31 See E. McParland, *Thomas Ivory, Architect*, Gatherum series, Ballycotton 1973, and Craig, *Classic Houses*, pp. 142-3.

32 See *Country Life*, 27 March 1969, p. 724, or Craig and Glin, *Ireland Observed*, Cork, 1970, p. 46.

33 Young, *Tour in Ireland*, Dublin, 1780, I, p. 44. I am obliged to Prof. L. M. Cullen for several particulars relating to the Slane Mill.

Chapter 13 - Provincial Towns and Churches (pages 200-231)

1 *A New History of Ireland*, III, Oxford, 1976, p. 473.

2 Typescript unpublished at the time of writing, for sight of which I owe thanks to the author.

3 J. Ferrar, *History of Limerick*, Limerick, 1787, pp. 85-6.

4 W. D. Girvan, *North Derry*, UAHS, 1975, p. 6.

5 C. Smith, *Ancient and Present State of the City and County of Cork*, ed. of 1815, I, p. 395. The Council book of Cork (4 Feb. 1705 and 16 Jan. 1706) is tantalisingly reticent about the 'able artist' and other 'persons' concerned.

6 C. E. B. Brett, *Court and Market Houses of the Province of Ulster*, UAHS, 1973, 25-6.

7 Ibid., pp. 60-62.

8 Colvin & Craig, op. cit. pl. LXIV.

9 Brett, op. cit. p. 6 and back cover.

10 Lanigan and Tyler, *Kilkenny*, 1977, p. 66.

11 Brett, op. cit. p. 75 ff.

12 Brett, *Buildings of Belfast*, 1967, pp. 3-4, 25.

13 Garner, op. cit. pp. 69-71. P. Shaffrey, *The Irish Town*, 1975, p. 81.

14 Smith, op. cit. (note 5 above).

15 *Co Down Survey*, pp. 397 sqq., pl. 196. Dunleath, Rankin, Rowan, *Downpatrick*, UAHS list, 1970, pp. 9 and 17.

16 Brett, *Court Houses*, p. 53.

17 L. M. Cullen, *Irish Towns and Villages*, 1979, pl. 28. Craig and Glin, *Ireland Observed*, p. 52.

18 Little of any value has been written on Cork. Apart from Smith's book of 1750 already cited, the following should be mentioned:

Cork: A Civic Survey (Cork Town Planning Association) 1925.

P. J. Hartnett (ed.) *Cork City, Its History and Antiquities*, Cork (*JCHAS*) 1943, with short chapter on the architecture by H. H. Hill.

T. F. MacNamara, 'The Architecture of Cork' in *RIAI Yearbook*, 1960.

Mark Bence-Jones in *Country Life*, 3 and 10 August 1967.

P. Dovell, *An Environmental Study of Cork* [Dublin] An Foras Forbartha, 1970.

Cork Corporation Draft Development Plan, 1979.

C. Lincoln, *Steps and Steeples: Cork at the Turn of the Century*, Dublin, 1980.

19 Four informative historical maps of Cork are reproduced in Hartnett, op. cit. (note 18).

20 *The Dublin Magazine*, September 1764.

21 For both Morrison senior and Roberts I have drawn on the unpublished thesis of the Knight of Glin. See also E. McParland on [Sir Richard] Morrison in *Country Life*, 24 May 1973. For Roberts, see Mark Girouard on Waterford in *Country Life*, 8, 15 and 22 Dec. 1966. For his Church of Ireland Cathedral, see Fallow, *The Cathedral Churches of Ireland*, [1894]: and Day and Patton, *The Cathedrals of the Church of Ireland*, 1932.

22 A. Rowan, *The Buildings of Ireland: North-West Ulster*, Harmondsworth, 1979.

23 *IGSB*, Jan-June 1974, pp. 19 sqq.

24 Brett, *Buildings of Belfast*, pp. 5-6 and pls. 8 and 9. *Historic Memorials of the First Presbyterian Church of Belfast*, Belfast, 1887.

25 Brett, *Belfast*, p. 6 and pl. 11.

26 D. Akenson, *The Church of Ireland ... 1800-1885*, New Haven and London, 1971.

27 In dealing with the Catholic churches at large I have had the advantage of using the (unpublished) unified list prepared by An Foras Forbartha in 1976, and derived from the county listings (for the 26 county area only) done by William Garner and myself during the previous four years. For the Church of Ireland churches at large, I have been able to use the material gathered by myself, mainly but not exclusively from the 26 counties, in an operation undertaken for and funded by the Representative Church Body and issuing in two brief reports of which the second was published in the *Reports of the General Synod* for 1977, pp. 48 sqq.

28 C. E. B. Brett, *Monaghan* list (UAHS and An Taisce) 1970.

29 Wheeler and Craig, *Dublin City Churches*, 1948, pp. 9, 22 and 34.

30 The plan is given in Addleshaw and Etchells, op. cit.

31 *Ireland Observed*, p. 18.

32 *Co Down Survey*, p. 330 (with plan) pl. 113.

33 C. E. B. Brett, *Glens of Antrim*, UAHS list, 1971, pp. 46, 48, 55. Ext. and int. ill. in de Breffny and Mott, *Churches and Abbeys of Ireland*, 1976, p. 127.

34 Ext. ill. in *IGSB*, July-Dec 1969, p. 95.

35 Fallow, op. cit. (see note 21 above) p. 40.

36 S. Lewis, *Topographical Dictionary of Ireland*, 1837, I, p. 344. Fallow (op. cit. p. 8) says the same, in his own words.

37 *County Down Survey*, p. 326 (plan) pls. 115, 117. Miller was involved also in the Hillsborough Fort nearby, for the same client. Brett, *Mid-Down*, UAHS list, 1974, pp. 9-11.

38 Fallow, op. cit. pp. 13-14. Day and Patton, op. cit. facing p. 42. Dunleath, Rankin, Rowan, *Downpatrick*, UAHS list, 1970, pp. 7, 13-14. *Co. Down Survey*, pp. 266 sqq. (plan on p. 269).

39 P. Rankin, *Irish Building Ventures of the Earl-*

Bishop of Derry, Belfast, UAHS, 1972, pp. 37 sqq.

40 E. McParland on Francis Johnston [and Cooley] in *IGSB*, July-Dec 1969, pp. 70, 73 sqq.

41 *The Treble Almanack* (Dublin) for the years in question.

42 J. Godkin, *Ireland and her Churches*, 1867, p. 5.

43 O.S. ref. 17 R 49 61.

44 O.S. ref. 8 H 21 17.

45 Spink Co Leix, near Abbeyleix. Compare Cullenagh, near Ennistymon Co Clare.

46 O.S. ref. 12 N 49 61, at 'Whitehall' ($\frac{1}{2}$-inch map) or 'Milltown' (1-inch map).

47 In Counties Cork, Kilkenny, Westmeath, Donegal, Kilkenny and Tipperary respectively. Since this was written Massmount has been totally ruined.

48 Ill. in *Ireland Observed*, p. 54.

49 In Louth, Meath and Meath respectively.

50 Dunleath, Rankin, Rowan, *Downpatrick* UAHS list, 1970, pp. 7, 19. *Co. Down Survey*, pp. 343-4 with plan, and pl. 130.

51 Brett, *East Down*, UAHS list, 1973, p. 33.

52 J. W. Kernohan, *Rosemary Street Presbyterian Church*, Belfast, 1923, frontispiece and pp. 45, 87. Brett, *Buildings of Belfast*, p. 19.

Chapter 14 – The Neo-Classic (pages 232-243)

1 McParland in *IGSB*, Jan-March 1972, pp. 1-32.

2 The history of the Dublin Society's Drawing School is as yet unpublished, but at the time of writing there is some hope that the work of Mr and Mrs Robert Raley on this subject will soon be given to the public.

3 J. Harris, *Sir William Chambers*, 1970, Chapters 4 and 5. The Casino in particular is such an important and elaborate building that justice cannot possibly be done to it in a work of this nature. See my *The Volunteer Earl*, 1948, Chapter VI.

4 McParland, 'James Gandon and the Royal Exchange Competition, 1768-9,' in *JRSAI*, 102, 1972, pp. 58 sqq.

5 Ibid., p. 59. From now on I have also made extensive use of Dr McParland's thesis 'The Public Work of Architects in Ireland during the Neo-Classical Period' (for Ph.D., University of Cambridge, 1975): unpublished as a whole but refined and extended in various articles which are cited as they become relevant.

6 See my *Dublin 1660-1860*, pp. 166, 166n and 195.

7 McParland in *JRSAI* (as note 4 above) p. 63.

8 Gandon and Mulvany, *The Life of James Gandon*, 1846 (reprinted ed. Craig, 1969) p. 40.

9 McParland, loc. cit. p. 69 and pl. 7.

10 Pool and Cash, *Public Buildings of Dublin*, 1780 (repr. ed. Craig 1970) p. 55 and plate. Craig, *Dublin*, p. 198 and pl. XXXIII.

11 McParland 'The Early History of James Gandon's Four Courts' in *The Burlington Magazine* CXXII, Nov 1980, pp. 727 sqq.

12 McParland, *Thomas Ivory Architect*, Gatherum series, Ballycotton, 1973, pp. 4 sqq.

13 Ibid., p. 6.

14 The Hibernian Marine School, now demolished, is variously credited to Ivory and to Cooley (Craig, *Dublin*, p. 197 and pl. XXXI) but is probably by Cooley, notwithstanding the resemblance between its wings and those of the Blue-Coat School.

15 J. Cornforth in *Country Life*, 28 Oct 1965, pp. 1128 sqq.

16 E. McParland in *IGSB*, July–Dec 1969, pp. 72–76.

17 Gandon, *Life*, pp. 43 sqq.

18 Craig, *Dublin*, p. 239.

19 McParland, unpublished thesis, Chapter III, note 32.

20 Gandon, *Life*, p. 112 sqq.

21 McParland in *IGSB*, Jan–March 1972, pp. 2–5.

22 Craig in *Trinity*, No. 11, Michaelmas 1959, pp. 14 sqq. McParland in *Country Life*, 20 May, 1976, pp. 1310 sqq.

23 Craig, *Classic Irish Houses*, pp. 154 sqq.

24 See the *Irish Architectural Drawings* catalogue, 1965, No. 3 (illus.).

25 McParland in *JRSAI*, 102, 1972, pp. 58 sqq. but especially pp. 66–7.

26 Reproduced by McParland in *The Burlington Magazine*, Nov 1980, p. 732 fig. 11.

27 Craig, *Dublin*, Appendix II, ii, p. 334.

28 Published by the Knight of Glin in *The Country Seat*, ed. Colvin and Harris, 1970, pp. 185 sqq.

29 C. P. Curran, *The Rotunda Hospital, its Architects and Craftsmen*, Dublin, 1945. I have also consulted the original records in the hospital's possession.

30 *Georgian Society Records*, III, 1911, pp. 99 sqq. and pls. LXII–LXXXIII. This early but by modern standards inadequate record has been supplemented by a magnificent survey made by the Irish Georgian Society in 1974 and now in the Irish Architectural Archive in Dublin (63 Merrion Square).

31 McParland, loc. cit. as note 21 above. Also same author in *Architectural Conservation*, ed. B. O'Connell, Dublin, 1975, pp. 24 sqq.

32 L. Réau, *St Pétersbourg*, Paris, 1913.

33 Summerson, *Georgian London*, 1945, p. 87 and idem. *Heavenly Mansions*, 1948, p. 96.

34 McParland thesis (as note 5 above) p. 103, and see *IGSB* Jan–March 1972, pl. 17.

35 Craig, *Dublin*, p. 247 and pl. L.

Chapter 15 – Neo-Classic to Romantic (pages 244–256)

1 J. Harris, *Sir William Chambers*, 1970, p. 236.

2 C. Hussey in *Country Life*, 31 Jan 1947 and J. Harris, op. cit.

3 *Country Life*, LXXX, pp. 654 sqq. and 682 sqq. (where it is inexplicably miscalled 'Castlecoole'. See also *Irish Architectural Drawings*, 1965, Nos. 39 and 40 (illus.) where the Johnston and Wyatt elevations may be compared.

4 P. Rankin, *Irish Building Ventures of the Earl-Bishop of Derry*, Belfast, UAHS, 1972. For Hervey's career generally, see B. Fothergill, *The Mitred Earl*, 1974. For Downhill, see W. D. Girvan, *North Derry*, UAHS list, 1975, pp. 53 sqq.

5 Rankin, op. cit. p. 25. Strictly, it is labelled 'Lounging Room'.

6 Rankin, op. cit. p. 49.

7 Brett, *Buildings of Belfast*, p. 13.

8 Colvin, ed. of 1978, pp. 718–9. Dr McParland has established that Sandys designed several fountains in Dublin, among them the Rutland Fountain in Merrion Square, formerly attributed (by me among others) to Henry Aaron Baker.

9 Mark Odlum in *Country Life*, 17, 24 and 31 July, 1980. A. J. Rowan in *IGSB*, Jan–March 1964, pp. 16 sqq. An important plan of 1703 is illustrated by Odlum, p. 200, the plan as existing by Guinness and Ryan, *Irish Houses and Castles*, 1971, p. 267. A Gandon drawing (erroneously attributed to Wyatt) is given by Betjeman in *The Pavilion* (ed. M. Evans) [1947], also, with another, in *Irish Architectural Drawings* catalogue, 1965.

10 Gandon, *Life*, pp. 99, 103.

11 M. Girouard in *Country Life*, CXXXII 1962, pp. 710 sqq. A. Rowan in *IGSB*, Jan–March 1964, p. 28 and pls. 15 and 18. McParland in *IGSB* July–Dec 1969, pp. 87 sqq and pls. 22–4. Photographs in *The Pavilion* (as note 9 above) pp. 34–5. See also *The Marlay Letters*, ed. Warwick Bond, 1937, pp. 110 sqq.

12 Guinness and Ryan, *Irish Houses and Castles*, p. 265.

13 Rowan in *IGSB*, Jan–March 1964, pp. 21 sqq. Guinness and Ryan op. cit. pp. 289 sqq.

14 J. Cornforth in *Country Life*, 13 July 1978, pp. 90 sqq.

15 Lecky, *History of England and Ireland in the Eighteenth Century*, 1883–90, VI, p. 590, VIII, p. 458.

16 M. Bence-Jones, *Burke's Guide to Irish Country Houses*, 1978, p. 74 (illus.).

17 Both Johnston and Morrison have been treated at some length by Dr McParland: Johnston in *IGSB*, July–Dec 1969, pp. 61–139 (the illustrations by ill-luck poorly reproduced) and Morrison in *Country Life*, 24 May 1973 (the villas) and 31 May 1973 (Lyons, Carton, Borris) followed by 13 and 20 Sept 1973 (Ballyfin). Prof M. McDermott has contributed an article on 'The Morrisons' to the *RIAI Yearbook* for 1977, pp. 81–4.

18 *Useful and Ornamental Designs in Architecture, composed in the manner of the Antique, and most approved Taste of the present day, the whole being peculiarly adapted for execution*. By Richard Morrison, Architect, Dublin: Robert Crosthwaite, 1793. A very long title for a very thin book which contains only 12 plates. See McParland in *Country Life*, 24 May 1973, pp. 1462–3: and Craig, *Classic Irish Houses*, pp. 34, 49.

19 *The Marlay Letters*, p. 113.

20 *Irish Architectural Drawings*, No 72, illus. p. 36.

21 Personal inspection, and drawings by Johnston still at Townley Hall. I cannot now recall the authority for the similar statement about Charleville.

22 Hall, *The Bank of Ireland*, 1949, pls. 64-65, which, however, give little idea of its scale and splendour.

23 McParland, *Country Life* articles (see note 17 above) and 20 Sept 1973, p. 775.

24 Colvin, ed. of 1978, p. 697.

25 *APS Dictionary*, s.v. Pain. M. McDermott in *RIAI Yearbook*, 1979, pp. 65 sqq.

26 *Irish Architectural Drawings*, 1965, No. 117 and ill. p. 44.

27 Accounts still in the house. There is also a large contemporary wooden model of the house, kept in an outbuilding.

28 Dixon, *Ulster Architecture* exhibition catalogue, 1973 p. 7.

29 McParland in *Country Life*, vol. 155, 1973, pp. 1274 sqq. and 1345 sqq.

30 McParland in *Country Life* (see note 17).

31 J. F. Fuller, *Omniana*, 2nd ed. n.d. [*c.* 1920] pp. 214-5.

32 Bence-Jones in *Burke's Country Houses*, I, 1978, p. 232.

Chapter 16 – The Early Nineteenth Century (pages 257-283)

1 For the Dublin Catholic churches generally, see N. Donnelly, *Short Histories of Dublin Parishes* [190?-1917]. See also Craig, *Dublin*, pp. 291 sqq.

2 For Cobden, see P. J. Brophy in *Carloviana* I, 3, 1949, pp. 125-6.

3 *Cork City, Its History and Antiquities*, ed. P. J. Hartnett, Cork, 1943, pp. 26, 98-7.

4 E. McParland, 'Who was "P"?' in *Architectural Review*, CLVII, 1975, pp. 71-3. Also the same author's unpublished doctoral thesis. See also *Irish Architectural Drawings*, 1965, Nos. 90 and 91 (illus.).

5 *Dublin Penny Journal*, 29 Dec 1832, p. 213.

6 Wheeler and Craig, *The Dublin City Churches*, 1948, pp. 18-20 and pl. XIX.

7 Ibid., p. 35 and pl. IX.

8 McParland thesis (unpub.) p. 225.

9 C. P. Curran 'Patrick Byrne: Architect' in *Studies*, XXXIII, 1944, pp. 193-203. P. Raftery 'The Last of the Traditionalists' in *IGSB*, Apr-Dec 1964, pp. 48-67.

10 Exterior illustrated in Richardson, *Monumental Classic Architecture in Great Britain and Ireland*, 1914, p. 47. Colour transparencies of the buildings within the curtilage were taken before demolition, but are at present inaccessible.

11 H. O'Sullivan 'The Court-house Dundalk' in *County Louth Archaeological Journal*, XV, 1962, pp. 131-143.

12 For Tinsley, see J. D. Forbes, *Victorian Architect: The Life and Work of William Tinsley*, Bloomington, Indiana, 1953.

13 McParland thesis (unpub.) p. 228 and note 46.

14 Craig, *Dublin*, pp. 295-6.

15 P. Henchy, 'Francis Johnston—architect' in *Dublin Historical Record*, Dec 1949-Feb 1950.

16 The book is in the library of the Royal Institute of the Architects of Ireland (at present deposited in the Irish Architectural Archive at 63 Merrion Square).

17 M. McDermott, 'The Deanes, an Irish Architectural Dynasty' in *RIAI Yearbook* 1975-6. See also *JCHAS*, 2nd ser. XXI, 1915, pp. 180 sqq.

18 R. B. McDowell, *The Irish Administration*, pp. 14 sqq.

19 A. Champneys, *Irish Ecclesiastical Architecture*, 1910, p. 34.

20 See Sir Samuel Ferguson in *Dublin University Magazine*, 1847, pp. 693 sqq.

21 A. Rowan, *The Buildings of Ireland, North West Ulster*, 1979, p. 348 and pl. 55.

22 Gandon, *Life*, pp. 68-70.

23 Lanigan and Tyler, *Kilkenny*, 1977, p. 83.

24 McParland thesis (unpub.) pp. 240 sqq.

25 C. E. B. Brett, *Court Houses and Market Houses of the Province of Ulster*, UAHS, 1973, p. 37. Drawings by Francis Johnston in the National Library dating from 1807.

26 See O'Sullivan as in note 77 above. An extremely fine set of contemporary drawings of the court house by Owen Fahy are kept in the building (photocopies in National Trust Archive). They do not in all respects tally with the building as constructed. The most revealing photograph (from the 'Lawrence' collection in the National Library) is reproduced in Harbison, Potterton and Sheehy, p. 191.

27 On W. V. Morrison, see the short biography, in *Weale's Quarterly Papers on Architecture*, I, 1843, Part I, Paper III. The plans of his, as of other court houses, are recoverable from the 1/500 Ordnance Survey plans of e.g. Carlow 1873 and Tralee 1878, at Mountjoy Barracks, Phoenix Park. See also M. McDermott, 'The Morrisons' in *RIAI Yearbook*, 1977, pp. 81 sqq., including a set of drawings of Carlow court house (modern) by an unknown hand.

28 McParland thesis (unpub.) pp. 246, 247, 248 and notes 98, 103 and 107. Cork itself was said at the time to have been influenced by Smirke's court house at Gloucester.

29 Little has been published on Irish bridges. I have used with profit T. A. Simington's Presidential Address to the Institute of Engineers in 1961 on 'Bridges in Ireland' typescript (through the courtesy of Joseph McCullough), and R. Cox, *Engineering Ireland 1778-1978*, exhibition catalogue, Trinity College, Dublin, 1978.

30 G. Semple, *The Art of Building in Water*, Dublin, 1776. See also Craig, *Dublin*, pp. 170 sqq.

31 Illustrated in Craig and Glin, *Ireland Observed*, Cork, 1970.

32 Quoted in Simington, loc. cit. (note 29 above).

33 P. Rankin, *Irish Building Ventures of the Earl-Bishop*, UAHS, 1972, p. 11. P. de la Ruffinière du Prey. 'Eighteenth-Century English Sources for a History of Swiss Wooden Bridges' in *Zeitschrift für Schweizerische Archäologie und Kunstgeschicht*, 36, 1979, pp. 51 sqq. Lewis's *Topographical Dictionary of Ireland*, 1837.

34 Colvin (ed. of 1978), p. 613 and the evidence of the print itself.

35 Colvin (ed. of 1978), p. 781. Illustrated in Craig, *Dublin*, pl. LXXII.

36 *Eddowes Salopian Journal*, 5 June 1816, kindly communicated to me by Mr Tony Byrne of the Ironbridge Gorge Museum Trust. The discovery was made by Dr Barrie Trinder.

37 Simington, loc. cit. (as note 29 above).

38 Cox, op. cit. (note 29) p. 28.

39 E. McCracken, *The Palm House and Botanic Garden, Belfast*, UAHS, 1971, pp. 35 sqq. For the Glasnevin houses, see *Country Life*, CLXVIII, 17 July 1980, pp. 192-3. *Taisce Journal*, 3, 1, Feb-April 1979 (E. J. Diestelkamp and C. Nelson) and *Glasra* no. 5, 1981, pp. 51 sqq. (E. J. Diestelkamp).

40 J. Gloag and D. Bridgewater, *A History of Cast Iron in Architecture*, 1948, p. 202. For further information tending to reduce Turner's claims, see J. Crook in Colvin (ed.). *The History of the King's Works*, VI, 1973, pp. 442 sqq., probably not the last word on the subject.

41 D. B. Hague and R. Christie, *Lighthouses, Their Architecture, History and Archaeology*, Llandysul, Dyfed, 1975.

42 Ibid., p. 86 (illus.).

43 Ibid., pl. 15.

44 Ibid., p. 128.

45 Ibid., pp. 210-11 (and illus.).

46 Ibid., pp. 133, 136 etc., and see *DNB*.

47 The fullest treatment of the Irish series of martello towers is by Paul Kerrigan in *An Cosantoir The Irish Defence Journal*, Apr 1974, pp. 107 sqq., May 1974, pp. 148 sqq., Aug 1974, pp. 285 sqq., May 1978, pp. 145 sqq., and (more peripherally) in his other articles on the defences of Ireland during the Napoleonic period. See also H. Mead in *The Mariner's Mirror*, XXXIV, 1948, S. Sutcliffe, *Martello Towers*, Newton Abbot 1972 (inadequate on the Irish material) and V. Enoch, *The Martello Towers of Ireland*, [1975].

48 Author's personal observations in the early 1960s.

Chapter 17 – The Later Nineteenth Century (pages 284-325)

1 B. M. Walker (ed.) *Frank Matcham, Theatre Architect*, Belfast, 1980.

2 John Sproule, *The Irish Industrial Exhibition of 1853*, Dublin, 1854, contains a very detailed description of the building and its construction, with plan, views etc.

3 Brett, *Buildings of Belfast*, p. 35.

4 See the invaluable list of office-holders from 1600 to 1730 given by Loeber in *The Irish Sword*, XIII, 50, 1977, pp. 34-5.

5 Craig, *Dublin*, p. 166.

6 The names of these office-holders are given in the directories for the years in question.

7 e.g. *I. Commons Journals*, ed. of 1797, Vol. VIII, pt. 1, p. 458 (1771), or an admission-ticket to Dublin Castle of 1780 in the possession of Ms E. Lane.

8 Malton's *Dublin*, text to 'Royal Infirmary Phoenix Park' 1794.

9 Dr McParland informs me that Ward, who had been second architect at the Tower of London, and was brought to Ireland by Lord Kildare, then Master of the Ordnance, died in 1788, apparently by his own hand, after a scandal the details of which are in *I. Common Journals*, 1789-90, App. CXLVI.

10 McParland in *IGSB*, Jan-March 1972.

11 R. B. McDowell, *The Irish Administration*, 1964.

12 Donald Akenson, *The Church of Ireland ... 1800-1885*, 1971.

13 *The Treble Almanack*, 1830, (*Watson's Gentleman's and Citizen Almanack*, p. 101).

14 *The National Monuments of the Irish Free State*, Dublin, Stationery Office, 1936, pp. 14-15. See also H. A. Wheeler in B. O'Connell (ed.) *Architectural Conservation, An Irish Viewpoint*, pp. 79-94 'The State's participation' (which is however mistaken on the genesis of the Board of Works). See also the annual reports of the Commissioners of Public Works from 1831 onwards, parts of which were often reprinted as guides to National Monuments.

15 Craig, *Classic Irish Houses*, p. 119 (illus.), and pp. 19-21.

16 See, for example, J. Meagher, *The Architecture of Ireland in drawings and paintings*, Dublin, 1975 (exhibition catalogue). Nos. 74-79 (illus.).

17 P. Stanton, *Pugin*, 1971, p. 37, and, more significantly, D. S. Richardson's unpublished thesis 'Gothic Revival Architecture in Ireland', Yale, 1970, of which I have made great use, here and hereafter. See, for Pugin, pp. 254 sqq.

18 Stanton, op. cit. pp. 70, 117.

19 Richardson, op. cit. pp. 504 sqq.

20 J. Sheehy, *J. J. McCarthy and the Gothic Revival in Ireland*, Belfast (UAHS), 1977.

21 McParland thesis (unpublished) pp. 210 sqq. Sheehy, op. cit. p. 5.

22 J. Morrison, 'Life of the Late William Vitruvius Morrison, of Dublin, Architect', in J. Weale's *Quarterly Papers on Architecture*, I, 1844, reprinted in *Dublin Builder*, 1 June 1859.

23 F. O'Dwyer and J. Williams, 'Benjamin Woodward' in T. Kennedy (ed.) *Victorian Dublin*, Dublin, 1980, pp. 38-63.

24 D. Dunlop, *A Memoir of the Professional Life of William J. Barre Esq.*, Belfast, 1868. The book is illustrated with numerous pasted-in photographs.

25 Ibid., text to plate of 'the Moat' (unpaginated).

26 For Lanyon, see *DNB*, xxxii, p. 140; Brett, *Buildings of Belfast*, pp. 24 sqq, Dixon, *Ulster Architecture 1800-1900* passim.

27 For Lynn, see H. Dixon in *IGSB*, Jan-June 1974, pp. 25 sqq.

28 Jordanstown Church is illustrated in J. Sheehy, *The Rediscovery of Ireland's Past*, 1980, p. 66.

29 J. F. Fuller, *Omniana*, 1916.

30 Sheehy op. cit. (as note 28) p. 63, illustrates Father Horgan's tower, and on p. 62 another, also beside a Catholic church, in Co Meath. I have made a rough tally of about 21 'revived'

Round Towers all over Ireland, fairly evenly divided into Catholic and Protestant, with the Protestant examples slightly preponderating. The earliest seems to be a Kelly mausoleum dated 1833 at Killeroran near Ballygar Co Galway.

31 Sheehy, op. cit. p. 64.

32 Fallow, *Cathedrals of Ireland*, pp. 93 sqq.; Day and Patton, *Cathedrals of the Church of Ireland*, 1932, p. 67; Sheehy, op. cit. p. 65.

33 Sheehy, op. cit. p. 128.

34 Ibid. See also [T. Cooke-Trench] *Church of St Michael and All Angels*, Dublin, 1894.

35 F. S. L. Lyons, *Ireland Since the Famine*, (ed. of 1973) p. 97. D. S. Richardson, thesis (as note 17 above) pp. 323 sqq.

36 Lanigan and Tyler, *Kilkenny*, p. 54.

37 Ferguson, Rowan and Tracey, *Derry*, pp. 33, 39.

38 R. Warwick Bond (ed) *The Marlay Letters*, 1937, pp. 111, M. Byrne, *A Walk Through Tullamore*, 1980, p. 297.

39 Craig, *Dublin*, pl. XXXIII.

40 Ibid., pls. XXIV and LI.

41 Dunleath, Rankin, Rowan, *Downpatrick* (UAHS), 1970, p. 17; Colvin (ed of 1978) p. 675. The attribution was first established by Dr McParland.

42 Craig and Glin, *Ireland Observed*, p. 23.

43 Ibid., p. 102.

44 Killanin and Duignan, *Shell Guide to Ireland*, ed. of 1967, p. 106.

45 For the Charter Schools, see K. Milne in *The Irish Journal of Education*, 1974, viii, 1, pp. 3-29. I am indebted to Dr Milne for further information also.

46 Lecky, *History of England and Ireland in the Eighteenth Century*, II, 1883, p. 202.

47 Illustrated in J.J. McGregor, *New Picture of Dublin*, 1821, p. 147. It was illustrated also in Warburton, Whitelaw and Walsh's *History of Dublin* of 1818. Its earliest appearance seems to have been in elevation in the *Dublin Magazine* for March 1762 (reproduced in *CARD X*, 1903). A perspective view appeared in the *Gentleman's Magazine*, Dec 1787, p. 1037.

48 The Hibernian Military School is now St Mary's Hospital. Johnston's elevation of 1808 is published by Betjeman in *The Pavilion* (ed. M. Evans), 1947, p. 35.

49 H. Dixon, *Soane and the Belfast Academical Institution*, Dublin, (Gatherum series) 1976.

50 M. Quane in *JRSAI*, July 1948, pp. 11 sqq.

51 Alexandra College seems to have moved at first into converted houses. Purpose-designed buildings by Kaye Parry followed in the 1880s, in flaming red brick and terracotta. The site was cleared in the late 1970s, following the migration of the school to the outer suburbs.

52 Rocque's map 1756. O.S. 5-foot (1:1056) 1847. Craig, *Dublin*, p. 27. Ormonde Bridge (which has no exact modern successor) gave access to the market.

53 Brett, *Buildings of Belfast*, p. 6 and pl. 11.

54 J. McGregor, *New Picture of Dublin*, 1821, pp. 302-3 (illus.).

55 McParland, 'The Contribution of History' in B. O'Connell (ed.) *Architectural Conservation An Irish Viewpoint*, Dublin, 1975, pp. 26-29. See also the same author in *IGSB*, Jan-March 1972, pp. 20 sqq.

56 W. and R. Mawson of Bradford won the competition in 1878, and the building was opened in 1881. *Irish Builder*, 20. 1 June 1878; 23 Nov 1881; 24, 15 June 1882; 34, 1 Sept 1892.

57 See the end-paper-map in *Brett's Belfast*, and contrast with the street (Clarence Street) as built.

58 Plan in P. Shaffrey, *The Irish Town*, Dublin, 1975, p. 24.

59 A. Rowan, *The Buildings of Ireland: North West Ulster*, 1979, pp. 485 sqq.

60 Plan and illus. in Shaffrey, op. cit. p. 25. See also G. Camblin, *The Town in Ulster*, Belfast, 1951, pp. 99-101.

61 Plan in L. M. Cullen, *Irish Towns and Villages*, Dublin, 1979 (unpaginated).

62 H. Butler in *JSRAI*, 1947, pp. 150 sqq.

63 Lewis, *Topographical Dictionary*, s.v. Belfast and Limerick. Census figures for populations of towns, especially growing towns, are always subject to the arbitrary limits of the municipal area at the time. See Craig's *Dublin* Appendix V, p. 341. See also P. Fitzgerald and J. J. MacGregor. *History of Limerick*, Dublin, 1827, II, pp. 485-7.

64 J. Milton, *Areopagitica* (*Selected Prose*, R. Garnett ed. of 1894, p. 43.)

65 In addition to Shaffrey (note 58), Camblin (note 60) and Cullen (note 61) there is much useful illustrative material in the journal *Irish Geography* (1944 onwards). There are, for example, plans of Tullamore, Birr and other Offaly towns in M. Byrne, *Sources for Offaly History*, Tullamore, 1978, and a plan of Mitchelstown (taken from *Irish Geography*) in R. A. Butlin (ed.) *The Development of the Irish Town*, 1977, p. 118. See also J. H. Andrews, *History in the Ordnance Map*, Dublin, Stationery Office, 1974. See also G. Darley, *Villages of Vision*, 1975, repr. 1979, pp. 193 sqq.

66 D. S. Richardson *Gothic Revival Architecture in Ireland* (Yale thesis 1970), pp. 504 sqq. Sheehy, *J. J. McCarthy*, pp. 57 and 59.

67 Ibid., pp. 25, 65 (pl. 55), 63.

68 Brett, *Belfast*, pp. 36-7.

69 Richardson, op. cit. pp. 506-8.

70 Ibid., pp. 575 sqq. Day and Patton, p. 43 (illus.)

71 Richardson, p. 579. Fallow, pp. 94-7 (illus.). Day and Patton, pp. 68-9.

72 Richardson, op. cit. pp. 582 sqq. Day and Patton, pp. 133 sqq. P. J. Hartnett (ed.) *Cork City, Its History and Antiquities*, 1943, pp. 30-31.

73 Richardson, op. cit. pp. 148 sqq. M. Bence-Jones, *Burke's Country Houses*, 1978 p. 144 (illus.).

74 M. Tierney and J. Cornforth, 'Glenstal Castle' in *Country Life*, clvi, 3 Oct 1974, pp. 934 sqq.

75 J. Williams in *Architectural Review*, August 1974, pp. 121 sqq.

76 Bence-Jones in *Country Life*, cxxxvi, 1964, 12 Nov, pp. 1274 sqq. Richardson, op. cit. pp. 694 sqq.

77 M. Girouard in *Country Life*, cvliii, 1968, 9 and 16 May, pp. 1212 sqq. and 1282 sqq., and in *The Victorian Country House*, 1971, pp. 116 sqq.

78 *Country Life*, 10 April 1969, p. 882.

79 D. Guinness, *Irish Houses and Castles*, 1971, p. 22.

80 B. Jones, *Follies and Grottoes*, 2nd ed. 1974, in which, however, the counties have got badly mixed up in the inventory on pp. 426 sqq. See also Mariga Guinness in *Ireland of the Welcomes* XX, 5, Jan–Feb 1972 (illus.).

81 Craig, *Dublin*, pp. 300–1.

82 J. Sheehy, *Kingsbridge Station*, Ballycotton, (Gatherum series) 1973.

83 On railway architecture generally, see J. Sheehy in the *Irish Railway Record Society's Journal*, Oct 1975, pp. 125 sqq.

84 On Irish mill-architecture generally, see D. Petherbridge 'Expressive Monuments of Industry and Order', Early Industrial Architecture in Ireland' in *Architectural Design*, 11 Dec 1977, pp. 742 sqq., generously illustrated. See also W. A. McCutcheon, *The Industrial Archaeology of Northern Ireland*, Belfast, HMSO, 1981, and occasional articles in *Technology Ireland* in the 1970s and 1980s, by divers hands, notably W. Dick.

85 V. and R. Delany, *The Canals of the South of Ireland*, Newton Abbot, 1966, and McCutcheon as in note 84.

86 An early attempt at a check-list of Irish mausolea is by the present author in *Studies*, Winter 1975, pp. 410. See also J. S. Curl, *A Celebration of Death*, 1980, especially pp. 169 sqq. and 266 sqq., and the same author in *Country Life*, 13 July 1978, pp. 126–7.

87 One particular graveyard, Clonenagh Co Leix, (OS 15S 38 96) has many cast-iron tombstones, cast at McCarthy's Foundry, Mountrath, which is still in business.

Book List

With the aim of keeping this list as short as possible, only works of a general nature are included, and books or articles on particular buildings excluded. A limited number of specialist studies of special significance have been listed, especially those which break new ground. Many other books and articles will be found cited in the appropriate places in the References. Purely topographical works, except for Lewis's *Topographical Dictionary*, have been omitted, nor are the large-scale Ordnance Survey maps, an indispensable aid to the enquirer in the field, here listed. The volume of local history published in recent years has been swelling rapidly, and the standard has been rising also, a very gratifying state of affairs. Books are published in London unless otherwise specified.

Abbreviations

APSD Architectural Publications Society's Dictionary.
CARD Calendar of Ancient Records of Dublin, 19 vols, Dublin 1889-1944
Co Down Survey, see *An Archaeological Survey*
Colvin, see COLVIN, Howard
Dunraven, see DUNRAVEN Earl of
Georg. Soc. Recs., see Georgian Society
Harbison, Sheehy, Potterton, see HARBISON, Peter
I. Arch. Drgs. see CRAIG, M. and GLIN, Knight of
IGSB Irish Georgian Society, Quarterly Bulletin
JCHAS Journal of the Cork Historical and Archaeological Society
JKAS Journal of the County Kildare Archaeological Society
JRSAI Journal of the Royal Society of Antiquaries of Ireland
Leask, *Churches* I, II, and III, see LEASK, H. G.
Leask, *Castles* see LEASK, H. G.
PRO Public Record Office
RIA Royal Irish Academy
RIAI Royal Institute of the Architects of Ireland
TCD Trinity College Dublin
UAHS Ulster Architectural Heritage Society
UJA Ulster Journal of Archaeology

Books and Journals

The Archaeological Journal, LXXXVIII, 1931 'The Summer Meeting at Dublin, 13th to 22nd July 1931' by R. A. S. Macalister, H. G. Leask, A. W. Clapham and others. Numerous illustrations, maps, plans.
The Architectural and Topographical Record, Vol. I (all published) Westminster, 1908.

An Archaeological Survey of County Down, Belfast, HMSO, 1966. Mostly by D. M. Waterman and A. E. P. Collins.

Architectural Publication Society, Dictionary of Architecture, 8 vols, 1848–92.

BARROW, G. L. *The Round Towers of Ireland*, Dublin, 1979.

BENCE-JONES, Mark, *Burke's Guide to Country Houses, Volume I, Ireland*, 1978. Also numerous articles by the same author in *Country Life* and elsewhere.

Board of Works, see Commissioners.

BRASH, Richard Rolt, *The Ecclesiastical Architecture of Ireland to the Close of the Twelfth Century*, Dublin, 1875.

BREFFNY, Brian de, and FFOLLIOTT, Rosemary, *Houses of Ireland*, 1975.

BREFFNY, Brian de, and MOTT, George, *Churches and Abbeys of Ireland*, 1976.

BRETT, C. E. B., *Buildings of Belfast 1700–1914*, 1967.

BRETT, C. E. B., *Court Houses and Market Houses of the Province of Ulster*, Belfast, UAHS, 1973. (Also much participation by the same author in the surveys published by the UAHS, 1968 onwards.)

The Builder, 1843 onwards. Contains a good deal of Irish material.

CAMBLIN, G., *The Town in Ulster*, Belfast, 1951.

CHAMPNEYS, Arthur, *Irish Ecclesiastical Architecture*, 1910. Reprinted Shannon Co Clare, 1970.

COLVIN, Howard, *A Biographical Dictionary of English Architects 1660–1840*, 1954. Revised and enlarged as *A Biographical Dictionary of British Architects 1600–1840*, 1978.

COLVIN, Howard, and CRAIG, Maurice, *Architectural Drawings by Sir John Vanbrugh and Sir Edward Lovett Pearce*, Oxford, for the Roxburghe Club, 1964.

Commissioners of Public Works in Ireland, *Annual Reports*, 1831 onwards. Extracts from these reports were sometimes published separately, e.g. *Ancient and National Monuments in County Cork*, 1908-9, ditto *in County Wexford*, 1909-10, *Glendalough*, 1911-12. *Clonmacnois*, 1906-1907. These are foolscap folios: after about 1919 they were published in octavo and soon ceased to be in form extracts from the Reports. Some were signed, e.g. *St Patrick's Rock, Cashel*, n.d. [1940] by H. G. Leask. One of particular value, by H. G. Leask but not signed, is *National Monuments, a Concise Guide to Ancient Irish Structures*, n.d. [1945]. See also H. G. LEASK, below.

COOPER, Austin, (ed. L. Price) *An Eighteenth Century Antiquary*, Dublin, 1942.

Country Life. Numerous articles of Irish interest, both on country houses, on Dublin and on provincial towns. An annual cumulative index (of country house articles only) is published.

CRAIG, Maurice, *Dublin 1660–1860*, 1952. Reprinted Dublin 1969 and 1980.

CRAIG, Maurice, *Classic Irish Houses of the Middle Size*, 1976 reprinted 1977.

CRAIG, Maurice and Glin, Knight of, *Irish Architectural Drawings*, Dublin, Belfast, Armagh, London, 1965. See also COLVIN, Howard, and GANDON, James.

CULLEN, L. M., *Life in Ireland*, 1968.

CULLEN, L. M. *Irish Towns and Villages*, Dublin 1979.

CULLEN, L. M. *The Emergence of Modern Ireland 1600–1900*, 1981.

CURRAN, C. P., *The Rotunda Hospital, its Architects and Craftsmen*, Dublin, 1945.

CURRAN, C. P., 'The Architecture of the Bank' in *The Bank of Ireland*, by F. G. Hall, Dublin 1949.

CURRAN, C. P., *Dublin Decorative Plasterwork of the 17th and 18th Centuries*, 1967.

DANAHER, Kevin (Caoimhín O Danachair), *Ireland's Vernacular Architecture*, Dublin, 1975.

DE PAOR, Máire and Liam, *Early Christian Ireland*, 1958, frequently reprinted, paperback 1978.

DIXON, Hugh, *Ulster Architecture 1800–1900* (catalogue of drawings exhibition), Belfast, 1972.

DIXON, Hugh, *An Introduction to Ulster Architecture*, Belfast, UAHS, 1975.

Dublin Builder, The (after 1866 *The Irish Builder*), 1859-66.

DUNLOP, Durham, *A Memoir of the Professional Life of William J. Barre*, Belfast, 1868.

DUNRAVEN, Earl of, *Notes on Irish Architecture*, 2 vols, 1875-. Mostly written, it would appear, by Margaret Stokes (q.v.).

ELMES, Rosalind, *Catalogue of Irish Topographical Prints and Original Drawings*, in the National Library of Ireland, Dublin, Stationery Office, 1943. Revised edition by Michael Hewson, Dublin 1975.

EOGAN, George, and HERITY, Michael, *Ireland in Prehistory*, 1977.

EVANS, E. E., *Irish Folk Ways*, 1957.

EVANS, E. E., *Prehistoric and Early Christian Ireland*, 1968.

FALLOW, T. M., *The Cathedral Churches of Ireland*, n.d. [1894].

Foras Forbartha, An (National Institute of Physical Planning and Research), architectural surveys of individual counties, of limited circulation and varying value, 1972 onwards. See also GARNER, W. and An Foras Forbartha's *Reference List of Reports and Documents*, February 1981.

GANDON, James (junior), *The Life of James Gandon*, prepared for publication by T. J. Mulvany, Dublin 1846. Reprinted with introduction, notes, appendices and index by Maurice Craig, London 1969.

GARNER, William. Cobh, *Architectural Heritage*, Dublin 1979. Kinsale, *Architectural Heritage*, Dublin 1980. Carlow, *Architectural Heritage*, Dublin 1980. Bray, *Architectural Heritage*, Dublin 1980. All published by An Foras Forbartha with the sponsorship of the Heritage Trust.

Georgian Society, *Records of Eighteenth-Century Domestic Architecture in Dublin*, 5 vols, Dublin 1909-15. (The fifth volume deals in fact with country houses). Reprinted Shannon 1969. See also SADLEIR, T. U., and DICKINSON, P. L.

GLIN, Knight of (Desmond Fitz-Gerald) and MALINS, Edward, *Lost Demesnes, Irish Landscape Gardening, 1660-1845*, 1976. See also CRAIG, Maurice

GLIN, Knight of (Desmond Fitz-Gerald), 'The Architecture of Davis Duckart' in *Country Life*, September 28th and October 5th, 1967.

GLIN, Knight of (Desmond Fitz-Gerald), 'Nathaniel Clements and Some Eighteenth-Century Irish Houses' in *Apollo*, October 1966.

GROSE, Francis, *The Antiquities of Ireland*, 2 vols., 1791-7.

GWYNN, Aubrey and HADCOCK, R. N., *Irish Monasteries and Religious Houses*, 1970.

GUINNESS, Desmond, and Ryan, William, *Irish Houses and Castles*, 1971.

HARBISON, Peter, Potterton, Homan, and Sheehy, Jeanne, *Irish Art and Architecture*, 1978.

HARBISON, Peter, *Guide to the National Monuments in the Republic of Ireland*, Dublin 1970, reprinted.

HENRY, Francoise, *Irish Art in the Early Christian Period*, 1965. *Irish Art during the Viking Invasions*, 1967. *Irish Art in the Romanesque Period*, 1970.

HERITY, Michael, *Irish Passage Graves*, Dublin 1974.

HILL, Arthur, *Monograph of Cormac's Chapel, Cashel*, Cork, 1874.

HILL, Arthur, *Ardfert Cathedral, Kilmalkedar and Temple na Hoe*.

HUNT, John, *Irish Mediaeval Figure Sculpture*, 2 vols., Dublin and London, 1974.

Ireland of the Welcomes, monthly, Dublin. This magazine of tourism contains from time to time authoritative articles by recognised authorities.

Irish Builder, The, 1867- (formerly *The Dublin Builder*).

Irish Georgian Society Bulletin, 1958 onwards.

JOHNSON, D. Newman, *Irish Castles* n.p., n.d. [Dublin 1979]

JOPE, E. M., (editor) *Studies in Building History*, 1961.

JOPE, E. M., 'Fortification to Architecture in the North of Ireland' 1570-1700' in *UJA* 1966 pp 97 sqq.

KERRIGAN, Paul, articles on fortifications of the Napoleonic period in *An Cosantóir*, April 1974, July 1974, August 1974, September 1974, February 1975, December 1975, May 1976, August 1977, May 1978, January 1981; in *The Irish Sword* xiii, 1979; and in *Journal of the Old Athlone Society* I, 4, 74-5.

KILLANIN, Michael (Lord) and Duignan, Michael V. *The Shell Guide to Ireland*, 1962. Enlarged and improved edition 1967.

LEASK, H. G., *Irish Castles*, Dundalk 1941. Third edition 1951.

LEASK, H. G., *Irish Churches and Monastic Buildings*, 3 vols, Dundalk, 1955-60.

LEWIS, Samuel, *A Topographical Dictionary of Ireland*, 2 vols and atlas, 1837.

LOEBER, Rolf, 'Irish Country Houses and Castles of the Late Caroline Period: an Unremembered Past Recaptured' in *IGSB*, January-June, 1973.

LOEBER, Rolf, 'Early Classicism in Ireland', typescript with illustrations, 1978 (partly published in *Architectural History* 22 1979).

LOEBER, Rolf, 'Sculptured memorials to the Dead in Early 17th Century Ireland', typescript with illustrations, 1978.

LOEBER, Rolf, 'Biographical Dictionary of Engineers in Ireland, 1600-1730' in *The Irish Sword*, XIII, 50, 1977, XIII, 51, 1977, XIII, 52, 1978-9 and XIII, 53, 1979.

LOEBER, Rolf, *A Dictionary of Irish Architects before 1730*, 1981.

LOEBER, Rolf, 'The Rebuilding of Dublin Castle, in *Studies*, Spring 1980.

MCCUTCHEON, W. A., *The Industrial Archaeology of Northern Ireland*, Belfast, HMSO, 1981.

MACNAMARA, T. F., *Portrait of Cork*, Cork 1981. (Appeared too late for consultation.)

MCPARLAND, Edward, 'Francis Johnston' in *IGSB* July-December 1969.

MCPARLAND, Edward, 'James Gandon and the Royal Exchange Competition 1768-9,' in *JRSAI*, 102, 1978.

MCPARLAND, Edward, *Thomas Ivory Architect*, Ballycotton Co Cork, 1973.

MCPARLAND, Edward, 'The Wide Streets Commissioners' in *IGSB* Jan-March 1972.

MCPARLAND, Edward, 'The Early History of James Gandon's Four Courts' in *The Burlington Magazine*, CXXII Nov 1980.

MCPARLAND, Edward, 'Trinity College, Dublin' in *Country Life* 6 May, 13 May and 20 May 1976, and 'The Provost's House, Trinity College' in *Country Life*, 14 and 21 October 1976, together constituting the only satisfactory account of the buildings.

MOONEY, Fr Canice, 'The Architecture of the Franciscan Order in Ireland' in *JRSAI*, vols 85, 86 and 87.

MURTAGH, Harman (editor) *Irish Midland Studies*, Athlone 1980.

NORMAN, E. R. and ST JOSEPH, J. K. S. *The Early Development of Irish Society*, Cambridge 1969.

O'CONNELL, Brian (editor) *Architectural Conservation, an Irish Viewpoint*, Dublin 1975. Nine papers read to the Architectural Association of Ireland during 1974 in preparation for European Architectural Heritage Year.

O'DWYER, Frederick, *Lost Dublin*, Dublin 1981. An exceedingly valuable record of the now vanished buildings in the capital from the year 1700 onwards.

O'DWYER, Frederick and WILLIAMS, Jeremy, 'Benjamin Woodward' in *Victorian Dublin* (ed. Tom Kennedy) Dublin 1980. Illustrated and with catalogue raisonnée of Woodward's works.

O'NEILL, T. P. *Life and Tradition in Rural Ireland*, 1977.

O'RIORDAIN, S. P. *Antiquities of the Irish Countryside*, Cork 1942. Reprinted London 1953 and 1964.

PETRIE, George, *The Round Towers and Ecclesiastical Architecture of Ireland*, Dublin 1845.

RAFTERY, Joseph, *Prehistoric Ireland*, 1951.

RAFTERY, Patrick, 'Patrick Byrne' in *IGSB*, April-December 1964.

ROTHERY, Sean, *The Shops of Ireland*, Dublin 1978.

ROTHERY, Sean, *Everyday Buildings of Ireland*, Dublin 1975.

ROWAN, Alistair 'Georgian Castles in Ireland' in *IGSB* Jan-March 1964.

ROWAN, Alistair, *The Buildings of Ireland, North West Ulster*, Harmondsworth 1979. The first in a projected series of eight or nine volumes in sequence with the famous English series of Pevsner.

RYNNE, Etienne (editor) *North Munster Studies*, Limerick 1967.

SADLEIR, T. U., and DICKINSON, P. L., *Georgian Mansions in Ireland*, Dublin, 1915. Uniform with the *Georgian Society Records*.

SHAFFREY, Patrick, *The Irish Town*, Dublin 1975.

SHEEHY, Jeanne, *J. J. McCarthy and the Gothic Revival in Ireland*, Belfast UAHS 1977.

SHEEHY, Jeanne, *The Rediscovery of Ireland's Past*, 1980. An account of the 'Celtic' revival in architecture, decoration and crafts. See also under HARBISON.

STALLEY, Roger, *Architecture and Sculpture in Ireland 1150-1350*, Dublin and London 1971.

STALLEY, Roger, 'Mellifont Abbey' in *Studies*, Winter 1975.

STALLEY, Roger, *Christ Church, Dublin, The Late Romanesque Building Campaign*, Ballycotton, 1973.

STALLEY, Roger, 'Boyle Abbey' in *Country Life*, May 6 1976.

STALLEY, Roger, 'William of Prene' in *Journal of the British Archaeological Association*, cxxx, 1978.

STOKES, Margaret, *Early Christian Architecture in Ireland*, 1878.

STOKES, Margaret, *Early Christian Art in Ireland, Part II*, (sculpture and architecture) Dublin, Stationery Office, 1932. See also DUNRAVEN.

Ulster Architectural Heritage Society. This society, founded in 1967, has to date (1981) published 26 volumes of building-lists for numerous towns and regions in the whole province of Ulster, as well as six monographs (some of which are separately noticed in this list) two volumes of quarto format, and other miscellaneous and occasional publications, all of value. This work has been carried on in circumstances often of the utmost difficulty by a devoted band of collaborators.

WAKEMAN, W. F. *A Handbook of Irish Antiquities*, Dublin 1848.

WAKEMAN, W. F. *A Survey of the Antiquarian Remains on Inismurray*, London and Edinburgh (for the Royal Society of Antiquaries of Ireland) 1893.

WATERMAN, Dudley, 'Some Irish Seventeenth-century Houses and Their Architectural Ancestry' in *Studies in Building History* (ed. E. M. Jope) 1961.

WATERMAN, Dudley, 'Sir John Davies and his Ulster Buildings' in *UJA* 1966, pp. 89 sqq. See also *Archaeological Survey of Co Down*.

WESTROPP, T. J. *Illustrated Guide to the Northern, Western and Southern Islands, and Coast of Ireland*, Dublin, 1905. Also many articles in antiquarian journals, of the highest value.

WILKINSON, George, *Practical Geology and Ancient Architecture of Ireland*, London and Dublin, 1845.

Since publication in 1982 the following have appeared:

BARRY, Michael, *Across Deep Waters, Bridges of Ireland*, Dublin 1985. A comprehensive review of bridges.

GAILEY, Alan, *Rural Houses of the North of Ireland*, Edinburgh 1984.

GLIN, Knight of, GRIFFIN, David and ROBINSON, Nicholas, *Vanishing Country Houses of Ireland*, Dublin 1988.

LARMOUR, Paul, *Belfast, an Illustrated Architectural Guide*, Belfast 1987. Supplements BRETT above.

MCCULLOUGH, Niall and MULVIN, Valerie, *A Lost Tradition*, Dublin 1987. Copiously illustrated with very many plans etc.

MCPARLAND, Edward, *James Gandon, Vitruvius Hibernicus*, London 1985. The definitive biographical and critical study.

SHAFFREY, Patrick and Maura, *Buildings of Irish Towns*, Dublin and London 1984; *Irish Countryside Buildings*, Dublin 1985. Very wide-ranging and admirably illustrated.

STALLEY, Roger, *The Cistercian Monasteries of Ireland*, London and New Haven 1987. The definitive work.

Index

Abbreviations: ch = early, mediaeval or ruined church; Cath ch = Catholic church built since the Reformation; C of I ch = Church of Ireland church; Presb ch = Presbyterian church. Numerals in *italic* refer to pages on which illustrations appear.